THE RISE OF
ANGLO-AMERICAN FRIENDSHIP

BOOKS BY LIONEL GELBER

The Rise of Anglo-American Friendship: A Study in World Politics 1898-1906 (1938)

Peace by Power: The Plain Man's Guide to the Key Issue of the War and of the Post-War World (1942)

Reprieve from War: A Manual for Realists (1950)

The American Anarchy: Democracy in an Era of Bigness (1953)

America in Britain's Place: The Leadership of the West and Anglo-American Unity (1961)

The Alliance of Necessity: Britain's Crisis, the New Europe and American Interests (1966)

THE RISE OF ANGLO-AMERICAN FRIENDSHIP

A Study in World Politics

1898–1906

BY

LIONEL GELBER

WITH A NEW PREFACE BY THE AUTHOR

ARCHON BOOKS
HAMDEN, CONNECTICUT
1966

FIRST PUBLISHED 1938
OXFORD UNIVERSITY PRESS

REPRINTED WITH PERMISSION 1966

LIBRARY OF CONGRESS CATALOG CARD NUMBER: 66–23449
PRINTED IN THE UNITED STATES OF AMERICA

CONTENTS

PREFACE TO THE 1966 EDITION

AT CRUCIAL turning-points in the twentieth century, Anglo-American friendship has been a mainstay of the West. The purpose of this book was to show how that factor took its modern shape. Two days after publication in London, in September 1938, the Munich Agreement had been signed. The West might have staved off the coming war, if it had had a better grasp of basic issues. But when the war did come it had to be won and here the Anglo-American factor served the free world as nothing else could.

This book was written at a time when, with the English-speaking peoples self-immobilized by appeasement on one side of the Atlantic and by isolationism on the other, it was hard to conceive of Anglo-American friendship as an instrument of power and action rather than as a residue of sentiment and myth. The writer had, nevertheless, suggested elsewhere that English-speaking solidarity—sympathy with Britain in the United States as well as in Commonwealth countries—was a factor that would tend to redress the world balance.* And a passage from its original preface may indicate the spirit in which this book was written:

"Today as first principles in foreign policy cease to be merely academic or even parliamentary issues and are again the common concern, history more than ever has a clarifying function to discharge. In any final crisis events must impel the English-speaking peoples to consider afresh not only their individual positions in the world, the kind of international order they each need or desire, but also their relation to each other, how those vital needs or desires can best be fulfilled. Woe to him that is alone when he falleth, said the gentle Preacher of old, for he hath not another to help him up. When there is so much at which to despair Anglo-American friend-

---

* "Britain and the European Balance", *The Fortnightly*, London, March 1, 1938. In that power analysis the writer warned that if Austria were allowed to go under the independence of Czechoslovakia would be undermined and a Nazi-Soviet Pact, dividing up Poland and putting the West at Germany's mercy, might follow.
Such, as a matter of fact, was the actual course of events—until Hitler struck at Russia in 1941 and the United States had been embroiled by Japan.

ship still gives hope of an hour less bleak; and it is the object of these pages to examine how from troubled beginnings it became an element of promise to all who cherish freedom and care deeply for the great and menaced heritage of Western society."

(London, S. W. 1
May 23, 1938.)

World War II had begun less than a year after those lines were first published. If Churchill's Britain had not stood fast, civilized society would have been vanquished, enslaved and debased. The stakes were high when, under Franklin Delano Roosevelt and within the limits of non-belligerence, "neutral" America provided the beleaguered British with support. But, despite an overriding community of interest, it was only after Pearl Harbor that the full weight of Anglo-American friendship could be brought to bear.

Nor has that factor, in the post-war era of American leadership, outlived its usefulness. The English-speaking peoples, with a cluster of allies, are once more the prime custodians of a free world order. Scope for the Anglo-American factor must therefore be preserved—an axiom at odds with policies that the United States has occasionally pursued and at variance with that outright merger between Britain and European neighbours which many of the British now favour. A new age calls for new measures. But it is still in the light of the past that these measures should be evaluated.

In later work the writer has dealt with more recent trends as well as with other general aspects of international affairs. Over the years there has been no reason for him to alter his pre-war and wartime view of world politics as a contest for power—one in which power must be the means through which the West might not only hold its own but strive towards nobler ends. On this score the change of outlook among the English-speaking peoples has been momentous. The broad imperatives of Anglo-American friendship remain unchanged.

Lionel Gelber

Spring 1966.

PREFACE

To-day as first principles in foreign policy cease to be merely academic or even parliamentary issues and are again the common concern, history more than ever has a clarifying function to discharge. In any final crisis events must impel the English-speaking peoples to consider afresh not only their individual positions in the world, the kind of international order they each need or desire, but also their relation to each other, how those vital needs or desires can best be fulfilled. Woe to him that is alone when he falleth, said the gentle Preacher of old, for he hath not another to help him up. When there is so much at which to despair Anglo-American friendship still gives hope of an hour less bleak; and it is the object of these pages to examine how from troubled beginnings it became an element of promise to all who cherish freedom and care deeply for the great and menaced heritage of Western society.

My chief obligation in writing this book is to my father, Mr. Louis Gelber, and to my uncle, Mr. Percy Hermant; without their support it could neither have been undertaken nor completed. The Rhodes Trustees have added to a debt already large by making a generous grant towards publication.

At an early stage in my studies I was privileged to have the advice and encouragement of Sir Alfred Zimmern, Montague Burton Professor of International Relations in the University of Oxford; of Mr. B. H. Sumner, Fellow of Balliol; and of Professor N. A. M. MacKenzie, Department of Law, University of Toronto. To Professor George de T. Glazebrook, Department of History, Toronto, I am very grateful for a valuable criticism of the first draft from which this later work has developed. In it, however, there is nothing for which any of them can be held in the least responsible. Lastly, it is a pleasure to acknowledge the kindness shown by every one connected with the Oxford University Press through whose hands the book has passed.

L. M. G.

London, S.W. 1.
May 23, 1938.

I

THE APPROACH TO AN UNDERSTANDING

TOWARDS the close of the nineteenth century, as in the days of Monroe and Canning, the New World was called into existence to redress the balance of the Old. At that time, in their relations with each other, Great Britain and the United States began to establish the enduring basis for their contemporary friendship. Both of these Powers were then on the threshold of an era marked by profound changes in their outlook abroad, and of those changes Anglo-American cordiality now emerged as a very conspicuous feature. For some of the tendencies of that age humanity has paid a terrible price. Yet whatever judgement may be passed on its other diplomatic accomplishments, one at least still redounds to the abiding good not only of the English-speaking nations but of all mankind.

Among the decisive events of modern history the achievement of an Anglo-American understanding must indeed take first rank. During the Great War of 1914–18, when the interests of the British Empire, as they might easily have been two decades earlier, were not exposed to American hostility, its supreme importance was manifest. Instead, despite grave difficulties over neutral rights, the way had been well paved for the United States ultimately to associate herself with the Entente Powers. At the testing-time of civilization the English-speaking peoples stood together.

It is when surveyed in this light that the *rapprochement* effected at the turn of the century between Great Britain and the United States assumes so deep and historic a significance. The formative years of Anglo-American understanding—from 1898 to 1906—were full of perplexity. For every advance there seemed at the start to be a corresponding retrogression. Yet both of the Governments continued to pursue a policy of adjustment. A twofold process characterized the creative period of Anglo-American friendship. First of all, conflict in their mutual relations had to be eliminated; the direct settlement of their differences was the basis of the transformation. But, secondly, a common front had been discovered on larger questions of world politics; an inclination towards unity tempered, however, by other British commitments and the tradition of American isolation. The first of these lines of progress was virtually complete during the autumn of 1903, while the second by the spring of 1906 had been definitely and repeatedly confirmed. Among the factors which constituted the diplomatic system before 1914 Anglo-American friendship thus took its place.

To a later generation, witnessing the durable results of this work, its existence causes no surprise. But at the time it was a very noteworthy departure. Since the American Revolution prejudice in her former colonies against England had never died out; the United States, they always recollected, owed her national independence to an Anglo-American quarrel. The memory of that was kept alive by the War of 1812 and the troubles of the Civil War. Nor did immigrants from Ireland and Germany help to repair the breach. Nevertheless, in the end the present advantage of amelioration—ceaselessly vivified by common cultural influences—overbore the fact and fancy of the past.

The year 1898 was the turning-point. But not long before there had been a disagreement that showed the serious dangers to which the English-speaking peoples were leaving themselves open. For in 1895 occurred one of those paradoxes, by no means the last, which demonstrated that the bonds between the two nations are strongest when they are most severely strained. The British and American Governments now took the lesson to heart and the ground was cleared for the new course.

For eighty years, since the Treaty of Ghent, Great Britain and the United States had been at peace with each other. But in 1895 a controversy about the boundary between Venezuela and British Güiana raised the threat of war. With the support of President Cleveland, Richard Olney, the American Secretary of State, enunciated a singularly extravagant interpretation of the Monroe Doctrine. He demanded that Venezuela and British Guiana, a British colony, should arbitrate their dispute without interference from Great Britain. In July 1895 Olney informed the Foreign Office that 'to-day the United States is practically sovereign on this continent, and its fiat is law upon the subjects to which it confines its interposition'. To his mind any permanent political union between a European and American State was unnatural and inexpedient.[1] Truly Napoleonic in his vision, Olney thus assailed the propriety of all British rights in the western hemisphere.

By Great Britain these far-reaching contentions could not be allowed to go unchallenged. The Marquis of Salisbury, both Prime Minister and Foreign Secretary, replied in November. The British Government saw no reason to bring in the Monroe Doctrine since,

---

[1] *Papers relating to the Foreign Relations of the United States*, 1895, Part I, pp. 552–62.

never having been accepted by other Powers, it was not part of international law. They moreover denied the existence of any rule which compelled Great Britain to arbitrate the question, something in any case for the two contestants alone to decide. The British Empire included Canada, Newfoundland, Jamaica, Trinidad, British Honduras, and British Guiana. Salisbury was consequently bound to dissent from Olney as to the unnatural and inexpedient character of any permanent union between a European and American State.[1] The Prime Minister, in fact, stoutly resisted American intervention.

The clouds gathered. In December President Cleveland delivered two angry messages to Congress. Great Britain had refused to arbitrate. It was therefore proposed that the American Government should themselves ascertain the frontier and defend it against a British violation.[2] Defiances were being hurled across the Atlantic, but men did not lose their heads and good sense prevailed. Crises elsewhere—the Jameson Raid and the Kaiser's telegram in January 1896 to the Boer President, Paul Kruger—rendered it all the more advisable to ignore Washington's bellicosity. Joseph Chamberlain, a member of the Cabinet, laboured for agreement, at home in company with Sir William Harcourt, the leader of the Liberal Opposition, and in the United States with Olney himself. Parliamentary spokesmen were unanimously pacific in utterance; towards the end of the year—Washington having granted the condition that there should be no change in the status of territory long occupied by British settlers—the two Governments came to an arrangement; and on February 2, 1897, Great Britain and Venezuela signed a treaty to set up an arbitral tribunal which would determine the boundary line. Its award was handed down in 1899 and largely favoured the claims of British Guiana, but the United States had nevertheless won her point that the dispute must be submitted to arbitration.[3]

The upshot of this affair was curious. The menace of war brought forth an instrument of peace. Negotiations were now conducted for a general Anglo-American arbitration treaty. Signed in Washington on January 11, 1897, by Richard Olney and Sir Julian Pauncefote, it was thereupon sent by President Cleveland to the Senate for ratification. But when the treaty was considered at the next session of Congress—William McKinley having become President of the United States—the senatorial amendments were ruinously drastic. Yet in its

[1] *U.S. Foreign Relations*, 1895, Part I, pp. 563–76.
[2] Ibid., pp. 542–5.
[3] Alfred L. P. Dennis, *Adventures in American Diplomacy*, pp. 17–62; R. B. Mowat, *The Life of Lord Pauncefote*, pp. 172–202; J. L. Garvin, *The Life of Joseph Chamberlain*, vol. iii, pp. 65–9, 92–6, 159–68.

provisions the agreement was most innocuous. Pecuniary claims and all other matters over which the two Governments might differ were covered but territorial questions were exempt. Should it nevertheless have been decided to arbitrate claims in that category, a majority of five to one was then required for settlement by the tribunal. National rights were carefully safeguarded. Still the Senate could not be mollified. Put to the vote on May 5 the treaty lacked the necessary two-thirds for ratification.[1] However keen the disappointment in both countries—and attempts were made to draft a new convention—the President felt unable to proceed further.

In spite of public opinion and the wishes of the Administration the Senate was master. That body may have disliked the State Department and insisted upon keeping jealous watch over its treaty-making powers. But among its motives were also suspicion of Salisbury and the British Government; the animosity against Great Britain of Irish-American politicians and opposition to her, as the champion of the gold standard, by advocates of free silver. The harmless arbitration agreement was the innocent victim of the currents of the age. For the structure of the American Constitution which gave a veto on treaties to a minority in the Senate—that is one-third plus one vote—was an obstacle to that smooth operation of the diplomatic machinery which distinguished the presidential from the parliamentary system. In the shaping of American foreign policy the opinions of individual senators and senatorial blocs were a negative factor as important sometimes as the positive desires of the Administration. Thanks to them a Secretary of State often oscillated between cowardice and martyrdom. The fate of the Olney-Pauncefote Treaty was a portent.

But the defeat of the general arbitration agreement mattered less than the spirit in which it had been negotiated. Following so closely on the heels of the Venezuelan episode, it was a token—the first of its kind in international relations—of the terms on which the two Governments hoped they might henceforth deal with each other. For at the end of the century, as in the days of the Holy Alliance, Great Britain, reacting against the policies of the continental Powers, seemed to gravitate once more towards the United States. What were the circumstances which lay behind this tendency?

Great Britain's position in the world may be seen from two angles. There was the diplomatic situation as a whole which affected the security of the British Empire everywhere, and there was one of its

---

[1] Mowat, *Pauncefote*, pp. 160–71; Dennis, *Adventures*, pp. 472–5; World Peace Foundation, *Arbitration and the United States*, pp. 500–13.

particular phases reflected in the problem of the Far East. Difficulties in China were to provide the first evidence that Downing Street sought the co-operation of the United States in international affairs. From that to the broader idea of an all-inclusive Anglo-American understanding was not a long step. It is against a wide background of world politics that the approach to friendship with the United States, now undertaken by Great Britain, must be reviewed.

In 1898 both of these countries were isolationist. Lord Salisbury was reluctant to abandon a time-honoured policy: to intervene when the diplomatic equilibrium had to be maintained or restored, yet to accept no obligations which might shackle British freedom of action. But the Concert of Europe was being undermined; the Powers were ranging themselves in antagonistic groupings. Could Great Britain afford to remain outside? There was first of all the constant, duel waged with Russia in the Far East, at the Straits and in middle Asia from where the safety of India might be endangered. To stop Russian encroachments British statesmen regarded as a primary task. Not until the Russo-Japanese War of 1904–5 did they perceive that the Muscovite Colossus stood really on feet of clay.

With France the story was similar. In the Far East, where she possessed Indo-China, the British Government bickered with her as with Russia. In western and central Africa, moreover, Great Britain and France were engaged in an acute colonial rivalry—finally settled in March 1899—while by the Quai d'Orsay the former had never been forgiven for succeeding to French pretensions in Egypt. During the autumn of 1898 friction on the Upper Nile was brought to a head by the Fashoda incident.[1] Acting singly, Russia and France were sufficiently vexing. But in 1894 the two chief opponents of Great Britain had begun to pool their resources.[2] To their common enmity the combination of Russia and France in the Dual Alliance imparted fresh strength.

Germany, the dominant military Power of Europe, was less hostile. She, too, nevertheless, displayed ill will and jealousy. The architect of the Triple Alliance of Germany, Austria-Hungary, and Italy, Bismarck had been unable to surmount the two great problems rooted in the German annexation of Alsace-Lorraine and Austro-Russian competition in the Balkans. Shortly after his fall, despite the brilliant adroitness with which he had staved it off; the *cauchemar des coalitions*,

[1] Garvin, *Chamberlain*, vol. iii, pp. 202–37; Viscount Grey of Fallodon, *Twenty-Five Years*, vol. i, pp. 7–25, 35–41.
[2] Sidney Bradshaw Fay, *The Origins of the World War*, vol. i, pp. 110–24.

the conjuncture of Russia and France, the fear of a war on two fronts, was no longer the bad dream of that statesman, but one of the inner-most realities of the European system. When the young Emperor dropped the 'old pilot' Englishmen felt a new epoch had been ushered in. Bismarck's ruling principle was to consolidate Germany's recent gains. For that reason he wanted to placate Great Britain and not challenge her supremacy on the seas. Only towards the end of his term was he prone to alter this programme for imperialist ventures in other continents.[1] But now a forward policy, aggressive and extra-European, supplanted Bismarckian conservatism.

Talented, vain and egotistical, William II well exemplified those neurotic characteristics which during the present century have been an invariable feature of German politics and diplomacy. To humour the many moods of their sovereign, to whet his appetite for fame and glory, there was, furthermore, seldom a deficiency of advisers—advisers who also endeavoured to implement the *Machtpolitik* of Baron von Holstein, the baleful head of the political department of the German Foreign Office. Setting out in a congested world to seek for his Empire a 'place in the sun', the Kaiser was dazzled, if not slightly maddened, by its sudden hot glare. To Berlin in 1895, believing that since the days of Disraeli England had backed the wrong horse, Lord Salisbury proposed the partition of Turkey. But the Wilhelmstrasse was chary of British offers and nothing came of the suggestion. Nor were matters improved when Dr. Jameson and his followers raided the Boers. By the message of sympathy which the Kaiser sent on January 3, 1896, to President Kruger Englishmen were bewildered and startled; into their relations with Germany a spirit of embitterment now began to creep.[2] The first German Navy Bill received its third reading in March 1898 and in the same year the Kaiser did not only proclaim that Germany's future lay on the water but in his travels through eastern lands attempted to secure Moslem friendship. Great Britain was the chief naval and colonial Power and suzerain of millions of Mohammedans. These activities seemed mainly to be directed at her. Long continued, they were bound to rankle.

Such, then, was the outlook which made some Englishmen, notably Joseph Chamberlain, doubt the expediency of further British isola-tion. The Great Powers of Europe had divided themselves into two vast coalitions opposed to each other but tending in the Near

---

[1] Erich Brandenburg, *From Bismarck to the World War*, pp. 18–19; J. A. Spender, *Fifty Years of Europe*, pp. 64–76.
[2] Brandenburg, *From Bismarck*, &c., pp. 72–90; Fay, *Origins of the War*, vol. i, pp. 127–8.

and Far East to combine against that one Power who held the balance between them. There were colonial feuds in the four corners of the earth; militarism was rampant and waxing; war loomed in South Africa; above all, Great Britain could not fail to be mindful of the fact that the two armed camps of Europe reserved for her a peculiar envy. Ahead of them she had gained a maritime and commercial start and the most splendid prizes of empire. To safeguard these far-flung interests at every point—either in diplomacy or war— might require her to muster alone an amount of sea-power which would over-tax even her immense resources. Could she therefore still refrain from deliberately cultivating outside support ? And in British calculations what part might Anglo-American friendship play ?

When William McKinley became President in 1897 the United States was isolationist in the tradition of her founders. For British and American isolationism were very dissimilar. Great Britain might intervene in international politics for an adequate reason; from European affairs the United States, on the other hand, stood entirely aloof. The Monroe Doctrine may have been designed to prevent interference by the Powers of Europe in the western hemisphere; but, conversely, it also emphasized the axiomatic principle of keeping the United States out of foreign entanglements. After the Civil War Americans were absorbed in the stupendous development of their domestic economy; geography and time endowed the Monroe Doctrine with an almost constitutional authority. As their trade, wealth, and national ambitions increased they were, however, unable to escape intimate contact with world affairs. Their interest in the Chinese situation pointed to this at the end of the century and it was especially evident when, as a sequel to the Spanish War, the United States, adding to her Samoan foothold, assumed extensive colonial responsibilities. Needing friends, Englishmen welcomed the change. The emergence of Great Britain and the United States from isolation appeared to coincide. The attempt was therefore made to arrange Anglo-American co-operation. Formal association proved impossible; informal association was sought.

In his memoirs Lord Grey of Fallodon reiterated the familiar warning against ascribing to British Ministers elaborate and far-sighted policies when they have been guided by immediate rather than future considerations.[1] Such historic empiricism seemed as true of Great Britain in her attitude towards the United States as in that towards other countries. Yet implicit in the new *rapprochement* between the English-speaking peoples was a sense of permanence; immediate and

---

[1] Grey of Fallodon, *Twenty-Five Years*, vol. i, p. 6.

future interests blended, practical and sentimental motives were one. For the entrance of the United States into world politics would obviously upset the balance of power. To capitalize that alteration in favour of Great Britain, to capture the goodwill of the United States for its own sake and before it was obtained by others, became now an object of British diplomacy. In their policies British Ministers were likely to follow no settled and premeditated scheme. The general drift of Great Britain towards an understanding with the United States can, nevertheless, infallibly be descried. And it was assisted by the fact that Europe regarded the United States as an English-speaking *parvenu*; a raw and mighty interloper capable of appropriating or protecting territory for which the Chancelleries hungered; a nation, moreover, whom a kindred culture and much common history brought closest to the British peoples. By the Government in London, anxious only to retain what they already possessed, the United States was encouraged as a counterpoise, a potential aid against other Powers improving their relative positions in the regions yet available while Great Britain stood still. And so American aggrandizement became a formidable, if secondary, counter in the British game to checkmate European competition. And thus, too, the United States—*tertius gaudens*—had everything to win and nothing to lose in the great age of imperialist politics.

Of this desire to draw the American Government into diplomatic activity on the British side the problem of China furnished the first concrete instance. The Celestial Empire was the focus of international rivalries and there the huge interests of Great Britain were exceedingly vulnerable. Overwhelmed in the Corean War of 1894–5, China had shown herself utterly defenceless. As a result of interference by Russia, France, and Germany, victorious Japan was, however, forced to relinquish whatever she had acquired under the Treaty of Shimonoseki on the Chinese mainland. The partition of China seemed to impend. For her services Peking rewarded Russia with the well-known concession to build the Chinese Eastern Railway across northern Manchuria—a land route of military and commercial importance which British sea-power, preponderant in Asiatic waters, could not affect. France was to get Kwang-Chow-Wan as a sphere of influence and Germany paid herself off in November 1897 when she seized Kiao-Chau—leased by treaty on March 6, 1898—a key to the trade of northern China, in the Shantung Peninsula. Not to be outdone in rapacity Russia took Port Arthur, the ice-free fortress on the Pacific, in December 1897—her formal agreement with Peking being signed on March 15, 1898. The Powers were robbing China of that which on her behalf they denied to Japan. In the English-speaking countries disquiet was widespread.

For Great Britain the situation contained a substantial element of political danger. Co-operating in the Far East with the Dual Alliance, Germany appeared as undependable as France and Russia. For it was her object not only to share in the plunder of China but also by diverting Russia to the Far East to mitigate Russian pressure on her own eastern frontier and to deflect Pan-Slavic agitation from the Balkan sphere of her Austro-Hungarian ally.[1] Nor did the challenge from St. Petersburg merely involve British predominance in China proper. The Pacific trade routes were controlled by Great Britain and she had to maintain her naval position as well as her prestige. Moreover, in Russian ascendancy there was also the risk that the security of her whole Eastern Empire—Hong Kong, Malay, Straits Settlements, Burma, even India—would be weakened and imperilled.

It may have been a political danger. It was also economic; or rather in it had been gathered all those mingled ingredients of politics and economics which the Industrial Revolution bequeathed to international relations. In that epoch Europeans and Americans thought that China offered rich opportunities for trade expansion. Power-politics and power-economics were linked inseparably with ready access to raw materials, communications, and markets. To attain something like the high estate of the British Empire the continental Governments hankered after exclusive zones for privileged exploitation—a policy repugnant to the Free Trade ideas under which Great Britain throve and prospered. And so when Germany, France, and Russia began to entrench themselves in China the menace arose of a partition which with the establishment of monopolies might threaten British interests. Of Chinese foreign trade Great Britain's share exceeded 70 per cent., its annual total being more than £32,000,000 and representing about one-sixth of her world commerce. Besides, British shipping also carried three-fourths of Chinese foreign trade and over half of the coastwise trade.[2] The bulk of British commerce in China was in the Yangtse Valley, with a market of over 150,000,000 people—Manchuria, the Russian sphere of influence, having as yet only a sparse population. It was therefore feared that Russia would push outside the limits of Manchuria and steal British trade in the Yangtse Valley. To thwart her had become imperative.

The British Government approached Russia herself first of all.

---

[1] Tyler Dennett, *Americans in Eastern Asia*, p. 635; H. B. Morse and H. F. MacNair, *Far Eastern International Relations*, pp. 636–7; Brandenburg, *From Bismarck*, &c., pp. 66–7.
[2] Chung-Fu Chang, *The Anglo-Japanese Alliance*, p. 56.

If Great Britain was going to be hampered in her policy of the Open Door she could not afford passively to hold off and watch the other Powers slice up China to the detriment of the enormous British trade in that feckless land. Lord Salisbury regretted that, however useless and expensive it might be, public sentiment now required 'some territorial or cartographic consolation in China'.[1] Before taking action the Government in London pursued nevertheless a dual programme: if possible to secure support that would guarantee the integrity of Chinese territory and the Open Door for foreign commerce and enterprise; but, failing that, to come to an arrangement with the Powers which—*faute de mieux*—might be a modification of her original principle yet which would at least preserve Great Britain's position in the Far East. With Russia only the second policy was feasible, and with that country Salisbury in January 1898 tried to arrive at an agreement. The scheme was to iron out differences wherever they occurred in the Near and Far East. The Prime Minister thus forsook a rigid interpretation of the Open Door doctrine. The British sphere of influence was to be in the Yangtse Valley, the Russian from the Hoangho northwards—the proposal being for a division of political preponderance rather than territory.[2] Eventually this may have constituted a very important diplomatic understanding. But the Russians dropped the negotiations and in March formally leased Port Arthur and Talienwan which they had previously occupied.

In Great Britain the Cabinet, now inwardly confused about the best plan to adopt, were outwardly optimistic. Ministerial speeches kept to the forefront the pure Open Door theory which an alarmed nation preferred; on March 1 both Unionists and Liberals registered in the House of Commons their demand for the maintenance of Chinese independence.[3] The Government were, however, less complacent than they seemed. With Russia they had not succeeded. They turned to the United States.

There were good grounds for expecting that such a move would yield useful results. By the end of the nineteenth century American industry, colossal in productivity, had begun to overflow the spacious banks of its internal market; the great mercantile countries were finding the United States a very serious competitor and in northern China she possessed over 50 per cent. of the import trade.[4] Nowadays

---

[1] Salisbury to Chamberlain, Dec. 30, 1897, Garvin, *Chamberlain*, vol. iii, p. 249.
[2] G. P. Gooch and Harold Temperley (eds.), *British Documents on the Origins of the War*, vol. i, pp. 5–41.
[3] The Earl of Ronaldshay, *The Life of Lord Curzon*, vol. i, pp. 276–81.
[4] Beresford to Hay, Nov. 28, 1898, Dennis, *Adventures*, p. 186.

it may be argued that the sanguine hopes once entertained were not realized for a vast increase of American commerce in the Orient. But at the time it was considered most urgent that to the exporters of the United States the avenues of Chinese business should not be barred. And besides, during the middle of the nineteenth century the American Navy had fostered and acted on a policy of Far Eastern trade expansion.[1] Remote from European questions, the Government in Washington were accustomed to deal more freely with China, Japan, and European Powers operating in the Orient. To many American missionary and religious bodies Chinese welfare was, in addition, a matter of deep concern. The Far Eastern interests of the United States were, in fact, already large and might presently be larger.

From a partition of China Great Britain, then, would not suffer alone. The interests of the United States, existing and prospective, were also endangered. A combination of three European Powers who might block their Chinese trade confronted Americans, British, and Japanese alike. In opposition to the Far Eastern grouping of Russia, France, and Germany, the United States, Great Britain, and Japan were thus thrown together.[2] Since 1895 official relations between the two English-speaking Governments had undergone a rapid improvement; in China neither of them had territorial aspirations. Threatened from a common source, they needed common measures to defend similar interests. Would they collaborate to devise a joint solution?

About public opinion in England Washington was being kept fully informed. Henry White, First Secretary of the American Embassy at London, reported the British attitude to John Sherman, McKinley's Secretary of State. He found Englishmen to be confident that in maintaining the freedom of the Chinese market, 'Great Britain will have the sympathy and support of the people of the United States and not improbably of our Government also'.[3] On the other side of the water Senator Henry Cabot Lodge echoed these views and from China the dispatches of the American Minister were making apparent the community of interest in the Far East of the English-speaking Powers.[4] The way was being prepared.

The negotiations with Russia had hardly come to naught when the British Government tried to buttress their position on the Pacific

[1] Charles A. Beard, *The Idea of National Interest*, pp. 60–3, 95–100.
[2] Dennett, *Americans in Eastern Asia*, p. 635; also Hay to Sherman, March 25, 1898, Dennis, *Adventures*, p. 198.
[3] Ibid., p. 197.
[4] Allan Nevins, *Henry White*, p. 166; Denby to Sherman, Jan. 31, 1898, Dennis, *Adventures*, pp. 203–5.

by a compact across the Atlantic. Joseph Chamberlain had suggested to Arthur Balfour in February that they should consult with the United States and Germany. Early in March—the American Ambassador, John Hay, being abroad—these two Ministers spoke to Henry White of their anxiety over the Far Eastern situation. They assured him that it was important for the United States to take 'some sort of action in support of England's policy in China'. Chamberlain told White that he distrusted Russian and German promises.[1] But John Sherman, the Secretary of State, was both a novice in diplomacy and too old for his post. The Germans had asserted that in their port there would be no restriction on foreign trade and the Russians soon did likewise.[2] With such affirmations the United States seemed content. In Washington the forebodings of the British Government were of small avail.

They made their overture to the United States on March 8, 1898. Two days before Germany had signed her lease of Kiao-Chau, and in the middle of the month Russia concluded with China her agreement about Port Arthur. What happened the British Foreign Office outlined many years later in the following terms:

'When His Majesty's Ambassador at Washington endeavoured in March, 1898, to ascertain the attitude of the United States Government on the possible complications in China and the Far East, he was verbally informed that the President was in sympathy with the policy of open trade in China, but saw no reason for the departure of the United States of America from its traditional policy respecting foreign alliances and of avoiding as far as possible any interference in the connexion of European complications.'[3]

This interrogation was no routine matter. Joseph Chamberlain, the most dynamic of British Ministers, fervently advocated Anglo-American co-operation. At the height of the Venezuelan crisis he had suggested to Lord Salisbury that Great Britain combine with the United States to rescue the Armenians from their Turkish persecutors. Some months later, when conciliation was the *mot d'ordre*, even Richard Olney, to whom it had been submitted by its author, applauded this proposal and, before laying down his office, deemed it fitting that the British and American peoples should stand side by side 'in support of a great cause'.[4] And now perhaps the Chinese

---

[1] Chamberlain to Balfour, Feb. 3, 1898, Blanche E. C. Dugdale, *Arthur James Balfour*, vol. i, pp. 252–3; Garvin, *Chamberlain*, vol. iii, pp. 251–2; White to Hay, Mar. 6, 1898, Nevins, *White*, pp. 162–3.

[2] Dennis, *Adventures*, p. 182.

[3] Tyrrell to Asquith, Sept. 6, 1922, The Rt. Hon. H. H. Asquith, *The Genesis of the War*, p. 33.

[4] Garvin, *Chamberlain*, vol. iii, pp. 68–9, 165–8; also Dennis, *Adventures*, pp. 58–62.

situation would provide the opportunity of which Chamberlain dreamed. By approaching Washington in March 1898 the British Government had clearly shown that they desired to collaborate with the United States in a major question of international politics. Was a joint move in China—where isolation then exhibited itself in its darkest colours—envisaged as merely the first step towards a real alliance? Out of a Far Eastern partnership one might have developed. In the event this object was achieved neither for limited nor for general purposes. Yet the ideal persisted and with the growth of Anglo-American friendship radiated throughout the English-speaking world an ever-widening influence.

Meanwhile it would appear that Great Britain had invited the United States not only to help maintain the Open Door, but also to defend the territorial integrity of China's seaboard. What occurred was described more completely in a report written by John Sherman. The Secretary of State recorded that:

> 'British Ambassador by a confidential and unofficial memorandum eighth instant, inquired whether British Government could count on the co-operation of the United States in opposing action by foreign Powers which may tend to restrict freedom of commerce of all nations in China either by imposing preferential conditions or by obtaining actual cession of Chinese coast territory. British Ambassador has been answered in like unofficial and confidential manner and with the reservation of ultimate determination of policy by Congress saying that the President is in sympathy with the policy which shall maintain open trade in China, that all his advices up to the present time indicate no foreign occupation which interferes with that trade or aims at exclusive commercial privileges, and that he does not see any present reason for the departure of the United States from our traditional policy of respecting [*sic*] foreign alliances and so far as practicable avoiding interference or connection with European complications.'[1]

The American refusal is not unintelligible. The United States was on the verge of war with Spain; her hands were full. Nor was the Chinese situation unrelated to the universal rivalry between Great Britain and the continental Powers. Why should the United States assist in the defence of British interests? On their behalf she was little disposed to infringe her cherished tradition of abstaining from foreign entanglements. They were, it is true, although to a lesser extent, American interests as well. McKinley and Sherman may, however, have suspected the inquiry of March 8 of being an artful ruse to inveigle them into fighting not their own but British battles in China. From the handicap under which it was thus placed

---

[1] Sherman to White, Mar. 17, 1898, Dennis, *Adventures*, pp. 170–1.

at the close of the century, American policy in the Far East never recovered. In the following years the Open Door would mean not only equal trading conditions for the commerce of foreign countries but also equal opportunities to make loans to the Chinese Government, to finance Chinese railways and to exploit Chinese natural resources. A decade later when the Administration of President Taft failed to receive from London the Far Eastern support they expected, they were nettled at the indifference of Great Britain to what they considered legitimate American rights. But in the interval the British Government had been constrained to look elsewhere—to Tokio, to Paris, and to St. Petersburg—and undertake other commitments. After the Russo-Japanese War, on much that happened in the Far East, Great Britain, strengthening her diplomatic ramparts against the Austro-German system, turned a blind eye.

The fact was that international affairs could not wait upon the sluggish evolution of American politics, finance, and statesmanship. Great Britain strove to act in unison with the United States on a strict basis of the Open Door and the territorial integrity of China. She made her offer in March 1898. It was bluntly rejected. An alliance or formal partnership between the English-speaking Powers might have brought stability to the Far East. Only the future could reveal that nothing less would suffice.

It may be idle to speculate on the might-have-beens of history, but in retrospect it is evident that the American refusal cut deeper than the channels of trade and commerce. British Ministers were beginning to think of an alliance with Japan—a combination that was finally arranged in 1902.[1] But if the United States had joined with Great Britain to maintain a common front in the Far East, the Anglo-Japanese Alliance, which became the diplomatic bedrock of Japanese imperialism, might have taken a shape less displeasing to the American people. Of this there were at first few signs and in the revision of that instrument President Theodore Roosevelt was in 1905 cordially to concur. With Anglo-American approval, Japan was then about to embark on her new career as a major Power. But after the Moroccan crisis, owing to their European preoccupations, the British Government did not want to antagonize their Eastern ally; nor indeed to shake the newly formed understanding between Russia and Japan which accompanied the recent Anglo-Russian *rapprochement*. Before 1914 when the United States and Japan were at cross-purposes it was incumbent upon Great Britain to keep

---

[1] Chamberlain to Salisbury, Dec. 31, 1897, Garvin, *Chamberlain*, vol. iii, p. 249; Ronaldshay, *Curzon*, vol. i, p. 278.

undamaged her connexion with both Tokio and Washington. How essential it had become for the British Empire that this should be done the second revision of the Anglo-Japanese Alliance attested; for in 1911 that proceeding was solely intended to release Great Britain and the Dominions from any obligation to participate in a war between Japan and the United States.[1] It is plain that a warmer response from Washington to the British overture of 1898 would throughout the present century have modified fundamentally Anglo-American, Anglo-Japanese, and American-Japanese relations. In the subsequent history of Pacific affairs, and that critical segment of world politics on which they are so interdependent, the negative effect of McKinley isolationism cannot be ignored.

Conjecture may wander farther afield. Would a combination of Great Britain, the United States, and probably Japan have constituted a third grouping of the Powers holding the balance between the Dual and Triple Alliances? Might it not have obviated or altered the fateful necessity for the British Government to cast their weight to one side or the other of the great European alignments? And towards Great Britain would it not again have induced Germany to change her attitude? How, too, would such an Anglo-American grouping have affected the internal governance of China herself? Would it not have long underpinned her administrative sovereignty and territorial integrity so enabling domestic forces of enlightenment and progress to work unmolested for her ordered unity? All that lay in the laps of the gods. It could not be expected that the United States, hindered by inexperience and isolationist by tradition, should see far ahead.

Nothing having come of Salisbury's soundings with Russia and the inquiry at Washington likewise proving fruitless, Joseph Chamberlain at the end of March accepted a German suggestion to discuss the possibility of an alliance between Great Britain and Germany. But this also yielded slender hope for British policy in the Far East or for an understanding with Berlin.[2] Meanwhile the news arrived in London of the Russian agreement with China. Knowing that their influence at Peking and in northern China was in jeopardy, the British Government now had to play the European game of counter-demands and counter-concessions. In the fourth week of March they therefore decided to occupy the last of the three ports available in the Gulf of Pechili; to equalize the action of Germany at Kiao-Chau and of

[1] Br. Docs., vol. viii, pp. 453–604.
[2] Garvin, Chamberlain, vol. iii, pp. 254–95; Blanche Dugdale, Balfour, vol. i, pp. 256–61; Brandenburg, From Bismarck, &c., pp. 103–22.

Russia at Port Arthur, Great Britain obtained a lease of Wei-hai-Wei.[1] During April France secured Kwang-chow-Wan and even Italy put in unrequited claims. Great Britain then enlarged her Hong Kong area and British groups were assigned concessions for railways traversing ten provinces with a pledge from Peking that her sphere of influence in the Yangtse Valley would not be alienated. In the next year London and St. Petersburg recognized each other's sphere of influence, the British in the Yangtse, the Russian north of the Great Wall.[2] Thus in the Far East the two principal contestants divided up commercially a huge portion of the Chinese Empire.

The economic dismemberment of China was under way. The British had occupied a port in the north of the China Sea and with France in southern China, Germany in Shantung, Russia in Mongolia and Manchuria, Great Britain took her place among them as the patron of the Yangtse Valley. Tangible assistance from the United States was not forthcoming for a Simon Pure policy founded on the territorial integrity of China and the Open Door; other precautionary measures ensued. In the autumn of 1899 when John Hay, then Secretary of State, formulated his Open Door notes Great Britain was already somewhat compromised. From the Russo-Japanese War, the period during which Anglo-American understanding in the Far East reached and passed its zenith, until after the Great War of 1914–18, the United States in Eastern Asiatic affairs could no longer rely on British support. The consequences of her earlier refusal were being encountered. In 1898, however, the United States was engrossed in matters nearer home. Events which preceded were but an introduction to the new chapters about to be opened up in relations between the English-speaking peoples.

[1] George Earle Buckle (ed.), *The Letters of Queen Victoria*, Third Series, vol. iii, pp. 237–8; Ronaldshay, *Curzon*, vol. i, pp. 283–5.
[2] Herbert Feis, *Europe The World's Banker*, p. 99; Sir A. W. Ward and G. P. Gooch (eds.), *The Cambridge History of British Foreign Policy*, vol. iii, p. 233.

II

THE NEW COURSE

In international affairs Anglo-American friendship first became a decisive factor during the Spanish War when the British Government, faithfully reflecting public opinion, manifested goodwill towards the United States and supported her growth as a colonial Power. The conflict itself was bred by a complex of incentives, some altruistic, others self-regarding: a genuine impulse on the part of Americans to liberate the downtrodden Cubans from Spanish misrule, an equal desire to protect the lives, property, and investments of their country-men from disorder and injustice in a neighbouring island; the revival in the United States of the urge towards economic expansion abroad and a movement towards the strengthening of her naval and coastal security.[1] In London the general situation was well appreciated. To John Hay, the American Ambassador, Lord Salisbury in October 1897 conveyed the view of his Government that British interests were purely commercial; on any policy which might restore tranquillity to Cuba Great Britain would look with favour. Reporting to President McKinley Hay pointed out that there was no need for the United States to fear British intervention.[2] And from that position, to the dismay of Europe, Great Britain would not recede. In the diplomacy of the period it was to be of capital importance.

A new Spanish Government assumed office too late to still the clamour for Cuban independence. Rioting broke out in Havana early in 1898 and to that city an American warship, the *Maine*, was now dispatched. Next occurred the recall from Washington of the Spanish Minister, some of whose correspondence had been published, followed on February 15 in the harbour of Havana by the explosion of the *Maine* with a heavy toll of casualties. It has never been proved that for this disaster the Spaniards were to blame, but the sensational press of the United States cried for revenge and swept the populace with it. Despite the temporizing of the American Administration war was imminent.

From the outset, and almost unanimously, British public opinion swung to the side of the United States. Such English-speaking solidarity was the more conspicuous because, against her, the French,

[1] Beard, *The Idea of National Interest*, pp. 65–70.
[2] Hay to McKinley, Oct. 6, 1897, Charles S. Olcott, *William McKinley*, vol. ii, p. 129.

the Austrians, and the Germans gave voice to strident antipathy. In Vienna the Habsburgs were connected by dynastic ties with the royal house of Spain, while at Potsdam the Hohenzollern Emperor upheld with them a common devotion to the monarchical principle. Moreover, the latter's chief mentor and Secretary of the German Admiralty, Admiral von Tirpitz, fancied that, with the United States otherwise distracted, Germany might purchase islands in the Danish West Indies and push forward her economic interests in South America. In his reminiscences Prince von Bülow, then Foreign Secretary, expatiated on the difficulty with which he had kept the German Government strictly neutral; his efforts to persuade William II— who once thought that 'the hidalgo will certainly cut Brother Jonathan to pieces'—that Spain and the Spanish Navy could not win.[1] In his own memoirs the Kaiser's comment was wholly nonsensical. For after his abdication he asserted that by a secret treaty the United States in 1897 had allied herself with Great Britain and France to encircle Germany.[2] The posture of international affairs at that time, the French attitude towards the English-speaking Powers and McKinley's undeviating isolationism, exhibited the crude untruth of the charge. But it did show the deep impression left on the Kaiser's mind by nascent Anglo-American friendship.

To many in the United States British goodwill came as an agreeable surprise. In February 1898 Theodore Roosevelt, the Assistant Secretary of the Navy, considered it desirable that the American continent should be rid of every European Power including Great Britain. He admitted, however, that the latter was not as hostile to the United States as Germany. But during the next month—the day after the British inquiry at Washington about co-operation in the Far East—Roosevelt uttered a totally different opinion. Now he was sure that in the Spanish question Englishmen sympathized with Americans. 'I am glad there seems to be so friendly a feeling between the two countries, though I don't believe that we ought to have an alliance.'[3] The atmosphere had been transformed and to that Theodore Roosevelt, no mean authority, bore witness.

The friendship of Great Britain presently saved the United States from diplomatic embarrassments. For it was expected in Europe that by jointly mediating at Washington the Powers might stay the declaration of war. Simultaneously behind the scenes in England the traditions of the nineteenth century struggled for a brief moment

[1] Prince von Bülow, *Memoirs 1897–1903*, pp. 143, 183–4, 215.
[2] Ex-Kaiser William II, *My Memoirs 1878–1918*, pp. 68–70, 302, 309.
[3] Roosevelt to Moore, Feb. 9, 1898, Joseph Bucklin Bishop, *Theodore Roosevelt and His Time*, vol. i, p. 79; Roosevelt to White, Mar. 9, 1898, Nevins, *White*, p. 132.

with the innovating forces of the twentieth. When the *Maine* was destroyed the Duke of York—trained in the Navy and later King George V—sent his condolences and those of the Duchess to the American Government.[1] But, on the other hand, a poignant appeal from the Queen-Regent of Spain inevitably filled Queen Victoria with compassion for her niece's tragic cause. Himself no stranger to the natural loyalties which animated his aged Sovereign, Lord Salisbury had thereupon to explain the unwisdom of a British intervention for peace. While Great Britain might associate herself at Washington with all the other Powers—and Queen Victoria replied to Maria Christina that this would be done—he doubted the expediency of any European action.[2]

What was the official British attitude ? In Salisbury's absence Arthur Balfour, the First Lord of the Treasury, deputized at the Foreign Office. About friendly relations between the English-speaking peoples his lifelong views had already been publicly expressed. During the Venezuelan crisis he had said in the first important address delivered by him on international affairs—and approved beforehand by his uncle the Prime Minister—that the idea of war with the United States carried with it 'some of the unnatural horror of a civil war'; as a bimetallist he had witnessed with sympathy the growth of that movement in the Republic and hoped it would lead the way towards the universal rehabilitation of silver.[3] Guided by such principles in the conduct of policy and enjoying Salisbury's entire confidence, Balfour, from 1898 onward, made a quiet contribution to the upbuilding of Anglo-American understanding the value of which cannot be overestimated. Together with his colleague Joseph Chamberlain, the Colonial Secretary, he effectually throttled whatever pro-Spanish influences might have still tended to revolve around the Court, the Foreign Office, and the Conservative Party. On April 6 a statement from Balfour to Hay revealed the Cabinet's decision. 'Neither here nor in Washington', he told the American Ambassador, 'did the British Government propose to take any steps which would not be acceptable to the Government of the United States.'[4] And this assurance must have enabled President McKinley to discount all attempts at combined interference. For, lacking

[1] White to the Duke of York, Feb. 20, 1898, *Letters of Queen Victoria*, Third Series, vol. iii, pp. 231–2.
[2] Queen-Regent of Spain to Queen Victoria, Mar. 17, 1898, *Letters of Queen Victoria*, Third Series, vol. iii, pp. 236–7; Salisbury to Queen Victoria, Apr. 1, 1898, ibid., p. 239; Queen-Regent of Spain to Queen Victoria, Aug. 30, 1898, ibid., p. 268; ibid., pp. 240, 244, 257.
[3] Blanche Dugdale, *Balfour*, vol. i, pp. 225–39.
[4] Hay to Sherman, Apr. 6, 1898, Dennis, *Adventures*, p. 72.

assistance from the greatest naval Power, the European Chancelleries were helpless.

In the meantime the representatives at Washington of Great Britain, France, Germany, Austria, Italy, and Russia, with the concurrence of the White House and the State Department, had drawn up a collective note which they submitted to McKinley.[1] But the danger of war had not been averted, and on April 14 the diplomatists made one more effort to preserve peace. Sir Julian Pauncefote, the British Ambassador, was prominent in drafting the final proposals and the part he played in these transactions became, four years later, the subject of an Anglo-German controversy. To the wording of the note, however, both London and Berlin objected.[2] The matter, accordingly, went no farther.

The European Powers were in the main being foiled by British abstention and the Austro-Hungarian Ambassador to the Quirinal gave vent to their wrath. Conversing in Rome with the correspondent of *The Times*, he spoke of the 'criminal shortsightedness of England in not opposing the designs of the United States'. It was the view of the German and Austrian Emperors that, against the high-handed attitude of Washington, Europe ought to take a stand and bring the Americans to reason. The Powers might turn against her if Great Britain encouraged the United States to flout Europe. The Austrian diplomatist wanted *The Times* to urge upon the British public an anti-American concert. In such a manifestation Germany, Austria-Hungary, France, and Russia were prepared to join, followed—should Great Britain enter—by Italy.[3] But in London the press and the Government were likely to yield neither to Austrian threats nor to Spanish entreaties once the United States was resolved upon war.

Nevertheless Balfour and Chamberlain had been alarmed by Pauncefote's proposal that Great Britain should adhere to the suggested European mediation. They did not wish to incur American ill will and sacrifice for the sake of Spain the welcome *rapprochement* with the United States. Balfour's difficulty—Salisbury being in the south of France—was one of rejecting categorically the advice of a respected Ambassador, of resisting the desire of the representatives of the Powers at Washington and the representative of Austria at London, that the British Government should give her 'a lecture on international morality'. He therefore instructed the Foreign Office to cable tactfully to Pauncefote that it seemed very doubtful whether

[1] *U.S. Foreign Relations*, 1898, p. 740; J. J. Jusserand, *What Me Befell*, p. 164.
[2] Mowat, *Pauncefote*, pp. 215–22; Dennis, *Adventures*, pp. 73–4; George W. Smalley, *Anglo-American Memories*, Second Series, p. 181.
[3] Henry Wickham Steed, *Through Thirty Years*, vol. i, pp. 131–2.

they ought to commit themselves to a judgement adverse to the United States and whether such action would advance the cause of peace.[1] In this fashion the serious blunder was avoided and the policy of April 6 remained uppermost: Great Britain, Balfour had informed Hay, would do nothing unacceptable to the American Government. By the Prime Minister himself the idea of a remonstrance at Washington had never been regarded with enthusiasm. The Powers now realized that no more could be done, and this Salisbury pointed out to Queen Victoria.[2] Spain was left to American mercies.

John Hay's delight knew no bounds at the friendly spirit of British public sentiment. Among American statesmen he was the chief advocate of English-speaking solidarity. With him at his country's Embassy in London—where he had the assistance of Henry White— Chamberlain could talk freely. So intimate had they become—it was recollected twenty years later—that, when the rumour spread of a European coalition against the United States, the Colonial Secretary dispatched a special emissary to tell the Ambassador that he would resign if the policy of the British Government were unfavourable. Since, however, Arthur Balfour—also in very close touch with Hay— remembered that there was practically no doubt of the Cabinet's decision, the incident may be interpreted as merely symptomatic of the prevailing temper.[3]

Chamberlain in fact during these months applied himself less to immediate political tactics and more to ultimate issues. For, early in April, the British Minister, then beginning with the Germans his famous discussions about an alliance, tried at the same time to combat the isolation of Great Britain by permanent Anglo-American unity. 'He is extremely desirous of a close alliance with us,' John Hay reported to President McKinley after conversing with Chamberlain on April 3, 'or if that is prevented by our traditions, of an assurance of common action on important questions. "Shoulder to shoulder", he said, "we could command peace the world over." He said again, "I should rejoice in an occasion in which we could fight side by side. The good effect of it would last for generations."' Chamberlain had his prescient dream and history will pronounce upon it as one of those which in the fortunes of mankind, soon or late, tend to their own fulfilment. But John Hay necessarily could only be conscious of almost

---

[1] Balfour to Chamberlain, Apr. 16, 1898, Blanche Dugdale, *Balfour*, vol. i, pp. 262–3; Chamberlain to Balfour, Apr. 16 and 17, 1898, ibid., p. 263; also Garvin, *Chamberlain*, vol. iii, p. 299.

[2] Salisbury to Queen Victoria, Apr. 22, 1898, *Letters of Queen Victoria*, Third Series, vol. iii, p. 244.

[3] Spring Rice to Thayer, Jan. 1918, Stephen Gwynn, *The Letters and Friendships of Sir Cecil Spring Rice*, vol. i, p. 253.

insuperable barriers at home—the remoteness of foreign affairs to a country priding itself in recent years on national self-sufficiency, the hard crust of anti-British prejudice which had yet to be broken. In his remarks to the President the Ambassador therefore continued: 'Of course I give no encouragement to any suggestion of an alliance, which seems to me impracticable; but I say what seems called for as reciprocation of so much friendliness. I think the present attitude of the British Government and people is most valuable to us, and may be still more so in the near future.'[1]

If Chamberlain's idea could have received a constructive response from the United States, would the Cabinet under the isolationist Salisbury have supported him ? The Colonial Secretary as the Minister most gifted with energy, imagination, and foresight was an indispensable colleague; there would have been no need for him to resign from the Government and rally the country to his standard. Salisbury and Balfour, however justified their scepticism, were willing to consider and carry on Chamberlain's negotiations with Germany;[2] it is inconceivable that they would cursorily have dismissed an infinitely more agreeable project. The policy of the Government expressed at Washington in the Far Eastern inquiry of March 8, the British outlook during the Spanish-American crisis, Chamberlain's national position—all these illustrate that he talked as no irresponsible visionary but as a leading Minister armed with immense official power and ready to do business. In this at least his former comrades of the Liberal Party would have backed him. The Germans, moreover, were aware of the fact that Anglo-American understanding constituted an integral portion of his scheme. When they first discussed an alliance the Colonial Secretary had asked Count Hatzfeldt, the German Ambassador, whether he believed that the United States would long continue her policy of non-interference in Europe, and neither of them thought it possible.[3] To associate the United States with Great Britain when the momentous shift occurred in American diplomacy was one of Chamberlain's cardinal ambitions. If he spoke as a man before his time, he yet could speak none too soon.

The United States in any case now profited from an Anglo-American alliance without its cost. Before and during the Spanish War British supremacy at sea paralysed intervention by the Powers.

---

[1] Hay to McKinley, Apr. 4, 1898, Olcott, *McKinley*, vol. ii, p. 130.

[2] Garvin, *Chamberlain*, vol. iii, pp. 254–95; Blanche Dugdale, *Balfour*, vol. i, pp. 256–61.

[3] Chamberlain's memorandum, Mar. 29, 1898, Garvin, *Chamberlain*, vol. iii, p. 260; also Willy to Nicky, May 30, 1898, N. F. Grant (ed.), *The Kaiser's Letters to the Tsar*, p. 54.

The friendship of England was important 'in the present state of things', Hay informed Senator Lodge, 'as it is the only European country whose sympathies are not openly against us. We will not waste time in discussing whether the origin of this feeling is wholly selfish or not. . . . If we wanted it—which of course we do not—we could have the practical assistance of the British Navy—on the *do ut des* principle naturally.'[1] But in fact, so far as a European coalition was concerned, the United States already enjoyed 'the practical assistance of the British Navy'. Its passive strength in reserve kept the way clear while the Americans wrought their victory and retained or disposed of their conquests. Short of finding an ally, what Great Britain thus gained was not to be fully manifest at once. Yet even then the process began of making the United States a friend who, while the British were otherwise engaged, would not disturb their outlying security, Dominion, colonial, or maritime, but might instead on the Pacific and in the western Atlantic oppose common adversaries. Such a policy—vague, tentative, and perhaps never precisely framed —which perceived in the United States an offset to hostile Powers was a form of reinsurance implicit in the diplomacy of the Spanish-American War. Neither Hay nor Chamberlain underrated the unifying force of their English-speaking heritage. But in a world of *Realpolitik* the great imponderables required from both sides the sanction of mutual advantage if they were to be an effectual bond.

On April 21, 1898, the United States was at war with Spain. The American Navy blockaded Cuba while Commodore Dewey proceeded from Hong Kong to Manila Bay in the Philippines, an enemy possession, to grapple with the Spanish fleet. American interests in Cuba and Spain were represented by Great Britain, and in Washington the French Ambassador acted for Madrid.[2]

So patent had been British goodwill that Henry White, visiting in the United States, was regarded as a negotiator for an Anglo-American alliance. In Washington he discovered that Congressmen were voicing their appreciation of the refusal of Downing Street to interfere or join the European mediators, while Senators Lodge, Frye, Morgan, and Davis, hitherto never very Anglophile, likewise expressed the change of sentiment—their colleague Senator Foraker even going so far as to regret that the United States had not combined with

---

[1] Hay to Lodge, Apr. 5, 1898, William Roscoe Thayer, *John Hay*, vol. ii, p. 165. Earl Grey had actually suggested that the United States borrow the British Navy to make a quick job of Cuba. She could, he told the Ambassador, return the favour another time. Hay to McKinley, Apr. 4, 1898, Olcott, *McKinley*, vol. ii, p. 130.
[2] *U.S. Foreign Relations*, 1898, pp. lxiv, 966.

Great Britain to stop the Russian advance in China. At London John Hay was therefore quick to grasp the opportunity and in April delivered a notable speech on the beneficent characteristics of Anglo-American friendship.[1] To the United States, confronted with general European obloquy, British sympathy had become a source of the utmost satisfaction.

The march of events was swift. At the end of April Dewey won his victory in Manila Bay and blockaded the city. With one stroke the United States enhanced her status in world politics and European apprehensions grew apace. In Berlin anti-American predilections were rife. The Kaiser hoped that in the altered circumstances on the Pacific the German Empire might obtain maritime compensations. His ideas were derived from Admiral von Tirpitz, who had expected that the Spaniards would beat the American fleet but fail to quell the Filipino insurrection: Manila, in Bülow's satiric phrase, would then drop like a ripe fruit into the German lap. Vigilant yet uncertain, Germany wondered in 1898 whether she could not cash some of the dividends of the American investment.[2]

Meanwhile Joseph Chamberlain was chafing at his country's impotence in the Far East and at her diplomatic isolation. John Hay had, moreover, suggested that he should not allow the Liberal Opposition to monopolize public utterances of goodwill towards the United States.[3] On May 13, in a speech at Birmingham, the Colonial Secretary lashed out. Referring to Russia's seizure of Port Arthur, he spoke admiringly of the proverb: 'Who sups with the devil must have a very long spoon.' He painted a sombre picture of the combination of Great Powers which menaced England. The same group was also unfriendly towards the United States and her recent triumph in Manila Bay gave Chamberlain an excuse for an exuberant passage. 'I go even so far as to say that, terrible as war may be, even war itself would be cheaply purchased if, in a great and noble cause, the Stars and Stripes and the Union Jack should wave together over an Anglo-Saxon alliance.' To Salisbury's policy the Colonial Secretary attributed the fact that the two nations now understood each other better than at any time since the American Revolution; but at home these remarks lost some of their effect in the furore aroused by Chamberlain's bold sally into European and Far Eastern affairs. The patience of the Prime Minister was sorely taxed and H. H. Asquith, its Liberal critic, derided the speech as touting for an ally

---

[1] Nevins, *White*, pp. 133–4; Tyler Dennett, *John Hay*, pp. 188–9.
[2] Bülow, *Memoirs 1897–1903*, p. 216; Brandenburg, *From Bismarck*, &c., pp. 123–4; Spring Rice to Hay, May 14, 1898, Gwynn, *Spring Rice*, vol. i, p. 248.
[3] Hay to Lodge, May 25, 1898, Thayer, *Hay*, vol. ii, p. 169.

in the highways and byways of Europe.[1] Nevertheless, its cordial reception in the United States gratified Chamberlain. A typical comment of his, quoted by John Hay, was that he did not 'care a hang what they say about it on the Continent'.[2]

Berlin professed to be unmoved. An alliance between Great Britain and the United States—with or without the adherence of Japan—might potentially limit and circumscribe Germany's mounting ambitions. That this would materialize was, however, not sufficiently probable to worry the Kaiser. To the British Ambassador he made some astute observations. William II agreed that British public opinion would now countenance an alliance, but he thought it injudicious to proclaim openly the need for one since the Power sought after might thus be enabled to demand heavier terms. About the prospects for an Anglo-American alliance the German Emperor, despite newspaper talk, preferred to remain sceptical. He admitted that a better understanding existed than ever before between the English-speaking peoples; so long as her war lasted with Spain the United States was doubtless anxious to secure the goodwill of Great Britain. But when it ceased—and here the Kaiser showed keener insight than Chamberlain—the United States would probably revert to her old habit of diplomatic independence and avoid anything in the shape of a European alliance.[3] Such too was the mood of complacency in which the Germans conducted their dilatory and evasive discussions with Salisbury and Chamberlain. Against the gloom of American tradition and British rivalry with France and Russia, they saw themselves shine forth as Great Britain's only conceivable ally. They might build their fleet with impunity, sell their neutrality to Salisbury for colonial concessions, cultivate St. Petersburg, and assert an ever-ascending claim in world politics. Eventually for their services the British Government would pay a high price.

At Madrid the speech of the Colonial Secretary played into the hands of the French. Spain was Anglophobe for one reason because the British held the Rock and controlled the Straits of Gibraltar—a viewpoint which met with no discouragement from France who wished to co-operate with her against Great Britain in Morocco. Nor in 1898 by British sympathy with the United States was French influence among Spaniards likely to be diminished. Chamberlain's proposal for an Anglo-American alliance, the British Ambassador reported from Madrid, 'has naturally created a great sensation. It

[1] Garvin, *Chamberlain*, vol. iii, pp. 282–4, 301–2; Alexander Mackintosh, *Joseph Chamberlain*, p. 219.

[2] Hay to Lodge, May 25, 1898, Thayer, *Hay*, vol. ii, p. 168.

[3] Lascelles to Salisbury, May 26, 1898, *Br. Docs.*, vol. i, no. 53, p. 34.

is supposed to imply hostility to Spain, and has increased, if possible, the bad feeling which our European friends have been stimulating for so many years'.[1] The Anglo-American *rapprochement* had entered into the calculations of continental statecraft. Between Great Britain and Spain there was during that summer to be a serious dispute.

The idea of an Anglo-American alliance had been flung by a member of the Government into the public arena. Defending himself in June before the House of Commons, the Colonial Secretary renewed his attack on British isolation and again predicted the European coalition with which one day Great Britain might be threatened. The Americans, he agreed, did not then desire an alliance. 'They do not ask for our assistance and we do not want theirs.' But his high aspiration Chamberlain refused to forsake. Could any one deny 'that the occasion may not arise, foreseen as it has been by some American statesmen, who have said that there is a possibility in the future that Anglo-Saxon liberty and Anglo-Saxon interests may hereafter be menaced by a great combination of other Powers? Yes, Sir, I think that such a thing is possible, and, in that case, whether it be America or whether it be England that is menaced, I hope that blood will be found to be thicker than water'.[2] Chamberlain's politics were better than his ethnology. It was an error for him to stress an identity of race. The forces of history and environment, the broad influence of English-speaking democracy and culture, the trend towards a community of international interests—these were some of the diverse strands out of which Anglo-American friendship would be composed. To the furtherance of that object the descendants of many stocks on both sides contributed.

Dewey's presence in the Philippines had, in the meantime, revived a long-standing controversy about annexation by the United States of the Hawaiian Islands. In American policy economic, naval, and political elements were inextricably mixed. But during the Spanish War it was especially important for strategic purposes to safeguard the western shore of the United States and consolidate her position on the Pacific. With Hawaii in the grip of another Power American ships in Manila Bay, no less than a free decision about the subsequent fate of the Philippines, would have been jeopardized. As a matter of fact in 1897 Theodore Roosevelt, the Assistant Secretary of the Navy, had prepared to move in advance of the Japanese, who were eager to

---

[1] Drummond Wolff to Salisbury, May 15, 1898, *Br. Docs*, vol. ii, no. 300, p. 253; also ibid., no. 301, p. 253; ibid., no. 302, pp. 253–4; ibid., no. 303, pp. 254–5.

[2] Garvin, *Chamberlain*, vol. iii, pp. 302–3. Chamberlain's appeal for an Anglo-American alliance, Balfour wrote to Queen Victoria, 'infuriated' Dillon, the Irish Nationalist leader. *Letters of Queen Victoria*, Third Series, vol. iii, pp. 25 .

expand and who in the end did protest against the American annexa-tion.[1] Of the British attitude towards the Hawaiian problem the Wilhelmstrasse had already received an intimation; in 1897 Salisbury rejected an offer of German support to oppose American acquisition of the islands.[2] And then in 1898, before the United States took the final step, there was British pressure of an unofficial character. Cecil Spring Rice, attached to the British Embassy at Berlin and a friend of John Hay, Theodore Roosevelt, and Henry Cabot Lodge, favoured the Americans as much as he detested the Germans. Anxious to have the United States forestall Germany on the Pacific, he wrote in that sense to John Hay. As a result, the American Ambassador cabled from London to his Government that an 'excellent authority in German matters suggests prompt action in annexation Hawaii before war closes as otherwise Germany might seek to complicate the question with Samoa or Philippine Islands'.[3] Such considerations presumably hastened developments. On July 8, 1898, President McKinley assented to the resolution for the annexation of Hawaii. It was the first ingathering of the harvest and Englishmen were not displeased.

The United States never forgot the lesson taught by the Spanish War, that sea-power had become vital to her security. Without the benevolent neutrality—sometimes very thinly disguised—of the British Navy she might have been hard-pressed. By the Spaniards all signs of assistance to their enemy were bitterly resented. In August the Queen-Regent sadly complained to Queen Victoria that coal had been supplied in British ports to American but not to Spanish ships and that the Filipino insurgents, in league with the United States against Spain, had procured their equipment at Hong Kong.[4] If Salisbury was at once inclined and obliged to observe his country's formal neutrality there were perhaps others both in and out of the Government somewhat less punctilious about diplomatic niceties.

At Manila, where Dewey with a small squadron had been maintain-ing the blockade, vessels of neutral Powers—a French, a Japanese,

[1] Henry F. Pringle, *Theodore Roosevelt*, p. 171; John Holladay Latané, *A History of American Foreign Policy*, pp. 563–4; also Beard, *The Idea of National Interest*, pp. 71–8.
[2] Brandenburg, *From Bismarck*, &c., p. 104.
[3] Hay to Day, May 3, 1898, Dennis, *Adventures*, p. 76; also Spring Rice to Hay, Apr. 30, 1898, Gwynn, *Spring Rice*, vol. i, p. 247; Hay to Spring Rice, May 5, 1898, ibid., p. 248.
[4] The Queen-Regent of Spain to Queen Victoria, Aug. 30, 1898, *Letters of Queen Victoria*, Third Series, vol. iii, p. 268. At Washington the British Naval Attaché, in company with his military colleague, apparently made himself available for con-sultation by the American authorities. J. M. Kenworthy and George Young, *Freedom of the Seas*, p. 52.

two British, and three German—arrived to hold a watching brief for their national interests. The Germans had publicly voiced the hope of obtaining a coaling-station in the eastern Pacific; the size of the force they now sent to Manila gave Spring Rice in Berlin a chance to warn a high diplomatist that their zeal might outrun their discretion. British opinion would, he said, oppose all German action repugnant to the United States. Dispatching an account of this colloquy to the American Ambassador at London, he reiterated in a further letter his belief that the Germans regretted the awkward situation they had created with their ships.[1] It is possible, though unlikely, that Spring Rice would have talked to the Germans and written to John Hay in this fashion without the knowledge of his official superiors at the Berlin Embassy and the Foreign Office. But in any case for the remainder of his career, in whatever post he occupied—and he himself from 1913 to 1918 was to be British Ambassador at Washington—he spared no effort to bring together the English-speaking peoples on the basis of the common danger from Germany.

Friction did arise in July between Dewey and the German Vice-Admiral, von Diederichs, when the latter protested against the fact that a German cruiser had been hove-to by an American ship and boarded to establish her identity. They accordingly appealed for a decision to Captain Chichester, the senior British naval officer, who, disagreeing with the German argument, thereupon upheld the correctness of Dewey's procedure under the rules of international law.[2] And then in August von Diederichs was suspected of endeavouring to intervene between the Spaniards and the Americans during the joint army and naval operations which led to the capture of Manila itself. Such interception, however, may have been blocked by Captain Chichester. The story was that at a critical juncture the British officer placed his command between the German and American vessels—a friendly act for which he received credit from McKinley's Secretary of the Navy.[3] In his memoirs Prince von Bülow tried lamely to explain away the Kaiser's motives and the ill-advised conduct of his countrymen. But even he had to admit that the German ships approached much too close to the battle with a consequent distrust in the United States.[4] The delicacy of the whole Manila

[1] Spring Rice to Hay, July 16, 1898, Gwynn, *Spring Rice*, vol. i, pp. 251–2; same to same, July 23, 1898, ibid., p. 252.
[2] The Admiralty to the Foreign Office, Sept. 29, 1898, *Br. Docs.*, vol. i, no. 126, pp. 105–7.
[3] John D. Long, *The New American Navy*, vol. ii, p. 112.
[4] Bülow, *Memoirs 1897–1903*, p. 216; also p. 413.

episode should not be exaggerated. It would have been rash for
Germany to misprize the latent naval strength which inhered in a
rapprochement between the English-speaking Powers. Her blunders
and intrigues were shorn of all peril through the insurance afforded
American arms, on land and afloat, by British mastery of the seas.

Late in the summer relations between Great Britain and Spain
went from bad to worse. In July a Spanish newspaper repeated a
rumour—which Chamberlain's speeches seemed to confirm—that
London and Washington had signed a convention for military and
other assistance. At Madrid this report was denied by the British
Ambassador.[1] But the fear of an Anglo-American alliance died hard.
Spain therefore undertook to protect herself by measures which
might prove useful in the event of such a union—measures directed
at the one nerve-centre of British sea-power to which she had access.
Near Algeciras, as elsewhere on their coast, ostensibly to defend
themselves against an American invasion, the Spaniards started to
erect batteries for heavy guns. The work was continued, however,
when the issue of the war appeared no longer in doubt and by it the
position of Great Britain at Gibraltar, her naval predominance in the
Mediterranean, might have been subjected to a potential disability
of the utmost gravity. And so at Madrid the British Government in
August employed extremely stern language.[2] Their representations
provoked a despairing letter to Queen Victoria from Maria Cristina,
the Queen-Regent of Spain. As if violations of her neutrality on
behalf of the United States had not been enough, Great Britain now
wished to divest the Spaniards of the means for ensuring the safety
of their country. Lord Salisbury, ignoring Maria Cristina's specific
charges, was indignant. His Government, he informed Queen Victoria,
had been absolutely neutral. Of the partiality of British newspapers
he was 'painfully aware', but in England the Executive had no
control over the press. In this vein Queen Victoria answered Maria
Christina; the Spaniards could only swallow their pride and abandon
the further construction of their fortifications.[3] As a phase of
European diplomacy Anglo-Spanish dissension did not arise solely
from the conflict then being waged overseas. It was none the less
in its immediate course governed by the repercussions on Madrid
of the British attitude towards the United States.

[1] Tyrrell to Asquith, Sept. 6, 1922, Asquith, *Genesis of the War*, pp. 33–4.
[2] *Letters of Queen Victoria*, Third Series, vol. iii, pp. 264, 266–7, 269–71.
[3] The Queen-Regent of Spain to Queen Victoria, Aug. 30, 1898, *Letters of Queen
Victoria*, Third Series, vol. iii, pp. 268–9; Salisbury to Queen Victoria, Sept. 11, 1898,
ibid., p. 279; Queen Victoria to the Queen-Regent of Spain, Sept. 12 (?), 1898, ibid.,
pp. 280–1; the Queen-Regent of Spain to Queen Victoria, Oct. 1, 1898, ibid., p. 289;
also ibid., pp. 244, 257.

Meanwhile, American troops having conquered Cuba and Porto Rico, negotiations were initiated for an armistice. Conducted under the good offices of France, they were finished in the middle of August. By them Spain agreed to the relinquishment of Cuba and the cession of Porto Rico and one of the Ladrones, leaving in the hands of the American Government the future disposition of the Philippine Islands.[1] Towards these latter what policy would it be best to adopt? Until Washington made up its mind and the treaty of peace had been signed at the end of the year there was from abroad no dearth of advice.

The German Government were at that stage in a high fever of excitement. Desiring to share in the new settlement of the Philippines, they sought to dissuade the United States from any plan to keep them exclusively as a possession of her own. In July the American Ambassador at Berlin intimated to Washington that in this matter close co-operation with Great Britain would result in a European coalition; the State Department assured him, however, that his apprehensions were illusory and indicated that continental interference was unacceptable. During the same month Count Hatzfeldt, the German Ambassador at London, conveyed to John Hay his country's colonial requirements, while Japan also was evidently willing to help administer the Philippines.[2] France, on the other hand, disclaimed aspirations in that quarter. But at the Quai d'Orsay M. Jules Jusserand—later Ambassador to the United States—in June and again in August warned the American Government through Henry White against the political and naval dangers of assuming the slightest responsibility for the distant Philippines.[3] Coming from the friend of Spain such solicitude could not be entirely disinterested. The situation was comic. For to the United States some of the Powers were solemnly suggesting that she should not reap the bountiful crop they had tried in the first place to prevent her from sowing.

The British Government knew what was afoot. Loaded with many burdens they did not then wish to shoulder new ones in the Pacific nor, by so doing, to face the prospect of having to find troublesome compensations elsewhere for those whose road they thus barred in the Philippines. Yet it would have been for them a distinct strategic and diplomatic setback if they allowed this Asiatic vantage-point, in part or as a whole, to fall to a Power such as Germany. Throughout 1898 Joseph Chamberlain, the most forcible of British Ministers, had

[1] *U.S. Foreign Relations*, 1898, p. 819.
[2] Dennis, *Adventures*, pp. 78, 81, 93–8; also J. Fred Rippy, *Latin America in World Politics*, pp. 167–73.
[3] Jusserand, *What Me Befell*, pp. 165–8; Nevins, *White*, pp. 137–8.

striven to out-manœuvre European rivals by sponsoring a friendly
United States in the sphere of world politics. The Prime Minister
himself may never have been so deliberate; in effect, nevertheless,
Salisbury's Cabinet had during the first half of the year sketched the
outlines of a consistent, purposive design. And now, by urging the
United States to keep what she could rightfully keep, it might best
be completed—a course which would be good not only for Anglo-
American relations but also serve British interests over against third
parties. For that reason no doubt Salisbury refused when Spain in
June invited his Government to occupy Manila. And then at the end
of July, several months before the American Administration had
themselves decided upon their policy, Great Britain made her attitude
explicit. From London John Hay cabled to the Secretary of State
that the 'British Government prefer to have us retain Philippine
Islands, or failing that, insist on option in case of future sale'.[1]
Writing to President McKinley, the Ambassador remarked that if
they abandoned the archipelago it would be a considerable disappointment to their British friends. Hay believed that the Germans
had been intriguing with Madrid and with Aguinaldo, the leader of the
rebellion in the Philippines. 'They are most anxious to get a foothold there; but if they do there will be danger of grave complications
with other European powers.'[2]

In broad perspective the British attitude is perfectly clear. Ever
since the opening of western trade with the Far East the two sea-
routes from Europe, either by way of the Cape of Good Hope or later
through the Suez Canal, had been under the control of the Royal
Navy and its strategic outposts. But now valuable seaports on the
coast of China, with access to the interior, were being seized by
expansionist European Powers. Against all that, however, could be
set off the rising strength on the Pacific of the United States. In
eastern Asia Anglo-American interests coincided so far as Great
Britain, without the help of Washington, was able to follow her
avowed programme of maintaining the Open Door and the territorial
integrity of China. During 1898—in Far Eastern and Spanish questions alike—a *rapprochement* between the English-speaking peoples
had been a notable feature of British diplomacy. If then the Philippines, an important naval station as well as stepping-stone to the
Orient, were no longer to belong to Spain, they must naturally be
transferred to that Power which had not only won them but also
possessed the supreme merit of being a friend. And indeed from this

---

[1] Hay to Day, July 28, 1898, Dennis, *Adventures*, p. 100; also ibid., p. 79.
[2] Hay to McKinley, Aug. 2, 1898, Olcott, *McKinley*, vol. ii, p. 135.

point of view, upholding the command of the eastern sea-routes, Great Britain could begin to consider the United States an associated part of her defensive system.

By October the Germans were more docile. Arthur Balfour told Henry White that so long as the United States kept them they would make no demands in the Philippines; should she, however, give up any portion of them Germany would take it over; and Balfour similarly expected German intervention if part of the islands were ceded to Great Britain or some other Power.[1] With Germany the British Government were assuredly not then looking for fresh quarrels. They were determined to purchase the Philippines only as a last resort if the Americans showed no willingness to remain there. During that autumn, just when President McKinley had reached his final-decision, Lord Salisbury himself observed to Henry White that, by annexing the whole archipelago instead of the single island of Luzon, the United States had avoided having on her hands 'another Kiau-Chau'.[2] And thus, too, the Germans were outwitted when Downing Street advised President McKinley to appropriate all the Philippine Islands. For in the final settlement of the Spanish War the British policy of informal strategic reinsurance with the United States was first successfully embodied.

There were many influences at work shaping McKinley's resolve to annex the Philippines in their entirety. Some of the most powerful were deep-rooted in the economic development of the United States and in the history of her naval and territorial expansion. But to the President's view that they must continue under American tutelage— once it was decided that they could neither be restored to Spain nor left to themselves—the ambitions of Germany and suspicion of France contributed weightily.[3] His attitude conformed to British policy; the pressure from London had doubtless not been disregarded. Signed on December 10, the treaty of peace included the preliminary terms of the August arrangement, and also for a payment of $20,000,000 the Philippines were ceded by Spain to the United States. Ratification had to be secured in the Senate over the votes of traditionally anti-imperialist groups; enough Democrats swung into line; the treaty was passed on February 6, 1899.[4]

It denoted great changes in the growth of the United States as a colonial Power and in her relations with the outer world. That these

[1] Nevins, *White*, p. 140.
[2] White to Hay, Nov. 2, 1898, Nevins, *White*, p. 165.
[3] Olcott, *McKinley*, vol. ii, p. 111; also Beard, *The Idea of National Interest*, pp. 78–83.
[4] Latané, *American Foreign Policy*, pp. 510–11.

synchronized with the rise of Anglo-American friendship was well understood in Washington by the imperially minded and in London by every shade of opinion from James Bryce to Joseph Chamberlain.[1] In November and December the latter had again delivered speeches advocating English-speaking solidarity. The hazards of war, however, were past; with Great Britain the United States was not now likely to move into a more formal association. Victory had been wrought by the single-handed prowess of the American nation; but thanks to the epoch-making cordiality of the British people and Government it was achieved without foreign interference. John Hay, who appreciated this better than any one else, had left the London Embassy to become in September the Secretary of State. Yet even with Hay at his side President McKinley exercised sober caution when, on December 5, in his annual message to Congress, he referred to Anglo-American goodwill during the Spanish War.[2] The neutrality of Great Britain could not be impugned in the eyes of Europe. But neither might risks be run with isolationist feeling and anti-British sentiment which in the United States, despite what had happened, were to exhibit themselves still lively and intractable.

In the history of the Republic 1898 was a dividing-year. Since the Civil War Americans had been absorbed in reconstruction and in exploiting the rich natural resources of their country. The struggle with Spain, however, extended the reach of the United States just when the last of her western frontiers had closed. In the American economy as urban industries took the lead over agriculture they needed commercial expansion outside home markets; at the end of the century the resumption of imperialist tendencies in the United States is, in a number of ways, explained by this fact.[3] At any rate she had now assumed responsibility for the welfare of Cuba, while Porto Rico, Guam in the Ladrones, Hawaii, and the Philippines provided problems for the governance of dependent races whom their new protector was genuinely anxious to assist. Added to them were international questions with which Washington had to deal, fantastic to those who thought the United States could still walk in the strait isolationist paths of her forefathers. The Philippines, which other Powers wanted, were near China, a base for American policy in the Far East. To their importance in that respect the British Government had been alert. They wished the United States to retain them;

[1] Lodge to White, Aug. 12, 1898, Nevins, *White*, p. 137; Lodge to Spring Rice, Aug. 12, 1898, Gwynn, *Spring Rice*, vol. i, pp. 250–1; Bryce to Roosevelt, Sept. 12, 1898, Bishop, *Roosevelt*, vol. i, p. 107.
[2] *U.S. Foreign Relations*, 1898, p. lxxvi.
[3] Beard, *The Idea of National Interest*, pp. 244–6, 274, 312, &c.

D

but if she hesitated, Great Britain, however reluctantly, would herself step in. They were also a possession to be defended in Asiatic waters seven thousand miles from American shores; situated far beyond Hawaii on the Pacific, they brought Japanese colonial rivalry more than ever into the diplomatic calculations of the United States. Nor, besides, could Germany be overlooked. For the upshot of contention with her about the disposal of the Spanish oceanic realm was the German purchase from Spain in February 1899 of the Caroline, the Pelew, and the remainder of the Marianne Islands.[1]

Most of these were matters with which Great Britain, desirous of a permanent *rapprochement* with the United States, would, in framing her policies during the twentieth century, have steadily to reckon. It is therefore pertinent to observe that at their birth she saw what was occurring and approved. Not least among recent events must be counted the regeneration of the American Navy. With sea-power coming to the forefront, a stimulus had been given in the United States to naval development. It was the age of Mahan, and his writings, read much abroad—and especially at Potsdam—were perused afresh by his countrymen. As a colonial Power the United States had outgrown her old coastal defence requirements; she therefore began to build ships which could serve far from home ports. After the Civil War the American Navy had been neglected, but in 1898 the fleet programme amounted to 36 vessels with a total of 59,570 tons and in 1899 it comprised 12 vessels of 105,084 tons.[2] Among those branching out with large naval armaments another nation thus made its modern début.

Europeans and Americans alike now recognized that henceforth the United States would have to be regarded as one of the Great Powers. There were, nevertheless, eminent public men in that country —notably Karl Schurz, William Jennings Bryan, Andrew Carnegie, Senators Hoar and Gray—who lamented the political changes of the period as a transgression of the Republic's fundamental ideals. But a puissant emotion had enveloped the United States, simultaneous with the widespread outburst of imperialism across the Atlantic, and their adjurations went unheeded. Then, quickly as it had flared up, the nationalist ardour died down. The ardour was quenched but not the nationalism. The altered circumstances, the final transition to world power, should logically have predisposed the American people towards collaborative diplomatic activity abroad. Instead

---

[1] Rippy, *Latin America in World Politics*, pp. 173–8.
[2] Clark, Stevens, Alden, and Krafft, *A Short History of the United States Navy*, p. 478; Hector C. Bywater, *Sea-Power in the Pacific*, p. 69.

the transformation engendered in them a strong sense of self-reliance militating against any reversal of their customary attitude. And so in the foreign policies of the United States there was after the Spanish War an awkward dichotomy. On the one hand as a Great Power she could not shirk participation in the wider spheres of international affairs; on the other all those economic forces and historic traditions were still vigorous which since the days of George Washington and Thomas Jefferson had induced Americans to be content with their fortunate geographical location and eschew outside entanglements. This conflict of interest presently displayed itself under John Hay in the Chinese question. The difficulty of sustained large-scale co-operation with the United States, Great Britain was but the first to experience. For the Government at Washington would work abroad spasmodically in only the loosest of association to attain their own immediate goals. That was self-defeating in the long run and crippled the potential effectiveness of Anglo-American friendship. But beyond it not even Theodore Roosevelt, in the Far Eastern crisis of 1904–5, dared to go—while to these two irreconcilable impulses in American policy events of the Wilsonian and post-Wilsonian era can also be traced. In the United States the obligations of world power were overridden by persisting isolationism, and from the turn of the century that fact constituted one of the central problems of international relations.

Henry Adams, humanistic, disenchanted, searching for some point of fixity in a bewildering modern society with which he could not cope, felt the spirit of his ancestors brooding over a consummation—the better understanding between the English-speaking peoples—which for two hundred years they had failed to effect. To have brought 'England into an American system' was the single proof he had ever discerned of 'the working of law in history'.[1] But did not the converse seem at least equally true—that the United States had been introduced into a British system? If Chamberlain defined the principle, Salisbury's entire Ministry accomplished the result. Having warded off European interference, Great Britain had pressed the Americans to keep for themselves the fruits of victory. By them colonial areas in the Pacific were thereupon annexed, vaster in extent than Germany was able to win throughout the whole period of her 'forward policy'.[2] Through friendship with the United States, Great Britain in several portions of the globe had managed to check rivals of her own. Out of the similarity of their imperial interests a permanent

[1] Henry Adams, *The Education of Henry Adams*, pp. 362–3.
[2] Parker Thomas Moon, *Imperialism and World Politics*, p. 393.

intimacy might emerge. Exposed to the chill blasts of Europe's hatred the British Government, for the interval, had triumphed. And besides, Anglo-American understanding was also welcomed by Lord Rosebery, Salisbury's predecessor in office and leader of the Opposition.[1] About that ideal in England, Liberals and Conservatives did not differ. This, moreover, was of peculiar significance at a time of increasing competition between the two countries in foreign trade. Economic difficulties abroad might be a source of union or contention. The political programme of Anglo-American solidarity remained paramount.

There was historically for the world in general a further aspect to the sudden appearance of the United States as a Great Power in Pacific and Far Eastern affairs. For a number of years the allotment of territorial compensations in Africa and the South Sea islands had been a kind of 'safety valve' through which escaped the steam of European expansion. But the entrance on the scene of the United States, soon to be followed by the growth of Japan, diminished the opportunities in the Pacific area for partitioning among the Powers. During the next decade and a half more attention was paid to Morocco and the crumbling realm of the Turks;[2] to regions, in short, where catastrophe approached and then in the Balkans actually arrived. In 1898 the international equilibrium had indubitably been upset; with encouragement from Great Britain an imperial and naval Power of the first class had thrust itself into the narrow room and crowded atmosphere of world politics. How to put Anglo-American cordiality to practical use was the task before the British Government. They had found that close relations enshrined in a treaty were not feasible. But to the United States the Spanish War demonstrated the reality and utility of British goodwill; perhaps in return she would always maintain an attitude of understanding and, wherever possible, in an age of intensifying animosities, become for Great Britain a sure and beneficent counterpoise. In the western hemisphere there was much which, once peace had been made, barred the way. To this British diplomacy now addressed itself. An alliance with the United States being ruled out, the informal policy of friendly reinsurance was as already adumbrated henceforth pursued.

[1] Oscar S. Straus, *Under Four Administrations*, p. 149.
[2] Brandenburg, *From Bismarck*, &c., pp. 521-2.

III

THE *RAPPROCHEMENT* IN SUSPENSE

THE new spirit in Anglo-American relations made the time ripe for the settlement between Great Britain and the United States of all their outstanding disputes. Would the sympathies of the period ease the process of liquidation? An early answer in the affirmative was expected. Then two problems—the Alaskan boundary and the isthmian canal—provided an unanticipated element of discord and delay. The main obstacle came from differences between Canada and the United States. The British Government were responsible for the external affairs of the self-governing Dominion. Differences between Canada and the United States were therefore differences between the latter and Great Britain. The Empire pulled one way, foreign policy another. But the controversies which resulted were neither barren nor wasted. For the Dominion occupied a position at the heart of any scheme of Anglo-American friendship and so far as that point could be driven home a major principle in the subsequent relations of the English-speaking peoples had been established.

Between Canada and the United States there was a long record of friction. Geography had ordained that their economic, and history that their cultural and social, contacts should be continuous. But their political relations were often unhappy. This fact, indeed, had strongly influenced the northern movement towards Confederation. For one thing: by the topic of annexation, upon which American public men were wont to discourse, Canadians, loyal to their national independence and to the British Empire, were frequently offended. They also had serious commercial grievances. The natural markets for the products of the various sections of Canada lay to the south; these, however, were closed by the high walls of the American protective tariff. It was, besides, a common complaint of Canadians that by the motherland their interests were usually sacrificed to their powerful neighbour. And so, for many reasons, against the United States the embers of their resentment perpetually smouldered.

In 1898 it was intended to adjust various differences between the Canadian and American Governments. With that object a protocol had been signed at Washington on May 30. By means of this agreement it was proposed to create a Joint High Commission to settle twelve of the questions which were most acutely troublesome. These were: fur seals, fisheries of the coast and contiguous inland waters, the Alaskan boundary, transit of merchandise in bond, alien labour laws, mining rights, reciprocity in trade, revision of the Rush-Bagot convention respecting naval vessels on the Great Lakes, the further marking of parts of the boundary, provision for the conveyance of criminals, and for wrecking and salvage. It was in addition a blanket arrangement, and matters not stipulated in the protocol could also be considered.[1]

There were twelve High Commissioners. The British members included Lord Herschell, late Lord Chancellor of England, and Sir Wilfrid Laurier, the Prime Minister of Canada. Newfoundland, interested only in fisheries and reciprocity, was represented by Sir James Winter. The United States sent, among others, Senators Fairbanks and Gray and John W. Foster, a former Secretary of State. The first session of the High Commission took place in Quebec City during the third week of August; it lasted a fortnight, being followed by a recess; then another two weeks' session was held. Further meetings were adjourned to Washington. On the fisheries and sealing questions the Anglo-Canadian delegation was accommodating, but the Americans would not come to terms.[2] It was, however, the problem of delimiting the Alaskan boundary that caused the final break-down of the Commission.

Between Canadian and American territory the drawing of a frontier from the Atlantic to the Pacific had taken about ninety years. Prolonged and acrimonious, that procedure gave birth in the Dominion to much of its mistrust of Anglo-American diplomacy. In 1867 Alaska had been purchased by the United States from Russia. This transaction was based on the boundaries prescribed by the Russo-British Treaty of 1825. According to it the dividing line of southern Alaska ran along the summit of a range of mountains parallel to the ocean or at a distance of thirty marine leagues inland if they were situated farther back than that from the coast. The Americans were to assert that, owing to the inexact language of the treaty, the specified mountains could not be determined. The ownership of some of the mountains at the mouth of the Portland Channel, the location of which became a subject of dispute, also had to be decided. The main difficulty was that the coast contained numerous fiords and indentations. The United States contended that the boundary should run in a line drawn round the heads of the inlets, that is, round the sinuous inland shores. Canada argued that the line should be drawn from the tips of the projections of land across the mouths of the inlets.

[1] *U.S. Foreign Relations*, 1899, p. xxi.
[2] Nevins, *White*, p. 187.

If the American view were correct the Canadian area would be shut off from the sea.

In 1897 gold had been discovered in the Yukon. It was essential to fix boundaries and jurisdiction—the land held hidden treasure. With prospectors and adventurers crowding to the territory, the Canadian Government found it an arduous task to maintain law and order. The Yukon could be reached by Arctic seas or almost impassable land routes, but the best approach to the region was over trails from several of the Alaskan ports on the Lynn Canal, which ran far from the coast into the mainland. For access to the territory Canada would have to control one of these ports.[1] Behind the Canadian claim as presented to the Joint High Commission lay this urgent need.

The Dominion Government could strive for no legalistic adjustment by the bare letter of the bond. They sought a generous settlement in exchange for other concessions. In the Canadian case there was a serious flaw; for over seventy years it had been assumed without challenge by Russia and the United States that the lisière, or coastline of the mainland, was unbroken: on British, Russian, and American maps the boundary of southern Alaska ran round the heads of the inlets.[2] In 1898 from a position so tactically advantageous the American Government and Commissioners could not easily be dislodged. They were no doubt afraid to provoke the taunt, still politically effective, of truckling to Great Britain; and one to which, as a champion of English-speaking co-operation, John Hay, the Secretary of State, was peculiarly susceptible. Besides, in Lord Herschell the Dominion had gained a redoubtable ally. At the beginning of December Hay thought Herschell was 'more cantankerous than any of the Canadians'; yet from Joseph Chamberlain at the Colonial Office some American Commissioners did not escape similar reprobation.[3]

On December 5, 1898, in his annual message to Congress, President McKinley was, nevertheless, bland and conciliatory. Such good humour sprang, however, from something more than an amiable temper. Despite the disagreement in the Joint High Commission the American Government were preparing to ask for British consent to a fundamental alteration in the Clayton-Bulwer Treaty of 1850. This treaty precluded the United States, without the permission of Great Britain, from building alone an isthmian canal across Central

[1] John W. Dafoe, *Clifford Sifton*, pp. 151–71.
[2] Oscar Douglas Skelton, *Life and Letters of Sir Wilfrid Laurier*, vol. ii, p. 135.
[3] Hay to White Dec. 3, 1898, Thayer, *Hay*, vol. ii, p. 204; Nevins, *White*, p. 188.

America. By a request to change it the dimensions of Anglo-American settlement would be at once enlarged. Could the isthmian and Alaskan problems be solved together ?

Between Great Britain and the United States the project of a canal across Central America was at the turn of the century the principal question at issue. The Spanish War had indicated the importance of sea-power in American strategy. Some means of inter-oceanic communication was necessary in order that the divided naval forces of the Republic could be transferred on short notice from the Atlantic to the Pacific or from the Pacific to the Atlantic; and in 1898 that had been conspicuously evidenced by the long voyage of the battle-ship *Oregon* round Cape Horn. On the Pacific, American policy now touched the rim of Asiatic and European diplomacy. Porto Rico and the protectorate over Cuba testified, again, to expansion from south-eastern shores. The United States was in fact tending to amplify the Monroe Doctrine by her theory of paramount interest in Central America, the sphere of the Caribbean Sea and the Gulf of Mexico. In this process the isthmian canal, through the domination of the Caribbean which it promised, would be a pivotal feature. For that colossal enterprise might become the link, commercial and strategic, unifying the responsibilities of the United States on the Atlantic, in Central and South America, with those on the Pacific and in the Orient.

The fulfilment of American policy was once more bound up with the British attitude. Since the collapse in 1889 of French endeavours under de Lesseps it had been apparent that the United States would herself have to build the canal. But she was restricted by the Clayton-Bulwer Treaty. For in 1850, defining the conditions under which the two countries might construct an isthmian waterway, Great Britain and the United States declared that neither of them would secure exclusive control. Equality was to be maintained throughout, and they were never to fortify such a canal nor assume dominion in the vicinity. Rights of commerce and navigation would also be shared equally; in case of war between the signatories the canal was to be a neutral area. All friendly States were, moreover, to be invited to agree to the treaty. The two contracting parties desired to establish a general principle as well as accomplish a particular object. They therefore extended their joint protection to all practicable communications, by canal or railway, across the isthmus of Central America.[1]

The recognition in this zone of equal Anglo-American rights pointed

[1] *U.S. Foreign Relations*, 1901, pp. 238–48.

at that time to the growing power of the United States. Yet British interests there were not only older than the Monroe Doctrine but even antedated the American federation itself. As the rival of Spain, England had planted herself on the east coast of Guatemala—later the colony of British Honduras—and on the Bay Islands off the coast of Spanish Honduras; and she also exercised a protectorate over the Mosquito shore of the eastern coast of Nicaragua. All these interests were not retained. Great Britain had nevertheless always to consider her colonies and bases in the West Indies and the Caribbean to which for many generations her proud argosies had plied; around which, since the days of Elizabeth, nations, princes, and freebooters had struggled; and where, above all, since the decline of Spain in the eighteenth century, her navy had been supreme. By the treaty of 1850 she had therefore ensured that in any trade route cut through the isthmian region she would be a partner.

In Central America, however, British interests could not withstand the rising predominance of the United States. To it the Clayton-Bulwer Treaty was soon regarded as an obstruction. But the more American statesmen protested against what they held to be a self-denying ordinance the less were British Ministers disposed to dissolve the partnership.[1] In point of fact during the years which had elapsed Anglo-American relations had scarcely been such as would prompt Great Britain to release the United States from the stipulations of the contract. Then came the Spanish War, and the *rapprochement* between the two countries was a fitting prelude to the renewal of negotiations. In 1898 the British Government, composing their differences with the United States, might now be willing to forgo that equality of rights in Central America upon which their predecessors had always insisted.

The treaty of peace with Spain had not been signed when, on December 5, the President, in his annual message, brought before Congress the need for speedy action on the isthmian project. In London McKinley's words at once attracted attention, since he had said that American policy called for the control of the canal by the Government of the United States.[2] The Clayton-Bulwer Treaty was still valid and in Washington the British Ambassador had to be assured that it would not be infringed. But the United States desired its modification. To that British Ministers, under the spell of the new Anglo-American friendship, did not object. Lord Salisbury told Henry White, the American Chargé d'Affaires, that the canal should

---

[1] Latané, *American Foreign Policy*, pp. 306–22, 517–26.
[2] *U.S. Foreign Relations*, 1898, pp. xxi–lxxii.

be built by the United States under whose single rule it could best
be protected. The Prime Minister thought that for Great Britain,
now that she had the Suez Canal, the other waterway would be
much less important. In December he merely asked that tolls
in the proposed isthmian canal be levied equally by the United
States and with no discrimination on the ships of all countries
passing through.[1] Without the cordiality prevailing at last between
the two Governments such talk was inconceivable. The events of
the period would be crowned by British consent to an American
canal.

Salisbury's attitude may have nourished the belief in Washington
that he would acquiesce unconditionally. Early in January 1899 Hay
and Pauncefote had actually drafted a convention. But it was also
an hour of vehement controversy; the High Commissioners were hotly
at variance over the Alaskan frontier. In London it seemed therefore
to be taken for granted that the revision of the Clayton-Bulwer
Treaty would depend upon a satisfactory treatment of the Canadian
problem. This was an erroneous assumption. With the vast concession now sought by the United States from the British Government
even the most favourable adjustment of the Alaskan boundary could
hardly be commensurate. Yet, though they made their proposal
while the High Commissioners were in sharp disagreement, the
Americans offered nothing of corresponding magnitude to the Anglo-
Canadian side. To Ottawa and London the United States thus handed
over a veritable armoury of bargaining weapons. None the less, her
recalcitrance in the Alaskan question barred the attainment under
Salisbury of an all-inclusive settlement.

Could the American Government have it both ways and receive
concessions without conceding? Demanding sympathy for their own
canal project they were in the end not very willing to appease Canada.
From that time onward it was beside the point to contest the legal
soundness of the Dominion's case; a general political arrangement,
as first contemplated by the convoking of the Joint High Commission,
had become the one rational solution. John Hay scented this. The
Secretary of State was infuriated with Lord Herschell, who wanted
to leave to the United States on the Alaskan coast only a few, separ-
ated, jutting promontories. Hay thought that, as a matter of common
sense, no nation would ever have allowed or another accepted 'the
cession of such a ridiculous and preposterous boundary line'. And
so at the beginning of 1899 he concluded that Herschell was putting

---

[1] Mowat, *Pauncefote*, pp. 272–3; Hay to White, Dec. 7, 1898, White to Hay, Dec.
23, 1898, Nevins, *White*, pp. 144–5; Thayer, *Hay*, vol. ii, p. 215.

forward a claim in which he himself had no confidence in order to trade it off for something substantial.[1]

The prospect of a diplomatic bargain did not constitute the limit of Canada's interest in American aspirations. The isthmian canal would inevitably affect the maritime approach to the Dominion's Pacific coast. That the Canadians desired to share in the control of the project had been reported to Washington in December; and it is recorded that Sir Wilfrid Laurier approved of a plan for the United States, Great Britain, and Canada to combine and construct the canal.[2] Nor was this idea incomprehensible or impracticable. Western Canada had just entered upon a stage of extensive development. In the Dominion some statesmen must consequently have been concerned about possible risks that might be run by sea-borne traffic to and from their Pacific ports should the suzerainty of the isthmian canal pass as a free gift to the southern Republic. Canada had long been apprehensive of American policy and the coastal shipping laws of the United States were not a good omen. Yet of this suggestion no more was heard. Great Britain did not wish to oppose American ambitions. Beset with many international difficulties, she was disinclined to weigh the future prosperity of western Canada, or even her own ancient rights and naval preponderance in the Caribbean, against her infant understanding with the United States.

But from the mind of the British Government Canadian considerations were by no means absent. The canal would eventually double the effective strength of the American fleet; Downing Street hesitated therefore to yield its consent when a frontier dispute off the northern Pacific coast troubled the relations of the three countries.[3] If this minor sore were healed, and it was within the power of the United States to apply the balm of peace, Canada would be content and Great Britain could agree to the revision of the Clayton-Bulwer Treaty.

At the outset Washington perceived the wisdom of so fair an adjustment. In January 1899 the American High Commissioners were ready to give Canada access to the sea on the Alaskan coast and a port under Canadian jurisdiction. The sovereignty of the territory thus transferred to the Dominion was, however, to remain with the United States. For that country, according to Senator Henry Cabot Lodge, would not permit its coast-line to be broken 'with another Halifax or Esquimault'.[4] Did Americans fear an Anglo-Canadian naval base

[1] Hay to White, Jan. 3, 1899, Thayer, *Hay*, vol. ii, p. 204.
[2] Nevins, *White*, p. 145.   [3] Mowat, *Pauncefote*, pp. 278–9.
[4] Lodge to White, Jan. 7, 1899, Nevins, *White*, p. 189. Halifax, Nova Scotia, on the Atlantic and Esquimault, British Columbia, on the Pacific, were the Canadian stations of the Royal Navy.

on the northern Pacific? If so, that anxiety was soon dispelled. Seattle and Tacoma, Pacific coast cities interested in trade with the Yukon, protested loudly against a solution which might entail commercial losses to a Canadian centre. President McKinley was standing for re-election in the following year and he would not gamble with far-western support. As a result of this pressure his Administration withdrew their offer. 'Our American fellow Commissioners', observed the Prime Minister of Canada, 'were at first and almost to the last disposed to come to a reasonable compromise.'[1] And then by sectional politics on a delicate issue of diplomacy the Government of the United States allowed themselves to be stampeded.

When matters went wrong between London and Washington there was, after the Spanish War, little sorrow abroad. The Tsar thought that the Canadian and isthmian questions would prevent Great Britain from forming 'a real alliance with the United States against Europe in general, and Russia in particular'. Nor was he frightened by the fact that the British wished to push the Americans against the Russians in China since, as he reminded the Kaiser, his empire sat entrenched at Port Arthur and touched the borders of Afghanistan.[2] In Washington Senator Lodge had also been keeping his eye on the Far Eastern situation. He regretted that the comparatively unimportant Canadian problems should disturb Anglo-American relations. Lodge wanted some agreement between Great Britain and the United States 'even if it is only a partial one, with a view to its effect upon other Powers'.[3] This the British Government had tendered in March 1898. But neither in regard to China or Alaska did the Administration of President McKinley feel themselves able to adopt policies that were really comprehensive and far-reaching. As a consequence Anglo-American co-operation was harder to achieve and seldom became the positive force in world affairs which events of the year before might have presaged.

In February the British Government made a conciliatory offer. Great Britain and Canada now asked for less than a definite concession in Alaska. They merely desired that the Alaskan boundary should be submitted to arbitration and in return a settlement about everything else could be attained. The procedure was to be along the lines of the adjustment that the United States had herself demanded and secured in the recent Venezuelan dispute; it would have meant the submission of the Alaskan controversy to an arbitral

---

[1] Laurier to Grant, Feb. 27, 1899, Skelton, *Laurier*, vol. ii, p. 131.
[2] Nicky to Willy, Dec. 2–14, 1898, Bülow, *Memoirs 1897–1903*, p. 267.
[3] Lodge to White, Jan. 7, 1899, Nevins, *White*, p. 190.

tribunal under an impartial chairman. About this Sir Julian Paunce-fote spoke to John Hay early in the month.[1] On February 15 Downing Street confirmed its programme of a general arrangement with the United States. 'I obtained assurances from British Minister for Foreign Affairs', Henry White cabled to the Secretary of State, 'that if High Commission should reach agreement British Government assent to your proposed Clayton-Bulwer Treaty would be given at once.'[2] Could the faltering negotiations be reinvigorated?

To the United States the British solution was unacceptable. Arbitration modelled upon the Venezuelan precedent might result in a compromise; if Canada thus received an Alaskan port the north-western and Pacific States would raise an outcry. Arbitration, moreover, jeopardized territory which had long been American and upon which towns had been established and enterprises founded. Hay's language here resembled that of Salisbury in 1895; but in 1899 the positions were reversed. It distressed the Secretary of State that on the Canadian question depended the building of a canal which would benefit the whole civilized world.[3] The British Government had, however, gone far to meet the isthmian request of the United States. Hay therefore devised an ingenious scheme.

His idea was that the frontier controversy should be submitted for judgement to a tribunal of six jurists. They were to be divided equally between the Anglo-Canadian and American sides and a majority vote would make decisions final. This suggestion did not provide for an impartial chairman; if a deadlock were to be avoided, and an award rendered, it would have been necessary for one member at least to vote against the case of his own country. The device was a travesty of the method of genuine arbitration; victory would go to the stronger party. John Hay himself subsequently admitted that, while by means of it the United States might win, she could never lose.[4] Canada rejected the proposal, her theoretical objections to it being amply justified by the manner in which it was applied four years later.

The negotiators were at loggerheads. Neither Great Britain nor the United States would surrender. On February 20 the Joint High Commission adjourned with nothing cleared up.

John Hay was indignant when the Canadians rejected his plan and caused the break-down of the discussions. Although agreement

---

[1] Memorandum, Feb. 4, 1899, Dennis, *Adventures*, p. 136; Hay to Choate, Apr. 28, 1899, Dennett, *Hay*, pp. 230-1.

[2] White to Hay, Feb. 15, 1899, Dennis, *Adventures*, p. 146.

[3] Hay to White, Feb. 14, 1899, Thayer, *Hay*, vol. ii, pp. 217-18.

[4] Hay to Roosevelt, July 14, 1902, Dennis, *Adventures*, p. 152. The year as printed (ibid.) is incorrect.

on the other matters seemed near the Dominion had baulked at separating the Alaskan problem from them for an independent settlement in the future.[1] To have done that would have been for the Canadians to fall into a trap. 'We wanted to arbitrate upon the terms of the Venezuela treaty,' Sir Wilfrid Laurier remarked. 'This they would not consent to do. . . . They offered to go on with the other subjects referred to us, but this we declined to do, and insisted, before we proceeded with the other articles, that they should either settle the boundary question by agreement or by reference to arbitration.'[2] Such being the state of affairs the British Government were not likely to acquiesce in the isthmian project. The American request constituted Canada's sole bargaining card and once deprived of it she was powerless. In that all-round accord with the United States which had become the aim of British policy, unrecompensed approval of the canal would have left the Dominion as an onerous and vulnerable exception. The Anglo-American *rapprochement* was making slow progress.

From Ottawa to Washington, the former now resolved, there would be no more pilgrimages. In both capitals tempers were frayed. Laurier and other public men of the Dominion delivered speeches that were indiscreet and of them American statesmen took note. Forgetting the influence of home politics on his own attitude, John Hay ascribed the intransigence of the Canadians to narrow partisan strife and condemned them for their consequent indifference to the interests of Great Britain.[3] The British Government, however, unlike that of the Dominion, could not afford to retire into a northern seclusion. The path to Washington was kept well-trodden.

The heat generated by the break-down of the Joint High Commission did not conduce to a rational settlement. During May the Canadian Government seem to have let one favourable proposal slip through their fingers. The American Administration were, for the moment, willing to adopt a plan for a commission of five—that is, a body over which an impartial chairman might possibly preside and discarding thereby the critical defect of the even-numbered Hay tribunal. But Canada asked firmly that Pyramid Harbour, the port she had almost secured in the Joint High Commission, should be assigned to her irrespective of the decision on the whole Alaskan boundary.[4] To this condition the United States would not agree,

[1] Hay to White, Feb. 21, 1899, Nevins, *White*, pp. 190–1.
[2] Laurier to Grant, Feb. 27, 1899, Skelton, *Laurier*, vol. ii, p. 132.
[3] Roosevelt to Spring Rice, Feb. 14, 1899, Gwynn, *Spring Rice*, vol. i, p. 293; Hay to Choate, Apr. 28, 1899, Thayer, *Hay*, vol. ii, p. 205.
[4] Dennett, *Hay*, pp. 229–30.

and John Hay now insisted upon his idea of an even-numbered tribunal, three on a side. In July the British Government accordingly
resumed the argument that the Venezuelan treaty was a precedent
relevant to the Alaskan controversy. At the State Department their
contention always occasioned discomfort. 'The position in regard
to arbitration is not altogether free from awkwardness,' Hay confessed. 'After we had put forth our entire force and compelled—
there is no other word for it—England to accept arbitration in the
Venezuela matter, we cannot feel entirely easy in refusing an arbitration in this.' The two cases, as he had pointed out to Lord Salisbury,
were, in his opinion, dissimilar; but the Secretary of State was worried
at the public impression thus created by denying to Great Britain
what, at the demand of Washington, she had granted to Venezuela.
He nevertheless continued to emphasize that, however clear their
claim might be, the Americans had to reckon with 'the fatal tendency
of all arbitrators to compromise'.[1] Such anomalous views were no
doubt dictated by domestic political circumstances. But so long as
they held sway the United States had only herself to blame for keeping
in abeyance British consent to her great isthmian undertaking.

Meanwhile the rush to the Yukon of lawless miners did not subside.
On the undemarcated frontier serious mischief, affecting the relations
of the three countries, might have been fomented. To obviate that a
modus vivendi for the Alaskan boundary was arranged. After somewhat disagreeable negotiations John Hay obtained the line for which
he had laboured and on October 20, 1899, notes were exchanged
between the British and American Governments.[2] But there was as
yet no permanent settlement in sight.

Would Anglo-American settlement prove to be a lengthy process of
piecemeal instalments or become an early and complete accommoda-
tion? Hay knew perfectly well that without a concession to Canada
Salisbury must turn a deaf ear to the isthmian request of the United
States; yet with the Foreign Office he still discussed the Alaskan
problem in a totally unyielding spirit.[3] On this subject the official
correspondence, which lasted until January 1900, seemed therefore
to possess an air of unreality. It was, in essence, simply an outer
façade for the trial of strength which went on behind it. Ineluctably
the winner of that contest would be the Government which had
the less immediate need of the other's friendship. Salisbury in the

[1] Hay to Reid, July 27, 1899, Thayer, *Hay*, vol. ii, p. 207; also James White in *The Canadian Historical Review*, Dec. 1925, vol. vi, no. 4, p. 337.
[2] *U.S. Foreign Relations*, 1899, pp. 320–2; Dennett, *Hay*, pp. 231–4.
[3] Hay to White, Sept. 9, 1899, Thayer, *Hay*, vol. ii, p. 220; Dennis, *Adventures*, pp. 141–3; James White, *Can. Hist. Rev.*, vol. vi, no. 4, p. 338.

meantime was waiting for Canada to be included within the orbit of Anglo-American understanding.

He waited in vain. For at the beginning of 1900 a dramatic event occurred when in the isthmian question Congress took a hand. Where diplomatists failed legislators might succeed. By the leisurely negotiations between Great Britain and the United States a more urgent character was thus abruptly acquired and, although in their fundamental policies of goodwill no change followed, the opportunity now vanished for a single comprehensive arrangement to embrace every outstanding difficulty, Canadian and Central American alike.

In January 1900 the Clayton-Bulwer Treaty was still fully binding. Into the House of Representatives a Bill had, nevertheless, been introduced empowering the American Government to undertake by themselves the construction of an isthmian canal. The route proposed ran through Nicaragua, the control of the necessary territory to be secured from that country and from Costa Rica. Measures for the defence of the project were authorized; in both Houses of Congress the passage of the Bill appeared certain.[1] Was the isthmian partnership of 1850 about to be rent forcibly asunder? Did the United States, just when relations with Great Britain had started to improve, intend that her treaty obligation should be trampled ruthlessly under foot?

To Congressional intervention the American Government responded with alacrity. At the unethical nature of the act John Hay expressed alarm. But, while not condoning that aspect of the Canal Bill, he yet seized upon it as a convenient means of eliciting the rapid consent of the British Cabinet to his own policy. Salisbury was therefore at once asked to sign without delay an isthmian convention such as Hay and Pauncefote had already drafted; the new canal agreement between Great Britain and the United States, which the Senate seemed willing to accept as an alternative, would replace the exclusively American Bill.[2] And in this fashion also any danger to English-speaking friendship could safely be overcome.

As American Ambassador John Hay had been succeeded at London by Joseph H. Choate. To him the Secretary of State wrote that the Congressional Bill was 'in many respects highly objectionable, especially as it absolutely ignores the Clayton-Bulwer Treaty, and, in fact, in many features, is an absolute violation of it'. The United States, he felt, would cut a poor figure before the world if the bill as then framed were passed. He suggested the possibility of his own resigna-

[1] Mary Wilhelmine Williams, *Anglo-American Isthmian Diplomacy*, p. 302.
[2] Pauncefote to Salisbury, Jan. 21, 1900, Mowat, *Pauncefote*, pp. 276–7.

tion. This may have been a hint meant for the Foreign Office: if Salisbury would not sign the draft convention he might find himself confronted with a new Secretary of State less Anglophile than Hay. It was also, more certainly, an endeavour to save his own and other political reputations. 'I think we ought to make an effort to arrange the matter through diplomatic channels, so that at least the Administration would have its skirts clear of any complicity in a violent and one-sided abrogation of the Clayton-Bulwer Treaty.'[1]

Hay wanted Salisbury to harbour no illusions. The building of the canal, he informed Choate, had become inevitable and the Treaty of 1850 would not prevent it. Nor could he say whether the Americans or the British were going to profit most from so great a benefaction for the whole of civilized mankind. 'It would be a deplorable result of all our labour and thought on the subject, if, by persisting in postponing the consideration of this matter until all the Canadian questions are closed up, England should be made to appear in the attitude of attempting to veto a work of such world-wide importance; and the worst of all for international relations is that the veto would not be effective.'[2] By the iron hand of Congress the velvet glove of the Secretary of State had been given a tighter grip.

The British Government were in a most embarrassing dilemma. The Boer War had broken out and the tale of conflict from South Africa—Black Week occurred in the middle of December 1899—was one of unredeemed disaster. In the Far and Middle East, moreover, the foreign pinpricks continued; continental Europe talked of combining to interfere with Great Britain in her distant struggle; and relations with Germany, after a speech at Leicester by Joseph Chamberlain, had again grown bad. This, plainly, was no season to destroy a promising *rapprochement*. Yet it was one thing to meet the United States more than half-way; it was another, when Great Britain had many grave preoccupations elsewhere, to be defied by Congress. Since 1898 the British Government had favoured the revision of the Clayton-Bulwer Treaty. Their sole stipulation was that the Alaskan controversy must also be settled. Differences on the northern Pacific as well as in the Caribbean area would be lifted simultaneously from the danger-zone. But the Administration in Washington, likewise seeking an Anglo-American adjustment, had not pursued for the various problems a single co-ordinated solution. The burden of Congressional initiative was instead now to be shifted from their backs—so that they might be acquitted of 'complicity' in the legislative

[1] Hay to Choate, Jan. 15, 1900, Thayer, *Hay*, vol. ii, p. 222.   [2] Ibid.

action—to the overladen shoulders of the British Government. Canada remained the stumbling-block.

The Prime Minister could scarcely conceal his annoyance. He was emphatic in telling the American Ambassador that the Dominion's case would have to be reviewed by the Cabinet. The canal proposal, Choate protested, did not concern Canada; but Salisbury in reply mentioned her anger at the American treatment of the Alaskan question. The Prime Minister was unimpressed when the Ambassador reminded him of the verbal consent he had frequently given to the modification of the Clayton-Bulwer Treaty. Since then the South African War had begun; the Dominion had volunteered assistance to Great Britain while public opinion in the United States was pro-Boer. Salisbury consequently asserted that the situation had been changed by the war and Canada's participation; it would have to be considered afresh in the light of these developments. And so from Ottawa resistance to the isthmian project was again expected.[1]

Canada made no trouble, for there was nothing she could do. By 'a violent and one-sided abrogation of the Clayton-Bulwer Treaty' more than the Anglo-American *rapprochement* might have been crushed; peace itself would hang in the balance. And with this as the grim issue she could not be a stickler for her contentions, whatever their merit in equity, about an obscure boundary on the coast of farthermost Alaska. In Anglo-American relations, by the cold logic of geography, Canada was a hostage to fortune.

On questions of foreign policy the right of a Dominion to be consulted had not yet been established. But in 1900 the situation was exceptional. First of all in the western hemisphere the British Government were endeavouring to handle their several problems as a single unit—it being accordingly recognized by them that even in the isthmian transactions Canada should make her voice heard. And secondly, such a procedure was not one which could be repudiated during the Boer War, at a moment when many Canadians were giving so warm an expression of loyalty to the British cause. To Ottawa at the end of January Whitehall therefore frankly explained its predicament. From the Colonial Office Joseph Chamberlain informed the Canadian Ministry of the dire effect upon Anglo-American relations if Great Britain refused to sign the Hay-Pauncefote draft convention. It 'would be regarded as an affront to the United States Government, and would tend to shake the position of the President, whose friendly attitude is in the present condition of public affairs of great importance'. And so Chamberlain hoped that Canada would agree

[1] Choate to Hay, Jan. 27, 1900, Dennis, *Adventures*, p. 158.

to the signature of the new canal treaty 'in the interests of the Dominion as well as those of the rest of the Empire'.[1]

Laurier was now in a worse quandary than Salisbury. At Downing Street Canadian influence had steadily been exercised to withhold British consent as a bargaining counter for an Alaskan concession. To sacrifice the Clayton-Bulwer Treaty without compensation meant gratuitously to forfeit the one chance left of pinning down the United States to a satisfactory adjustment. The Dominion Government did, nevertheless, what they were requested to do. They answered the Colonial Office that they would no longer object to the signature of the isthmian convention. All they desired was that at Washington Salisbury should still urge vigorously the Canadian case.[2] By Congress, in the dark period of the Boer War, Great Britain's hand was being forced. Towards the conduct of British policy Canada thereupon added to her moral and military support a valuable diplomatic contribution.

On February 5, 1900, Hay and Pauncefote signed the new isthmian treaty. Of the magnanimity shown by the British Government the Secretary of State expressed his appreciation; the Prime Minister told Joseph Choate that Canada had been very considerate; and in London the American Ambassador himself thought that the Dominion deserved a large credit mark.[3] By the introduction into Congress of the Canal Bill extraordinarily quick results had been produced. It gained more for the American people, at less cost and in a shorter space of time, than all the voluminous dispatches of generations of Secretaries of State and half the battles of the war with Spain. For unenacted legislation this surely constituted a record. But something also had been lost. The first Hay-Pauncefote Treaty was the last important negotiation directed in person by Lord Salisbury before relinquishing his post at the Foreign Office. The attempt to include Canadian problems in a general arrangement had been characteristic of his broad and temperate methods. As a truly 'graceful concession' the isthmian agreement might have then become the coping-stone of the Anglo-American *rapprochement*. In Washington, however, his policy had not been accepted. The piecemeal process of settlement held the field.

To the Senate the Hay-Pauncefote Treaty was immediately submitted for ratification and referred to its Committee on Foreign Relations. The agreement authorized the United States to construct,

[1] Chamberlain to Minto, Jan. 30, 1900, Mowat, *Pauncefote*, pp. 279–80.
[2] Skelton, *Laurier*, vol. ii, pp. 139–40.
[3] Pauncefote to Salisbury, Feb. 5, 1900, Mowat, *Pauncefote*, pp. 280–1; Choate to Hay, Feb. 7, 1900, Dennis, *Adventures*, p. 166.

regulate, and manage a canal across the isthmus of Central America. From its predecessor it adopted the fundamental principle of neutralization—the rules for free navigation being modelled on those of the Suez Canal Convention. But it did not abrogate or supersede the Clayton-Bulwer Treaty; the new pact merely modified and supplemented.[1] The Senators, however, wanted the United States to have complete control over the canal and an amendment was brought in explicitly superseding the earlier contract of partnership. The first article of the Hay-Pauncefote Treaty stipulated that the canal, in peace and war alike, should be free and open on equal terms to all vessels, commercial and naval, of every nation; there were to be no discriminating charges or conditions in the waterway against the traffic of any country. And then the second article added that the canal could never be blockaded nor belligerent acts committed within it. To these articles also the Senators objected, for by them the United States would be pledged to the neutrality of the canal when she was at war. One of the prime motives in undertaking the project had been to strengthen the system of American naval strategy and coast protection. This, therefore, was a self-imposed limitation which the Senators were swift to attack.

As a matter of fact the amendments to the Hay-Pauncefote Treaty well exemplified those conceptions of national interest which, after the war with Spain, Americans felt their country now capable of putting into practice. A rough passage was thus encountered by a clause in the third article which laid it down that upon ratification Great Britain and the United States would invite other Powers to adhere to their isthmian agreement. For this meant that European Governments were to share in maintaining the use and neutrality of the canal. The Monroe Doctrine had only to be invoked to demonstrate that a rule borrowed from the Suez Canal Convention did not apply in Central America to the expanding sphere of paramount interest of the United States. At a time when Great Britain was yielding valid rights in the western hemisphere the Senate would never permit the creation of new ones for other European Powers. Similarly, by the seventh article no fortifications were to be erected commanding the canal or the adjacent waters; the United States could, however, keep there such military police as she required to protect it against lawlessness and disorder. In other words, the general principle of neutralization carried over from the Clayton-Bulwer Treaty would be perpetuated. But that, precisely, was the principle which the Senate assailed. With fortifications debarred

---

[1] *U.S. Foreign Relations*, 1901, pp. 241–3.

the defensive potentialities of the canal would be hamstrung. This restriction was accordingly also singled out for censure.

Great Britain had already granted to the American Government everything they had requested. The Senate, nevertheless, without offering any equivalent whatsoever, strove for a maximum concession. The Hay-Pauncefote Treaty may have been signed to improve friendly relations between the English-speaking Powers. During 1900 the debate over the amendments threatened unexpectedly to have the opposite result.

The ablest arguments against the agreement came from Theodore Roosevelt, then Governor of the State of New York. The Hay-Pauncefote Treaty clashed with his view of the Monroe Doctrine and American naval strategy. In war-time the neutralization clauses would be a needless handicap. Left open to an enemy fleet, the canal gave it an advantage; while the United States would furthermore have thereby taken upon herself an additional point for her navy to guard. But if the isthmian waterway were equipped to protect itself American war-vessels, liberated from that extra task, would be free for offensive action elsewhere. Only when fortified could the canal really become, as desired, a tower of strength to the sea-strategy of the United States. Roosevelt also criticized the plan for a joint guarantee of the neutralized waterway by foreign nations. If, he contended, she invited European Governments to accede to this, in a neighbouring area where American interests were so obviously vital, the United States could not object to similar co-operation in more distant regions—for example, in southern Brazil or the Argentine. 'If Germany has the same right that we have in the canal across Central America, why not in the partition of any part of Southern America? To my mind, we should consistently refuse to all European powers the right to control, in any shape, any territory in the Western Hemisphere which they do not already hold.'[1] Such were the ideas of American security which Theodore Roosevelt was shortly to bring with him to the White House; and of them Downing Street would be bound to take cognizance. Meanwhile Great Britain had consented to the construction of the canal. But the United States was to bear the whole cost herself. The Senate therefore demanded that she acquire the entire use of the canal for her own defensive purposes.

When the Hay-Pauncefote Treaty was signed, nothing for which they asked had been denied by Salisbury to the American Government. Why, then, from the start did they not adopt the full-blown nationalist position? Perhaps the answer was that Great Britain

[1] Roosevelt to Hay, Feb. 18, 1900, Bishop, *Roosevelt*, vol. i, pp. 144–5.

had engaged herself to forfeit large privileges; without offering compensation the State Department could not ask for more. Besides, until the actual treaty had been published, many American notions about the naval potentialities of the isthmian canal were probably vague or inchoate. And yet another reason can possibly be found in the existence of the *rapprochement* with Great Britain which, during the Spanish War, was at the centre of strategic considerations. Admiral Dewey and Captain Mahan, significantly enough, were not only Anglophile in their outlook, but also approved of the new canal agreement. Framed in part by a statesman with sympathies so pronounced as John Hay, it was postulated doubtless on a continuing Anglo-American friendship, and the undiminished pre-eminence of the Royal Navy. From European countries such as Germany, or from Great Britain herself, no danger would thus arise. But the opponents of the treaty, perceiving the imperial power of the United States, believed that she should be exclusively self-dependent. Their contention, moreover, and the British standpoint—though not in 1900—gradually coincided. Soon Great Britain would be increasingly absorbed elsewhere, in other political and defensive problems. In such circumstances it was in the hands of a friendly rather than hostile Power that the command of the projected canal might best repose. At first the Rooseveltian conception of American naval security may have seemed a high price to pay. On second thought it might have been regarded as an important reinforcement in the western Atlantic for that policy implicit since 1898 in British support of American colonial expansion. Although Great Britain wavered early in 1901 this second thought tacitly prevailed. By 1904 the British policy of naval reinsurance with the United States had been founded exactly upon the supremacy of that Power in the western hemisphere of which Rooseveltian imperialism was a contemporary expression.

The attacks on the treaty did not all spring from a legitimate appraisal of American security. Agitation against England had during the Boer War been given a new lease of life; for the ancient sport of twisting the tail of the British lion any excuse would serve; and as the presidential elections were to be held in that year politicians of moderate opinion maintained a cautious silence. It was with the most intense disgust that John Hay witnessed the intimidating effect of the press campaign on Senators who had promised to back his treaty. Would it be wrecked by the amendments? Successful in gaining the isthmian agreement without yielding over Alaska, he now saw his work being wantonly undone. To Hay the Anglophobia then running riot was intolerable; in March when the amendments were introduced into the Senate by its Committee on Foreign Relations, he tried to resign. Persuaded, however, by McKinley to remain at the State Department, Hay hoped Great Britain would accept the treaty as amended.[1] If she did not, the future was dark. For the Senate, flagrantly overriding British rights still intact in the Clayton-Bulwer Treaty, would thereupon pass the Bill to initiate American action on the canal project. Ratification was postponed until the end of 1900.

The flood-gates of anti-British prejudice had been let down, and during the summer John Hay felt utterly disheartened. In China the Boxers were creating havoc; to protect American interests, Far Eastern co-operation between London and Washington was desirable. But that Hay did not dare to attempt. 'All I have ever done with England', he cried, 'is to have wrung great concessions out of her with no compensation.'[2] Nevertheless, the popular legend that he was excessively pro-British hindered him at every turn. From England an acute German observer, Count Paul von Wolff-Metternich—soon to be Ambassador at the Court of St. James's—reported the situation to the Chancellor of the Reich. Before this, in the previous year or two, he had thought that trouble between Germany and the United States furnished the only danger of an Anglo-German war. By the summer of 1900 a change had occurred. 'The Americans have shown their dislike of England too clearly and though the English will not admit this fact to themselves or anyone else, they know it perfectly well.' But it was also realized that from such misunderstanding European Governments could derive no advantage. 'England will stand far more from America than from any other Power, and even in purely diplomatic issues it is more difficult to make England take sides against America than to make any other Power do so.'[3]

In November William McKinley was re-elected to the Presidency and he invited John Hay to carry on as Secretary of State. During the autumn of 1900 the British Government also appealed to the country—the opportunity not being missed by Joseph Chamberlain to tell the electors of one constituency that he wanted Great Britain 'if possible to be something more than friends with the United States of America'.[4] The Unionists were returned to power, but the Cabinet underwent reconstruction. While Lord Salisbury continued as Prime Minister he retired from the Foreign Office, where he was

---

[1] Hay to White, Mar. 18, 1900, Nevins, *White*, p. 152; Hay to McKinley, McKinley to Hay, Mar. 13, 1900, Thayer, *Hay*, vol. ii, pp. 226–8.
[2] Hay to Foster, June 23, 1900, Thayer, *Hay*, vol. ii, pp. 234–5.
[3] Bülow, *Memoirs 1897–1903*, p. 422.
[4] Garvin, *Chamberlain*, vol. iii, p. 598.

succeeded by the Marquis of Lansdowne. Associated with Lansdowne's name are the Japanese and French agreements which terminated the policy of British isolation. But under him likewise, and as part of this same far-reaching diplomatic process, the chief differences between the English-speaking peoples were finally to be erased.

· In December the Senate sat again and during the middle of the month passed the Davis amendment to the Hay-Pauncefote Treaty. This stipulated that the neutralization clauses should not apply to measures which the United States might find it necessary to take in the canal for securing by American forces her own defence and the maintenance of public order.[1] A basic principle of the old and new isthmian agreements was thus impaired and with the latter the Senate had not yet finished. Through Henry White in London the views of that body were conveyed privately by Senator Lodge to Arthur Balfour.

> 'If England should reject the Senate amendments it is just as certain as the coming of the day that we shall abrogate the treaty by resolution of Congress and go on with the building of the canal. The American people mean to have the canal and they mean to control it. Now England does not care enough about it to go to war to prevent our building it, and it would be ruinous if she did make war on us.'[2]

Standing behind John Hay, Congress in January had levelled a diplomatic pistol at Salisbury's head. Resistance fell flat. Brushing Hay aside, and with passions waxing, the Upper House at the end of the year prepared to repeat the performance.

On December 20, 1900, the Senate ratified the Hay-Pauncefote Treaty after it had incorporated the amendments recommended by its Committee on Foreign Relations. The Clayton-Bulwer Treaty of 1850 was declared to be definitely superseded. The Davis amendment that the neutralization clauses should not apply to American defensive measures in the canal had been added to the fifth article. The provision in the third article for obtaining the adherence of other Powers was omitted. The clause debarring fortifications had been nullified by the preceding Davis amendment and did not, therefore, need to be eliminated.[3] The isthmian canal project was preserved from any connexion with Europe. The principle of neutrality had been fundamentally compromised. By substituting a national monopoly

---

[1] *U.S. Foreign Relations*, 1901, p. 243; Thayer, *Hay*, vol. ii, p. 259.

[2] Lodge to White, Dec. 18, 1900, Nevins, *White*, pp. 154–5. For other indications of Lodge's attitude, *Proceedings LVIII Massachusetts Historical Society*, p. 336, 'Memoir of Henry Cabot Lodge'; Hay to Choate, Dec. 21, 1900, Dennett, *Hay*, p. 258. ·

[3] Williams, *Anglo-American Isthmian Diplomacy*, p. 304; *Proceedings LVIII Mass. Hist. Society*, p. 335, 'Memoir of H. C. Lodge'.

for an international partnership the Senate had in fact rewritten the treaty.

What would Great Britain do ? The Secretary of State, pressing her to accept the agreement as amended, glossed over the alterations. He pretended to Choate that its substance was unchanged and wanted Salisbury to say to the United States: 'Take your treaty, Brother Jonathan, and God send you better manners.' But this was a pose of gay insouciance which Hay did not really feel. He had again offered to resign, President McKinley again making him stay.[1] Lodge's nostrils breathed fire. To Henry White he wrote that if Great Britain rejected the amendments Americans would conclude that her motive in hampering their country by means of the Clayton-Bulwer Treaty was a sinister one; and as a result construction of the canal by the United States would receive a tremendous impetus.[2] Like a thunder-cloud over Anglo-American friendship brooded the Congressional threat of unilateral action.

By the British Government the amendments were nevertheless rejected. Lord Lansdowne reminded the United States—in a dispatch submitted to John Hay on March 11, 1901—of their conciliatory attitude in negotiating the new isthmian agreement. He then pointed out that the Clayton-Bulwer Treaty was a contract which could only be changed with the consent of both signatories. In spite of that, however, without any previous effort to ascertain their views, the British Government were now confronted with a proposal to abrogate this contract. Even more unacceptable was the second amendment. It provided for American naval and military control of the canal in war-time and marked thereby a distinct departure from the principle of neutralization which had always been sought for the project and upon which the Clayton-Bulwer Treaty had been founded. To the omission of the clause for inviting the adherence of other Powers Lansdowne also objected. He argued that without their adherence the neutralization of the canal would depend solely upon the guarantee of the two contracting parties. As compared with other Powers not subject to such a limitation, Great Britain would thus be put in a position of considerable disadvantage. For all these reasons, in place of the amended Hay-Pauncefote Treaty, the British Government preferred to maintain in force the unrevised terms of the Clayton-Bulwer Treaty. But by them further discussion of a new isthmian arrangement was not excluded.[3]

---

[1] Hay to Choate, Dec. 21, 1900, Dennis, *Adventures*, pp. 161–2; Thayer, *Hay*, vol. ii, p. 233.
[2] Lodge to White, Dec. 24, 1900, Nevins, *White*, p. 155.
[3] Williams, *Anglo-American Isthmian Diplomacy*, pp. 305–6.

The high hopes for the settlement of their differences, which the English-speaking Governments entertained in 1898, had not yet been fulfilled. Like Mohammed's coffin the Anglo-American *rapprochement* seemed to hang in mid-air, suspended between earth and sky. The two Governments were, however, still fully determined to bring their mutual relations into harmony. The rejection of the amended treaty was a natural diplomatic move; such drastic alterations could not be adopted without a formal protest. By the early renewal of negotiations for another canal treaty the deeper lines of policy would speedily be disclosed. And besides, from 1899 to 1901, while the Alaskan and isthmian questions were proving so difficult, Anglo-American understanding was also being weighed in the larger scale of world politics. But here, too, the results were less satisfactory than might have been expected. Yet whatever divergences cropped up between the English-speaking peoples, their ultimate community of interest was abundantly evident. For the next few years the Canadian problem would remain unadjusted. Nevertheless, the final canal treaty was shortly to become a symbol of goodwill rather than dissension. By British acquiescence in the isthmian ambitions of the United States the progress of Anglo-American friendship soon stood revealed.

IV

THE MEASURE OF CO-OPERATION

The Spanish War had not been long concluded before Anglo-American friendship was confronted by a number of diplomatic questions outside the western hemisphere. In international affairs they provided the first post-war test of general co-operation between Great Britain and the United States. The latter, it was clear, could never be again islanded off from the main stream of world politics. But would the English-speaking Governments uphold each other in the spirit of their new understanding, or would the dualism in the policy of the United States—the isolationist and anti-British traditions hampering her attitude as a Great Power—assert itself?

That a reaction had set in the Canadian and isthmian difficulties well illustrated. As a matter of fact at the beginning both of the Hague Conference and of the Samoan troubles the two Governments seemed to be working hand in hand; in the end, however, they stood no closer together. But the trends were plainer during the South African War and when the United States formulated her staple policy in the Far East. They showed in international affairs—as did the current disagreements in the settlement of their direct relations —the handicaps under which an Anglo-American understanding laboured. Nevertheless, these also served a useful purpose. The *rapprochement*, heralded in the transient flush of the Spanish War, could now be adjusted to permanent political realities. In 1899 and 1900 it might almost have appeared that the sudden improvement in Anglo-American relations had come to a halt. The reverse happened. Profiting by the lessons of the two intervening years, Anglo-American friendship—too circumscribed for its proponents, more definite than its enemies desired—again moved forward.

The first Hague Peace Conference, which sat from May 18 to July 29, 1899, could not surmount the opposition of Great Britain, the chief naval Power, and of Germany, the chief military Power— an opposition in which the United States also partook—to a limitation of armaments. The Russians failed therefore to accomplish the object for which they had invited the nations to assemble. But the Conference did succeed in establishing the Permanent Court of Arbitration, and here the British and American representatives were in substantial accord. Sir Julian Pauncefote, experienced at Washington in arbitration matters, had been sent to The Hague as head of his country's delegation. And it was his scheme, supported by Russia and the United States, which the Conference finally adopted.[1]

From Germany the plan to create an international tribunal met with stiff resistance. Pauncefote, however, made it possible for her to adhere by supplanting Russian and American proposals for obligatory arbitration with one for voluntary and optional arbitration.[2] The Hague Convention went further in principle than in fact. Yet on the eve of the twentieth century, in the organization of the modern machinery of peace, it signalized an important advance.

Having been granted modifications, Germany decided to sign the agreement. In so doing one of her foremost reasons was the fear of grouping together the English-speaking Powers. Bülow argued that by rejecting the scheme she might endanger her policy of friendship with Russia and the United States; should she, however, join the others, 'a fresh leaning of the Americans towards England' would be rendered difficult; her Foreign Secretary indeed expected, and the Kaiser hoped, that they would instead turn towards Germany.[3] Conspicuous in the history of English-speaking friendship is the perennial feature of German jealousy, the ceaseless efforts of Potsdam and the Wilhelmstrasse to dissolve the Anglo-American *rapprochement* by currying favour with the United States. And to this in 1899 the successful establishment with German consent of the Hague Tribunal may partly be attributed.

About the arbitration project Anglo-American relations were cordial, yet by the delegates from the United States Pauncefote was afforded considerable anxiety. They did not wish to be accused at home of mixing in European affairs or of qualifying their country's exclusive paternalism over Central and South America. Pauncefote pleaded with Dr. A. D. White, the chief representative of the United States, to enter no caveat on behalf of the Monroe Doctrine: 'It will be charged against you that you propose to evade your duties while using the treaty to promote your interests.' And so when the Final Act was read the American delegates—as they had promised Pauncefote—merely added a verbal reservation that nothing in the Hague Convention should be construed as marking a departure from the American policy of non-interference abroad; nor to imply a relinquishment by the United States of her traditional attitude towards

---

[1] Andrew Dickson White, *Autobiography*, vol. ii, p. 273; Mowat, *Pauncefote*, pp. 226–45.

[2] Ibid., pp. 233–8; *Br. Docs.*, vol. i, pp. 223–33.

[3] Bülow to the Kaiser, June 21, 1899, *Grosse Politik*, xv. 304; E. T. S. Dugdale (ed.), *German Diplomatic Documents*, vol. iii, pp. 80–1.

purely American questions. None of the other delegates at the plenary session dissented.[1] But, despite the devotion of their compatriots to the ideal of international arbitration, the representatives of the United States were alone in thus demanding special treatment. And by the temper of this reservation the whole development of Anglo-American understanding was to be affected.

Over one critical problem at the Hague Conference the United States and Great Britain were on opposite sides. The British representatives refused to discuss the proposal of the American and other delegations for the exemption from capture of private property at sea.[2] This disagreement reflected an historic division of opinion between the English-speaking peoples which, again becoming acute in 1914, remained for them one of the principal questions of contemporary world politics. Eager to extend her friendship with the United States, Great Britain could scarcely have been happy in contesting American ideas about the freedom of the seas. Not that the United States stood altogether for the humanization of war. American abstention kept the British delegates—who would have adhered had there been a unanimous vote—from accepting a declaration against the use of projectiles containing asphyxiating or deleterious gases.[3] The truth was that immunity of private property at sea meant the forfeiture by Great Britain of the efficient exercise of her naval supremacy. If notions as old as those of the War of 1812 had not lingered so long the American Government would have realized that, in both the western hemisphere and the Far East, British maritime power constituted the one sure bulwark for their policy. And perhaps in Washington at the turn of the century that fact was not really overlooked. At any rate, in Anglo-American relations this difference of views—ventilated once again at the second Hague Conference—then produced no ill effects.

Into the comments of British naval and military experts on American claims at The Hague there now crept, however, a less complaisant, more sardonic tone. Admiral Sir John Fisher told the German naval delegate that the suggestion originated in a desire to obtain British overseas trade when Great Britain was at war. Always an extremist in utterance, Fisher's opinions were not unalterable; at the Admiralty five years later he himself initiated the great reforms in naval strategy for a branch of which Anglo-American goodwill was the political foundation. Yet in 1899 he averred that, since so many

---

[1] White, *Autobiography*, vol. ii, pp. 263, 267, 271, 340–2.

[2] *Camb. Hist. of Br. Foreign Policy*, vol. iii, pp. 259–60; White, *Autobiography*, vol. ii, p. 287.

[3] Charles Carlisle Taylor, *The Life of Admiral Mahan*, p. 97.

of their interests conflicted, the new friendship between the English-speaking peoples could not endure.[1]

A report on the obstacles to a limitation of armaments submitted to his Government by Lt.-Col. Charles À Court, British military adviser at the Hague Conference, trenchantly analysed the position of the United States. He observed that her new policy and the rapid growth of her fleet were bringing to the front a fresh set of considerations.

'The American Delegates have, it is true, stated that they stand apart from Europe, and that their naval policy has not relation to, and can have no importance for, the Powers of Europe. Mr. White indeed made an eloquent speech in defence of the policy of protection for private property at sea, and laid stress on the sentimental side of American character; but it is difficult to get credit for good intentions, and the French Admiral remarked to me at the close of the speech that the Americans had destroyed the Spanish navy and commerce, and now wanted no one to destroy theirs.'

The British attaché had conversed with the famous American naval adviser.

'Captain Mahan has not only stated that his Government will on no account even discuss the question of any limitation of naval armaments; he has also informed me that he considers that the vital interests of America now lie East and West, and no longer North and South; that the great question of the immediate future is China, and that the United States will be compelled, by facts if not by settled policy, to take a leading part in the struggle for Chinese markets, and that this will entail a very considerable increase in her naval forces in the Pacific, which again must influence the naval arrangements of at least five Powers.'[2]

The technical experts of the fighting services had turned commercial prophets. But if similar trade interests did not result in effective combination between Great Britain and the United States, as British Ministers had expected they would in the Far East, neither did dissimilar ones elsewhere lead to the evil consequences foreseen by those who over-emphasized their general economic rivalry. The first Hague Conference—a review-ground of all current international problems—had indicated that the United States would not modify her attitude of formal non-co-operation and that in dealing with her Great Britain would have to make allowance for special psychological factors no less than for policies confined to particular regional applications. By these circumstances the possibilities of intimate Anglo-American collabora-

[1] Report by Captain Siegel, June 28, 1899, *Grosse Politik*, xv. 226; Dugdale, *Germ. Dip. Docs.*, vol. iii, pp. 78–80.
[2] Lt.-Col. Charles À Court, 'Note on the Limitation of Armaments', July 29, 1899, *Br. Docs.*, vol. i, no. 282, p. 231.

tion in world affairs were diminished. But they did not invalidate the assumption that, although an alliance was impracticable, friendship between the two countries should be extended and strengthened. Great Britain welcomed the naval and colonial responsibilities which the United States had recently undertaken. So far as they were common to each the English-speaking nations might discharge them together. At the Hague Conference nothing of an economic or political nature had demonstrated that the disunion of the past was better than the maintenance and furtherance of their good under-standing.

Meanwhile Great Britain, the United States, and Germany had been struggling with complications in Samoa. The condominium through which they jointly governed that archipelago was established in 1889—it being there that both the United States and Germany had first committed themselves to a form of colonial expansion abroad. But the Samoan arrangement did not work well. The native king of the principal island, Malietoa of Upolu, had died; the election held to choose his successor was disputed; with the Chief Justice, an American, rested the final decision. The chieftain Malietoa Tanu being selected, the other candidate, Mataafa, took up arms. The latter was backed by the Germans, the former by the British and the Americans. The English-speaking consuls were, moreover, at odds with the German consul and the German President of the munici-pality of Apia. Severely disapproving of her officials, John Hay requested Germany to dismiss them; at the beginning of 1899 Paunce-fote cabled to Salisbury that in the Samoan matter the Secretary of State expected the support of Great Britain.[1] And then in March, over the protest of the German consul, British and American marines prevented the victorious Mataafa from ascending the throne. During their bombardment of Apia damage had been done to the German consulate. Although Malietoa Tanu was crowned king, the party of Mataafa again triumphed in battle. With the state of confusion in Samoan affairs the three Powers were by the spring of 1899 thoroughly dissatisfied.

Germany was especially agitated. To Samoa she had a sentimental attachment as the cradle of her colonial aspirations and the death-bed of many of her sons. But Bülow considered that the game was not worth the candle if it caused the other two Governments to combine against her. With the United States, still keyed up by the successes of the Spanish War, Germany did not want to quarrel; on the

[1] Pauncefote to Salisbury, Jan. 27, 1899, *Br. Docs.*, vol. i, no. 131, p. 110; also ibid., pp. 100–31.

contrary, her Foreign Secretary desired to solve the Samoan problem as a way of improving German-American relations. For it had been perceived by him that between the English-speaking Powers, even in the absence of a formal alliance, an 'undoubted *rapprochement*' existed. He thought, furthermore, that, despite their isthmian and Canadian differences, such a result would always follow any disturbance in their relations with Germany and suspected that in order to drive her out of Samoa the Americans were being egged on by the British. In April Bülow therefore suggested to the Kaiser that the United States be treated with more circumspection than Great Britain, on whom, in any case, the Wilhelmstrasse had better means of exerting pressure.[1] Germany, in other words, would attempt, as she often attempted in the years which lay ahead, to separate the two English-speaking Governments. And so when the Powers discussed plans for a settlement, it was at London but not at Washington that her rancour was henceforth unleashed. Meanwhile, the United States denounced the conduct of the German officials and energetically defended what had been done in Samoa by her officers and naval forces.[2]

The proposal was now made, and accepted by the Governments concerned, that a Joint High Commission should be sent out to investigate the situation and pacify the islands. By the middle of May the three Commissioners—a British, an American, and a German representative—were at their task. They confirmed the choice of Malietoa Tanu and then induced him to renounce his kingship; the Chief Justice resigned; the consuls were left to govern; a change among the officials occurred. By July peace had been restored.

How should the Powers dispose of the Samoan Islands? At Salisbury's procrastination Potsdam and the Wilhelmstrasse took offence. American guns had accidentally demolished German property and the United States tendered apologies; but Great Britain, not having been involved, said nothing and the Kaiser was enraged. During May, in conversation first with the British Military Attaché and then with the British Ambassador, he struck a defiant note. Great Britain, the Emperor declared, apparently treated Germany as a nonentity. But her attitude would alter when his country, no longer weak at sea, possessed a great fleet. He hoped, moreover, that the constant disregard and contempt for German interests shown by Great Britain would not by then have forced his Government into combinations

---

[1] Bülow's memorandum, Mar. 14, 1899, *Grosse Politik*, xiv. 185; Dugdale, *Germ. Dip. Docs.*, vol. iii, p. 53; Bülow to the Kaiser, Apr. 1, 1899, *Grosse Politik*, xiv. 590; Dugdale, *Germ. Dip. Docs.*, vol. iii, pp. 56–7.

[2] Department of State to the German Embassy, Apr. 13, 1899, Dennis, *Adventures*, p. 113.

inimical to her. Alive to the assurance and strength which the good-will of the United States might afford to British policy in the Pacific, William II feared an Anglo-American understanding wholly to eliminate the Germans from Samoa. He sought, therefore, to belittle the idea that Great Britain could depend upon her new friend. Sir Frank Lascelles, the British Ambassador, made the appropriate disclaimers when the Kaiser charged her with having bribed the American press to attack Germany. 'Her Majesty's Government', he retorted 'must have known of it and had taken no steps to counter-act this evil influence which, however, had not prevailed, as the relations between Germany and the United States had now been put on a satisfactory footing. All this was known in Germany and increased the ill-feeling towards England.'[1] About the Prime Minister the Kaiser dispatched a letter of vitriolic reproach to Queen Victoria herself. The Queen replied in June, soundly reproving her grandson and sending him Salisbury's denial that British gun-fire had hit the German consulate.[2] Their dispute over Samoa was another reflection of the growing world rivalry between Great Britain and Germany. Although the two English-speaking Powers had acted together, the vials of the Emperor's wrath were consequently poured out on the British alone.

What Germany desired was soon evident. In July 1899 the Samoan High Commission advised that the condominium be aban-doned and that in future the islands be singly and not jointly ad-ministered.[3] In brief, it favoured a partition. At Washington the Germans thereupon proposed a solution which the American Govern-ment would almost certainly deem acceptable. They suggested that Tutuila—the harbour of which she had held by treaty since 1878—should go to the United States, Upolu to Germany, and Savaii to Great Britain. And this scheme the Wilhelmstrasse asked the American Government to recommend in London.[4] From Samoa the Germans did not intend to retire.

At Downing Street their soft speech had become harsh bluster. But the more they fumed with impatience, the more Salisbury temporized; he would not, he said, be dictated to by Berlin with a stop-watch.[5] Nor was it only on general grounds that the Prime Minister objected to German manners and German policy. In the

[1] Lascelles to Salisbury, May 26, 1899, *Br. Docs.*, vol. i, no. 141, pp. 117–18; also *Letters of Queen Victoria*, Third Series, vol. iii, pp. 357–60.
[2] Ibid., pp. 375–82.
[3] *U.S. Foreign Relations*, 1899, p. 636 et seq.
[4] German memorandum, Dennis, *Adventures*, pp. 114–15; also *Br. Docs.*, vol. i, nos. 146 and 147, pp. 122–3.
[5] Baron von Eckardstein, *Ten Years at the Court of St. James'*, pp. 106–7, 109–16.

southern Pacific, New Zealand and the Australian colonies were opposed to any colonial expansion by Germany. Samoa lay on their direct route to North America and the projected isthmian canal—a fact which, when the position of Hawaii was also considered, made it so essential for the United States to possess a naval base in the archipelago. They complained that by Germany and her agents the Samoan Act of 1889 had been repeatedly violated; to the last they protested against annexation by her of all or part of the islands.[1] In London no Imperial Government could ignore such representations.

Meanwhile the Wilhelmstrasse had succeeded in conciliating the United States and thereby dispelled the prospect of closer Anglo-American co-operation. During September John Hay described relations with the Germans as being perfectly civil and courteous even though to bully and swagger was in their nature. About Samoa the United States and Germany were most friendly; by his German colleague the American High Commissioner had been given full support. To the amazement of Washington matters were arranged harmoniously and the British Commissioner, if any one, was the more stiff in attitude. 'The Emperor is nervously anxious to be on good terms with us—on his own terms, *bien entendu.*'[2] Withdrawn from Europe, the United States could yet prosper by its jealousies and dissensions.

Unable to do business with Salisbury, the Germans turned to Joseph Chamberlain. Upon the mind of the Colonial Secretary the Australasian contentions were bound to exercise great influence; he therefore suggested that, in return for other British islands in the Pacific and valuable compensation in West Africa, Germany should cede to Great Britain all her rights in Samoa and Tonga.[3] But since he wanted his own Government to establish a Samoan naval base Admiral von Tirpitz disapproved of this proposal. As a key-point in a chain of possessions stretching across the Pacific from Kiao-Chau to South America, Samoa might then be useful when the isthmian canal, constructed by the United States, created new trade and naval routes and could even provide a station for a German world cable.[4] The directors of policy in Berlin seemed thus to be contemplating the necessity of keeping watch on American as well as British sea-strategy. But in Washington the Administration were unaware of

---

[1] Colonial Office to the Foreign Office, Jan. 24, 1899, *Br. Docs.*, vol. i, no. 130, p. 110; also ibid., vol. iii, Appendix A, p. 411.
[2] Hay to White, Sept. 9, 1899, Thayer, *Hay*, vol. ii, p. 229.
[3] Garvin, *Chamberlain*, vol. iii, pp. 336–41; also ibid., pp. 324–43.
[4] Tirpitz to Bülow, Oct. 11, 1899, *Grosse Politik*, xiv. 660; Dugdale, *Germ. Dip. Docs.*, vol. iii, p. 73.

that. Refusing to depart from Samoa, the Germans rejected the British offer.

The outbreak of the Boer War presented them with their opportunity, for then William II could threaten, unless the Samoan dispute were settled in their favour, to reconsider the question of his country's neutrality.[1] In the autumn of 1899, with South Africa requiring her undivided attention, it would have been a dangerous risk for Great Britain to leave this problem unsolved and so add the deepening ill will of Germany to that of France and Russia. Furthermore, until agreement could be reached, an important visit had been postponed which the Kaiser was to make to Queen Victoria. His journey to England would be a salutary diplomatic gesture: in the face of Europe's pro-Boer sentiment a tacit proclamation of German disinterestedness. But upon that visit a price had now been set. Chamberlain spoke of German 'blackmail'; Salisbury, who said that he did not work for the King of Prussia, was constrained to yield. Australian and New Zealand protests could be no longer heeded; by two conventions in November and December 1899 Great Britain surrendered her claims to any of the islands in the Samoan archipelago. Germany received both Upolu and Savaii, Tutuila going, as the Wilhelmstrasse had proposed, to the United States. Tonga and some of the German Solomon Islands were in exchange transferred to Great Britain and a small adjustment was effected in Zanzibar. The Germans, having obtained more than they had demanded two months before, were delighted.[2] Their correct neutrality was assured and the Kaiser proceeded to Windsor. The Samoan episode had finished.

Nevertheless, John Hay believed that Germany got the worst of a bargain in the making of which he had not been consulted. American interests in Samoa, the Secretary of State explained, were very meagre except for those at Pago Pago in the island of Tutuila. The finest harbour on the Pacific, it was absolutely indispensable to the United States. With an arrangement they had long desired the American Navy Department were therefore exceedingly pleased.[3] The three Powers had been concerned in the affairs of the archipelago because of its strategic value. But whatever the outcome of their controversies the United States alone was certain in advance to maintain— and improve—her Samoan position. On the Pacific without serious discomfort or embitterment abroad she thus picked up a permanent addition to her colonial and naval system.

[1] *Br. Docs.*, vol. iii, Appendix A, p. 411.
[2] *The Letters of Queen Victoria*, Third Series, vol. iii, pp. 416–17; Bülow, *Memoirs 1897–1903*, pp. 280–3.
[3] Hay to Choate, Nov. 13, 1899, Thayer, *Hay*, vol. ii, pp. 281–3.

In this respect she was more fortunate than Great Britain. Although at the start the English-speaking Powers had acted together, the change at Washington in German tactics enabled her to sit back while the British Government, with the advent of the South African crisis, were compelled to relinquish their Samoan interests. As a result of Anglo-German competition for American goodwill her share in the partitioning of the archipelago had never been questioned. Some of it she owed to joint action with Great Britain during the first half of 1899, but no compensation had been asked of her, as it was of Germany, when the British withdrew. To the Spanish War the Samoan incident stood out in sharp contrast. At that time, in the teeth of German opposition, Great Britain urged the United States to secure and retain all her conquests. A year later the British Government, distracted elsewhere, were forced to look on while Germany planted herself more firmly in the South Seas. Yet no matter what happened, the United States on both occasions profited by a rivalry which allowed her with a comparative economy of effort to make swift strides. Samoan difficulties did not increase Anglo-American collaboration. They indicated, however, that on the Pacific, whichever way the colonial waves flowed, the United States rode the crest.

That English-speaking friendship was one of the first principles of British policy the Wilhelmstrasse had lately been driven to take into account. By the immediate sequel to the Samoan agreement, the Kaiser's visit to Windsor, this object was brought into high relief. For in November William II and Count von Bülow, resuming in person the diplomatic conversations of 1898, discussed with British representatives not only the idea of an Anglo-German alliance but also the question of an understanding with the United States. The Prince of Wales—soon to be King Edward VII—and his sisters told Bülow that a *rapprochement* between Great Britain, Germany, and the United States was to their common interest and would be the best guarantee of the world's peace. The German Foreign Secretary also had a talk with Arthur Balfour, whose opinions were neither as anti-isolationist as those of Joseph Chamberlain nor as isolationist as those of Lord Salisbury—the latter, freshly bereaved of his wife, not being present at Windsor. To Bülow Balfour said that in Great Britain all parties desired a *rapprochement* with Germany and simultaneously, if possible, with the United States.[1] Members of the Royal Family and a Minister so highly placed as Arthur Balfour, within a few

[1] Bülow's memorandum, Nov. 24, 1899, *Grosse Politik*, xv. 413; Dugdale, *Germ. Dip. Docs.*, vol. iii, pp. 108–14.

years to be Salisbury's successor, would not have spoken in this fashion unless they knew beforehand the considered attitude of the Government. In the special circumstances of the Windsor discussions, views thus expressed were a tribute to the political stature of the United States and the weight attached by Englishmen to her goodwill.

Nor had Chamberlain's outlook altered, so that in his conversations with the Kaiser and Count von Bülow the topic of a general tripartite understanding figured prominently. Trying to sell their collaboration in the dearest market, the German visitors contended, however, that, unlike Great Britain, they were not threatened from Paris or St. Petersburg. Chamberlain, on the other hand, argued that for help in the Far East against Russia the British, lacking a large body of troops, would have to turn to the Germans and to the Americans. While the United States had no standing army she could, as during her Civil War, recruit vast masses of volunteers. Of American assistance in Eastern Asia the Colonial Secretary seemed to feel assured. He told Bülow that in his policy a *rapprochement* with the United States was a cardinal point and that he would do nothing to displease her. Despite the existence of tempting regions in South America he proposed therefore to steer clear of that continent. To this Bülow replied that if Chamberlain really wanted a triple *rapprochement* he ought to prevent further misunderstandings between Germans and Americans, and that on the United States, in the matter of their political and trade relations, he should exercise a soothing influence. Such remarks invited the obvious retort: it would be a British interest to keep Berlin and Washington in good humour with each other if Great Britain and Germany were more friendly.[1]

Emboldened by these interviews, Chamberlain, on November 30, delivered at Leicester another of his famous speeches. Count von Bülow, he was later to record, 'expressed a wish that I might be able to say something as to the mutual interests which bound the United States to a triple understanding with Germany as well as to Great Britain'.[2] During the Boer War anti-British vituperation saturated the Parisian press and with an angry reprimand the Colonial Secretary warned the French that there would be serious consequences if they did not mend their manners. He wanted to terminate British isolation; the most natural alliance—and he recognized that a firm under-

[1] Bülow's memorandum, Nov. 24, 1899, *Grosse Politik*, xv. 413; Dugdale, *Germ. Dip. Docs.*, vol. iii, pp. 108–14.

[2] Chamberlain to Eckardstein, Dec. 1, 1899, Eckardstein, *Ten Years at the Court of St. James'*, p. 130; Chamberlain to Lascelles, Dec. 12, 1899, Garvin, *Chamberlain*, vol. iii, p. 512; also ibid., pp. 496–517.

standing might be preferable to a written treaty—was that of Great Britain with Germany, supported, he hoped, by the United States. 'If the union between England and America is a powerful factor in the cause of peace, a new Triple Alliance between the Teutonic race and the two great branches of the Anglo-Saxon race will be a still more potent influence in the future of the world.' As a result of this sensational utterance a torrent of criticism assailed Chamberlain. It was audacious of him, when British arms in South Africa were undergoing reverses, to castigate the French and advocate a partnership with a Power so hostile and pro-Boer in sentiment as Germany. At home both Unionists and Liberals regretted that he had mistaken the Colonial for the Foreign Office; Chamberlain really must be kept out of foreign politics, observed Sir Edward Grey, 'or he will make everything impossible, even friendship with America'.[1] Outside Great Britain the effect was likewise the opposite of that intended.

Germany seethed with Anglophobia and Chamberlain's sanguine words came too soon after the Windsor visit. Addressing the Reichstag, Bülow within a fortnight deemed it expedient therefore to repudiate him. With the Triple Alliance and Russian friendship the Foreign Secretary was content; to Great Britain his references were decidedly frigid. Of the favourable situation abroad, moreover, Germany had to take advantage in order to strengthen her fleet. In the twentieth century her role would be that of hammer or anvil. Though Bülow attempted in London privately to explain away his Reichstag speech its meaning was plain.[2] Chamberlain's spectacular *ballon d'essai* had been regarded as a confession of British weakness; it was pricked open by the trident which, according to the Kaiser, had to be grasped in the German fist. Seizing upon the *Bundesrath* incident—British men-of-war having searched for contraband German steamers travelling to South Africa—the German Government in the winter of 1900 introduced their second Navy Bill. When adopted this enactment would double the fleet programme of 1898. It was a bold challenge from the chief military nation to the two-Power naval standard maintained by Great Britain against Russia and France. In March Bülow cited to the Reichstag British conduct during the Samoan affair as an example of conditions which justified the increase. The Manila episode, attributed by him to American chauvinism, furnished another instance. These were the dangers, the Minister

---

[1] Grey to Haldane, Dec. 4, 1899, George Macaulay Trevelyan, *Grey of Fallodon,* p. 77; also J. A. Spender, *The Life of Sir Henry Campbell-Bannerman*, vol. i, pp. 258–9.

[2] *Camb. Hist. of Br. Foreign Policy*, vol. iii, p. 278; Eckardstein, *Ten Years at the Court of St. James'*, pp. 144–7; *Letters of Queen Victoria*, Third Series, vol. iii, p. 440.

announced, to which peace was exposed with Germany inferior at
sea.[1] And so, contrary to sage Bismarckian counsel, she began to
build warships which upset British naval calculations. Her maritime
and political aims impelled Great Britain to seek friends elsewhere.
And from that quest it became progressively more and more improbable that the United States could be excluded.

In Washington no such train of evil followed Chamberlain's speech.
But the Secretary of State had been hard put, even before war was
declared, to resist domestic sympathies with the Transvaal. Irish
and German members of the population were demanding that the
United States associate herself with the Boers against Great Britain.
In their attitude towards the South African War American statesmen
like John Hay and Theodore Roosevelt were, however, very pro-
British.[2] Nevertheless, many of the native-born remembered that
fighting the Boers was the same enemy from whom in the eighteenth
century their ancestors had wrested their national freedom. On the
other hand, the United States, suppressing the Filipino rebellion
under Aguinaldo, could not then preach to Great Britain a loftier
political morality. That Chamberlain's suggestion about a tripartite
understanding was greeted without enthusiasm by the American
press the Germans were quick to notice.[3] Yet as a matter of fact
President McKinley and John Hay admired the Leicester speech,
although the latter said that he would never employ the term
'alliance'. It was therefore an act of friendship towards Great Britain
for an American Government, vexed by pro-Boer vehemence, to
point at this time to their impartiality and neutrality—something
upon which, on December 5, in his annual message to Congress,
President McKinley insisted.[4] If the isolationism of the United States
was not to be modified as Joseph Chamberlain desired, neither would
it be compromised in favour of Paul Kruger. By the American
Government the cause of the Boers could scarcely be espoused during
a period of negotiation with Great Britain over Canadian and isthmian difficulties. Besides, it is inconceivable that they would have
forgotten how, throughout the Spanish War, the British Cabinet had
helped pilot them through the shoals and reefs of European diplomacy.
But the public memory was short, and it seldom recalled that only

---

[1] *Camb. Hist. of Br. Foreign Policy*, vol. iii, pp. 279–80; Bülow, *Memoirs 1897–1903*,
p. 413.
[2] Hay to White, Sept. 24, 1899, Thayer, *Hay*, vol. ii, p. 221; Roosevelt to Mrs.
Cowles, Dec. 17, 1899, Anna Roosevelt Cowles, *Letters from Theodore Roosevelt to
Anna Roosevelt Cowles*, p. 226.
[3] Bülow, *Memoirs 1897–1903*, p. 327.
[4] *U.S. Foreign Relations*, 1899, p. xxii; Hay to White, Dec. 27, 1899, Dennett, *Hay*,
p. 331.

a year or two ago Great Britain, alone among the Powers, had manifested goodwill.

Meanwhile, between the British and the Boers, Russia had been attempting to organize some sort of European mediation. But her ally, France, held back and waited for Germany to take the lead. The Germans, however, were satisfied with the drift of events. France would not pledge herself to renounce Alsace-Lorraine ;[1] and so Germany, before her fleet was ready, showed no inclination, for the sake of the Dual Alliance, gratuitously to antagonize Great Britain. Moreover, in January and February 1900 the American Government— whose suitability as a mediator had been discussed during the preceding summer by the Germans, the Dutch, and the Boers—made it perfectly clear to Berlin and St. Petersburg that the United States did not support the Russian proposals. The ruin of the British Empire, John Hay emphasized to the German Ambassador, would be a misfortune for the whole world.[2] With the Government of the United States refusing to be drawn in and with the Quai d'Orsay vouchsafing no advantages, Germany was well advised to keep her promise— given to Great Britain upon the settlement of the Samoan dispute— that she would stand aloof.

So long as no signs of their benevolent attitude reached the public, McKinley and Hay were free to act in consonance with Anglo-American friendship. But when, following a series of defeats, the Boers applied with mediation proposals direct to Washington, the Government of the United States, in complying with their request, went further than any of the European Powers. On March 5 the Presidents of the Boer Republics submitted to Lord Salisbury an offer, rejected by him on March 11, to treat for peace on a basis which would have recognized both Republics as sovereign international States. Approaching the other Powers they were rebuffed at Berlin and Vienna on the grounds that third-party intervention was acceptable only to one belligerent.[3] Downing Street regarded the war as internal to the British Empire, and Russia, working for the Boers, could not induce the Kaiser and the Wilhelmstrasse—or now even the French—to interfere. At St. Petersburg the soundings which Count Mouravieff, the Russian Foreign Minister, had undertaken were confided by the American Ambassador to his British colleague.[4]

[1] Brandenburg, *From Bismarck*, &c., pp. 141–4.
[2] Dennis, *Adventures*, pp. 125–7; Holleben to the German Foreign Office, Feb. 2, 1900, *Grosse Politik*, xv. 510; Dugdale, *Germ. Dip. Docs.*, vol. iii, p. 122.
[3] Lascelles to Salisbury, Mar. 17, 1900, *Br. Docs.*, vol. i, no. 315, pp. 254–5; *Letters of Queen Victoria*, Third Series, vol. iii, pp. 503, 507–9, 512, 519–20, 527.
[4] Scott to Salisbury, Mar. 19, 1900, *Br. Docs.*, vol. i, no. 317, pp. 255–6.

This was evidence of his Government's goodwill. But in Washington itself they had a harder furrow to plough.

What European Governments could do with their outright, or almost outright, control of foreign policy the more democratic character of American institutions did not permit. In the autumn of that year the presidential election was to be held and among voters pro-Boer elements were too numerous to be ignored. To London on March 10 the Secretary of State therefore proceeded to forward the South African message, expressing at the same time McKinley's hope that a way would be found to bring about peace and towards the accomplishment of that object volunteering his friendly assistance. In Washington the British rejection arrived three days later. To the Germans Salisbury frankly described the American offer as an electoral move.[1] Hay was anxious that in London the President's suggestion should not be misinterpreted, but from press reports he judged that at the Foreign Office it had been received without much warmth. Yet to St. Petersburg the independent action of the United States, destroying the possibility of combined intervention, was also unwelcome. Identic representations, remarked the American to the British Ambassador in that capital, had been spoiled by the reply which Washington had elicited from London.[2] That McKinley and Hay did not wish to help the Boers against Great Britain is unquestionable. Nevertheless, the Kaiser and the German Government rather than her American friends were the ones who had most decisively scotched interference.

Hay's disquietude was intelligible. Germany, Austria, and France —the three anti-American Powers with whom, on the eve of the Spanish War, Great Britain refused to unite—would not handle so delicate a proposal; while such mediation as Russia, a corrupt and oppressive autocracy, might have contrived could spring from no sympathy with a harried minority, but was designed to embarrass and obstruct the British Empire. With American opinion inflamed the Government in Washington were, however, unable to pursue a public line as unequivocal as that of the principal European Chancelleries. Although he foresaw the British rejection, Hay defended to Henry White at the London Embassy the step they had taken. For the first time, so far as he knew, the Irish and German groups seemed 'to have joined their several lunacies in one common attack against England and incidentally against the Administration for being too

---

[1] Dennis, *Adventures*, pp. 127–8; Metternich to the German Foreign Office, Mar. 14, 1900, *Grosse Politik*, xv. 521; Dugdale, *Germ. Dip. Docs.*, vol. iii, p. 125.

[2] Hay to White, Mar. 18, 1900, Nevins, *White*, p. 151; Scott to Salisbury, Mar. 19, 1900, *Br. Docs.*, vol. i, no. 317, p. 256.

friendly to England'. In the Senate, moreover, this anti-British spirit had been influencing the amendments to the isthmian treaty. Devoted to the preservation of Anglo-American understanding, the Secretary of State believed that in her South African struggle Great Britain was promoting the cause of progress and he felt that her success would benefit his own country. But it would have been self-defeating if, instead of allowing it to blow itself over, the Administration outwardly opposed the tempest of Anglophobia then raging. And that was why with 'an expression of the President's platonic desire for peace' he had transmitted the Boer message to the British Government. Had he done otherwise 'there would have been a joint resolution rushed through Congress advising us to do it, couched in language which could not have failed to be offensive and injurious'.[1] Thus explained, his action appears less in the light of a narrow electoral expedient and more in that of broad political principles. As with the signature of the isthmian treaty, so now the Executive undertook a swift manœuvre at London in order to deflect from the realm of diplomacy a dangerous legislative irruption. For, despite the reasoned attitude of the White House and the State Department, American foreign policy was still liable to be twisted and distorted by domestic considerations which in the long run ill served the United States as a Great Power.

After this, however, she did not swerve from her true course. In May when a Boer mission visited Washington it secured none of the official assistance that popular acclaim led it to expect—a fact to which so shrewd an observer as Count von Bülow attached special significance. In his view it was a warning for the European Chancelleries to treat with care—a policy followed by his own Government—the question of helping the Boer delegates or of supporting their cause; according to him, the opportunity had been grasped by the United States to stress the interests she possessed in common with Great Britain.[2] Detecting Anglophile tendencies in Washington, many Americans suspected hidden entanglements. The United States had been entirely neutral, Hay was compelled to reassure one of the Senators, and no secret alliance between her and Great Britain existed.[3] Wherever they might dwell the opponents of English-speaking friendship perhaps now appreciated its central paradox: although in world politics it had not shown itself to be an effective

---

[1] Hay to White, Mar. 18, 1900, Nevins, *White*, pp. 151–3.

[2] Bülow to Pourtalès, May 28, 1900, *Grosse Politik*, xv. 544; Dugdale, *Germ. Dip. Docs.*, vol. iii, p. 125; also Dennis, *Adventures*, pp. 128–9. To the Boer President, Paul Kruger, the Kaiser at the end of 1900 denied an audience.

[3] Hay to McMillan, July 3, 1900, Thayer, *Hay*, vol. ii, p. 233.

instrument, nevertheless to each other the British and American Governments stood closer than either of them to the rest of the Powers.

Against the yoke of domestic prejudice and tradition Hay chafed incessantly. About the Boer War his distress was an offshoot of his general diplomatic programme. In it Anglo-American collaboration occupied first place, and he was therefore saddened to discover that as fighters the British had not been very skilful. If Russia and Germany were to arrange things, Hay ruminated gloomily, the balance for peace and civilization would be lost for ages.[1] Such pessimism arose from developments not only in South Africa but also in China, where, during the past year, he had been laying down the insubstantial foundations of his Far Eastern policy. In various diplomatic activities since the Spanish War—those marked by the Hague Conference, the Samoan episode, the Kaiser's visit to Windsor, and the South African conflict—Anglo-American understanding was reckoned among the important factors of international relations; and yet at no time between the English-speaking Powers had a full measure of co-operation been produced. China was the acid test. Would the American Government decide to work in association with Great Britain, as the British proposed in March 1898, or would they adopt some other plan? To this query the answer was supplied by Hay's notes on the Open Door and the policy they pursued during the Boxer Rebellion.

Of the American attitude towards China the interested capitals had been apprised in the autumn of 1899 and the winter of 1900. The United States now had possessions stretching across the Pacific to the Philippines; about the prospective partition of the Chinese Empire she could as a great Far Eastern Power no longer remain silent. Towards her, moreover, the European Governments were conducting themselves with a new deference; after the Spanish War a pronouncement from Washington seemed bound everywhere to carry weight on behalf of the territorial integrity of China and equal opportunities in that country for foreign trade. As with Great Britain the danger confronting the United States was that her imports would be forbidden entry into China's exclusive spheres of influence and special privilege—imports which recently had shown a large expansion, particularly in the north and in Manchuria, the Russian zone. And even if she also should desire a port or sphere of influence—to which public opinion at home might not have consented —these were difficult to procure, most of them having already been

---

[1] Hay to Adams, June 5, 1900, Thayer, *Hay*, vol. ii, p. 232.

leased or pre-empted by non-alienation agreements.[1] For the fact
was that on the Far Eastern scene at the close of the nineteenth
century American diplomacy appeared over a year too late.

In the winter of 1899 Hay watched the situation and did nothing.
From Hong Kong the Consul-General of the United States reported
that assistance for the British policy of the Open Door would not be
warranted—at any rate until the isthmian canal had been built—
by the amount of her trade with China.[2] But American exporters
expected it to increase in the near future and for them, during a
period of rapid industrial growth, the Administration had to safeguard potential Chinese markets. Besides, in 1898, under the auspices
of the British Chambers of Commerce, Lord Charles Beresford went
to the Far East, where he spoke of a combination of Powers to rescue
China from Russian and French clutches and framed a scheme for
internal order in which Chinese troops were to receive British,
American, German, and Japanese instructors. An advocate of an
Anglo-American commercial alliance in the Far East, Beresford,
returning to England through the United States, saw Hay in February.[3] Before that, in December 1898, in his annual message to Congress, President McKinley had declared himself in favour of the Open
Door; this statement, coupled with the speeches of Joseph Chamberlain and Beresford's propaganda—presently embodied in his book
The Break-up of China—naturally prompted inquiries at Washington
about the intentions of the American Government. These, however,
continued to be strictly isolationist and of that in January 1899 Great
Britain had been again informed.[4] Nevertheless, by the Secretary of
State a definition of policy was soon to be devised which, within
the narrow compass available, might yet preserve politically and
commercially the American stake in China.

During that summer it took shape. For guidance Hay turned to an
American expert on China, W. W. Rockhill, and the two of them were
advised by an Englishman, a former member of the Chinese Maritime
Customs, Alfred E. Hippisley. Rejecting the idea of concerted Anglo-
American action in the Far East, their exchange of views was of
historic importance. How could McKinley and Hay elude the
strictures of anti-British and isolationist elements? Let the United
States assume the lead, Hippisley suggested, and Great Britain

[1] Dennett, *Americans in Eastern Asia*, p. 648; Conger to Hay, Mar. 1, 1899, Dennis, *Adventures*, pp. 207–8.
[2] Wildman to Hay, Jan. 6, 1899, Dennett, *Hay*, p. 287.
[3] Dennett, *Americans in Eastern Asia*, pp. 641–2; Dennis, *Adventures*, pp. 185–6.
[4] Dennett, *Hay*, p. 288; Dennis, *Adventures*, pp. 198–9; Hay to Dana, Mar. 16, 1899, Thayer, *Hay*, vol. ii, p. 241; also *U.S. Foreign Relations*, 1898, p. lxiii.

merely follow.[1] With Beresford's proposals Rockhill's final memorandum—a document on which Hay based his procedure—found fault. What China needed was not to adopt modernized armed forces for the protection of her territorial integrity but to reform her system of government. According to Rockhill, conditions were less serious than had been supposed. While Englishmen called for trade equality in China, Great Britain herself, along with France, Germany, and Russia, recognized spheres of influence; as existing facts these latter had to be accepted. The attitude towards them of the British Government was, however, explained by diplomatic exigencies, and so they also tried to secure the Open Door for which their business classes clamoured. But with Russian and German promises Rockhill felt more content than with British behaviour at Kowloon. Spheres of influence had come to stay; the United States could only bow to the inevitable. Upon what the American Administration should insist, he contended, was equality of commercial treatment in the foreign zones; equality of opportunity might still be pursued although, since concessions were assigned to the subjects of the privileged Powers, Rockhill had little hope that it would be obtained. In conclusion, the policy best suited to the United States was, he observed, 'not a British one—for England is as great an offender in China as Russia itself'.[2]

Such were the premises upon which Hay now undertook to model his programme. Since the winter of 1898 it had been evident that without American co-operation the incongruities in British Far Eastern policy were not likely to diminish. But in Washington the means were still declined which Great Britain offered to help keep open the closing Chinese door. By the United States, for hastening inside before it was bolted and barred irrevocably, could the British Government be therefore altogether blamed?

In September 1899 to Great Britain, Germany, and Russia John Hay sent the first of his celebrated notes on Chinese trade. From each of the Powers claiming a sphere of influence he requested a declaration for equality of commercial treatment. His initial stipulation was that in its sphere or leased territory it should not interfere with any treaty port or vested interest. He asked secondly that, in all except free ports, the prevailing Chinese tariff be applied to incoming merchandise, irrespective of national ownership, and that duties thus levied be collected by the Chinese Government. Thirdly and lastly, in the ports and on the railways of its sphere he suggested

[1] Hippisley to Adee, Aug. 16, 1899, Dennett, Hay, p. 291; ibid., pp. 290–1.
[2] Rockhill to Hay, Aug. 28, 1899, Dennis, Adventures, pp. 186, 208–14.

that the dominant Power, in imposing harbour dues and charges on the transport of such merchandise, avoid discrimination between its subjects and non-subjects.[1] After the alarums and excursions of the past few years these, then, were the lines along which Hay proposed to deal with the Chinese problem.

From the British overture of March 1898 they fell far short. Great Britain had invited the United States to co-operate in opposing the 'actual cession of Chinese coast territory' as well as the establishment by foreign Powers of preferential conditions.[2] By the British Government an Anglo-American combination was apparently envisaged which would maintain intact China's political independence and territorial integrity. A year and a half later Hay's enunciation of policy tended to disregard that aspect of affairs. In his notes, it is true, the second stipulation recognized China's right to levy and collect her own tariffs; this, however, could scarcely suffice as a guarantee of her territorial integrity and governmental sovereignty. The fact of the matter was that Hay had been compelled to resort to a makeshift expedient of little more than verbal intervention, and at Washington in the diplomatic method he employed there would subsequently be no lack of imitators.

The United States had now framed an abstract and individualist policy to support principles which in the British view would have to be enforced concretely and collectively. Of the paralysing defect in his programme no one was more keenly aware than John Hay himself. The first of his notes on the Open Door were dispatched a month before the outbreak of the South African War; struggling with the pro-Boer sympathies of the American public, the Secretary of State had to deny the existence of an Anglo-American alliance. This, he wrote, was impossible, for the Senate would turn it down. 'As long as I stay here, no action shall be taken contrary to my conviction that the one indispensable feature of our foreign policy should be a friendly understanding with England. But an alliance must remain, in the present state of things, an unattainable dream.'[3] And yet, as he soon realized, unless that dream were somehow attained, with no threat in reserve of ultimate backing from the associated navies of the English-speaking Powers, his Far Eastern efforts would in the long run prove ineffective. Since its earliest days the Monroe Doctrine had derived much of its strength from the benevolent attitude of the British fleet; but in 1899 by refusing the

---

[1] *U.S. Foreign Relations*, 1899, pp. 128–42.
[2] Sherman to White, Mar. 17, 1898, Dennis, *Adventures*, p. 170.
[3] Hay to White, Sept. 24, 1899, Thayer, *Hay*, vol. ii, p. 221.

formal aid of the Royal Navy and by omitting any sanction of its own the Hay programme was born congenitally feeble. So favourable an opportunity did not again occur for Great Britain and the United States to merge their sea-power and on the East Asiatic mainland anchor their influence more securely. Until it passed to the Japanese, foreign primacy there was held by the Russians; in the resultant contest for supremacy of continental land-power China's confusion is writ large. But in that country events would doubtless have taken a different turn if at the end of the nineteenth century by the English-speaking peoples an unparalleled chance had not been lost for contributing together to the stabilization of Far Eastern politics.

To Hay's notes the adherence was announced in March 1900 of all the foreign Powers concerned in China. Great Britain and France acceded after certain demurrers, Germany, Japan, and Italy agreed entirely, while Russia answered with a studied evasiveness.[1] For several years the British Government had hoped that in the Far East the United States would take a stand. To them the American proposals were therefore very welcome as well as to the Parliamentary Opposition and the general public.[2] For now in China, during the troubled period of the Boer War, the United States had become a fellow champion of the cause of freer foreign trade. And since by European Governments, bent upon the cultivation of American goodwill, the assurances they had given would not be immediately violated, the disruption of the Chinese Empire had been again deferred. In the Hay policy, even if it were merely a stop-gap, Downing Street must thus have found no inconsiderable advantage.

Yet it probably accomplished less than the mutual checkmating in which the Powers indulged and the delimitation agreements at which they arrived. By means of it the United States only obtained most-favoured-nation treatment; preferential railway and mining privileges were undisturbed; on all sides the status of spheres of influence was recognized and confirmed.[3] Henceforth declarations on the Open Door usually appeared in the major Far Eastern treaties; but in the domain of international politics and finance commercial equality was subject to many curious interpretations. To British Far Eastern endeavours the United States had at last made her public rejoinder. Active collaboration with Great Britain might have accorded the trade of both English-speaking countries the liberal opportunities it sought; above all, from some of the prodigious evils

[1] Dennett, *Americans in Eastern Asia*, pp. 646–7; Dennis, *Adventures*, pp. 187–93.
[2] Choate to Hay, Nov. 3, 1899, Dennis, *Adventures*, p. 189; Salisbury to Choate, Nov. 30, 1899, *U.S. Foreign Relations*, 1899, p. 136; also Nevins, *White*, p. 167.
[3] Dennett, *Americans in Eastern Asia*, p. 647.

that have since befallen her China would perhaps have been saved. But instead the American Government were constrained to choose a quasi-co-operative course which, while independent of Great Britain and involving no direct obligations, left them floundering in the end.

Of that the Boxer uprising furnished early proof. Thirsting to avenge the spoliation of their country, numerous bands of Chinese attacked the lives and property of resident foreigners; at Peking in June 1900 the legations were besieged; and with the Powers suspecting each other of mischievous designs the partition of China again became a burning issue. In the new crisis the provisions of the Hay notes on the Open Door—an economic solution for a political problem—were not likely to be an adequate remedy. To preserve their respective positions in the Far East would the English-speaking Governments therefore take common counsel?

This Hay did not dare to attempt. Surrounded by the anti-British agitation of the Boer War and harassed by the hostile amendments in the Senate to the isthmian treaty, the Secretary of State rebelled against the isolationist strait jacket to which his diplomacy was confined. He complained bitterly that the American Administration would be accused of 'subservience to Great Britain' if they did anything in China to protect their endangered interests. France, he gibed, was Russia's harlot—to her own grievous damage. He believed that with sufficient concessions they could probably win over Germany and then in a grouping of the Americans, the British, the Japanese, and the Germans they might manage to save their skins. By some of his correspondents Hay was cursed for doing nothing and by others for 'being the tool of England against our good friend Russia'. Every Senator he met said, 'For God's sake don't let it appear we have any understanding with England.' But how, he asked in despair, could he make bricks without straw? He was utterly exasperated by the fact that the American Government were compelled to refuse the 'assistance of the greatest Power in the world, *in carrying out our own policy*'.[1]

Such was the domestic outlook when he decided that the turmoil in China demanded an amplification of his Far Eastern programme. In the circumstances he had to restrict himself to a further description of the American attitude and with this on July 3, 1900, he circularized the Powers concerned. The policy depicted by Hay was one which aimed at bringing peace to China, at preserving her territorial and administrative entity, at protecting treaty rights, and at safeguarding within her boundaries the principle of equal and impartial

---

[1] Hay to Foster, June 23, 1900, Thayer, *Hay*, vol. ii, pp. 234–5.

foreign trade.[1] These were all very laudable objects and in asserting them at that time the United States may have again helped to avert the awaited dismemberment. Besides, in intent the July circular was much more far-reaching than the notes on the Open Door. Having specifically mentioned the preservation of China's 'territorial and administrative entity', the American Government now defended on paper the sovereignty and integrity of the Chinese Empire. It was, nevertheless, still only a paper defence. To the Powers Hay had merely submitted a unilateral definition unsecured by formal partnership with Great Britain and possessing no sanction or authority of its own. With this fresh statement of American policy Lord Salisbury fully concurred. At home, however, the Secretary of State exerted scrupulous care to assure critics that with the British Government there had been no previous consultation.[2] In the Far Eastern intervention of the United States the main shortcoming thus persisted.

During August the beleaguered legations were relieved. Contrary to the German view, the British and American Governments did not regard themselves as being in a state of war with China;[3] but as part of the international expedition for suppressing the Boxer disturbances they both sent troops. Of this force the command had been taken by a German general, Count Waldersee, and when the contingent of his own compatriots departed for China it was with the exhortation of the Kaiser ringing in its ears to act as Huns and give no quarter.

At the end of the summer chaos reigned in Far Eastern diplomacy and with each other the English-speaking Powers were not in close touch. Before the Boxer uprising had been quelled, in order to be suitably rewarded by China, Russia sought to withdraw from Peking her troops and legation and in August she invited the United States to follow her example. Although President McKinley, anxious for electoral purposes to evade the charge of foreign entanglements, favoured the proposal, Hay persuaded the Cabinet to resist Russian intrigues.[4] The rumour, however, had been propagated—and it was one of which vestiges lingered—that in Chinese matters the United States would now be friendlier with Russia than with Great Britain. At this idea members of the American Government scoffed.[5] Yet

---

[1] *U.S. Foreign Relations*, 1901, Appendix, 'Affairs in China', p. 12.

[2] Choate to Hay, July 7, 1900, *U.S. Foreign Relations*, 1900, p. 345; Dennett, *Hay*, pp. 308–9.

[3] Salisbury to Queen Victoria, July 5, 1900, *Letters of Queen Victoria*, Third Series, vol. iii, p. 571.

[4] *U.S. Foreign Relations*, 1901, Appendix, 'Affairs in China', p. 20; Dennis, *Adventures*, pp. 230–4; Dennett, *Hay*, pp. 311–15.

[5] Radolin to Bülow, Aug. 2, 1900, *Grosse Politik*, xvi. 208; Dugdale, *Germ. Dip Docs.*, vol. iii, pp. 131–2; Root to Hay, Sept. 2, 1900, Dennis, *Adventures*, p. 231.

Hay felt it necessary—through Henry White at the London Embassy —to correct in Downing Street any false impression. 'We have steadily withstood every overture—and there have been many—on the part of Russia and Germany for a more intimate understanding to the disadvantage of Great Britain.'[1] In spite of some momentary impatience with British policy, it was improbable that the Russians and Germans could offer Washington better satisfaction. And so by the autumn on the principal Far Eastern questions Hay and Salisbury were in accord.[2] While between them active co-operation was not achieved, the friendly attitude towards each other of the English-speaking Governments remained unshaken.

In the meantime with the Russians sweeping across Manchuria the search for safeguards had to be renewed. To Great Britain the United States was of small use. With the Powers she might associate herself temporarily, as when her troops joined the international force to subdue the Boxers; yet she also insisted upon being independent of all ties. This Hay himself bewailed unceasingly, perceiving that if, for the protection of their identical interests, Downing Street could not obtain assistance from Washington—owing to the 'morbid state of the public mind toward England'—it would at least try to come to terms with Germany.[3] Between London and Berlin negotiations had in point of fact already been started. The result was that on October 16, 1900, Great Britain and Germany signed an agreement pledging themselves not only to maintain the Open Door and the territorial integrity of China but also, in case the latter principle should be jeopardized, to consult each other about the preservation of their interests. By it the Germans thought that they had secured equality of treatment in the Yangtse Valley, the British sphere of influence, and that it would enable their legion in China to complete its mission without a humiliating loss of support from Great Britain; while for the British Government a Far Eastern engagement with Germany during the Boer War was, on many grounds, highly opportune. The agreement, nevertheless, soon led to serious Anglo-German embitterment. Germany did not wish to attenuate her connexion with Russia whom she wanted—for sound geographical and diplomatic reasons—to keep diverted to Eastern Asia and away from Europe or the Balkans. Early in 1901, when St. Petersburg pressed China for additional concessions in the north, the German Government refused therefore to construe their recent agreement as

[1] Hay to White, Sept. 7, 1900, Nevins, *White*, pp. 172–3.
[2] Ibid., pp. 173–8; Dennis, *Adventures*, pp. 229–39.
[3] Hay to Adee, Sept. 14, 1900, Olcott, *McKinley*, vol. ii, p. 259; also *U.S. Foreign Relations*, 1900, p. 143.

applying to Manchuria.[1] The dispute which thus arose was no trifling matter. It meant that in the Far East Great Britain could look to Germany even less than to the United States for reliable co-operation.

Towards the signature of the Anglo-German agreement John Hay did not profess to be indifferent. At first he assumed it was the kind of arrangement he had been offered by Salisbury in 1898 before leaving the London Embassy. Then he feared a secret provision. Finally, although the United States gave partial adherence to it, Hay saw that the omission of Manchuria rendered the agreement almost worthless.[2] His country, he remarked, was at any rate spared the infamy of a German alliance. The Secretary of State would rather have been 'the dupe of China, than the chum of the Kaiser'. Nor did the British Government seem to know what a horrible practical joke had been played upon them. About John Bull, said Hay, his heart was heavy.[3]

A singular event now occurred which detracted from the avowed impeccability of American intervention in Far Eastern affairs. By the War and Navy Departments of the United States, the Administration had been induced to attempt to obtain a coaling-station at Samsah Inlet, north of Foochow; from their effort wider territorial ambitions were not excluded. But Japan, who had acquired from Peking a non-alienation engagement for Fukien Province, sturdily opposed a project which affected her own interests and which would accelerate the partition of China. Such a move, she also warned the State Department, might bring into operation the Anglo-German agreement. It was an ironical circumstance that only six months after his July circular—in December 1900—it should have been necessary for Tokio to remind John Hay of the accepted American attitude towards the territorial integrity of China.[4] And so, with Japan standing guard, the United States on the Chinese sea-coast did not follow in the footsteps of the other Powers. From London the news of this endeavour, which perhaps put Tokio in a somewhat cynical mood about American diplomacy, may have been withheld. But on the development of the Far Eastern policy of the United States it threw strange light. By Hay's advisers Great Britain was criticized—and formal British collaboration rejected—for doing in China what his own Government had themselves just proposed to do at Samsah Bay.

[1] *Br. Docs.*, vol. ii, pp. 1–31; Brandenburg, *From Bismarck*, &c., pp. 147–53, 160; *Camb. Hist. of Br. Foreign Policy*, vol. iii, p. 289; G. P. Gooch, *History of Modern Europe*, pp. 325–6.
[2] Dennett, *Hay*, pp. 320–1; Nevins, *White*, p. 179.
[3] Hay to Adams, Nov. 21, 1900, Thayer, *Hay*, vol. ii, pp. 248–9.
[4] *U.S. Foreign Relations*, 1915, pp. 113–15; also Dennis, *Adventures*, pp. 251–2; Beard, *The Idea of National Interest*, pp. 83–4.

Meanwhile the Germans were never slow to unearth evidence of Anglo-American misunderstanding. A settlement had to be reached of the problems raised by the Boxer outbreak, and the United States suggested that the Powers confer either in Washington or somewhere in Europe. Russia and France approved but Germany, supported by Great Britain and Japan, preferred Peking; and the upshot was that for the negotiations, which did not conclude until September 1901, the Chinese capital remained the centre. During January, however, a report of a 'pronounced *rapprochement*' between the Americans and the Russians had been dispatched to the Wilhelm-strasse from the German Embassy at London. According to it not only was the flotation of a large loan in the United States being planned at St. Petersburg, but with the British Foreign Office the relations of Joseph Choate, the American Ambassador, were less cordial than usual.[1] European diplomatists thus talked—the wish being father to the thought—of a cooling-off in English-speaking friendship. And by the manner in which the Senate had lately adopted its amendments to the isthmian treaty they doubtless were not silenced.

In the Far Eastern attitude of the United States there had, as a matter of fact, been no outward change. The incident of Samsah Bay was a brief and secret aberration; on the maintenance of the Open Door and the territorial integrity of China the American Government continued to base their policy. Like Great Britain, therefore, they did not witness with equanimity Russia's sustained aggression in Manchuria and her brazen infringement of pledges. Yet Hay was helpless when the Japanese asked what steps they intended to take. On February 1, 1901, he informed Tokio that the United States would not attempt to enforce her views by a hostile demonstration either alone or in concert with other Powers.[2] Of the programme to which Hay had been restricted such diplomatic passivity was the logical and ultimate consequence. Because of it, however remarkable the early improvement in their direct relations, Great Britain in the Far East could not depend upon the United States. If international rights in China were to be conserved something more substantial than solemn admonitions would be required. But that Washington was not prepared to give. Only to Japan could the British turn, and with her during the next year Great Britain became allied.

Since the Spanish War the English-speaking Governments had

---

[1] Eckardstein to Holstein, Jan. 10, 1901, Eckardstein, *Ten Years at the Court of St. James'*, pp. 180–2; also Dennis, *Adventures*, pp. 240–1.

[2] Memorandum of Feb. 1, 1901, Dennis, *Adventures*, p. 242; also ibid., pp. 241–5.

acknowledged their new understanding and it entered into the calculations of the European Chancelleries. Yet between Great Britain and the United States positive co-operation seldom mounted to the high level dictated by their common interests. In mutual affairs Anglo-American friendship was soon to make notable progress; in general world politics, however, it assumed forms that were timid, ineffectual, and disappointingly negative. But there, too, even a modicum of Anglo-American goodwill was valuable and important. All recent experience seemed, nevertheless, to point to the inescapable conclusion that, for active assistance outside the western hemisphere, Downing Street could not look to Washington. In Anglo-American collaboration the limiting factors had been revealed and by them practical statesmanship would in the future have to shape its course. But others also of a more constructive character had again emerged, and as these grew increasingly manifest the advance in friendly relations between the English-speaking peoples was now resumed.

V

THE GROWTH OF THE UNDERSTANDING

FOR three years British policy had been in a state of experimentation, but in 1901 under Lord Lansdowne at the Foreign Office a new phase began. Great Britain failed with Germany and succeeded with Japan in negotiating an alliance. Re-examining the fundamental issues of their external security, the British Government at the same time clarified their attitude towards the United States: although she did not see fit effectively to co-operate abroad, they would do nothing in international affairs that might cause her offence. During the fateful months when they were critically taking stock of their diplomatic position they seem to have resolved once and for all to consolidate Anglo-American understanding. The next stage in the final settlement with the United States of their mutual disputes coincided significantly with activities—the last of the discussions about an alliance with Germany, the negotiations with Japan—which culminated in Great Britain's definite abandonment of isolation. The permanent pattern of Anglo-American friendship was gradually becoming visible. Since 1898 domestic traditions and prejudices in the United States had forced the two Governments to draw back; but this, on the whole, was a case of *reculer pour mieux sauter*. By 1902—following a complete adjustment of the isthmian question—English-speaking goodwill had won the consent of both nations.

In 1901, when Great Britain and Germany for the last time officially explored together the possible terrain of an alliance, Anglo-American friendship was indelibly charted on the map of British policy. Joseph Chamberlain—with the support in the Cabinet of the Duke of Devonshire—had been again urging his views upon Berlin. Conducted by Lord Lansdowne, the negotiations, however, petered out mainly because the two Powers distrusted each other and considered their respective terms incompatible. Germany was pleased that the British and Japanese should attempt to protect China from the designs of St. Petersburg; but with the Tsardom on her borders she could not, for the sake of the Far East or political stability elsewhere, afford to incur Russian enmity in Europe. The alternative idea of a British understanding with Paris and St. Petersburg the German Foreign Office dismissed as entirely unattainable. It was true that with the fixed hostility of Russia Great Britain had to contend in many parts of Asia, while in the period of the Boer War the malevolence of the French and rivalry with them in Morocco seemed almost as irremediable. The Wilhelmstrasse had therefore strong grounds for reasoning that only in Berlin could the British Government purchase a sympathetic hearing; that they would inevitably return to the Germans and be compelled to offer better colonial and defensive conditions. This, moreover, was expected to happen after peace had been restored in South Africa, when, towards an Anglo-German constellation, the public sentiment of both countries might have shed some of its anti-pathy.[1] But the British did not come back and turned instead to their grouping with Japan, then with France, and ultimately with Russia.

In order to enhance the value of their goodwill the Germans in 1901 over-emphasized to Great Britain her diplomatic friendlessness. One way of doing this was to exaggerate the fragility of Anglo-American understanding. In January, as Queen Victoria lay on her death-bed, the Kaiser visited Osborne and the conversations then held were a dress-rehearsal for those which started in March. With the Chinese Boxer situation in mind William II spoke to the new King about 'the symptoms of a *rapprochement* between the United States and Russia' —a coalition which Edward VII believed would be a great danger for the whole of Europe. The Kaiser, in fact, was blandly suggesting that the Americans might form an entangling alliance to exploit China and close the door to the commerce of other nations. To Lansdowne he said that the United States hated Great Britain and repeated his prophecy of a combination between Washington and St. Petersburg. While the Russians were bankrupt, Wall Street would provide the money they desired; it was their object, he argued, to direct American enterprise towards the British sphere of influence in the Yangtse Valley.[2] Whatever the 'symptoms' of the German diagnosis the malady went no further. Nobody was deceived by this transparent endeavour to play upon trade rivalries or by allegations of sympathy in the United States with Great Britain's most implacable adversary. Any wedge would do if the Germans could drive it into English-speaking friendship. They were thus sedulously assuring themselves and others that the British and American Governments had drifted apart. But they were none too certain. So having brought their ser-vices to market they tended to disparage the wares of a still potential competitor.

Nevertheless, towards Great Britain, in the various problems which had arisen since the Spanish War, large sections of the American

[1] *Br. Docs.*, vol. ii, pp. 60–88; Brandenburg, *From Bismarck*, &c., pp. 154–81; Fay, *The Origins of the World War*, vol. i, pp. 137–41.
[2] Eckardstein to Holstein, Jan. 28, 1901, Eckardstein, *Ten Years at the Court of St. James'*, p. 191; Lord Newton, *Lord Lansdowne*, p. 199.

people, as distinguished from their Government, had shown themselves hostile. In March 1901, at the outset of the Anglo-German
negotiations, the Imperial Chancellor, Count von Bülow, therefore
favoured an alliance the *casus foederis* of which would apply only
when one of the signatories was attacked by two or more Powers. By
doing this he proposed, among other things, to exempt Germany from
an Anglo-American war about Canada.[1] The Wilhelmstrasse accordingly declined in advance an obligation it never would have been
invited to assume.

How were such matters regarded by Americans ? Did they feel that
against them Germany would fight alongside Great Britain or Great
Britain alongside Germany ? At the end of March these precise questions were discussed by Senator Lodge and Theodore Roosevelt, then
Vice-President of the United States. In the view of the latter Germany
was the one serious menace. Roosevelt expected that, planning to
defy the Monroe Doctrine in the West Indies or South America, she
would strike when work ceased on the upbuilding of the American
Navy; and as a result of the way in which Congress had treated the
canal agreement and the consequent weakening of British goodwill,
she counted, he thought, on Great Britain standing aloof. He also
observed that if a suitable isthmian arrangement were not conceded
—and he wished to be friendly with Great Britain from whom the
United States had nothing to fear—his compatriots would have to
act on their own; for this eventuality he desired the armed forces to
be ready. Roosevelt said he had reason to believe that, if the United
States violated her existing isthmian engagements, Germany would
support a British protest. 'Before we abrogate the Clayton-Bulwer
Treaty we want to be sure of the position we intend taking should
Germany and England combine against us. Of course such a combination would be one of the utmost folly for England, because she is
certain to have her paws burned, while the nuts would go to Germany.' On the other hand, during the past two years Roosevelt had
discovered—and his opinions were of the highest importance since
within the next six months he was to occupy the White House—that
British statesmen could commit the 'wildest follies'.

When Great Britain rejected the amendments to the new isthmian
treaty a resolution was introduced into the Senate to abrogate the
old one. Replying to Roosevelt, Lodge pointed out that the Canal
Bill would be passed unless, by December of that year, the British
Government had yielded to American demands. About the prob-

---

[1] Bülow to Hatzfeldt, Mar. 24, 1901, *Grosse Politik*, xvii. 48; Dugdale, *Germ. Dip.
Docs.*, vol. iii, pp. 143–4.

ability of a German attack he was, however, less convinced than the Vice-President. Yet one could occur in Brazil—the Kaiser being capable of anything; it was therefore necessary, by increasing her navy, for the United States to be prepared to defend the Monroe Doctrine throughout the southern continent. According to Lodge, American economic pressure on Europe would be the basic cause of the conflict. But Germany had nothing to do with the Clayton-Bulwer Treaty and in a quarrel over it the Senator did not expect her to back Great Britain. 'That the English should undertake to go to war about the canal seems impossible, although, I admit, they have done a good many impossible things lately. If, however, there is any danger of that kind, now is the time to take the step, for England is too exhausted by the African war to enter on any new struggle, and Germany has all she can handle in China at the present moment.'[1] Was it this sort of realistic calculation that had been actuating the Senate? On the British side, at any rate, the resumed negotiations for the final canal treaty quickly disposed of the dark hypotheses raised by Roosevelt and Lodge. In London, moreover, and unknown to the American Government, additional testimony of their utter irrelevance was soon to be furnished.

The Anglo-German discussions about an alliance were a jealously guarded secret. But of a pro-American policy defined in those circumstances the authenticity was all the more incontestable. In May 1901 the British Foreign Office reached the stage of drafting a convention for a defensive alliance between Great Britain and Germany. The outlines of the treaty, as suggested in conversation with Lord Lansdowne, were sketched by Sir Thomas Sanderson, Permanent Under-Secretary of State for Foreign Affairs. In the first draft, which was dated May 27, 1901, Article IV stipulated: 'It is agreed that this Convention shall not apply to any questions arising in the American Continent or involving war with the United States.' In the alternative draft Article III declared: 'It is agreed that this Convention shall not apply to questions on the American Continent, nor bind either High Contracting Party to join in hostilities against the United States of America.'[2] In each draft there were but five clauses; apart from the proposed signatories the United States was the only Power accorded special mention. The Anglo-German negotiations were abortive—for one reason because Lord Salisbury, the Prime Minister, still cherished

---

[1] Roosevelt to Lodge, Mar. 27, 1901, Lodge to Roosevelt, Mar. 30, 1901, Henry Cabot Lodge (ed.), *Selections from the Correspondence of Theodore Roosevelt and Henry Cabot Lodge*, vol. i, pp. 484-8.

[2] Sanderson's memorandum, May 27, 1901, *Br. Docs.*, vol. ii, no. 85, Enclosures 1 and 2 in no. 85, pp. 66-8.

his country's diplomatic independence.[1] Great Britain and Germany were then at the parting of the ways. But from these months of grave decision, so big with the destiny of the twentieth century, the one palpable fact of British goodwill towards the United States had again emerged.

With that may be contrasted two important expressions of opinion —the first an American and the second a German. In June Roosevelt's tone had been modulated, presumably by the progress of the renewed negotiations for a canal treaty. To Senator Lodge he now wrote that he was friendly towards Great Britain; to her the United States stood closer than to any other nation; and that in the future their interests would probably run on parallel lines. It was less than a month since the draft convention of an Anglo-German alliance had been drawn up in the Foreign Office. Roosevelt seems therefore to have been tilting at windmills when he remarked that he did not care whether Great Britain accepted or rejected the Monroe Doctrine. She was the one Power with whom a struggle over that principle of policy, while a calamity for both sides, would be to the immediate profit of the United States: the loss of Canada to the British Empire could never be compensated by the possible seizure of the Philippines and Porto Rico.[2] About Anglo-American relations the German Emperor also held strong views. At Wilhelmshöhe in August he spoke of them once more to King Edward VII and to Sir Frank Lascelles, the British Ambassador. By him the latter was advised against putting too much faith in the United States. In commercial matters their chief rival, she would throw over the British as soon as it paid her to do so.[3] At the Foreign Office these words of warning do not appear to have caused alarm. Never did the Kaiser learn how vain is the net spread in the sight of any bird.

By the end of 1901 the negotiations had finally ceased for an alliance between Great Britain and Germany. As résumés of the ground traversed several accounts were composed in the Foreign Office—one by a high permanent official, another by Lansdowne himself—which, among other things, briefly depicted British policy towards the United States. In these summaries the wishes of the Dominions were also scrupulously appraised. The fact was that in Whitehall a new custom had developed—one more fully exemplified in 1911 when the second Anglo-Japanese Alliance underwent revision and which since the Great War of 1914–18 has been a central feature

[1] Salisbury's memorandum, May 29, 1901, *Br. Docs.*, vol. ii, no. 86, pp. 68–9.
[2] Roosevelt to Lodge, June 19, 1901, *Correspondence of Roosevelt and Lodge*, vol. i, pp. 493–4.
[3] Lascelles to Lansdowne, Aug. 25, 1901, *Br. Docs.*, vol. ii, no. 90, p. 73.

in the conduct of the external affairs of the British Commonwealth. For in far-reaching departures the Foreign Office had begun always to scrutinize their probable consequences—consequences often juxtaposed and occasionally even fused—upon the autonomous sections of the Empire and the United States alike. In doing this the British Government were not deserting Europe: it was overseas addition rather than continental subtraction. Thus Francis Bertie, the Assistant Under-Secretary of State for Foreign Affairs, reviewing the Anglo-German negotiations, pointed out in November that a defensive alliance would cost Great Britain more than Germany; it might mean the sacrifice of her 'liberty to pursue a British world policy'. Besides, their respective aims were neither identical nor capable of being reconciled. As an example of that, Bertie cited the position in the Indian and Pacific Oceans where the 'Colonies of Australasia' had interests which they sometimes felt were adversely affected by German and French proceedings. Whenever 'Colonial interests' arose in questions between Great Britain and foreign Powers, the Dominions, having taken part in the South African War, would now expect their desires to prevail.[1]

As for relations with the United States, Bertie was not apprehensive on that score. During the summer and autumn of 1901 the British and American Governments had been concluding another canal treaty which fulfilled the demands of the Senate. Less than a fortnight before it was signed the Assistant Under-Secretary of State revealed a defensive motive which underlay the concession. In his memorandum on the Anglo-German discussions he had observed that with those of his own country the interests of Germany were irreconcilable. He continued: 'I do not mention her ambitions in the American Seas. They may safely be left to be dealt with by the United States.'[2] Here, in two pregnant sentences, was epitomized the frame of mind in which, at the turn of the century, Great Britain had encouraged American colonial expansion. And now, in 1901, they expressed for the Caribbean region the same British policy of reinsurance with the United States. The isthmian treaty of that year did not only permit full American control over the proposed canal; it also constituted the British seal on the ascendancy of the United States in the New World. Great Britain was to find herself more and more preoccupied elsewhere; her trans-Atlantic interests—her trade routes and her dependencies—which, in any case, merely required the maintenance of the *status quo*, would soon have to be less vigilantly watched. It

---

[1] Bertie's memorandum, Nov. 9, 1901, ibid., no. 91, pp. 73–6.
[2] Ibid., p. 75.

therefore seemed best, as a counter-balance in the western hemisphere to the intrusion of other Powers, to help strengthen her new friend— in such informal reinsurance strategic economy blending with political wisdom. And thus, too, the project which the combative fancy of some Americans had conjured up as likely to rupture the good understanding between Great Britain and the United States became presently a buttress of their joint security.

On Lord Lansdowne the fact had especially impressed itself that, in terms of English-speaking friendship, British and German *weltpolitik* were antithetical. During November he also surveyed in a memorandum the impediments to a closer understanding with Germany. The idea of Count Hatzfeldt, the German Ambassador, was that the liability of the Triple Alliance should be to support the British Empire in any of its disputes; Great Britain would have been no more obliged to defend the frontiers of Germany and Austria-Hungary than those two Powers to defend Australasia, the African colonies, and British America. Lansdowne differed from Salisbury, whose characteristic opinion was that his country had fared well in spite of her international situation. The Foreign Secretary argued that the safety of Great Britain in the past did not warrant complacency about the future results of isolation. To German diplomatists he had, nevertheless, indicated difficulties in the way of a 'full-blown defensive alliance' which were, as he stated, 'virtually insuperable'. Of these, Lansdowne enumerated five. The first was the impossibility of defining the *casus foederis* so that it would not be too rigid, thereby hampering British freedom of action, or too vague, thus depriving the alliance of its practical value. Next came the certainty of alienating France and Russia. Then Lansdowne, fearing complications with the 'Colonies', appears to have foreseen the rise of nationalist opposition in the Dominions to European commitments; they might, he said, not want to be 'hanging on to the skirts of the Triple Alliance'. The fourth difficulty involved the United States, while the fifth was that of gaining the approval of Parliament at a time when the Government had so little reason to be satisfied with the position at Westminster. His fourth difficulty the Foreign Secretary described in weightier language than the others. It was: 'The risk of entangling ourselves in a policy which might be hostile to America. With our knowledge of the German Emperor's views in regard to the United States, this is to my mind a formidable obstacle.'[1]

The importance of Lansdowne's statement can hardly be over-

---

[1] Lansdowne's memorandum, Nov. 11, 1901, *Br. Docs.*, vol. ii, no. 92, p. 78; also ibid., pp. 76–9.

rated. The United States had been singled out as the one Power with whom the prospect of war or antagonistic engagements would not be entertained. During the Anglo-German negotiations, by the Foreign Secretary and his chief officials, peace and friendship with the American people was treated indeed as a cardinal maxim of British policy. To current and subsequent events their confidential and authoritative evaluations furnish a noteworthy clue.

Meanwhile the immediate centre of interest for British diplomacy had been shifting from Berlin to Tokio. And in the Japanese capital relations with the United States were then such that towards the maintenance of Anglo-American understanding no hindrance was likely to be encountered.

Plans for an alliance between Great Britain and Germany had often included Japan as a prospective partner. When these failed to materialize a direct connexion was discussed by the British and Japanese Governments. After the Boxer Rebellion, instead of withdrawing her troops, Russia had occupied the whole of Manchuria and from her all countries which stood for the territorial integrity of China and equality of commercial opportunity were faced with a growing menace. Germany, too, with Russia as bait, had not ceased to fish in the troubled waters of the Far East. In the Kaiser's angling, moreover, the United States constantly figured. In August 1901, when he conversed at Wilhelmshöhe with King Edward VII and Sir Frank Lascelles, he did not only reiterate his warnings about the alleged *rapprochement* between Washington and St. Petersburg and the American threat to British interests in the Yangtse Valley; he also inquired whether Great Britain could oppose alone and without Japanese aid both the United States and Russia. The French, said William II, would not assist her against their own ally, and for that sort of mission the Germans had no fleet.[1] At what was he driving? The Kaiser evidently wanted Great Britain to combine if not with Germany then with Japan so that, while he remained hand in glove with the Tsar, these two Powers would keep open the Chinese door for German commerce. Nor could the opportunity be resisted, by crowing over the supposed cleavage in the Far East between the English-speaking Governments, to stress the British need of a friend.

For Japan the Anglo-Japanese Alliance became the diplomatic lever with which she lifted herself to the rank of a Great Power. Upon the encroachments of Russia towards the ice-free ports of China she had long looked with scant composure—her own eyes being

---

[1] The Kaiser's memorandum, Aug. 23, 1901, *Grosse Politik*, xvii. 97; Dugdale, *Germ. Dip. Docs.*, vol. iii, pp. 154–5.

riveted not only on Corea, to which the Russians had access from Manchuria, but on the latter province as well, where it was hoped she would herself find a valuable market, a source of raw materials, a territory to be colonized. And so after some initial hesitation, forsaking the idea of coming to an agreement with St. Petersburg itself, the Japanese consented at London to play the part cast originally for others. On January 30, 1902, when Lord Lansdowne and Count Hayashi signed the Anglo-Japanese Alliance an Oriental Power had helped terminate Great Britain's formal isolation.[1]

The treaty affirmed a Far Eastern policy with which in general the United States might have associated herself. Consisting of six articles, it was to last five years. The preamble registered the desire of the signatories to maintain the independence and territorial integrity of the Chinese and Corean Empires and to uphold within them the principle of equal opportunities for the commerce and industry of all nations. Disclaiming aggressive tendencies and supporting the *status quo*, they reserved the right, however, by the first article to safeguard their own 'special interests'—those of Great Britain in China and those of Japan in China and Corea—against foreign interference or internal unrest. In 1905, when Japan took Corea under her wing, the preamble and the first article were to be modified with the explicit approval of President Theodore Roosevelt. Establishing the diplomatic conditions upon which the Japanese fought the Russians, this alliance, for Anglo-American relations in the Far East, was, as a matter of fact, soon to be of primary importance. By the second article, if either Great Britain or Japan, defending their respective interests in Eastern Asia, were to become involved in war with a third Power, the fellow-signatory would observe strict neutrality and seek to prevent other Powers from joining in against its ally. Should two or more Powers attack one of the allies the other contracting party was, under the third article, to come to its assistance, conduct the war in common and make peace in concert with it.

The British Government, in short, having informally localized the American conflict with Spain, would now localize formally any future struggle between Russia and Japan. For the protection of India, nevertheless, they only derived an indirect advantage: in the event of war there the Japanese would not be on the Russian side in China. The major weapon in the hands of Great Britain was her fleet, and a diplomatic note about the disposition of naval forces and their peace-time co-operation accompanied the treaty. According to it,

[1] *Br. Docs.*, vol. ii, pp. 115–18; also ibid., pp. 89–137.

so far as possible, each signatory intended to maintain available for concentration in Far Eastern waters a naval force superior to that of any third Power.[1] In this provision the French and Russian were the squadrons contemplated—they, after the British, then being strongest off the coast of Eastern Asia. But in 1905, following the formation of the Entente Cordiale and the defeat of Russia, the British Government considered that it had become superfluous. Persuading Japan at that time not to renew it, they were to a large extent influenced in their view by the friendly attitude in the Far East of the American Navy.

In 1902 nothing on the political horizon seemed to portend that by Anglo-Japanese naval arrangements the United States could ever seriously be affected. But to the maritime aspirations of Japan they were a lively stimulus and as such served to foster subsequent difficulties over sea-power on the Pacific. Until Russia, however, was vanquished and the Japanese had freer scope in the Orient, Tokio and Washington were not troubled by rival naval ambitions. Yet, on the course of European affairs, separate British negotiations in 1901–2 with Japan and the United States were, in their results, to have a common unforeseen effect. For while Great Britain had been preparing the basis for her naval withdrawal from the Far East, the way was also being cleared, through the parallel conclusion of a final canal treaty, for a similar move from the Caribbean. What the diplomatists began the admirals finished. Within the next three or four years the Anglo-American and Anglo-Japanese maritime relationships, supplemented later by the Anglo-French —the Mediterranean agreement differed in time but not in intent—were knit together by the British Government into a single policy of concentration in the North Sea.

During the Anglo-Japanese negotiations the United States had not been forgotten. In January 1902, responding to an inquiry from Marquis Ito, the Elder Statesman of Japan, Lord Lansdowne was confident that of the treaty there would be neither American nor German disapproval. Of the United States he said that the British Government 'had every reason to believe that she desired the maintenance of the *status quo* in the Far East'.[2] The Wilhelmstrasse, as a matter of fact, was gratified with what had been done, and in the United States the press proclaimed its satisfaction that for American trade other Powers should gratuitously keep open Chinese markets. Nevertheless the tell-tale reference in the first article of the agreement

[1] Ibid., pp. 119–20.
[2] Lansdowne to MacDonald, Jan. 7, 1902, ibid., no. 120, pp. 109–10.

to the 'special interests' of Great Britain and Japan in China and Corea did not escape the attention of the State Department. The American Government therefore expressed their pleasure that the treaty sought to uphold the independence and territorial integrity of China, but reserved full liberty to protect their own interests in that country and in Corea.[1]

In the Far East the Russians were thus confronted with a new combination, and they feared that it might include the United States. Nor was their apprehension decreased by a protest from the State Department against some of their recent demands on China. At St. Petersburg Count Lamsdorff, the Russian Minister for Foreign Affairs, spoke to the American Ambassador of reports he received that the United States was being pressed to join the Anglo-Japanese Alliance. He had heard likewise that towards this idea the Government in Washington were not ill disposed. Such a step, Lamsdorff declared, would have been regarded by Russia as an unfriendly act. These rumours, however, John Hay speedily denied. The Secretary of State told Count Cassini, the Russian Ambassador, that the United States had never been approached about the agreement or asked to adhere to it. Hay hoped Cassini was wrong and that the Far Eastern situation would not end in war; by Great Britain and Japan his Government had been assured that the objects of their treaty were entirely peaceable. Russia, he added, could anticipate the friendship of the United States so long as she respected the Open Door, equality of opportunity for American commerce and enterprise, and the territorial integrity of China.[2]

The Germans, on the other hand, were glad that the Alliance had been concluded as it reduced the danger of a *rapprochement* between London and St. Petersburg. Yet the Wilhelmstrasse was anxious to ascertain whether British self-confidence—enhanced by the emergence from isolation—would lead to greater activity in the Far East, where the ambitions of Germany might be opposed by the Anglo-Japanese group. And in the event of that happening Count von Bülow wanted her Ambassador to watch in London for indications of American sympathy or support.[3] The Germans, apparently, were now less prone to aver that in China the English-speaking Powers had parted company.

---

[1] Lascelles to Lansdowne, Feb. 7, 1902, *Br. Docs.*, vol. ii, no. 128, pp. 122–3; Chang, *The Anglo-Japanese Alliance*, pp. 86, 241–2; *U.S. Foreign Relations, 1902*, p. 931.

[2] Hay's memorandum, Mar. 6, 1902, Dennis, *Adventures*, pp. 374–6.

[3] Bülow to Metternich, Mar. 13, 1902, *Grosse Politik*, xvii. 149; Dugdale, *Germ. Dip. Docs.*, vol. iii, pp. 157–8.

Russia did not redeem her pledges to evacuate Manchuria so that in the Far East the British and American attitudes remained substantially unaltered. What had been procured by Tokio in 1902 Washington might have had at any time during the past four years. Yet towards Great Britain John Hay could only adopt a policy of benevolent detachment. In 1903 he acknowledged that the British and Japanese Governments would support and follow such suggestions as the United States might make;[1] but these were invariably hedged in by the strict tradition of American diplomatic independence. And from that state of affairs there was no change until President Theodore Roosevelt, absorbed in the fortunes of the Russo-Japanese War, intervened in the grave international crisis which it evoked.

Meanwhile, during her negotiations with Germany and Japan, Great Britain had consistently assumed the existence in world politics of permanent friendship between the English-speaking Powers. It would, however, have been impossible to do this without the vast improvement in their mutual relations bred of a settlement of the isthmian problem. In March 1901 Lansdowne's rejection of the amendments to the new canal treaty had revived the danger of the Clayton-Bulwer Treaty itself being violated—a resolution towards that end having been at once introduced into the Senate. By Senator Lodge John Hay was informed of the conditions upon which his fellow-legislators would sanction a further agreement with Great Britain. If the American people were to build, protect, and administer the canal impartially for the passage of ships of all nations—equal tolls on domestic and foreign commerce alike—they also intended to have its control 'absolutely within their own power'. The Senate, Lodge said, would ratify a treaty which superseded that of 1850, assigned the defence of the canal to the United States alone, and accorded her the right to maintain its neutrality when she herself was not at war.[2] Demanded by the Senators without previous diplomatic consultation, these extra requirements the British Government might rigorously disallow. But if properly negotiated between the two sides could they be still refused?

The earlier situation seemed to be recurring when, to Hay's proposals, the Colonial Office had first been impelled to secure Canada's hasty acquiescence. And now nothing was better calculated than continued obduracy in Whitehall to goad the Senate into authorizing

[1] Hay to Roosevelt, May 12, 1903, Dennis, *Adventures*, pp. 376–7.
[2] Lodge to Hay, Mar. 28, 1901, Thayer, *Hay*, vol. ii, p. 260; also Williams, *Anglo-American Isthmian Diplomacy*, pp. 306–7.

H

American construction of the canal; an act which would inflict on British prestige not only an intolerable blow but also entail the loss of a new and valued friendship as well as a tragic resurgence of ill will between the English-speaking peoples. Again threatening forcibly to abrogate the Clayton-Bulwer Treaty, the Senate held the whip-hand.

In Washington, however, the Executive were determined not to let the initiative slip from their grasp. The Secretary of State set therefore to work on the draft of a treaty which might satisfy the Senate and yet preserve unharmed the policy of a good understanding with Great Britain. His ideas were acceptable to so notable a critic as Theodore Roosevelt, and in the spring of 1901 the outlook was much brighter. At the end of April through Lord Pauncefote—whose elevation to the peerage had occurred in 1899—John Hay submitted his new plan to the British Government. In London at the same time Joseph Choate inquired of the Prime Minister whether negotiations might start afresh. Salisbury consented. He merely asked once more that, in the tolls charged for the use of the canal, there should be no discrimination against the ships of any country.[1] The victory of the Senate being foreshadowed, the trans-Atlantic wire could now be repaired.

Since in principle the major concession had been made, the exchange of views forged steadily ahead. In the treaty-making powers of the Senate Lord Lansdowne was not very well versed, and that presented a slight difficulty. Senator Lodge, however, visiting England during the summer, explained the American case first to the Foreign Secretary himself and then to a small group of Cabinet Ministers which included Arthur Balfour.[2] In many ways this private discussion resembled that of Joseph Chamberlain with Richard Olney at the time of the Venezuelan controversy. It was in line, moreover, with the Anglo-American expedient of employing special emissaries such as Cecil Spring Rice in 1905, Sir William Tyrrell and Colonel House in the early years of Woodrow Wilson's Administration, to bring the two English-speaking Governments into closer touch. While the official diplomatic representatives still had their normal duties to perform, the informal conversations of men like these helped to correct misapprehensions and unify policies. Nor is it improbable that nowadays when some of the Powers appoint Ambassadors-at-Large they are, in the conduct of international affairs, simply carrying out a

---

[1] Dennis, *Adventures*, p. 162; Nevins, *White*, pp. 156–7; Mowat, *Pauncefote*, pp. 284–5; Thayer, *Hay*, vol. ii, p. 258.

[2] *Proceedings LVIII Mass. Hist. Society*, 'Memoir of H. C. Lodge', pp. 336–7; also Nevins, *White*, p. 158.

wider and more formal development of this same Anglo-American practice.

Hay's anxieties were legion. In London he did not allow it to be overlooked that Congress would tear up the Clayton-Bulwer Treaty unless agreement were reached before the end of 1901. In July the old idea of compensation on the Alaskan frontier was suggested by Lord Salisbury to Henry White. When the latter objected the Prime Minister said: 'Well, there would be this advantage in dealing with the canal question alone, that we should have only one antagonist, whereas in respect to Alaska there would be two—yourselves and Canada.' Lansdowne transmitted his proposals to Washington in August and during the summer Hay prudently attempted to forestall opposition by conferring with various Senators. According to him the British Government had shown a very fair and reasonable spirit.[1]

The negotiations were thus well advanced when, in September 1901, William McKinley was assassinated and Theodore Roosevelt succeeded to the Presidency. That event signified no mere change of personalities. In the history of the United States as a Great Power it completed the passage from the epoch of becoming to the epoch of being. President McKinley had bridged two ages. Under him, in the period of the Spanish War, Americans were awakened to a new consciousness of their place among the imperial nations. This feeling it was Roosevelt's mission to deepen and confirm. As Assistant-Secretary of the Navy, as warrior in Cuba, and as post-war politician, he had taken a leading part in the great issues of his time. A man of versatility, he gave voice to strong convictions. Since his youth he had detested 'Anglo-maniac mugwumps', pacifists, and 'futile sentimentalists of the international arbitration type'. Peace with honour, he tirelessly declared, could be maintained only by constructing a big efficient navy—the basis of American security and his extended theory of the Monroe Doctrine. Against national sloth and timidity he frequently inveighed, while he praised military preparedness and the righteous pursuit of martial virtues.[2] This philosophy he never altered and his actions often suited his words. Yet, as President, such were his manifold contradictions, he submitted to the Hague Court its first case—the Pious Fund dispute with Mexico;

---

[1] Hay to White, June 18, 1901, White to Hay, July 24, 1901, Nevins, *White*, p. 158; Samuel Flagg Bemis (ed.), *American Secretaries of State and Their Diplomacy*, vol. ix, p. 158; Williams, *Anglo-American Isthmian Diplomacy*, pp. 307–9; Thayer, *Hay*, vol. ii, p. 261.

[2] *Correspondence of Roosevelt and Lodge*, vol. i, p. 218; Bishop, *Roosevelt*, vol. i, pp. 75–6; Henry Cabot Lodge (ed.), *Addresses and Presidential Messages of Theodore Roosevelt, 1902–1904*, p. 328.

his Administration arranged a number of arbitration treaties; and, although head of a Government wedded to non-interference, he nevertheless intervened for peace abroad in the widespread diplomatic crises of 1904–6. With Theodore Roosevelt, the articulate focus of American nationalism, British representatives did not always find it easy to cope. And indeed English-speaking friendship might meet almost any danger if it could survive the hazards of his masterful temperament. During Roosevelt's terms of office, in their mutual relations and in world politics as a whole, Great Britain and the United States were to be confronted both with serious difficulties and large opportunities for the furtherance of their common interests. The outcome was that by the middle of his Presidency Anglo-American understanding had never reposed on more solid foundations.

Installed in the White House, Theodore Roosevelt, a critic of the first of the new canal treaties, became a sponsor of the second. By him John Hay had been invited to continue as Secretary of State and the draft then being framed received his enthusiastic approval. Meanwhile Lord Pauncefote, who was visiting England, advised the British Government to concede everything—except the right to impose differential charges on foreign and American traffic—and with the Foreign Secretary Senator Lodge again discussed matters.[1] From London Joseph Choate bore witness to the consideration and generosity with which Lord Lansdowne had treated him; nor could agreement be prevented by the publication of details which Senators divulged prematurely to the triumphant American press. Towards Great Britain, Salisbury told Henry White, there was, in the way the previous treaty had been amended, 'nothing necessarily offensive'.[2] The British Government were patently resolved to let bygones be bygones. Even so, for a delay of over two years, the United States could blame no one but herself. Had she assented in 1899 to a simultaneous adjustment of the Canadian problem additional privileges might have been provided ungrudgingly and at once. But now conciliation was uppermost, the bludgeoning of Congressional diplomacy muffled, and on November 18, 1901, John Hay and Lord Pauncefote signed their second isthmian treaty.

Its real authors were the opponents of its immediate predecessor. They had demanded that the Clayton-Bulwer Treaty should not be modified but superseded; this was done in the first article. Then by

---

[1] Hay to Choate, Sept. 21, 1901, Dennis, *Adventures*, p. 163; Hay to White, Oct. 14, 1901, Nevins, *White*, p. 159; Mowat, *Pauncefote*, pp. 285–6; *Proceedings LVIII Mass. Hist. Society*, 'Memoir of H. C. Lodge', pp. 336–7.

[2] Choate to Hay, Oct. 2, 1901, Hay to White, Oct. 14, 1901, Dennis, *Adventures*, pp. 163–4; White to Hay, Nov. 25, 1901, Nevins, *White*, p. 222.

the second article Great Britain specifically yielded to the United States the power to construct an inter-oceanic canal and the exclusive right of managing it. From the Clayton-Bulwer Treaty the 'general principle' of neutralization was retained; as in the first Hay-Pauncefote Treaty, the Suez Canal rules for the regulation of the isthmian waterway were again included. But it also exhibited important differences. According to the agreement of 1900 European Governments were to be asked to adhere, so guaranteeing the neutralization of the canal. The Senate, in the name of the Monroe Doctrine, discarded that stipulation and it was not restored. Nevertheless in the treaty of 1901, by the first rule of the third article, the British Government did secure one international right: the canal was to be open for the use of vessels of all flags—if they observed the regulations —under conditions of absolute equality.[1] From these terms Great Britain, as the chief sea-faring Power, would benefit most; yet they were in the interest no less of every maritime nation. During the Administration of President Taft Panama Tolls were a source of Anglo-American controversy, but in 1914 Congress was persuaded by Woodrow Wilson to revoke legislation which discriminated against foreign shipping.

With the second Hay-Pauncefote Treaty the United States could now establish effective control over the projected isthmian canal. By the agreement of 1900 fortifications were prohibited, but through the Davis amendment the Senators had sought to exempt measures which might be necessary to ensure in the canal the defence of their country and the preservation of public order. In 1901, however, the reference to fortifications was entirely deleted. On the other hand, in the second rule of the third article the contracting parties agreed that the canal should never be blockaded and that within it no right of war could be exercised nor act of hostility committed. Yet along the waterway, to protect it against lawlessness and disorder, the American Government were at liberty to maintain military police. In 1901 the disappearance of the ban on fortifications may have been understood as implying silent British consent to their erection; the police clause was, in any case, capable of an elastic interpretation; and by means of it Washington later justified military measures taken in the Canal Zone. Moreover, the fourth article provided—a timely stipulation in view of subsequent dealings by the Roosevelt Administration with Colombia and the new State of Panama—that by changes in territorial sovereignty the Anglo-American treaty would not be affected. From Great Britain the United States had clearly gained a stupendous

[1] *U.S. Foreign Relations*, 1901, pp. 244–6.

victory. For her policy in Central America, and subject to no compensation whatever, she had been given a free hand.

The signature of the isthmian treaty was announced by Theodore Roosevelt on December 3 in his first annual message to Congress. He said that on the American continent no single work of such consequence to the people of the United States remained to be undertaken. The treaty, he added, guaranteed them every right in the canal for which they had ever asked. Through the Senate it was propelled by Senator Lodge; in the same month an overwhelming majority of that body advised that it be ratified. With Great Britain there were no further difficulties and in February 1902 the Hay-Pauncefote Treaty was proclaimed.[1] To Henry Adams, turning over in his mind the long and stormy record of Anglo-American disputes, the event appeared peculiarly auspicious. Of John Hay he wrote: 'With infinite effort he had achieved the astonishing diplomatic feat of inducing the Senate, with only six negative votes, to permit Great Britain to renounce, without equivalent, treaty rights which she had for fifty years defended tooth and nail.' About England, he continued, the Senate had nothing left to oppose, for England was won, and Canada alone could give trouble.[2]

England had been won, but so perhaps was the United States. What the British Government abandoned might only have been held at the cost of Anglo-American goodwill; what they secured was the possibility of endowing it with fresh strength. At first glance they seemed to have surrendered privileges of incalculable value when they relinquished an equal share in the construction and management of the isthmian sea-route between the Atlantic and Pacific Oceans. Ordinarily the maritime responsibilities of Great Britain would have been augmented and not diminished by a project comparable in importance with the Suez Canal; because of it the Royal Navy ought presently to have engaged in an increasing rather than decreasing surveillance of her West Indian colonies, her lines of Imperial communications and oceanic trade in the waters of the Caribbean. Yet, in spite of that, by transferring her rights in the isthmian canal she also sacrificed her naval preponderance in the region of Central America. This was done primarily to placate the United States; but with the deepening complexity of international affairs it became doubtful whether she could in any case protect by herself all her far-flung interests. On the other hand, the Venezuelan controversy

[1] *U.S. Foreign Relations*, 1901, p. xxv; ibid., 1902, pp. 517–19; also *Proceedings LVIII Mass. Hist. Society*, 'Memoir of H. C. Lodge', pp. 337–8.
[2] *Education of Henry Adams*, p. 423.

had tended lately to show—a truth more cogently demonstrated in 1902–3—how resolutely in the New World, against the intrusion of non-American Powers, the United States would stand on guard. Between the former disputants an era of friendlier relations then ensued, and in the policies of adjustment which accompanied the change there could be detected direct territorial implications. For now the Monroe Doctrine would preserve rather than menace existing British interests in Central America and beyond—a prospect of which the Foreign Office had not altogether been oblivious when the final canal treaty was signed and the negotiations terminated for an alliance with Germany.[1] What in fact Great Britain had ceded were rights which European conditions as much as the attitude of the United States were making it awkward to maintain: the right to expand—which she had long ceased to exercise; the right to control; but not the right to remain in and about Central America. When, therefore, during the next three or four years, British war-vessels were withdrawn from this area, the Admiralty was merely expressing in terms of naval strategy the recent accomplishments of Anglo-American diplomacy. For in the western hemisphere, by her *rapprochement* with the United States, Great Britain had been reinsuring the *status quo*.

The many separate threads in Anglo-American understanding were thus being gathered up on the loom of events and woven—in effect if not by design—into a single fabric. The United States might refuse precise obligations to co-operate in international affairs; nevertheless, across the Atlantic, she would in her own interest cover the rear of the British Empire against a foreign invader; and in return for that vital service Great Britain shunned pledges to other Powers to which her friend might reasonably object. Nor would the Canadian problem—a lesson crisply impressed on Ottawa in 1903—be allowed to check the improvement in their relations. There was in such matters no exception to the characteristic British habit of moving without preconceived plans or according to rigid theories. But one step led to another—steps still sufficiently haphazard to enmesh Great Britain in the Venezuelan fiasco of 1902–3—and on the whole the Government in London were seldom bereft of the general sense of direction by which they had been guided since the last few years of the nineteenth century. Of the meaning of these tendencies, so richly to her advantage, the United States could not fail to take cognizance. For, continuously interacting on each other, the settlement of mutual disputes and the search in world politics for a common

[1] Bertie's memorandum, Nov. 9, 1901, *Br. Docs.*, vol. ii, no. 91, p. 75.

outlook were bound to draw the English-speaking peoples closer together. The second Hay-Pauncefote Treaty, seen from both angles, indicated the sturdy growth of Anglo-American solidarity.

To the isthmian project of the United States the main hindrance had now been overcome. It would give her a passage-way connecting her own Atlantic and Pacific coasts with each other and with those on the opposite sides of South America; furnishing a quicker route from the Atlantic seaboard to Hawaii and the Philippines, the canal affected intimately her defensive and offensive position on the Pacific and in the Far East; to her divided fleet it could indeed, by rapid union in an emergency, afford off either coast double the striking-power. If, moreover, being ultimately fortified, it were to consolidate American security, it needed support from outposts and naval bases. For such a purpose the recent occupation of Cuba and Porto Rico was especially useful. But the ascendancy of the United States over the Caribbean and Central America, bolstered up by capital investment, resulted also elsewhere in that region in intervention of a tutelary nature. The roots of this development were embedded in her geographical situation and her national history. Yet from the alleviation of Anglo-American isthmian differences which it followed, it received a further impetus. By the new friendship between the English-speaking Powers the international aggrandizement of the United States was thus again facilitated.

Meanwhile among Germans the notable improvement in Anglo-American relations caused disquiet. Any policy intended to cut it short was, however, weakened by rumours current in Washington about their own ambitions in the western hemisphere. The American Government would not permit the establishment of German foot-holds or naval bases on the approaches to the projected canal, and in 1901 the State Department addressed a frank warning to Berlin against an alleged proposal to acquire the Venezuelan coast-island of Margarita. Although vigorous denials were made the suspicion lingered that Germany wanted to infringe the Monroe Doctrine. In 1902 the frustration of American efforts to purchase from Denmark the Virgin Islands in the West Indies had been ascribed by the agent of the United States to German intrigues; Joseph Choate thought that the Kaiser was seeking two harbours in southern California; while President Theodore Roosevelt seems to have informed the British Prime Minister that, if Germany subjugated the Netherlands, he would take over Dutch Guiana.[1] For the rash designs attributed

[1] Hay to Jackson, Apr. 10, 1901, J. Reuben Clark, *Memorandum on the Monroe Doctrine*, p. 174; Dennis, *Adventures*, p. 284; Nevins, *White*, pp. 205–8.

to it the Wilhelmstrasse, in all probability, had no stomach. But for a number of years German activities were distrusted by Theodore Roosevelt, John Hay, Senator Lodge, and important members of the American Diplomatic Service.[1] With this state of affairs, undermining confidence between Washington and Berlin, Great Britain had no reason to be dissatisfied. Nevertheless, for the conduct of British policy it was temporarily to have some very embarrassing consequences.

What these were would be fully demonstrated in 1902-3 during the Anglo-German coercion of Venezuela. That undertaking, however, was preceded by a curious episode, a retrospective controversy over the course pursued by the Powers prior to the Spanish War. Seldom placid for long, Anglo-German relations had been disturbed of late by recriminations between Joseph Chamberlain and Count von Bülow concerning the comparative behaviour of the British troops in South Africa and the Prussian forces in 1870. In January 1902 fuel was added to the flames when a spokesman for the British Government replied to a parliamentary question about diplomatic endeavours at Washington just before the Spanish-American conflict. Lord Cranborne, the Under-Secretary of State for Foreign Affairs, had then explained that in April 1898 the representatives of the Powers made their first attempt at collective mediation with the consent of President McKinley; but he also said that with other subsequent proposals Downing Street declined to associate itself, as these might have appeared to be putting pressure on the American Government or offering an opinion on their attitude.

This answer was given on the eve of a visit to the United States by Prince Henry of Prussia, at a time when the Germans were particularly anxious to acquit themselves of any responsibility for the 'other subsequent proposals' and thus combat the damaging belief that in 1898 they had been actuated by ill will. Eager to court American favour at the expense of Great Britain and to smooth the path for Prince Henry, they decided therefore to play a trump card. In February 1902 the German Government published dispatches from their Ambassador at Washington in which Pauncefote, his British colleague, was disclosed as one who took the lead in striving to prevent a declaration of war between the United States and Spain.[2] At

---

[1] Charles Callan Tansill, *The Purchase of the Danish West Indies*, pp. 373-453; Rippy, *Latin America in World Politics*, pp. 142-53; Mary Evelyn Townsend, *The Rise and Fall of Germany's Colonial Empire*, pp. 201-8; also *Correspondence of Roosevelt and Lodge*, vol. ii, pp. 120, 136.

[2] Mowat, *Pauncefote*, pp. 213-22; Smalley, *Anglo-American Memories*, Second Series, pp. 179-82.

Anglo-American friendship they had aimed point-blank. Would so straight a shot pierce its target?

In Washington the German revelations were treated with contempt. Whatever Pauncefote may have said or done at a moment of confusion in 1898, upon his labours for Anglo-American understanding a high value had been set by the White House and the State Department. And so the German Government overreached themselves when they complained in a memorandum to John Hay that the British were jealous of good relations between the United States and Germany. 'Is this the speech of great nations,' he asked the President disdainfully, 'or the shrieks of angry housemaids pulling caps over the policeman?' To the Wilhelmstrasse Hay accordingly submitted evidence of Germany's bad faith when she conspired against the United States with the Filipino insurrectionists. Theodore Roosevelt, pleased with the ratification of the isthmian treaty, had been equally undeceived and for Lord Pauncefote lost none of his esteem.[1] The German effort to rake over old coals was a dismal failure.

In their wooing of the United States the Kaiser and Count von Bülow were, nevertheless, exceedingly diligent. William II had a medal conferred on the President, gave a Germanic Museum to Harvard University, presented the American people with a statue of his ancestor Frederick the Great, arranged exchange professorships, and appealed to the racial sentiment of German stock in the country. He even ordered a yacht from an American shipyard and invited Alice Roosevelt, the daughter of the President, to christen it. France, too, vied for the friendship of the United States: she likewise established exchange professorships and, by presenting the nation with a statue of Rochambeau, sought to arouse fraternal memories of the American Revolution.[2]

It was, moreover, as part of this campaign that the Kaiser's brother, Prince Henry of Prussia, embarked on his mission of goodwill to the United States. Impressing upon him the significance of the journey, the Chancellor took care in advance to prime the royal emissary with tactful replies to inconvenient questions about the relations of Germany since 1898 with the English-speaking Powers; and to the Tsar the Kaiser expressed his amusement at the 'toothache' being felt across the Channel because of his brother's trip.[3] Although the

[1] Hay to Roosevelt, Feb. 15, 1902, Hay to A. D. White, Feb. 17, 1902, Dennis, *Adventures*, p. 74; Smalley, *Anglo-American Memories*, Second Series, p. 185; Mowat, *Pauncefote*, p. 220.

[2] Pringle, *Roosevelt*, p. 281; Jusserand, *What Me Befell*, pp. 278–81; Carl Russell Fish, *The Rise to World Power*, p. 241.

[3] Bülow, *Memoirs 1897–1903*, pp. 567–8; Willy to Nicky, Jan. 30, 1902, *The Kaiser's Letters to the Tsar*, p. 87.

President was not inclined to meet the Prince the mission proved to be a success. A few months afterwards the British diplomatist, Cecil Spring Rice, on a private visit to Washington, discovered that, among Germans in the United States, there existed organized political propaganda against Great Britain. But on the American people foreign flatteries were, he thought, largely wasted as they knew how different the European attitude would have been had they not won the Spanish War.[1]

In May 1902 Pauncefote died. He had been a devoted servant of English-speaking solidarity and to the excellence of his work the American Government now testified with fine ceremonial courtesies.[2] At Washington Sir Michael Herbert, by whom he was replaced, had been twice Chargé d'Affaires; his wife, like Joseph Chamberlain's, was an American; and an old friendship of his with Theodore Roosevelt had not a little to do with the appointment. Senator Lodge used his influence with Lord Lansdowne, who consulted him, to procure it; and Cecil Spring Rice hoped that by similar means and for somewhat similar reasons he might obtain the secretaryship of the Washington Embassy.[3] The British Government, however, did not send him to the United States and in Anglo-American diplomacy during the Russo-Japanese War their decision was to have an important sequel. His friends were then in the presidential circle, but when a decade later Spring Rice took over the Embassy itself power rested in other hands.

At the end of May peace was concluded with the Boers. John Hay wrote privately to congratulate Joseph Chamberlain, who, responding, mentioned the discouragement of his compatriots that they had been maligned abroad 'and especially in the United States, with which it is the first object of my public life to cultivate a good and even an affectionate understanding'. He was, nevertheless, heartened by support from the Dominions and 'in this politic vision of the Empire' he perceived a promise for the future. Chamberlain applauded— perhaps with a touch of irony—the suppression of the Filipino rebellion; the governance of dependent populations, he told Hay, would help the people of the United States to understand 'our world-work'.[4] Of the British Imperialist creed Anglo-American friendship had, at the beginning of the twentieth century, become in fact a

[1] Roosevelt to Robinson, Feb. 3, 1902, Pringle, *Roosevelt*, p. 282; Spring Rice to Miss Lascelles, June 2, 1902, Gwynn, *Spring Rice*, vol. i, pp. 351–2.

[2] Mowat, *Pauncefote*, pp. 294–7.

[3] *Proceedings LVIII Mass. Hist. Society*, 'Memoir of H. C. Lodge', p. 341; Gwynn, *Spring Rice*, vol. i, pp. 358–9; Smalley, *Anglo-American Memories*, Second Series, p. 354.

[4] Chamberlain to Hay, July 5, 1902, Dennis, *Adventures*, p. 129.

striking feature. By Cecil Rhodes, who died in 1902, that ideal was embodied in the munificent benefaction of his Will. Wishing to come to terms with Germany, he included the German Rhodes Scholarships. But he wanted above all to promote the unity of the British Empire and tighten the bonds with the American nation in a great English-speaking fellowship to lead mankind. From the most distant corners of the King's Dominions and the United States Rhodes Scholars would foregather at Oxford, the ancient shrine of their common culture, and upon leaving it pursue the high tasks of which he dreamed. His legacy was the substance of a spiritual aspiration which in that age now animated far-sighted statesmen on both sides of the Atlantic.

VI

SEA-POWER AND THE MONROE DOCTRINE

By 1902 British policy in Central and South America was founded in
principle on friendship with the United States. Would the theory be
borne out in practice ? To this question the blockade of Venezuela by
Great Britain and Germany shortly supplied an unequivocal answer.
During the winter of 1902–3 the coercion of that Caribbean Republic
subjected to a thorough test not only English-speaking understanding
but its effect also on Anglo-German diplomacy. Never again in the
western hemisphere would European Governments thus exercise their
sea-power, and the lesson afforded by the episode—a lesson already
foreshadowed in the Hay-Pauncefote Treaty—was soon incorporated
by Great Britain in the redistribution of her fleet. For now in the
chain of British security, so transformed were Anglo-American relations since the days of Olney and Cleveland, the Monroe Doctrine
had become an important link.

At the turn of the century Venezuela, rent by faction, groaned
under the dictatorial rule of Cipriano Castro. During the civil disturbances the persons and property of foreign residents had suffered
severely, but their demands for compensation were ignored. Payment, moreover, was refused by his Government on the Venezuelan
external debt and they winked at the widespread violation of con-
tractual engagements. The claimants were citizens of many countries,
not excluding the United States; it was felt, however, by Great
Britain and Germany that the grievances of their nationals were the
most serious. In February 1901 matters were aggravated when the
Venezuelan authorities seized four British ships near Trinidad. Six
months later Germany proposed a scheme, which Castro would not
consider, for the arbitration of her claims. Then early in 1902 the
Ban Righ, a British ship connected with the Government of Colombia,
was used to aid Venezuelan rebels. At Caracas representations from
Lord Lansdowne were consequently spurned and British shipping
continued to be ill-treated.[1] By peaceful methods, London and
Berlin appeared at last to realize, satisfaction was unobtainable.

Great Britain and Germany were perfectly aware of the fact that,
without taking into account the susceptibilities of the United States,
no South American Government could be brought to book. But

---

[1] Howard C. Hill, *Roosevelt and the Caribbean*, pp. 106–10; *Camb. Hist. of Br.
Foreign Policy*, vol. iii, pp. 294–5; also *Br. Docs.*, vol. ii, pp. 154–6.

President Roosevelt's attitude had done much to dispel their fear of obstruction from Washington. In December 1901 he told Congress that the Monroe Doctrine allowed every country in the western hemisphere to direct its own commercial relations. 'We do not', he added, 'guarantee any state against punishment, provided that punishment does not take the form of the acquisition of territory by any non-American Power.'[1] For the British and German Governments this pronouncement seemed a fair enough licence to proceed with the chastisement of the defaulting Venezuelans. The problem which was afterwards to arise must be more narrowly defined. Public opinion in the United States then objected not only to the final act of conquest. The mere creation of circumstances which might have enabled Germany—and against her declared policy—to establish herself on the shores of the Caribbean sufficed to put the American people vigilantly on guard.

From the outset, nevertheless, the Germans had reckoned with mistrust in the United States of their trans-Atlantic ambitions. One way of counteracting that was to collaborate with the British— Anglo-American friendship might give some shelter should trouble occur; another was by explaining beforehand to Washington the genuine moderation of their views. In December 1901, when they discussed with the State Department the probable coercion of Venezuela, the scheme suggested came well within the limits of the Monroe Doctrine as expounded by Theodore Roosevelt; that Germany sought no acquisitions in the western hemisphere the Kaiser had asserted emphatically in a recent message which the President accepted. As a result of such preliminary assurances the Imperial Chancellor thought himself free to draw up a programme of co-operation with Great Britain and Italy for a pacific rather than a belligerent blockade of Venezuela. This proposal meant that ships which ran the blockade were not to be confiscated but only held or turned back for the period of the naval operations. The Kaiser, however, vetoed Bülow's approach to the British Government until Prince Henry in the winter of 1902 had returned from his mission of goodwill to the United States. William II was afraid that by Great Britain the plan for employing force in the Caribbean might be used as a means of inciting the Americans against Germany and so mar the effect of his brother's visit.[2] The Chancellor therefore had to wait.

[1] *Addresses and Messages of Theodore Roosevelt, 1902–4*, p. 322; also Roosevelt to Sternburg, July 13, 1901, Pringle, *Roosevelt*, p. 283; Roosevelt to Sternburg, Oct. 11, 1901, Bishop, *Roosevelt*, vol. i, p. 158.

[2] *U.S. Foreign Relations*, 1901, pp. 192–6; Bülow to the Emperor William, Jan. 20, 1902, *Grosse Politik*, xvii. 241; Dugdale, *Germ. Dip. Docs.*, vol. iii, pp. 160–1.

At Caracas during the summer of 1902 British protests were still of no avail. Lansdowne's patience was exhausted and to him in July Count Metternich, the German Ambassador, broached the whole subject. Metternich conveyed his Government's opinion that it might soon be necessary for the interested Powers to exercise pressure on Venezuela. The Foreign Secretary thereupon voiced the readiness of Great Britain to confer with Germany, although to the Ambassador's inquiry about a pacific blockade in the autumn he made no definite response. Because of this understanding for joint action British Ministers were subsequently to find themselves in a most unhappy dilemma. Yet at the end of the Boer War Anglo-German relations had undergone a momentary improvement and common sense decreed that whenever feasible these two Powers should work together. The British Government accordingly warned Castro, who remained defiant, that they might be compelled to resort to strong measures and the Admiralty was consulted.[1]

During the autumn the steps to be taken were more fully discussed. The Wilhelmstrasse agreed to a British proposal for the seizure of the Venezuelan gunboats. Lansdowne, however, rejected a pacific blockade on the grounds of its ineffectiveness, while a belligerent blockade might produce complications with other Powers. To the British plan the German Government reluctantly consented hoping that, if it failed, their own programme would be tried. They also perceived that the diffidence of Great Britain was due to her friendship with the United States. And so they reminded Lansdowne of similar pacific blockades in which Great Britain had participated; precedents in which the Monroe Doctrine might have been, but was not, regarded as an obstacle. That with the growth of Anglo-American goodwill such examples were no longer apposite the history of the next few months afforded abundant proof. Nevertheless, Metternich told Lansdowne that, when apprised by Germany of the action contemplated, the United States did not object. On November 11 the Foreign Secretary was therefore in a position to send his final warning to Caracas.[2]

Nor, at the same time, had he neglected to communicate with Washington. The Secretary of State was informed by Sir Michael Herbert, the British Ambassador, that, if Castro did not relent, his Government would adopt the measures required. On November 13

[1] Lansdowne to Buchanan, July 23, 1902, *Br. Docs.*, vol. ii, no. 171, pp. 153–4; *Camb. Hist. of Br. Foreign Policy*, vol. iii, pp. 294–5.
[2] Lansdowne to Lascelles, Oct. 22, 1902, *Br. Docs.*, vol. ii, no. 172, p. 154; Lansdowne to Buchanan, Nov. 11, 1902, ibid., no. 174, pp. 156–7; *Camb. Hist. of Br. Foreign Policy*, vol. iii, p. 296.

John Hay cited in reply President Roosevelt's interpretation of the Monroe Doctrine. Regretting that European Powers should exert force against Central and South American countries, the Administration of the United States could not, however, oppose anything done—provided there was to be no acquisition of territory—for redress of injuries.[1] By this initial suspension of outward disapproval the Foreign Office must have again been lulled into a false sense of wellbeing. Afterwards, when Washington doffed its mask of disinterested acquiescence, Great Britain was too deeply committed to Germany instantaneously to abandon the operations without a loss of honour and prestige. No doubt the British Government were misled by a certain instability in the policy of the United States. And yet if Lansdowne had listened to Sir Michael Herbert he might have gauged the extent to which Americans distrusted Germany and been more wary about the idea of a joint enterprise.[2] On the other hand, the German case was as sound as the British, while at Washington the two partners had taken every diplomatic precaution. It is in the light of these facts that later events must be judged.

Since Lansdowne's final warning to Venezuela was fruitless the Anglo-German preparations went steadily ahead. In November, by promising an independent settlement of her claims, Castro attempted craftily to detach Germany from Great Britain; with exemplary good faith the Wilhelmstrasse rebuffed him and, instead, reported the offer to London. The British Government now suggested, if more stringent measures were essential, that a belligerent blockade—a pacific blockade being incompatible with their conception of international law—be added to the seizure of the Venezuelan gunboats. But the Germans still preferred a pacific blockade as they wished to avoid a declaration of war—for which the sanction of their Bundesrath had to be secured—and the search of neutral vessels on the high seas. As it happened, each side was contending that its proposals seemed the less likely to bring them into conflict with the United States.[3] Upon two points, however, both were agreed: the first, to apply naval force; the second, that nothing should be done to antagonize the American people. Yet of the character of the blockade the British and German Governments were maintaining different views even when they actually had begun to coerce Venezuela.

[1] Lansdowne to Herbert, Nov. 11, 1902, *British and Foreign State Papers*, vol. xcv, pp. 1081–2; Herbert to Lansdowne, Nov. 13, 1902, ibid., p. 1084.

[2] Newton, *Lansdowne*, p. 256.

[3] Metternich to the German Foreign Office, Nov. 26, 1902, *Grosse Politik*, xvii. 256; Dugdale, *Germ. Dip. Docs.*, vol. iii, p. 162; Lansdowne to Buchanan, Nov. 26, 1902, *Br. Docs.*, vol. ii, no. 175, pp. 157–8; Lansdowne to Metternich, Dec. 2, 1902, ibid., no. 177, p. 160.

To President Castro they presented their ultimatums on December 7. His rejoinder was unsatisfactory and the Ministers of the two Powers were withdrawn from Caracas. Venezuela's four gunboats were then immediately seized—some of them being sunk—and her ports blockaded. By the vigour of this castigation the outside world was startled, the British and American press at once leaping to the conclusion that for it Germany bore the chief blame. In Great Britain the ill will she displayed during the South African War had not been forgotten and from a common Anglo-German venture of that sort the public mind wholeheartedly recoiled.

Washington, moreover, objected to a pacific blockade in which neutral rights and commerce might be adversely affected. Sensitive to accusations of German severity in British and American newspapers, resenting the allegation that they were the prime instigators, the Government in Berlin accordingly decided that henceforth they must let Great Britain take the lead. To Lansdowne's plan for a belligerent blockade they thereupon acceded; but with the United States, Germany was already somewhat out of step.[1] The two European Powers, however, being now in agreement with each other, were subsequently able to announce a belligerent blockade to go into effect towards the end of the month, and they were joined in their operations by Italy. Meanwhile on December 13—principally because of British grievances—the forts of Puerto Cabello were bombarded. When that happened American opinion became exceedingly restive about the Monroe Doctrine and in Great Britain sentiment was profoundly stirred.

By the action of the Powers, nevertheless, Castro had been brought to his senses. Although the Monroe Doctrine had not yet protected him he turned naturally to Washington; through American diplomatic channels Venezuela suggested that a portion of the Anglo-German claims should be arbitrated.[2] As it did not cover all the foreign debts this offer was very inadequate; at that juncture its rejection would have been justified. But within less than a week the British and German Governments accepted Castro's proposal. What were the considerations by which they had been influenced?

One of the most decisive arose from the fact that American public opinion was being fanned to a high degree of excitement. Situated

---

[1] Hay to Tower, Hay to White, Dec. 12, 1902, *U.S. Foreign Relations*, 1903, pp. 420, 452; Bülow to the Emperor William, Dec. 12, 1902, *Grosse Politik*, xvii. 258; Dugdale, *Germ. Dip. Docs.*, vol. iii, pp. 162–4; Lansdowne to Buchanan, Dec. 13, 1902, *Br. Docs.*, vol. ii, no. 179, p. 161.

[2] Hay to Tower, Hay to White, Dec. 12, 1902, *U.S. Foreign Relations*, 1903, pp. 420, 453.

on the Caribbean approach to the projected isthmian canal, Venezuela occupied a position which the United States regarded as of vital importance to her defensive system. Among Americans, ever since the Spanish War, suspicion of Germany had been rife; the many rumours of her desire for naval bases and territorial footholds in the New World were now revived by the blockade and given fresh credence. Of where the British Government stood there could, after the signature of the Hay-Pauncefote Treaty, be no question; such keen annoyance as was expressed about them sprang from the belief —to which numerous Englishmen also subscribed—that their limited partnership might have furnished Germany with a cloak behind which lurked more far-reaching aspirations. During November, for the guidance of the American Administration, a secret naval memorandum had been drafted which analysed the possible course of the German coercion of Venezuela. In it references to Great Britain were significantly lacking. The United States, it pointed out, had to keep a force in and near Culebra, Porto Rico, equal or superior to the whole German squadron. She was to aim at being always better prepared for war than Germany; every move of the latter would have to be met by corresponding preparatory action from the former. And this advice seems to have been followed. While the Powers were blockading Venezuela, Admiral Dewey, in command of a large fleet, was stationed at the American base in the Caribbean with orders from Washington to be ready to advance at a moment's notice.[1] Of these precautionary measures taken against the Germans, or of their real nature, Downing Street may have had no exact knowledge. But for Great Britain the general outlook was fraught with peril. On the one hand she did not wish to impair English-speaking solidarity; on the other, in the coercion of Venezuela, she was bound to her European associate. And so as the danger grew of a clash between the United States and Germany the difficulties multiplied for the preservation of Anglo-American friendship.

Did President Roosevelt in the middle of December 1902, repudiating his policy of non-interference and manifesting the national displeasure, compel the Kaiser to accept Castro's proposal for arbitration? In the contemporary records of the blockading Powers there is no evidence to substantiate his famous story—not disclosed in detail until 1916—that he had threatened the German Ambassador with action by Dewey; the incident, Roosevelt's account of which many investigators dismiss as either mythical or at least a gross

[1] Naval memorandum, Nov. 1902, Dennis, *Adventures*, pp. 291–2; Latané, *American Foreign Policy*, p. 493.

exaggeration, may have occurred in December or more probably on a critical occasion at the end of the next month.[1] Nevertheless, even if the President had not as yet intervened, it was clear that, tò pacify the official and public opinion of the United States, Great Britain and Germany would be well-advised to make some quick and conciliatory gesture.

At home the widespread dissent from their policy had not been foreseen by the British Government. Sir Thomas Sanderson, Permanent Under-Secretary for Foreign Affairs, deplored the anti-German outcry, but the Liberal Opposition were mainly concerned with the repercussions of the Venezuelan enterprise on Anglo-American understanding. Sir Henry Campbell-Bannerman called it privately 'a blunder with the seed of a war in it', while John Morley hastened to forward to the Cabinet a message of grave perturbation that he had received from Andrew Carnegie.[2] The absence of Salisbury's restraining hand, Arthur Balfour having become Prime Minister in the summer of 1902, may help to explain how the Government under-estimated the strength of popular prejudice in the English-speaking world against Germany. Yet neither Balfour nor Lansdowne could plead inexperience in American matters, and so celebrated an advocate of close relations with the United States as Joseph Chamberlain only departed on his trip to South Africa when arrangements with Berlin were practically complete. In the meantime Henry White, the American Chargé d'Affaires, had been urging the Prime Minister and the Foreign Secretary to do nothing that might estrange his country. Such representations and the distaste in Great Britain for co-operation with Germany—intensified by the sinking of the Venezuelan ships—now shaped events.[3]

At Westminster in the third week of December Ministers addressed Parliament in no bold Palmerstonian fashion. Lord Cranborne, the Under-Secretary of State for Foreign Affairs, told the House of Commons that, in the estimation of the Government, the claims of bond-holders did not bulk largest; they were coercing Venezuela because of attacks upon the lives, liberty, and property of British subjects. He also adverted to the crucial question of American interests. The

---

[1] Roosevelt to Thayer, Aug. 21, 1916, Thayer, *Hay*, vol. ii, pp. 411–16; Bishop, *Roosevelt*, vol. ii, pp. 221–6. For earlier references to this or a similar incident Jusserand, *What Me Befell*, p. 321; Gwynn, *Spring Rice*, vol. ii, p. 10. Nevins, *White*, pp. 499–500; Royal Cortissoz, *The Life of Whitelaw Reid*, vol. ii, p. 415. Also Hill, *Roosevelt and the Caribbean*, pp. 123–38, 143–6; Rippy, *Latin America in World Politics*, pp. 182–99; Pringle, *Roosevelt*, pp. 287–8; Dennett, *Hay*, pp. 388–94.

[2] Sir Almeric Fitzroy, *Memoirs*, vol. i, p. 117; Spender, *Campbell-Bannerman*, vol. ii, p. 85; Burton J. Hendrick, *The Life of Andrew Carnegie*, vol. ii, pp. 176–83.

[3] White to Hay, Dec. 13 and 15, 1902, Nevins, *White*, p. 210.

view of the United States was reasonable; Cranborne quoted the pronouncement made by President Roosevelt before the blockade had been undertaken: that there was no infringement of the Monroe Doctrine if European Powers insisted on South American Republics meeting their international engagements. Speaking on behalf of the Government, the Under-Secretary acknowledged the validity of the Monroe Doctrine; in maintaining it no nation had, he said, been more anxious than Great Britain to assist the United States. The Cabinet was nevertheless resolved to allay all disquiet. In the two Houses of Parliament Lansdowne and Balfour announced therefore that territory would not be occupied—the Commander-in-Chief of the North American and West Indies squadron being at the same time instructed that without the authority of the Admiralty vessels operating off the coast of Venezuela were neither to land men, bombard forts, nor sink any ships.[1]

As a further step in the restoration of confidence the British Government accepted Castro's offer. From Washington on December 16 Sir Michael Herbert had cabled to Lord Lansdowne the first of a series of reports and entreaties which must have contributed weightily to the formation of policy. Although in the attitude of the Administration the Ambassador discerned no change he did observe 'a growing feeling of irritation in Congress, especially in the House of Representatives against the action of the two Powers, chiefly owing to the bombardment and the sinking of Venezuelan ships'. While not suspicious of Great Britain the American Government were 'undoubtedly apprehensive as to German designs'. Herbert's conclusion was significant and it coloured his advice throughout the period of the blockade. 'The impression prevails in Washington that Germany is using us, and our friends here regret, from the point of view of American good feeling towards us, that we are acting with her.'[2] Thus Great Britain discovered that the comparatively unimportant object of collecting debts from a Caribbean republic might involve a risk of serious damage to a cardinal principle of her international relations. Moreover, on December 17 at London and Berlin the American representatives were directed to repeat with 'strong commendation' Venezuela's proposal for arbitration. To it the British Cabinet had already decided to agree and Germany promptly followed suit.[3]

The German Government showed prudence when they overcame

[1] Latané, *American Foreign Policy*, p. 495; Alejandro Alvarez, *The Monroe Doctrine*, p. 92; *Br. Docs.*, vol. ii, footnote, no. 187, p. 166.
[2] Herbert to Lansdowne, Dec. 16, 1902, *Br. Docs.*, vol. ii, no. 180, p. 162.
[3] *U.S. Foreign Relations*, 1903, pp. 421, 424, 453, 798; Hill, *Roosevelt and the Caribbean*, pp. 120–2.

their reluctance and, as suggested by their Ambassadors in Great Britain and the United States, likewise accepted Castro's offer. They had declared that they would confine themselves to a belligerent blockade and John Hay told their Chargé d'Affaires that he and the President trusted them. But the Secretary of State also indicated that he wished for an early settlement as the American public was nervous about the Monroe Doctrine and, upon the Administration, Congress might make extreme demands.[1] Berlin, in any case, now hoped that, if the initiative were left to the British, the clamour would subside in the English-speaking world against the conduct of the German forces; always jealous of Anglo-American understanding, the Wilhelmstrasse did not want Great Britain, by playing up to the United States in a sudden volte-face, to gain an advantage. And so on December 18 Count Metternich informed Lord Lansdowne that his Government would do nothing to provide additional 'ammunition' for those opponents of the partnership who were placing British Ministers in such an awkward predicament. 'They recognised', the Foreign Secretary noted, 'that resort to arbitration would be likely to produce a salutary effect, and they considered that action should be taken upon the Venezuelan proposal at once, without waiting until Washington "exchanged the rôle of post-office for one of a more active character".'[2] The sharp disapproval of the British people may have led to this swift change of front, but influencing them and the two Governments were the dangers which obviously inhered in a prolonged exacerbation of American opinion.

The first stage of the imbroglio was over. Rational and decorous in its diplomacy, Downing Street had disregarded in international relations the ever-mounting strength of undisciplined mass sentiment. During the Venezuelan episode British and American opinion exemplified the unknown, the incalculable element of surprise, which periodically convulses the foreign affairs of modern democracies. Between the Governments in London and Berlin, for the defence of their respective interests, the coercion of Venezuela had been concerted amicably. From the start they did not ignore American policy and well in advance duly communicated their intentions to the State Department. There had, it is true, been much violence, but if this kind of intimidation was to be applied, what else could be expected? Yet the blockade had scarcely begun when the Powers were enveloped in a whirlwind of public indignation—and one which threatened to

---

[1] Hill, ibid., pp. 134–5; *U.S. Foreign Relations*, 1903, p. 421; Quadt to the German Foreign Office, Dec. 18, 1902, *Grosse Politik*, xvii. 269; Dugdale, *Germ. Dip. Docs.*, vol. iii, p. 164.

[2] Lansdowne to Lascelles, Dec. 18, 1902, *Br. Docs.*, vol. ii, no. 181, p. 162.

increase in velocity. On both sides of the Atlantic its main cause was somewhat, but not altogether, analogous. Neither in Great Britain nor in the United States did it flow from sympathy for the sufferings of downtrodden Venezuela. Thanks to it, nevertheless, Castro was saved from a punishment not wholly undeserved.

The agreement to arbitrate excluded part of the foreign claims and until completely suitable terms could be arranged the blockade continued. The United States being one of the creditor countries, Theodore Roosevelt declined to act as arbitrator; the questions were therefore referred to the Hague Tribunal. To Andrew Carnegie the British Prime Minister now sent a reassuring letter which its recipient passed on to the President and to John Hay. Great Britain, Balfour remarked, had the reverse of any objection to the Monroe Doctrine; he wished that by the United States herself—towards whom he was most warmly disposed—the troublesome republics of South America would be taken in hand. Meanwhile, from Washington Sir Michael Herbert wrote that the Administration and the Senate were maintaining a correct and sensible attitude but public unrest in the United States, as manifested through the House of Representatives, made responsible officials anxious for an early settlement. For that reason, too, Roosevelt would have been an admirable choice as arbitrator and when he refused Lord Lansdowne was highly disappointed; an award by him must have carried with it 'a strong moral sanction'. The Foreign Secretary was also sorry to see in Great Britain so bitter an antagonism against co-operation with Germany, and he believed that, while profoundly impressing the German mind, its expression had been overdone.[1]

At the end of December 1902 the reports from London and Washington of the American and British representatives reflected a deep similarity of interest. Henry White had found Lord Lansdowne eager to conform as much as possible to the views of the United States. To John Hay he pointed out that for over a week Englishmen were very uneasy lest the association with Germany bring them into conflict with American public opinion and thus diminish 'the good feeling which they hope exists on our side towards this country'. Added to that was the anti-German prejudice produced by the Boer War. The fact that British Ministers were astonished by the unpopularity of the partnership—the outburst in the United States being combined with a stronger and more hostile sentiment in Great

---

[1] Balfour to Carnegie, Dec. 18, 1902, Hendrick, *Carnegie*, vol. ii, p. 180; Carnegie to Morley, Jan. 18, 1903, ibid., p. 182; Herbert to Lansdowne, Dec. 19, 1902, Newton, *Lansdowne*, p. 256; Lansdowne to Herbert, Jan. 2, 1903, ibid., p. 258.

Britain—only furthered the acceptance of American advice as to how they might best deal with the situation.[1]

Sir Michael Herbert was also watching the effect of the coercion of Venezuela on English-speaking understanding. According to him, after the ministerial explanations in Parliament and when the press attacks on the Government became known across the Atlantic, Great Britain began to swing back into favour. The Ambassador even informed Lansdowne that by some Americans the presence of the British blockading squadron was looked upon as a guarantee that the Germans would be prevented from following a course which might result in a collision with the United States. Describing the explosion of wrath in that country against Germany, Herbert said that 'suspicion of the German Emperor's designs in the Caribbean Sea is shared by the Administration, the press, and the public alike'. By the American naval authorities, who had not forgotten the Manila episode of 1898, such distrust would, moreover, be fostered; along with the influential ship-building firms they wanted to enlarge their fleet. And at this turn of events the British Ambassador was gratified, especially when he remembered the Kaiser's recent campaign to flatter the American people, the persistent German attempts to discredit the late Lord Pauncefote, and the efforts to sow dissension between the English-speaking Powers. 'The Administration has been most friendly throughout, and, if the dispute be referred without delay to arbitration . . . it will be almost safe to affirm that the friendly relations between Great Britain and the United States, instead of being impaired, have, if anything, been strengthened by the Venezuelan incident.'[2]

The British Government now endeavoured to liberate themselves as rapidly as their own prestige and an honourable commitment to Germany would allow. They were, for purposes of both domestic politics and English-speaking goodwill, in bad diplomatic company. During January 1903 negotiations were undertaken in Washington and, with the consent of the Powers, Herbert W. Bowen, the American Minister at Caracas, represented Venezuela. But until a final settlement could be concluded the blockade remained in force, so that in the Caribbean the state of affairs was still precarious. And besides, it seemed likely that, unless agreement were reached before Parliament reassembled, the Government would fail to weather the storm of criticism, protest, and opposition. Neither at home nor abroad had their difficulties ceased.

[1] White to Hay, Dec. 31, 1902, Nevins, *White*, pp. 211–12.
[2] Herbert to Lansdowne, Dec. 29, 1902, *Br. Docs.*, vol. ii, no. 184, pp. 163–4.

For Great Britain the discomfort of riding in double-harness with Germany became more acute when, in the middle of January, the Germans renewed the severity of their coercive measures. The fort of San Carlos on Lake Maraçaibo fired on the German ship *Panther*, legitimately engaged in maintaining the blockade; the Venezuelan fort had in retaliation been heavily bombarded. This move American public opinion angrily condemned and from it, to the immense relief of the Foreign Office, the Commander-in-Chief of the British North America and West Indies squadron dissented. To him, at Lansdowne's request, the Admiralty sent word expressing satisfaction that he was carrying out the policy of his Government. 'It is of the utmost importance,' the message ran, 'that His Majesty's ships should not be implicated in any indiscreet or violent action, and that matters should be kept as quiet as possible pending negotiations.'[1] Meanwhile, as the discussions with Bowen, the Anglophobe spokesman for Venezuela, were making little headway, Sir Michael Herbert decided towards the end of January to strike a warning note. 'There is', he cabled to the Foreign Secretary, 'a feeling of intense irritation in the United States against Germany, and in default of an early settlement there may be an outburst of feeling which may produce a strained situation and place the President in a position of serious embarrassment.'[2]

With the Germans at this point Lansdowne became quite stern. They had suggested that the blockading Powers hold the customs-houses of the two Venezuelan ports until the Congress in Caracas could give the appropriate sanction to any contract made with President Castro. Rejected by the Foreign Secretary, their proposal seemed to indicate that they did not fully appreciate the British attitude towards the United States. 'It would be a pity at the last moment', Lansdowne told the German Ambassador, 'to take a step which we had from the first deprecated, for reasons which were familiar to his Excellency.' He next showed his disapproval of the excessive reprisals which Count Metternich defended. While the Foreign Secretary did not want to hurry over the last part of the negotiations with Venezuela, the Ambassador must have known that 'a great deal of irritation had been created both in this country and in the United States by the German bombardment of San Carlos'.[3] It was, as a matter of fact, late in the day for the British Government to consider the possible ruthlessness of their partner. In the English-

---

[1] Commander-in-Chief to the Admiralty, Jan. 23, 1903, *Br. Docs.*, vol. ii, no. 186, pp. 165–6; Admiralty to Commander-in-Chief, Jan. 24, 1903, ibid., no. 187, p. 166.
[2] Herbert to Lansdowne, Jan. 26, 1903, ibid., no. 189, p. 166.
[3] Lansdowne to Lascelles, Jan. 27, 1903, ibid., no. 190, p. 167.

speaking world German unpopularity had for some years been nourished by the sabre-rattling of Potsdam. Nor was Whitehall, the administrative centre of a vast colonial Empire, unaccustomed to the occasional use of punitive force. The Foreign Secretary must therefore have cared less about the morality or justice of the German bombardment—an occurrence difficult in the circumstances to avoid —than the political and diplomatic consequences which co-operation with Germany entailed. At the outset the two Governments had agreed to support each other throughout the blockade.[1] By the winter of 1903 this mild understanding, however proper at the start, was threatening to become an inordinately burdensome entanglement.

At Washington, in his anxiety to dissolve the Anglo-German partnership, Sir Michael Herbert strove hard to achieve a speedy settlement. With that object in view he was prepared to tolerate the overbearing conduct of Herbert Bowen, Venezuela's American representative, but as Germany kept putting forward fresh conditions its attainment seemed more and more remote. By the anti-German sentiment in the United States which followed the bombardment of San Carlos he had been rendered particularly impatient of delay since, as he wrote apprehensively to Lansdowne, 'complications with Germany mean trouble for us'. And lest he be regarded as over-zealous to come to an arrangement with Bowen, Herbert reminded his chief that it was the Ambassador's business to think first of Anglo-American relations. For that reason he preferred to let the claimants and bondholders wait for a few years rather than 'embarrass the Administration here, which is so friendly to us, and alienate good feeling towards England'.[2] The truth was that in Washington, owing to the coercion of Venezuela, the British Government had already incurred considerable disfavour—enough, at any rate, again to postpone a permanent adjustment of the Alaskan question. Meanwhile from London whatever could be done King Edward VII and Arthur Balfour were doing to assure Americans of their special esteem for the United States.[3]

And now Theodore Roosevelt himself attempted to accelerate matters. Henry White had cabled that an influential quarter in the Cabinet was strongly advising the Prime Minister to terminate the situation by raising the blockade even if it were necessary for them to sever themselves from Germany. He also reported that in Great

[1] Lansdowne to Buchanan, Nov. 11, 1902, ibid., no. 174, p. 157.
[2] Herbert to Lansdowne, Jan. 30, 1903, Newton, *Lansdowne*, p. 259.
[3] Skelton, *Laurier*, vol. ii, pp. 142–3; White to Mrs. White, Jan. 29, 1903, Nevins, *White*, p. 212; Balfour to Carnegie, Jan. 30, 1903, Hendrick, *Carnegie*, vol. ii, p. 183.

Britain popular discontent and pressure were increasing.[1] From this the American Government could at least deduce that, to expedite the slow-moving negotiations, they must tackle not the British but the Germans. Dr. von Holleben, the German Ambassador, had, moreover, departed and a personal friend of the President's, Baron Speck von Sternburg, was, with rare tact, sent to replace him at Washington. To Sternburg Roosevelt spoke on January 31. 'I have seen the German Minister,' Herbert wired to Lansdowne, 'who informs me that the President told him this morning that he earnestly hoped that a prompt settlement of the Venezuelan dispute would be arrived at as public opinion in this country was growing more and more irritated.'[2] That interview may have marked the occasion—or one of the occasions—on which Roosevelt privately threatened interference in the Caribbean by the American fleet with the German blockading squadron. And even if he only employed language as temperate as Herbert recorded the gravity of the crisis was unmistakable.

The Germans, nevertheless, were more concerned about the attitude of Great Britain than of the United States. It was not altogether their fear of Washington but British solicitude for American goodwill which brought them ultimately into line. They could not afford to hazard a break-down of the Anglo-German partnership; without its continuance there was no way of securing their Venezuelan claims while protecting themselves against a conflict with the United States and averting further opprobrium abroad. At the beginning of February 1903 in a dispatch from London the German Ambassador depicted how, for the coercive measures, Englishmen saddled Germany with the major responsibility; but, trusting Lansdowne to stick to his bargain, Metternich expected that Bowen's arrogant behaviour would prevent Great Britain from yielding too readily to Venezuela. Yet he also noted that if, prior to the reassembly of Parliament on February 17, a sharper difference of opinion were to arise between the Foreign Secretary and the United States, the Balfour Ministry would be overthrown; and this might happen should Roosevelt lose patience, surrender to his country's yellow press, and demand the lifting of the blockade. Contending that the British Government could not resist the 'American fetish' coupled with animosity against Germany, the Ambassador predicted that relations with Great Britain would be menaced if, because of their co-operation with the Germans, the Conservatives were ousted by the Liberals. With these arguments the Kaiser and Bülow were in

---

[1] White to Hay, Jan. 28, 1903, Dennis, *Adventures*, p. 303.
[2] Herbert to Lansdowne, Jan. 31, 1903, *Br. Docs.*, vol. ii, no. 192, p. 168.

accord. For Anglo-German diplomacy, the Chancellor observed, the Liberal Rosebery was much more dangerous than a Cabinet which included Balfour, Chamberlain, and Lansdowne.[1]

And so the Wilhelmstrasse decided not only to indulge in no recriminations but to do nothing that might jeopardize the life of the Unionist Ministry. To American warnings it doubtless paid heed; against them Germany could stand out so long as she was certain of British support. But the advent at Westminster of a Liberal Government might have been followed by the defection of Great Britain from the blockade with the German squadron being exposed single-handed to Dewey's fleet in the Caribbean. The Wilhelmstrasse, therefore, though still seeking to wrest adequate terms from Venezuela, was as desirous of keeping Balfour and Lansdowne in office as were these latter to preserve English-speaking friendship. The British policy of Anglo-American understanding, and not Rooseveltian thunderings at Berlin, thus chiefly prevailed.

During the first week of February the prospects for an early settlement seemed poor. Trying to tempt Germany into an independent arrangement, Bowen circulated statements in the American press that Baron Speck von Sternburg differed from Herbert and his Italian colleague. But to the partnership the Germans reaffirmed their loyalty and, struggling against the spectre of separation, appealed subtly to the sportsmanlike instincts of the British Government. By Lansdowne it was thereupon announced that Great Britain fully intended to maintain joint action. And when the Wilhelmstrasse thanked him for this declaration, it quoted Bowen's remark that he had as the main object of his diplomacy the fomenting of discord between the British and German representatives.[2]

These tactics brought Berlin a brief success. For a few days the intrigues of Venezuela's American agent enabled the Germans to recover in London some of the ground they had lost. Influenced by them, Lansdowne, on February 7, cabled to Herbert that Bowen wanted to arouse dissension among the Powers and not to facilitate an equitable adjustment. With him the British Government would therefore have been glad to break off negotiations. For 'parliamentary and other reasons', however, a complete solution was needed without further delay. And so, if that could not be reached in Washington, the Foreign Secretary proposed—a plan previously submitted to the Wilhelmstrasse—that they should abandon all attempts at direct settlement with Bowen and refer the disputed

[1] Metternich to Bülow, Feb. 4, 1903, *Grosse Politik*, xvii. 288; Dugdale, *Germ. Dip. Docs.*, vol. iii, pp. 164–5.   [2] *Br. Docs.*, vol. ii, nos. 194–7, pp. 169–71.

questions to the Hague Tribunal. He also reminded the Ambassador that, in arranging such a reference, President Roosevelt had at the end of 1902 offered to be of service. As soon as the preliminaries for this were fixed, the blockade would be raised.[1]

But from Washington Sir Michael Herbert now delivered a counter-blast which rushed everything in less than a week to an agreement. Bowen's conduct would not be allowed by him to provide an excuse for any last-minute digression; as compared with the future of Anglo-American understanding the German and Italian claims were of meagre importance. To Lansdowne the Ambassador cabled back in a fighting mood. Bowen, he expostulated, would have at once signed the protocol with Great Britain; most of her terms had already been granted; German and Italian conditions, not properly presented at the outset, were the stumbling-block. 'Consequently, in view of public opinion here, it would be folly on our part to take the lead in breaking off the negotiations with Mr. Bowen.' Deeming the German and Italian demands to be unfair, Herbert insisted, if the British Government were obliged to support them, that the suggestion should be sponsored by Germany and not Great Britain. But he advised instead that Lansdowne urge Berlin and Rome to show more leniency. The Ambassador was exceedingly disturbed.

'I feel myself bound to warn your Lordship that a great change has taken place in the feeling of this country towards us since I wrote my despatch No. 355 of December 27th last, and that our good relations with this country will be seriously impaired if this Alliance with Germany continues much longer. The time has almost come, in American opinion, for us to make the choice between the friendship of the United States and that of Germany.'[2]

Language so unguarded seldom crept into formal communications from an Embassy to the British Foreign Office. Herbert sent unsolicited counsel; with Lansdowne's whole Venezuelan policy he did not disguise his acute personal dissatisfaction. Yet for his candour the Ambassador was rewarded by attaining his object. Confronted with the stark alternatives which he outlined, the British Government could decide only in one way. In its final significance the brisk conclusion of the Venezuelan episode was an effort by them to preserve English-speaking solidarity.

When he next saw the German Ambassador, Lansdowne did not mince words. The Foreign Secretary explained the gravity of the situation and the importance of an immediate settlement. Bowen had conceded Great Britain's demands, and it would have been

[1] Lansdowne to Herbert, Feb. 7, 1903, *Br. Docs.*, vol. ii, no. 198, pp. 171–2.
[2] Herbert to Lansdowne, Feb. 7, 1903, ibid., no. 199, p. 172.

'almost intolerable' for her to break off the discussions because the Germans could not secure from Venezuela terms of a very different character. Nor, as Lansdowne told Metternich, did he think the 'position of Germany would be enviable if negotiations fell through under such circumstances'. He added, however, that to Germany the British Government were willing to yield priority in some of their claims. But there was a sting in his remark that, although they did not intend to desert their partner, a solution had become absolutely essential—thus hinting inversely at a contingency which the Wilhelmstrasse had resolved at all costs to avoid.[1] Herbert's adjurations were about to bear fruit.

By obstinacy the Germans would have been ill repaid and an agreement was at last visible. Had they remained adamant Arthur Balfour's Government might have been supplanted by one even less favourable towards Berlin and more acquiescent towards Washington. English-speaking friendship would then be strengthened—an eventuality never attractive to the Wilhelmstrasse—and Anglo-German embitterment revived. The negotiations with Bowen would, besides, not only have failed; the German squadron, coercing Venezuela, would also have been isolated in the Caribbean and at the mercy of the American fleet. Berlin gave way. When to President Roosevelt the question of preferential claims was submitted for adjudication, he suggested that it be referred to the Hague Tribunal.[2] On February 13 Venezuela and the Powers signed their protocol and a day later the blockade was lifted.

At the same time Balfour set British and American opinion at rest. The Monroe Doctrine, he now declared, had no enemies in Great Britain of whom he knew; in the coercion of Venezuela it had, in fact, not really been involved. By Great Britain, said the Prime Minister, any increase was welcomed in the influence of the United States upon the western hemisphere; nor did she desire further to colonize there, to alter the balance of power, acquire territory, or interfere with the mode of government of trans-Atlantic countries. And from London Henry White, the American Chargé d'Affaires, emphasized how widely in Great Britain these sentiments were shared; the deference shown throughout by the British Government to the views of the United States; the relief, after the partnership with Germany, which all Englishmen experienced at the signature of the protocol.[3]

[1] Lansdowne to Herbert, Feb. 9, 1903, ibid., no. 200, pp. 172–3.
[2] *U.S. Foreign Relations*, 1903, pp. xviii–xix.
[3] Alvarez, *The Monroe Doctrine*, p. 92; White to Hay, Feb. 14, 1903, *U.S. Foreign Relations*, 1903, pp. 475–6.

To the appeasement of American public anxiety Theodore Roosevelt also contributed. On April 2, in an address at Chicago, he observed that during the Venezuelan episode the policy of the United States had been disinterested and confined to preventing a breach of the Monroe Doctrine. Geography dictated the offer of American services; their acceptance was helped by the explicit assurances of the Powers, kept with an honourable good faith which the President acknowledged, that the Monroe Doctrine would not be violated.[1] But this pretence of aloofness could scarcely have deceived the Chancelleries. Roosevelt's anger with Great Britain came to the surface when he made his brusque demand for a swift and maximum settlement of the Alaskan controversy. 'The English behaved badly in Venezuela,' the President then wrote, 'despite the fact that we had behaved with scrupulous impartiality during the Boer War. I don't intend that they shall do any shuffling now.'[2] And of this imperious temper neither London nor Ottawa had in 1903 heard the last.

After the blockade had been lifted mixed commissions met at Caracas to decide upon the claims. Those still in dispute were submitted subsequently to the Hague Tribunal, which handed down its award in February 1904. While it did not give the Powers everything for which they asked, it upheld and vindicated the coercive measures. A nice point for future policy, a problem in international relations rather than of international law, had, nevertheless, been raised. Because of the Monroe Doctrine, from defaulting nations in Central and South America, European Powers could not forcibly collect their legitimate debts. For the acts of these republics would the United States therefore hold herself responsible? To that question—discussed in the House of Lords—the British Government, with an eye on Anglo-American friendship, could provide no satisfactory answer. From European views, moreover, Dr. Drago, the Argentinian Foreign Minister, vigorously dissented. The Calvo Doctrine which forbade coercive operations to secure pecuniary claims was elaborated by him, and the United States presented it in modified form to the second Hague Conference.[3] Actually, as between trans-Atlantic criticism and Latin-American protest, Washington pursued a middle course. For, having barred the European bailiff, the United States herself assumed police duties, her southward ascendancy being in turn thus further enhanced.

[1] *Addresses and Messages of Theodore Roosevelt, 1902–4*, pp. 118–20.
[2] Roosevelt to Lodge, June 29, 1903, *Correspondence of Roosevelt and Lodge*, vol. ii. p. 37.
[3] Alvarez, *The Monroe Doctrine*, pp. 92–3; Latané, *American Foreign Policy*, pp. 495–7.

Over the merits of the Venezuelan partnership a division of opinion afterwards persisted in the British Foreign Office. By the older school of officials, which still hoped to work with Germany, the hostility in Great Britain then manifested towards her was not condoned; while of this episode Lansdowne himself said in later years that 'the Germans, upon the whole, ran straight as far as we were concerned'.[1] The Wilhelmstrasse, in fact, had begun to feel the effect of its smug refusal at the turn of the century to take seriously the changes either pending or already introduced in British policy. In the Far East its support of Russia was being neutralized by the Anglo-Japanese Alliance; and now elsewhere a temporary association with Great Britain had been crippled by the common adverse sentiment of the English-speaking world. In 1903, when Berlin offered it a share in the Baghdad Railway concession, Downing Street was unable to agree to suitable terms. Of British public antagonism against further co-operation with Germany the signs, following the Venezuelan partnership, had been too plainly evidenced.[2]

For Great Britain it was no trivial matter that, during the blockade, Anglo-German relations should have suffered a setback. Unlike the United States, and more than other Great Powers, the British Empire lacked geographic or territorial coherence. In the twentieth century, for the better enforcement of her policies, Great Britain was consequently obliged to enter into both limited and general commitments. She had, nevertheless, scarcely engaged herself in the first of her general commitments—that with Japan—before she had been impelled to becloud a limited one with her troublesome German rival. The British Government risked an affront to their partner to a considerable extent in order to preserve American goodwill—and of this German diplomatists were not unaware.[3] So far as they ever were to make a choice between Germany and the United States that choice had been made. Strangely enough, in 1901, at the end of the negotiations for an Anglo-German alliance, Lord Lansdowne had himself adverted to the danger of entangling Great Britain in a policy which might be inimical to her American friend. To remain disentangled from Germany on account of the United States was then visualized by the British Foreign Secretary as a theoretical necessity.[4] Within the next year and a half a singular turn of the wheel converted it into a desideratum of political action. If the plot of the drama was different

---

[1] *Br. Docs.*, vol. iii, pp. 413 and 429; Newton, *Lansdowne*, p. 260.
[2] *Camb. Hist. of Br. Foreign Policy*, vol. iii, pp. 299–301; also *Br. Docs.*, vol. iii, p. 429.
[3] Count Bernstorff, *My Three Years in America*, pp. 13–14.
[4] Lansdowne's memorandum, Nov. 11, 1901, *Br. Docs.*, vol. ii, no. 92, p. 78.

the protagonists and *dénouement* were identical. That play had
finished. But there were other boards which the same actors would
again soon tread together.

And yet the joint coercion of Venezuela served unexpectedly a
salutary purpose. If any doubts survived about the British attitude
towards the United States they could finally be dismissed; before the
Monroe Doctrine Great Britain had made her solemn obeisance. That
the American people would resist a German challenge to its paramountcy in the western hemisphere was fully shown; and on the
British Admiralty this demonstration must have had a very appreciable influence when it planned the naval reorganization initiated in
1904 under Sir John Fisher. For by the alterations then inaugurated,
and which until 1914 constituted the basis of her sea-strategy, the
defensive value to Great Britain of Anglo-American understanding
would clearly be revealed.

These new arrangements were caused by the one European problem
of that era, Germany's irrepressible ambition to construct a large fleet,
which more than anything else quickened the contemporary changes
in British policy. Admiral von Tirpitz, with the passionate support
of William II, did not only believe that his country must furnish
additional protection for its expanding interests, colonial and commercial. The fleet which he envisaged was also to be strong enough to
earn the cautious respect of Englishmen at critical moments, to prevent them, restricted by world-wide responsibilities, from venturing
into conflict with it. Employing the naval threat, Germany could then
extort concessions and, as she hoped, exercise in world politics a role of
undisputed pre-eminence. According to Tirpitz, the danger for Great
Britain would not be that of outright defeat but one of such a decrease
in her maritime supremacy as the outcome of an Anglo-German
struggle that the command of the seas would fall to a coalition of
other hostile Powers. His thesis assumed fallaciously the lasting enmity towards her of France and Russia; among his compatriots it was
often accompanied by less subtle manifestations of pan-German
ideals.[1] Great Britain, however, would not allow herself to be thus
overtaken in naval capacity; as distinguished from Germany, her
very independence, power, and prosperity rested upon that maritime
superiority by means of which she could defend her international
trade, safeguard the importation of foodstuffs and raw materials, and
freely control the lines of communication with her scattered Empire
overseas. By geographical necessity and historic precedent German
military predominance in Central and Western Europe would in any

[1] E. L. Woodward, *Great Britain and the German Navy*, pp. 11, 32–4, 36–9.

case render her insular safety relatively less secure. The greatest land-Power on the neighbouring continent, Germany could not be permitted also to catch up in maritime resources to the greatest sea-Power. And so between them, in the building of bigger and bigger naval armaments, the calamitous race began.[1]

It was Lord Salisbury who once pointed out that the British fleet could not climb the mountains of Armenia. His successors likewise perceived that in the new circumstances the constant patrol by the Royal Navy of the world's oceanic routes would have to be diminished. It had become essential to reform the maritime strategy of the Empire; the scheme followed reflected the recent achievements of British diplomacy. The Japanese Alliance and the Anglo-French Entente of 1904 were to have direct naval consequences; and a similar result ensued—to which the settlement in 1903 of the Alaskan question had lately contributed—from the progressive improvement in Anglo-American relations. By these favourable developments the First Sea Lord was enabled to adopt Mahan's view that the secret of naval warfare is concentration, concentration in defence at home and in offence while attacking. The front had shifted from abroad, from the south coast and the Channel to the East and the North Sea; here, then, against Germany Fisher levelled his maritime spear-head. During the Russo-Japanese War an Anglo-Russian naval crisis—the Dogger Bank incident—gave the British Government their chance to announce the Admiralty's project for the instantaneous mobilization of a renovated and more homogeneous fleet. In December 1904 the proposals—the first of their kind since 1812—were laid before Parliament.[2] To the German Emperor they came as a rude shock; with his Naval Chief of Staff he thought the British were preparing for war.[3] England, as the ancient Halifax had enjoined, again looked to her moat.

Affecting British sea-power in the western Atlantic and in the eastern and western Pacific, the fleet reorganization could not have been devised without reference to Anglo-American friendship. Its principal feature was the withdrawal of naval vessels from outlying parts of the world. Fisher strengthened the Home Fleet—now named the Channel Fleet—reduced the Mediterranean Fleet based on Malta, and created an Atlantic Fleet based on Gibraltar; a process of redis-

[1] Grey of Fallodon, *Twenty-Five Years*, vol. i, pp. 47–8, 242–3, 249–50; ibid., vol. ii, pp. 48–9, 272–4.
[2] Sir Sidney Lee, *King Edward VII*, vol. ii, pp. 327–9; Admiral Sir R. H. Bacon, *The Life of Lord Fisher of Kilverstone*, vol. i, pp. 293, 300; ibid., vol. ii, pp. 59–61; also Lord Fisher, *Records*; Lord Fisher, *Memories*.
[3] Prince von Bülow, *Memoirs 1903–1909*, pp. 69, 187–9.

tribution which would be accentuated as France and Great Britain drew together and Germany away from them. Through the Alliance with Japan and the destruction in May 1905 of the Russian Navy the need had disappeared for the China Battle Fleet—composed of six battle-ships, six first-class cruisers, and six second-class cruisers—to be centred round Hong Kong.[1] Most British ships were therefore recalled from the Far East—although in agreement with Australia and New Zealand arrangements were subsequently made for squadrons to be stationed in Chinese, Australian, and East Indian waters. To her Japanese Ally, whose naval growth had been rapid, Great Britain thus assigned the major share of policing the coast of China. She could do this, moreover, confident that in the Pacific the augmented naval forces of the United States would not be ranged against her. And in the summer of 1905, when the Anglo-Japanese Alliance was being revised, that fact entered into the negotiations; for then the British Government stipulated that from their naval calculations in the Far East the American fleet must be exempt.[2] So deliberate an omission was, obviously, of the highest significance. Anglo-American understanding seems to have been considered a secondary factor—with the Anglo-Japanese Alliance as the primary safeguard—in the British system of Far Eastern maritime security. And of Great Britain's informal reinsurance with the United States this indeed was but one aspect—another, as will be seen, being indicated at the same time by the altered strategy in the Caribbean and West Indies. Later, as ill will sprang up between Washington and Tokio, the state of affairs in Europe required that British interests should remain pledged to Japan. The diplomatic and naval obligations of Great Britain to her Far Eastern Ally were hard to reconcile with Anglo-American friendship. The attempt was made in 1911, but only after the Great War of 1914–18, by terminating the Anglo-Japanese Alliance entirely, could a more comprehensive effort be undertaken to adjust harmoniously the triple relations on the Pacific between the British Commonwealth, the United States, and Japan.

Of President Monroe and John Quincy Adams it was said that they had blown 'a blast on the republican trumpet while sheltered behind the shield of England'. That held true of American policy so long as the Royal Navy showed its flag everywhere and the United States did not equip herself with a sure shield of her own. But now Great Britain, concentrating her Grand Fleet nearer home, left her naval interests in the western hemisphere to the benevolent protection of

---

[1] *Br. Docs.*, vol. iv, nos. 122–4, pp. 133–4.
[2] Ibid., no. 126, p. 137; ibid., note A, p. 169.

the sea-power of the United States. The withdrawal of British war-vessels from the New World was a logical sequel to the Anglo-American *rapprochement*. The whole naval strategic situation, observed the First Lord of the Admiralty, had undergone a thorough revolution: 'That revolution is the birth of the American Navy.'[1] The seminal teachings of Captain Mahan, the impetus of the Spanish War, the acquisition of colonies and protectorates, the political leadership of men such as Theodore Roosevelt and Henry Cabot Lodge—all these influences were at work. Among the principal Naval Powers the United States quickly took her place.

The attitude adopted by Great Britain towards that development may be viewed from two angles. The first was to ensure that the American Navy, ineluctably growing stronger in waters of extreme importance to the British Empire, should never be hostile. The second—to the extent that the isolationism of the United States would permit—had been exhibited by the co-operative policy of Great Britain during and after the Spanish War, her approval of American expansion in the Pacific and Caribbean, the waiving of equal rights in the isthmian canal. If the Hay-Pauncefote Treaty completed in outline the strategic programme—now put into full effect—the Anglo-German coercion of Venezuela furnished the test-case. For it had disclosed that by the American people the Caribbean was regarded as *mare nostrum* in no mere rhetorical sense. In trans-Atlantic regions Germany or any other new-comer would summarily be repelled and from this clear resolution the territorial integrity of British possessions derived an automatic guarantee. English-speaking friendship, the increased Navy of the United States, and the popular reassertion of the Monroe Doctrine were, in fact, all constituents of that informal defensive reinsurance on which Great Britain could henceforth rely as she turned away to face whatever might arise across the North Sea. For in the New World it was to the benefit of the British Empire that against the possibility of an *imperium Germanicum*, colonial or naval, there should be set up the *pax Americana*.

The redistribution of the Royal Navy was accordingly framed to include the recall of vessels stationed in the Atlantic as well as in the Pacific which had been avilable for service in the waters of the western hemisphere. The abolition of the North American squadron was, moreover, facilitated by the Franco-British Entente; in the West Indies it would no longer be necessary to keep watch on the French naval division. In that area a reduction also ensued of British armaments on land. The head-quarters of the North American squadron

[1] Algernon E. Aspinall, *The British West Indies*, p. 396.

were in Bermuda and it was supported there by a big naval establishment which had been enlarged—a legacy of the Trent affair—after
the American Civil War. The naval importance of Bermuda henceforth declined and so did that of Port Royal in Jamaica situated near
Guantanamo—the naval base leased recently from Cuba by the
United States. The decision of the British Government to withdraw
infantry stationed in the West Indies was announced in February
1905. Port Royal and the coaling-station of St. Lucia were transformed into cadres with a small peace-time expenditure; the work on
the dockyard then being constructed at Bermuda—and finished in
1907—was, however, allowed to continue. With these arrangements
British colonists in the islands affected were naturally displeased;
nevertheless all that they could be promised was a yearly visit by a
naval squadron and the permanent allocation to West Indian waters
of a fast cruiser. Sir John Fisher therefore organized a training unit
of six cruisers, which had an English base, annually to show the flag
of the Royal Navy in the West Indies and off the coast of South
America—this squadron in an emergency being free to join either the
Channel or the Mediterranean Fleets.[1] And with that the colonists
had to be satisfied, for in the Americas Great Britain was depending
upon the friendly supremacy of the United States.

In Canada the new strategic arrangements do not appear to have
excited comment. The chief problems of the Dominion were internal.
Where the Royal Navy was less disposed to patrol the Monroe Doctrine would protect. The Alaskan question, settled finally in 1903, produced acrid polemics but no irremediable enmity. More than ever, as
Anglo-American understanding grew, Canada's security was hinged on
the state of her relations with Washington. British naval and military
withdrawals coincided with the Dominion's advancing autonomy. At
the Colonial Conference of 1902 Canadian Ministers had already agreed
to take over the upkeep of the garrisons at Halifax on the Atlantic
and at Esquimault on the Pacific; four years later Canadian soldiers
alone were doing duty on the soil of the Dominion. The naval station
at Halifax was turned over to Canada in 1910. There, as at Esquimault, which overlooks the Straits of Juan de Fuca and where a large
base had been proposed, the Dominion merely obliged itself to care
for Admiralty property so that war vessels could be afforded coaling
and docking facilities.[2] In Canadian public life, during the years immediately preceding the Great War of 1914–18, sea-power was, never-

---

[1] Bacon, *Fisher*, vol. i, pp. 276, 296–8; Aspinall, *The British West Indies*, p. 396.
[2] J. H. Rose and others, *The Cambridge History of the British Empire*, vol. vi, p. 718;
Hector C. Bywater, *Navies and Nations*, pp. 35, 196.

theless, a subject of profound contention. Opinion, however, did not divide over the likelihood of hostilities with the United States. The controversy was provoked by the desire of Great Britain, concentrating her fleet against Germany in home waters, to obtain contributions from the Dominions for the defence of their own sea-borne commerce and the collective safety of the British Empire. Several cruisers were purchased; at Ottawa ship-building programmes were promulgated and submitted to Parliament; a plan was mooted for units of the new Canadian Navy to be stationed on the Pacific and Atlantic coasts. In the prolonged discussion partisan strife mingled with Dominion nationalism and Imperialist sentiment. Yet there was underlying it no fear of war with the United States but the changed circumstances brought everywhere into being by German aspirations at sea.

To the naval importance of Anglo-American friendship frequent references in debates at Westminster presently attested. With the introduction of Dreadnoughts into Anglo-German rivalry the difficulties were intensified for the maintenance by the Asquith Government of the two-Power standard—in other words, the traditional scale of British superiority in capital ships over the pooled strength of the next two largest navies. Since the United States had now emerged as one of the greater Naval Powers she should ordinarily have been included in their calculations; although Ministers admitted this they explicitly refused time and again to estimate their requirements by the size of the American fleet. The danger was primarily European in character, and in parliamentary pronouncements and diplomatic intercourse the British Government made no attempt to conceal from Germany the special position which the United States occupied. Eventually, in the light of Anglo-American and Anglo-French goodwill, they abandoned the two-Power standard altogether and sought merely to retain an adequate lead over German naval construction.[1] It was out of the question, said Sir Edward Grey in 1912, for Great Britain to maintain over other Powers a margin of naval strength in the Mediterranean, in the West in the Atlantic, in the Pacific and the Far East as well as at home. Her superiority in home waters over a neighbouring fleet or fleets was, he declared, the sole means, diplomatic and defensive, by which the policy of his country as a Great Power could continue to prevail.[2] These were observations of exceptional gravity and they never could have been uttered if Great Britain had not depended upon her friendships abroad—with Japan, with

[1] Woodward, *Great Britain and the German Navy*, pp. 169, 244, 289–90, 368–9, 464, 467–8, 471–3.
[2] Paul Knaplund (ed.), *Speeches on Foreign Affairs 1904–1914, Sir Edward Grey*, pp. 203–4.

France, with the United States. The absence of a more cordial feeling between the English-speaking nations would have left Canada and all British interests in the western hemisphere seriously vulnerable. The fleet concentration in the North Sea might have proceeded, Japan and France providing the other main political features of the naval redistribution. Without Anglo-American understanding the strategic system as a whole would nevertheless have been materially impaired: in 1914 the entire scheme might have met with disaster. But that, fortunately, did not occur. For, however vexed on the high seas relations between Great Britain and the United States then became, such contingencies were dwarfed by their ultimate co-operation in a supreme task common to them both.

In point of fact the strategic advantages of Anglo-American friendship were not one-sided but reciprocal. For this reason the leading naval officers of the United States now dissented from the historic policy of their country to abolish the capture of private property at sea ; a proposal which, had it been adopted before 1914—the Declaration of London, rejected in 1911 by the House of Lords, being a step in that direction—would have hindered the war-time naval dominance of Great Britain. Domestic politics probably intervened—a mixture of the peace movement with pro-German elements and the traditional American attitude towards this problem—for at the second Hague Conference the advice tendered by the experts, in which Elihu Root as Secretary of State concurred, was not followed by the Administration.[1] But in the long run events justified the counsel they had given. It was believed that Germany, with her growing maritime and commercial ambitions, wished the Powers to accept inviolability, and to the Navy Department German designs in Central and South America were a source of anxiety. Great Britain and the British Navy, as Captain Mahan wrote in 1904 to President Roosevelt, lay right across her carrying trade. 'Exempt it, and you remove the strongest hook in the jaw of Germany that the English-speaking people have—a principal gage for peace.' While British and American interests diverged, Mahan yet argued that fundamentally they were identical. 'The United States', he affirmed, 'has certainty of a very high order that the British Empire will stand substantially on the same lines of world privileges as ourselves ; that its strength will be our strength, and the weakening it injury to us.'[2] To insist for the sake of American

---

[1] Br. Docs., vol. viii, no. 167, pp. 197–8; ibid., no. 207, pp. 250–1. A British diplomatic observer then stated that the Americans acted 'often obviously in a sense quite opposed to their own interests'. Crowe to Tyrrell, Oct. 11, 1907, ibid., no. 254, pp. 287–8.

[2] Mahan-Roosevelt correspondence, Taylor, Mahan, pp. 145–7.

commerce upon the doctrine of the freedom of the seas might be to enfeeble rather than safeguard the larger liberties of mankind.

With these views the General Board of the United States Navy, over which Admiral Dewey presided, expressed full agreement. Reporting in 1906 that Anglo-American relations had never been better, they anticipated, in case of war between their country and Germany, the passive goodwill of Great Britain, perhaps even a protective treaty with her. The General Board likewise disapproved of the inviolability of private property, since it might relieve the Wilhelmstrasse of the fear of American molestation with German shipping. If, moreover, the British were allied to the United States, and the Royal Navy could paralyse the Germans at sea, it would diminish 'the immense assistance we might expect to receive from Great Britain'. The Board mentioned the supposed aims of Germany in the New World—aims which might cause war when her fleet was ready to strike—to which London and Washington were both opposed. Their support was therefore withheld from changes in international law that would deprive the Royal Navy of belligerent rights at sea. 'The welfare of the United States', they concluded, 'and its immunity from entanglements with the other Powers is greatly strengthened by strong ties of friendship and by unanimity of action with Great Britain.'[1]

Mahan, Dewey, and the General Board thus looked to the Royal Navy to check Germany in home waters as much as the Foreign Office and the Admiralty, for a guarantee of the *status quo* elsewhere, seemed to rely on the Monroe Doctrine and Anglo-American understanding. If, early in the twentieth century, Great Britain was informally reinsured in the western hemisphere, the chief naval authorities of the United States counted on British sea-power as one of the principal foundations of American world security. And, that being so, in 1917 the final alignment of forces would occasion no surprise. For behind the joint defence by the English-speaking peoples of their common civilization were also arrayed those less impalpable and more immediate national interests of which Anglo-American friendship was the unifying spirit.

[1] Ibid., pp. 148–52.

VII

THE CANADIAN QUESTION

IN Anglo-American understanding there had of late been so notable
an advance that men may have forgotten the Alaskan dispute which
still lurked in the background to harass, envenom, and disrupt. But
by Great Britain and the United States a settlement of this problem
in their mutual relations could not be postponed indefinitely ; without
a solution of the Canadian question further progress in English-
speaking friendship was bound to be impeded. Washington allowed
the matter to rest because it had confidence in its own case and because it knew that the British Government, supporting the Dominion
from duty rather than conviction, would again yield on grounds of
policy and expediency as they had been doing in the western hemisphere since the turn of the century. Moreover, with the signature
of the first Hay-Pauncefote Treaty for the building of the isthmian
canal, Canada had lost, in the shape of influence exercised at London,
the one bargaining counter she possessed. Meanwhile in both the
Dominion and the United States some extraordinary fears were
entertained—in the latter, that Ottawa sought an impregnable port
on the Lynn Canal in order that the British Navy might dominate the
northern Pacific and the western seaboard of the American continent ;
in the former, that Washington, with a view to the strategic control
of north-western Canada, had naval and military designs upon a
group of islands off the Alaskan coast. Although by such suspicions
the controversy was rendered more acrimonious they soon vanished
from the relations of the two North American countries whose un-
defended frontier stretched over three thousand miles in length. For
the adjustment of the Alaskan problem—by methods fair or unfair—
had the priceless merit of their complete exorcism.

The *modus vivendi* of 1899 was not a success. A stray shot by one
of the turbulent miners, the discovery of gold in the no-man's-land
of the region, might easily have led to incidents of a grave nature ;
with the temporary arrangement American States in the north-west
were as little satisfied as Canadian Ministers. In June 1901 a dis-
courtesy to the British flag occurred at Skagway, but no serious harm
was done.[1] In the diplomatic exchanges the whole issue now began
to reappear. In 1899 at the end of the Joint High Commission—and
again in May 1901—the Secretary of State had proposed that it be

[1] *U.S. Foreign Relations*, 1902, pp. 546–9.

submitted to a tribunal of six jurists, three on a side. The Canadian Government were anxious to secure a reference to arbitration, but to his judicial scheme they at last decided to agree—with the proviso, however, that two members of the tribunal should be neutral commissioners. Of this condition, upon which the Hay plan would be accepted, the State Department was informed by Lord Lansdowne early in February 1902.[1] But the American Administration were in no hurry. Three years later President Theodore Roosevelt told a distinguished company, which included two members of his Cabinet, that out of friendship for Great Britain he did not wish to press the Alaskan dispute during the Boer War. Nevertheless, in the event of gold being found nearby, 'he had intended to occupy the boundary'. Joseph Choate, as Roosevelt remembered, favoured arbitration, but the Ambassador, like most of his predecessors and educated Americans generally, had become 'pro-English'. Rejecting the advice of his representative, the President never seemed to appreciate how unflinchingly in London Choate upheld the contentions of the United States. Roosevelt instead preferred—and instructed the Ambassador accordingly—to let sleeping dogs lie.[2] From Washington, therefore, the Canadian suggestion elicited an unsympathetic response.

If the Alaskan problem was ostensibly dormant, the American Government had not been slumbering. The President often quoted the proverb: 'Speak softly and carry a big stick, you will go far.' To the Naval War College he had once declared that diplomacy is utterly useless without force behind it and that the diplomatist is the servant, not the master, of the soldier. These ideas Roosevelt was disposed to apply to the Canadian situation. In March 1902 orders were issued from the White House for Elihu Root, the Secretary of War, to have 'additional troops sent as quietly and unostentatiously as possible to Southern Alaska'; and Root obeyed his instructions within a few days.[3] Early in 1898 Canada had dispatched a constabulary detachment of more than forty men to establish Alaskan claims; Senator Lodge admitted subsequently that the American military body consisted of eight hundred cavalrymen. 'There is nothing so dangerous', he recollected sagely, 'as a controversy about land.' To a member of the British Embassy the President said in May 1902 that he was 'going to be ugly' over the Alaskan

[1] Oscar Douglas Skelton in the *Queen's Quarterly*, Feb. 1932, p. 6; James White, *Can. Hist. Rev.*, vol. vi, no. 4, Dec. 1925, p. 338.
[2] M. A. De Wolfe Howe, *James Ford Rhodes*, p. 121; Cortissoz, *Reid*, vol. ii, p. 442; Dennis, *Adventures*, p. 143.
[3] Cortelyou to Root, Mar. 27, 1902, Root to Cortelyou, Mar. 29, 1902, Pringle, *Roosevelt*, p. 290.

question.[1] Roosevelt intended to wield the Big Stick; the soldier rather than the diplomatist or statesman would be uppermost. All of this occurred shortly after the Hay-Pauncefote Treaty, signalizing the isthmian concession, had been ratified and many months before a strain would be put on Anglo-American relations by the blockade of Venezuela. Over the heads of the British and Canadian Governments the presence in Alaska of American troops hung like a Damoclean sword. English-speaking friendship, peace itself, had to be preserved. An immediate settlement was imperative.

During the summer of 1902 the scene shifted to London. Sir Wilfrid Laurier, the Prime Minister of Canada, was about to attend the Colonial Conference and some members of his Cabinet were apprehensive lest the British Government persuade him to surrender to the United States. 'A self-constituted sub-committee' which included Clifford Sifton, the Minister of the Interior, had therefore visited Laurier before he departed from Ottawa. This delegation, according to Sifton, warned the Prime Minister that in London pressure would be brought to bear to make him accept the Hay scheme of a judicial tribunal—a reference of the Alaskan dispute to an even-numbered commission with neither an impartial chairman nor neutral members. Laurier, however, promised not to back down.[2] When the matter was discussed at the Foreign Office three of his ministerial colleagues were also present; the essence of what Lord Lansdowne told them can be gathered from the moves which followed. Lord Minto, the Governor-General of Canada, was likewise in London. At the end of June the British Foreign Secretary asked the American Ambassador to see Minto and Laurier, and the President granted Choate permission to interview them. Nevertheless Roosevelt felt that 'the Canadian claim has not a leg to stand on and that compromise is impossible'.[3] Negotiations were resumed.

Meanwhile the Canadian Prime Minister had already spoken to Henry White and in July there were several conversations between him and the American Ambassador. Emphasizing the dangers of the situation, Laurier left these two diplomatists with the impression that the course he was attempting to pursue had been dictated by domestic political circumstances. Should the United States agree to arbitrate and the decision then go against the Dominion he could at least tell the Canadian people that he had done his best; if, however, the result

[1] Dafoe, *Sifton*, pp. 214–15; *Proceedings LVIII Mass. Hist. Society*, p. 339, 'Memoir of H. C. Lodge'; Newton, *Lansdowne*, p. 263.
[2] Dafoe, *Sifton*, p. 217.
[3] Hill to Choate, June 28, 1902, *American Secretaries of State and their Diplomacy*, vol. ix, p. 168; also Skelton, *Queen's Quarterly*, Feb. 1932, p. 6.

were to be favourable to Canada, Laurier did not propose to take over the Skagway district; the Dominion would instead be entitled to pecuniary or territorial compensation elsewhere. But with the Canadian statesman so obviously softening in his attitude John Hay was encouraged to remain firm. 'It is evident', he remarked to the President, 'that Lansdowne is also anxious to have some settlement'; and he thought the Foreign Secretary was convinced 'that if anything is to be done, it must be done on our own lines'.[1] The American Government held and were resolved to maintain the upper hand.

Laurier now went far to conciliate them. During his first conversation with Choate he hinted that in return for early American consent to an adjustment he would no longer oppose the type of tribunal advocated by John Hay. About the motives of Laurier and Lansdowne in sounding the retreat the Ambassador himself professed a curious scepticism; nevertheless, his apparent indifference served only to make the British Foreign Secretary more eager for a prompt arrangement. Lansdowne spoke to Choate in July about the urgent need for a settlement in order to avoid conflict should gold be discovered within the disputed area; he therefore regretted that the Ambassador had 'thrown cold water upon Sir Wilfrid'. But Choate merely repeated the uncompromising views of the President and his belief that the contentions of Canada were legally baseless.[2] It was clear that to the Dominion, from the successive expressions of British friendship towards the United States, no profit had accrued.

In their efforts to rid themselves of the Alaskan incubus Laurier and Lansdowne wisely persevered. In July the President of the United States informed John Hay that he foresaw the possibility of complications. His Secretary of War was, however, prepared for every eventuality. 'Root has been quietly strengthening the garrison', Roosevelt wrote apropos of Alaska. In a spirit of 'bumptious truculence' the Canadians had put in a false claim which, he observed, England for years had resisted. 'They now say that trouble may come if it is not acted on. I feel like telling them that if trouble comes it will be purely . . . their own fault; and although it would not be pleasant for us, it would be death for them.'[3] Upon a man of Hay's temperament, outlook, and methods such Rooseveltian pugnacity was calculated to jar; yet about the boundary question he himself had, during and since the Joint High Commission, been nearly as obdurate

---

[1] White to Hay, June 28, 1902, Nevins, *White*, pp. 192–3; Hay to Roosevelt, July 7, 1902, Dennis, *Adventures*, pp. 143–4.

[2] Choate to Hay, July 5, 1902, Dennett, *Hay*, pp. 457–9. The year as printed, ibid., is incorrect; Choate to Hay, July 19, 1902, Dennis, *Adventures*, p. 144.

[3] Roosevelt to Hay, July 16, 1902, Pringle, *Roosevelt*, p. 291.

as the most intransigent Senator. It was his judicial scheme against which Canada struggled, and in the summer of 1902 he still suggested the plan by which the United States could not lose and quite probably might win.[1] For Washington insisted that the interpretation of the Anglo-Russian Treaty of 1825, under which Alaska was acquired in 1867, must not be made by the Hague Court, a neutral umpire, or a tribunal with two foreign participants; there would be a commission of six, three on each side, a majority decision requiring one member to vote against his own case—or nothing. Unable to risk further delay, the British and Canadian statesmen agreed in London to accept the American proposal. Whatever its drawbacks, it was better than border skirmishes which might culminate in war. About that neither Laurier nor Lansdowne had any doubts. The process of concessions to the United States would be renewed.

The Prime Minister of Canada had next to meet his own Cabinet. His recital to them, when back in Ottawa, of the arrangement contemplated was reprehensible to those of his colleagues who expected him to maintain an inflexible attitude. Nevertheless, beyond reporting that he had pledged himself to adopt the Hay proposal, Laurier in October merely explained that 'he had no option but to yield the point'.[2] This was the capitulation long dreaded by the Dominion. Most of the disputed territory the United States already held in her possession; towards ceding desired portions of it no American member of the tribunal was likely to cast his vote. Nor would a deadlock leave matters where they were: to prevent armed conflict Canada must again retire from the field. It was, besides, all the more galling that, just when a new sense of Imperial unity had begun to develop, the chief of the Dominions should be faced with such a prospect—so soon, indeed, after the aid given during the Boer War and the tariff preference accorded by her in recent years to Great Britain. And yet from the standpoint of her immediate safety Canada had no higher interest than the preservation of Anglo-American goodwill. Would Laurier's change of front enable Great Britain to harmonize friendship with the United States and Imperial responsibilities?

It was at this time, in the autumn of 1902, that Sir Michael Herbert proceeded to Washington to take up his post as British Ambassador. The preliminaries having been settled, an Alaskan convention was, in accordance with Hay's scheme, thereupon drafted. Guarding against compromise, Senators, moreover, now made sure—Henry Cabot Lodge in particular advising the President—that in it should

---

[1] Hay to Roosevelt, July 14, 1902, Dennis, *Adventures*, p. 152. The year as printed, ibid., is incorrect.   [2] Dafoe, *Sifton*, p. 217.

be included no definition of the tribunal as arbitral in character.[1] For the negotiations which followed Lord Herschell was dead not only in flesh but in spirit.

Early in 1903, a fortnight before the signature of the Alaskan convention, Canada, however, ventured upon a last half-hearted endeavour to obtain a real form of arbitration. On January 12 the Colonial Office cabled to Ottawa that Herbert suggested as a tribunal which would command general confidence one consisting of three Judges of the American Supreme Court, the Lord Chief Justice, the Chief Justice of Canada, and a Judge of the High Court of Great Britain. What were the views of the Dominion about the terms of the draft treaty, the finality of the tribunal's decision and its 'composition'? By 'composition' the Canadian Cabinet understood that the structure of the tribunal was meant rather than its membership. And so they reopened a matter about which with Laurier an agreement in principle had previously been reached. The Governor-General replied to the Colonial Office on January 13. While the Government in Ottawa were satisfied with the questions to be presented to the tribunal they still objected to its 'composition'. Before consenting to the treaty Canadian Ministers hoped therefore that another effort would be made to have the questions 'submitted either to a Board of Arbitrators composed in part of independent jurists, not subjects of either State . . . or to the Hague tribunal'.[2] But the American Administration, refusing to countenance an impartial judgement or settlement, were at that stage less minded than ever to abandon by one jot or tittle the advantage they had gained.

Hay was adamant. When the British Ambassador visited him on January 18 he spoke of his hope—especially as alterations had on their behalf been introduced into the terms of reference—that the Canadian Government would accept the treaty 'spontaneously'.[3] To Herbert the Secretary of State could only reiterate what he had been telling him since the Ambassador had first arrived in Washington: no 'form of arbitration' would be approved by the President other than that proposed in the draft; and the Senate would certainly reject any treaty which provided that the Alaskan boundary dispute be submitted either to foreign arbitration or to the international court at The Hague. Hay, presumably, was not asked for what purpose in

[1] *Proceedings LVIII Mass. Hist. Society*, p. 339, 'Memoir of H. C. Lodge'; Dennett, *Hay*, pp. 355–6.
[2] Colonial Office to Minto, Jan. 12, 1903, Minto to the Colonial Office, Jan. 13, 1903, John S. Ewart, *The Kingdom of Canada and Other Essays*, p. 303.
[3] In December 1902 Herbert had written to Hay about changes in the draft which were 'inadmissible' since they excluded the contentions of the Dominion. James White, *Can. Hist. Rev.*, vol. vi, no. 4, Dec. 1925, p. 343.

1899 the establishment of the latter institution had been fostered at the Hague Conference by the United States. Washington declined to modify the nature of the Alaskan tribunal. To the signature of the draft the British Government were therefore compelled to cable for Canadian assent.[1]

The fact was that for a strong assertion of its views the Dominion could not then turn to Great Britain. Since the close of the nineteenth century the cultivation of American friendship had been influenced by the exigencies of world politics, and in the winter of 1903 relations between the 'English-speaking Powers were for the interval being affected adversely by the Anglo-German coercion of Venezuela. Nor did the German bombardment of San Carlos just when the 'composition' of the Alaskan tribunal was under debate serve to generate in Washington a more congenial atmosphere. From that capital Sir Wilfrid Laurier heard in January how the Chairman of the Senate Committee for Foreign Affairs had said that he could not be accommodating towards Canada because the Caribbean expedition had for the moment undermined Anglo-American understanding.[2] One result of this attitude was during the next month the hasty signature of the Venezuelan protocol followed at once by the lifting of the blockade. The British Government had shown their desire to propitiate the American people; and of that expiatory temper they tried for the remainder of the year, so far as Canadian recalcitrance would allow, to offer further proof. For the Dominion the conjuncture of the Venezuelan enterprise with a decisive part of the Alaskan discussions was thus a most unfortunate circumstance. Yet what happened did not differ fundamentally from the manner in which the isthmian concession had been treated. To Canada no doubt British policy was a handicap. But the United States regarded her claims with undissembled impatience. The opportunity to negotiate in peace was furnished by Anglo-American goodwill. Without it, in the absence of all British support, the Dominion's plight would have been even more unenviable.

The treaty was signed by John Hay and Sir Michael Herbert on January 24, 1903. After prolonged disagreement the former had won his point about the plan to be adopted for solving the Alaskan problem; in her string of diplomatic victories over Great Britain the United States had scored once more. Hay, nevertheless, seemed to feel that London and Washington tacitly understood each other; and he

[1] Herbert to the Colonial Office, Jan. 18, 1903, the Colonial Office to Minto, Jan. 19, 1903, Ewart, *Kingdom Essays*, pp. 303–4.
[2] Farrer to Laurier, Jan. 1903, Skelton, *Laurier*, vol. ii, pp. 142–3.

deemed it an act of friendship to have given the British Government a dignified means of extricating themselves from an 'untenable position'.[1] The treaty stipulated that there should be a judicial and not an arbitral settlement; an even-numbered tribunal without a neutral umpire would be set up to render a majority award—three of its members being selected by Great Britain and three by the United States. This body was to 'consist of six impartial jurists of repute who shall consider judicially the questions submitted to them, each of whom shall first subscribe an oath that he will impartially consider the arguments and evidence presented to the tribunal and will decide thereupon according to his true judgement'.[2] That condition could be evaded only by flouting the explicit terms of the article. In such matters, ever since the Alabama Claims, the English-speaking Powers had always resorted to arbitration—a method which by the Jay Treaty of 1794 they had introduced into the modern world and one, significantly, which Great Britain had never pursued when at variance with other nations.[3] From that method this mechanism for settling international disputes marked an unhappy departure. And yet, however conspicuous its structural defects, these were overshadowed by the commission's value as a public symbol of high policy. In Anglo-American adjustments the ways not of force but of peace would again prevail.

What were the questions to be considered by the tribunal? It had to make a judicial interpretation of the Anglo-Russian Treaty of 1825 which defined the boundaries between Russian territory and British North America and under which the United States had succeeded by purchase to Russia's territorial rights in Alaska. Being vaguely described, the southern, but not the northern, line was difficult to determine; and here the Canadians and Americans locked horns. Southward the line was to follow the crests of mountains running parallel to the coast where they were found not more than 10 marine leagues from the sea. But where they were found farther back from the sea than 10 marine leagues the boundary—so it had been stated— 'shall be formed by a line parallel to the windings of the coast, which shall never exceed ten marine leagues therefrom'. If the boundary were to follow the summits of the mountains it would intersect some of the bays; pursuing the general contour of the mainland it would then furnish the Canadian Yukon with access to and from the sea. Although the Dominion was convinced that certain mountains did in

---

[1] Hay to Seward, Jan. 30, 1903, Thayer, *Hay*, vol. ii, p. 211; also Roosevelt to Holmes, July 25, 1903, Bishop, *Roosevelt*, vol. i, pp. 259–61.

[2] *U.S. Foreign Relations*, 1903, pp. 488–9; also ibid., pp. 488–549.

[3] Sir James Headlam-Morley, *Studies in Diplomatic History*, pp. 11, 13, 15.

fact come within the scope of the Anglo-Russian Treaty the United States denied their existence. She affirmed, therefore, that the fringe of the coast must conform faithfully and without a break to its numerous curvatures and indentations measured from the heads of the inlets; from the sea, by a strip 10 marine leagues in width, Canadian territory would thus everywhere be excluded. At the extreme south the location of the Portland Canal, giving an interior approach to the Klondike, was also disputed: did the line run south of four small islands in that channel as the Americans argued, or did it run north of them as the Canadians countered? Since the Alaskan boundary was not to be arbitrated but settled judicially upon its legal merits it might have been pertinent to assess the respective cases. But the organization of the tribunal and the use to which it was put precluded a judicial decision. The procedure, despite the Treaty of January 1903, soon became largely diplomatic. It is not in the litigation but in the politics of the settlement that Anglo-American relations are to be appraised.

The Hay-Herbert Treaty of January 1903 had to be ratified by the Senate. Many years afterwards, and with disarming simplicity, Senator Lodge recalled how this was accomplished. Some of his colleagues, especially those from the American north-west, intimated to him that before casting their votes they must learn whom the President proposed to select—'they could not agree to having anybody on the tribunal who would yield on the Canadian claim'. Lodge thereupon spoke to Roosevelt who permitted him to reveal to his fellow-Senators the names of the prospective nominees. The President intended to appoint Elihu Root, the Secretary of War, Senator George Turner from the State of Washington on the Pacific coast, and Lodge himself. 'When these selections were made known in confidence to the Senators', Lodge recollected, 'there was no further objection to the treaty and it was ratified by the Senate, unanimously as I remember, on the 11th of February, 1903.'[1]

Could political expediency palliate the immediate breach of an international contract to which a great country had just pledged its honour? The treaty stipulated that the commissioners were to take an oath to consider the arguments and evidence impartially and to decide upon them according to their true judgement. Yet at senatorial behest the President chose three commissioners precisely because they had prejudged the case and could be depended upon to maintain policy rather than law. Senator Lodge was an eminent politician but not 'a jurist of repute'; he had been connected with the Joint High

[1] *Proceedings LVIII Mass. Hist. Society*, p. 340, 'Memoir of H. C. Lodge'

Commission; he had participated privately in the framing of the new treaty; his speeches and activities were a notorious disqualification. Senator Turner had once held judicial office but he represented in the Upper House that section of the United States—its ports seeking the Canada-Alaska coastal trade—which clamoured most vociferously against the Dominion. At the Bar Elihu Root enjoyed the highest renown, yet the Cabinet in which he sat was a direct party to the dispute; during 1902 as Secretary of War he had moved additional American troops to Alaska; in the same lawsuit he could scarcely be both claimant and judge. Root's acceptance of the nomination and his acquiescence in the subsequent Alaskan transactions are hard to reconcile with other features of an illustrious public and professional career. On every count the appointments were quite indefensible.

The treaty was Hay's but not the selections. To Henry White he expressed his regret that Judges of the Supreme Court declined to serve on the tribunal; but were there in the United States no other impartial jurists of repute? As a matter of fact Hay's own account— apart from Lodge's astonishing reminiscences—makes it doubtful whether members of the Supreme Court were invited with sincerity or at least expected to accept appointments. For 'the President thought it was impossible to get the treaty through the Senate without the earnest and devoted assistance of Lodge and Turner and of the groups which they represented'. Lodge insisted, Hay wrote, that his friend Roosevelt nominate him to the tribunal. That the Secretary of State had protested to the President the Senator himself—who in a public speech had been again attacking the Canadians—later put on record.[1] Nor could Hay have stood alone in perceiving that the American attitude towards the sanctity of treaties was undergoing rapid and contradictory changes. For the Anglo-Russian agreement of 1825— on which her purchase of Alaska had been based—the United States in the current controversy demanded the most literal and scrupulous respect. On the other hand, during 1900 and 1901 the violation of the Clayton-Bulwer Treaty had repeatedly been threatened by the Senate and that body might have now refused to ratify the Alaskan treaty without a convenient, unilateral interpretation of its own. To Anglo-American friendship such confusing alternations of strict legalism and political manœuvre in support of national self-interest were a perpetual menace. Only by completing the settlement of mutual differences, however it might be contrived, could this major source of

[1] Hay to White, Apr. 10, 1903, Nevins, *White*, p. 195; *Proceedings LVIII Mass. Hist. Society*, p. 340, 'Memoir of H. C. Lodge'.

discord be eliminated from the relations of the English-speaking peoples.

These proceedings, nevertheless, were not likely to fortify the faith of Canadians in any award rendered by the tribunal. Although they had striven for arbitration or fair adjudication they were constrained to accept a scheme the character of which must in the end have required sacrifices from them for the sake of a peaceful adjustment. And then in the middle of February the unofficial announcement of Roosevelt's nominations heaped coals upon the fire. Ottawa was furious. Yet at Westminster, as if the American appointments had in no manner altered the situation, the British Government declared their intention to ratify the treaty and blandly asked for the views of the Dominion about suitable British commissioners. To this inquiry from the Colonial Office the Canadian Government replied with their opinion of the President's selections. The condition upon which they had agreed to the treaty was that the tribunal would be composed of impartial jurists and they had hoped that the American members would be judges of the highest courts in the United States; unless that condition were now fulfilled they might decide wholly to abandon the arrangement—a step which, since the treaty had not yet been ratified by Great Britain, they were still perfectly free to take.[1]

In London, however, there was little that could be done. The Anglo-German blockade of Venezuela had just been terminated and the British Government assuredly were in no mood for the staunch advocacy at Washington of treaty stipulations on behalf of Canada. The Colonial Office, responding to the Dominion's remonstrance, struck a sympathetic note. But it argued that Great Britain was unable to press for a cancellation of Roosevelt's appointments; complaints against the personal fitness of Root, Turner, and Lodge would produce no useful effect. 'His Majesty's Government are, therefore, virtually in the position of having to choose between breaking off the negotiations altogether or of accepting the American nominations.' It was, nevertheless, suggested that the Anglo-Canadian selections should be appropriate to the changed circumstances. To drop the negotiations, the Colonial Office cabled, would be 'a grave misfortune to the interests of Canada'.[2] The Dominion was powerless. To Hay Laurier had addressed a private appeal, but in vain. And so, finally, the Canadian Government resolved to show the world that they would

---

[1] Colonial Office to Minto, Feb. 18, 1903, Minto to the Colonial Office, Feb. 21, 1903, Ewart, *Kingdom Essays*, p. 307.
[2] Colonial Office to Minto, Feb. 26, 1903, ibid., p. 308.

'stick to the bargain like gentlemen'.[1] But could Downing Street run the risk of waiting for the advent in Ottawa of such temperate counsels?

From Washington the tidings did not bode well. Labouring to retain their goodwill, the British Ambassador had, throughout the Venezuelan crisis, steadily acknowledged the friendly attitude of the Administration which he beseeched Lansdowne not to hazard by protracting the partnership with Germany. Yet no sooner were the American nominations divulged than Herbert's language was transformed. 'The President's Alaska appointments, with the exception of that of Root, are more than unfortunate,' he wrote to the Foreign Secretary, 'and I am naturally disgusted and disheartened. Moreover, all my illusions are gone in regard to men in whom I believed. Everything in this country is subservient to politics, and really an Ambassador in Washington needs more than an ordinary stock of patience.' Herbert knew Hay was helpless, while Roosevelt contended that, Judges of the Supreme Court having refused to serve, his selections conformed to the terms of the treaty. The Ambassador quoted the President—who had 'got his back up'—as having remarked that he consented to the tribunal only in order to afford England a way of escape from the difficulty in which the Dominion had placed her. By Herbert the views of Senator Lodge were discovered to be farcically irresponsible.[2]

What the British Government now feared was that Canada might do something rash. They had been warned by Herbert against the danger, in making their appointments, of imitating the American example, while the consequences of suspending negotiations 'would be too grave to contemplate'. The more he appreciated the temper of the politicians in Washington, the Ambassador informed Lansdowne, the more he realized the paramount importance of an Alaskan settlement.[3] By Downing Street there was from this advice but one line of action to be inferred. An impulsive withdrawal on the part of Canada might result in disaster. For reasons of high Imperial policy—to save the Dominion from a worse humiliation and preserve intact English-speaking friendship—the Canadian Government would have to be outflanked. Without more ado, on March 3, Great Britain and the United States exchanged ratifications of the Alaskan treaty.[4] Another crisis was thus met—and passed.

The grievances of Canada were accumulating. She had surrendered

---

[1] Laurier to Hay, Feb. 24, 1903, Dennett, *Hay*, pp. 357–8; Minto to Elliott, Mar. 1, 1903, John Buchan, *Lord Minto*, pp. 171–2.
[2] Herbert to Lansdowne, Feb. 21, 1903, Newton, *Lansdowne*, pp. 262–3.   [3] Ibid.
[4] Ewart, *Kingdom Essays*, p. 309; Skelton, *Laurier*, vol. ii, p. 155; *U.S. Foreign Relations*, 1903, p. 488.

loyally to British urgings so that the first isthmian agreement could be signed and then she had given way on the structure of the tribunal. Yet in 1903, before the new Alaskan treaty entered into force, its intended infringement was evident. In spite of that, however, by exchanging hurried ratifications with the United States, Great Britain had deprived Canada of the opportunity—even if she continued the negotiations—of demanding a formal protest at Washington. But although the Foreign Office did not bring Roosevelt's appointments officially to the notice of the American Ambassador, the Colonial Secretary, fresh from his trip to South Africa, talked outspokenly to Henry White. The very strength of the American case, said Chamberlain, ought to have made it easier for the President to select jurists unaffiliated with the Administration and uncommitted publicly against the claims of the Dominion.[1] Laurier, nevertheless, did not adopt Whitehall's proposal that the Anglo-Canadian appointments should be likewise of a political nature; their obligations under the treaty his Government sedulously discharged. As suggested from London, Lord Alverstone, the Lord Chief Justice of England, was accepted and Ottawa itself nominated to the tribunal two Canadians: Mr. Justice Armour of the Supreme Court of Canada and Sir Louis Jetté, a former puisne judge of the Quebec Supreme Court and Lieutenant-Governor of the Province of Quebec—Allen B. Aylesworth, K.C., a Toronto barrister who had declined promotion to the Supreme Court of Canada, succeeding Judge Armour when the latter died in London.[2] To the United States the selection of such men must have seemed a quiet yet eloquent rebuke. But that the dice were loaded against the Dominion was a sentiment burning deep in the Canadian mind.

The prejudging persisted. At Ottawa Sir Wilfrid Laurier had spoken on the Alaskan question in Parliament and the President assumed that the speech of the Prime Minister was a mandate given to the Canadian members of the tribunal. In March instructions to Root, Lodge, and Turner were thereupon dispatched from the White House. The claim of the Dominion to a port on the Lynn Canal Roosevelt did not regard as open to discussion. There was, however, room for adjustment whether in any locality the boundary should be placed back 10 marine leagues or whether nearer the coast a chain of mountains actually existed marching parallel to the sea. This view of the President's, frequently reiterated, his more illiberal representatives in London were, during the final transactions, disinclined to admit. But the American commissioners—whose oath required them to be

---

[1] White to Hay, Apr. 1, 1903, Nevins, *White*, pp. 194–5.
[2] Skelton, *Laurier*, vol. ii, pp. 147–8.

guided by their own true judgement—were, nevertheless, directed by Roosevelt that 'in the principle involved there will of course be no compromise'.[1] Troops had been sent to Alaska; for the tribunal were selected, as impartial jurists, hand-picked partisans. And to these latter the head of their Government now added the impropriety of communicating in broad detail the arguments of the case they would be expected to uphold.

Senator Lodge was presently in the thick of the negotiations. Anxious to protect American commerce in China, he wanted the United States to co-operate with the allied British and Japanese in protesting against Russia's Manchurian activities. Yet this did not inhibit his ceaseless Anglophobia, his desire in the Alaskan dispute to harry Great Britain and Canada to the utmost. In the meeting of the tribunal he would brook no delay and, detecting in British procrastination a clandestine conspiracy, invoked the assistance of the President. Like the Senator, Theodore Roosevelt had also to take care of his political engagements; he too wished to see the Alaskan problem settled before the approaching presidential campaign. Did they both anticipate that by an early victory over Canada they would be furnished with a popular electoral advantage? Still, in reply to the Senator, the President observed that it was a question whether the boundary line at the mouth of the Portland Channel ran on one side of the four islands or the other. To their possession, contrary to the opinion later manifested by his commissioners, he attached no importance. But Roosevelt thought that in coercing Venezuela the British had behaved badly and he would tolerate no further postponement. The Anglo-Canadian counter-case was, as a matter of fact, submitted on time and Lodge departed for the sessions of the tribunal in London. During the summer, however, the President reminded the Senator that the commission marked 'the last chance of coming to an agreement by the free act of both parties'—something he had said in June to Joseph Choate, John Hay, and Elihu Root. To them as to Lodge he had, moreover, also stated that if it failed there would not only be no arbitration but Congress would be asked to make an appropriation to enable him 'to run the line on our own theory'. By the middle of July the President felt that he had gone very far in his endeavour 'to come to a friendly understanding with England'.[2]

---

[1] Roosevelt to Root, Lodge, and Turner, Mar. 25, 1903, *Correspondence of Roosevelt and Lodge*, vol. ii, pp. 4–5.

[2] Lodge to Roosevelt, May 21, 1903, ibid., p. 15; Lodge to Roosevelt, June 23, 1903, ibid., pp. 32–3; Lodge to Roosevelt, June 27, 1903, ibid., p. 35; Roosevelt to Lodge, June 29, 1903, ibid., p. 37; Lodge to Roosevelt, July 5, 1903, ibid., p. 38; Roosevelt to Lodge, July 8, 1903, ibid., p. 38; Roosevelt to Lodge, July 16, 1903, ibid., p. 39.

About Roosevelt's intentions the British Government were not left in the dark. To Hay, from whose hands the conduct of foreign policy had in this instance been practically removed, he expressed the hope that England would appreciate what the situation was; if there were no agreement the United States would have 'to act in a way which will necessarily wound British pride', and of that danger Ministers in London were being informed by Henry White.[1] On July 25, 1903, Roosevelt sent privately to Mr. Justice Holmes of the American Supreme Court, then visiting England, a famous letter destined for perusal by Joseph Chamberlain, the Colonial Secretary. 'Nothing but my very earnest desire to get on well with England', the President wrote, 'and my reluctance to come to a break made me consent to this appointment of a Joint Commission in this case; for I regard the attitude of Canada, which England has backed, as having the scantest possible warrant in justice.' And so if the tribunal now failed to agree he would 'request Congress to make an appropriation which will enable me to run the boundary on my own hook'. The major portion of the Canadian claims was inadmissible; on lesser points adjustment might be considered. Of the latter he cited the islands in the Portland Channel and the precise location of the chain of mountains parallel to the coast. But Roosevelt flatly disallowed Canadian access to the sea from the Yukon and further discussion about the line through the Portland Channel. The choice of the American commissioners was defended by him, and he wanted the British Government to realize his purpose. In the event of disagreement the course he would adopt ruled out every subsequent possibility of arbitration; authorized by Congress, he proposed to establish the boundary 'without any further regard to the attitude of England and Canada. If I paid attention to mere abstract right, that is the position I ought to take anyhow. I have not taken it because I wish to exhaust every effort to have the affair settled peacefully and with due regard to England's dignity'.[2]

To such intervention the President afterwards attributed great weight. Two years later, in the presence of Secretaries Taft and Root, he observed that Holmes had shown this letter to Chamberlain and added that he wrote 'substantially the same thing to Henry White to be imparted to Balfour'. The British Government, he thought, 'tipped the wink to the Chief Justice'.[3] Even Roosevelt's discursive pen could on occasion become a Big Stick.

The United States may have had the sounder case, but the President

[1] Roosevelt to Hay, July 29, 1903, Dennis, *Adventures*, p. 145; Nevins, *White*, pp. 197, 199.
[2] Roosevelt to Holmes, July 25, 1903, Bishop, *Roosevelt*, vol. i, pp. 259–61.
[3] Howe, *J. F. Rhodes*, p. 121.

appeared now to doubt the efficacy of her own judicial scheme and employed its direct negation in curt diplomatic interference. American nationalism was in ferment during the isthmian controversy; this time, however, the British Government would have to reckon not so much with an ebullient legislature and Anglophobe sections of the public as with the White House itself. Nor were they likely to offer resistance. After the Boer War, apart from her Manchurian aggression, the encroachments of Russia in the Persian Gulf, central Asia, and Tibet were causing concern; the safety of India rather than the Canadian question was for the British Empire the chief problem overseas. And besides, in the spring of 1903 King Edward VII went on his historic mission to Paris and in July President Loubet returned the visit. Confronted in Europe by the common German peril, the British and French Governments were about to sink their differences. To the Wilhelmstrasse in May the German Chargé d'Affaires reported from London the trend towards a new grouping to consist of Great Britain, France, and the United States. In a combination of that kind the 'British Philistine' would be attracted by an evident sense of freedom; and it was noted that, in the view of Englishmen, Joseph Choate, as the Anglo-Saxon cousin, occupied first ambassadorial rank.[1] Lansdowne's foreign policy seemed to be crystallizing. The Alliance with Japan had been signed. The Anglo-French Entente was beginning to mature. If at all possible friendship with the United States would not be marred but steadfastly maintained.

To that aim the British Prime Minister was devoted. Chamberlain's campaign for Imperial tariff reform had been initiated in the spring of 1903 and his critics, deploring its potential effect on Anglo-American relations, feared the growth of trade reprisals between Ottawa, London, and Washington. To Andrew Carnegie, however, Arthur Balfour wrote in July that against a British preference to Canada the United States could not reasonably complain—having regard to the high protective duties levied by her on the manufactures of Great Britain and the nature of her commercial arrangements with Cuba. Nevertheless, as the Prime Minister also remarked, there was no wish nearer his heart than to secure and preserve Anglo-American understanding.[2] By economic conflict the English-speaking peoples were not, in fact, divided. In that era, with the defeat of Chamberlain's doctrine, the issue was postponed, and when it again arose Anglo-American friendship had progressed far beyond the trials of

---

[1] Bernstorff to Bülow, May 17, 1903, *Grosse Politik*, xvii. 575; Dugdale, *Germ. Dip. Docs.*, vol. iii, p. 174.

[2] Carnegie to Balfour, July 23, 1903, Hendrick, *Carnegie*, vol. ii, pp. 190–3; Balfour to Carnegie, July 28, 1903, ibid., p. 194; also ibid., pp. 183–96.

these formative years. But in 1903 nothing could better exemplify Balfour's attitude towards the United States than the treatment shortly accorded by him to the settlement of the Alaskan boundary.

On the gates of London Roosevelt did not pound in vain. Yet when Lodge first arrived in England he was uncertain whether the British Government, acting through Lord Alverstone, would have the courage to decide against the Dominion. Nor did it strike the Senator that 'impartial jurists' should deal with the matter in any fashion except as advocates for their respective sides. To the President he wrote that the land in dispute would remain under the American flag and observed further that with his country England would not go to war—'slavish as she is to Canada she will draw the line there'.[1] In other words, Lodge knew that he and his American colleagues could with impunity submit the most uncompromising demands. The early meeting of the tribunal upon which they insisted was duly obtained. But before it assembled Lodge expected Canada to relinquish none of her claims and in London he found that to be the general opinion; she possessed power, he pointed out to Roosevelt, unaccompanied by any responsibility.[2] In external affairs the Dominion's lack of responsibility would by Laurier and his Ministers have been even more severely deprecated. Events, however, had shown, and were soon to show again, that of the power thus ascribed to her Canada was almost wholly destitute.

Meeting at the Foreign Office on September 3, 1903, the members of the tribunal took their oath to consider the questions impartially. The circumstances in each consecutive stage of the Alaskan controversy had, however, scarcely been such as might have induced in the Canadian commissioners, Allen Aylesworth and Sir Louis Jetté, a judicial frame of mind. What would Alverstone do ? His views were the deciding factor. If he favoured the Canadian claims a deadlock would ensue to which President Roosevelt was threatening at once to respond with action on the Alaskan frontier; but, on the other hand, a vote now cast for those of the United States would be tantamount to yielding to American pressure. For after what had happened few imagined that on the sheer merits of the dispute there could, in accordance with the Treaty of January 1903, be a strictly legal pronouncement. Alverstone's task would be invidious whatever he did; an incorruptible judge, he had, in the eyes of Canadians and Americans alike, become the mediating agent of the British Government. And

[1] Lodge to Roosevelt, July 30, 1903, *Correspondence of Roosevelt and Lodge*, vol. ii, pp. 41–2; Lodge to Roosevelt, Aug. 20, 1903, ibid., p. 46.
[2] Choate to Hay, Aug. 14, 1903, Dennis, *Adventures*, p. 146; Lodge to Roosevelt, Aug. 30, 1903, *Correspondence of Roosevelt and Lodge*, vol. ii, p. 48.

as this was so, since an objective award on the law of the Anglo-Russian Treaty of 1825 had already been prejudiced, the Lord Chief Justice pursued the only prudent course available, that of safeguarding peace and friendly relations between the English-speaking peoples.

In the formal sessions of the tribunal the Canadian commissioners participated as much as any of the others. With what went on behind the scenes, however, they were totally unacquainted. The decision was reached between Alverstone and his American colleagues back of whom stood their Governments watching the negotiations, not with entire detachment, as they swayed and see-sawed towards an inevitable goal. Counsel began the oral argument in the middle of September and within a week Henry White wrote to the Secretary of State that the Lord Chief Justice was on close terms with Lodge and Root. 'There seems to be unanimity in thinking the Canadians have a good case upon the Portland Canal or channel, and Alverstone has intimated that he is with us on the main question.'[1] At the end these early opinions about the Dominion's claim to the Portland Channel were to undergo an abrupt metamorphosis. Meanwhile to White, for the benefit of British Ministers, John Hay ominously recapitulated the policy and plans of the President. From Laurier and Pauncefote he had himself heard that Canada had no case; he could not believe that over this problem might be annulled all recent efforts to further Anglo-American friendship.[2] One contention, underlined by Roosevelt, Hay, and the American lawyers, Alverstone refused to accept. This was the plea based on long occupation and on recognition by the Powers concerned of the right of the United States to the disputed territory. It applied exclusively to arbitration which Washington had rejected; in 1903 a judicial interpretation of what the Anglo-Russian Treaty of 1825 actually conferred was alone permissible.[3] But by the Canadians from that technical success not much solace could be derived.

The letters of Senator Lodge to President Roosevelt portrayed the bargaining process in the Anglo-American adjustment of the Alaskan boundary. On September 24 he reported Alverstone to have been discussing matters with Elihu Root and himself. The Lord Chief Justice felt 'bound on the law and the facts as at present advised to hold that the line goes round the heads of the inlets, which is, of course, the main contention. He takes very decisively the British view on the Portland Canal'. The Canadians asserted that there were

[1] White to Hay, Sept. 19, 1903, Nevins, *White*, p. 197.
[2] Hay to White, Sept. 20, 1903, ibid., p. 198; also Hay to Roosevelt, Sept. 25, 1903, Dennett, *Hay*, p. 361.
[3] Dafoe, *Sifton*, p. 226.

mountains as contemplated by the Treaty of 1825; the Americans rejoined that such did not exist and therefore the coastal fringe which belonged to the United States would extend everywhere 10 marine leagues in width from the sea. Alverstone, Lodge wrote, wanted to answer question 7 'by picking out a series of mountains which will reduce the strip running round the heads of all the inlets to as narrow bounds as possible, his idea being, I presume, to try to let the Canadians down as easily as possible in this way, after having decided against them on the main point'.[1] By the Lord Chief Justice some form of compromise was being sought.

If Alverstone strove to arbitrate the American commissioners were also attempting to square politics and law. At London, in the framing of an unbiased judicial award, their Ambassador should have had no share. On September 23 with Joseph Choate the American members of the tribunal had, nevertheless, a long conversation. 'We all agreed', Lodge informed Roosevelt, 'that if Alverstone decided in our favor on the main contention, namely, the heads of the inlets, that we could afford, with a slight modification, to accept their Portland Channel; but we were also agreed that we could come to no definite conclusion as to a complete decision on all questions until we saw what line he proposed to make under question 7'—that is to say, on the width of the American coastal fringe. 'We cannot afford', Lodge added, 'to have the territory cut down too much, even if we win the great point of the line running round the heads of the inlets. Moreover, in answering question 7 we must, as Turner well pointed out, rest whatever line we are conceding, upon a *tenable* theory on which we can stand at home.' And for that reason Lodge and Root did not then perceive how they could assent to Alverstone's solution.[2]

Yet in accordance with Canadian ideas the opinion of the Lord Chief Justice confirmed, and the American position hardly denied, the existence of a chain of mountains parallel to the coast within the limit of 10 marine leagues. To that possibility Theodore Roosevelt had often referred, and even in the statement dispatched by him to Mr. Justice Holmes for communication to the British Colonial Secretary he had admitted a margin of doubt.[3] But the American commissioners were more extreme than the President and let slide the opportunity of pacifying Canada on this debatable issue. By them neither

---

[1] Lodge to Roosevelt, Sept. 24, 1903, *Correspondence of Roosevelt and Lodge*, vol. ii, p. 58.

[2] Ibid., pp. 58–9.

[3] Roosevelt to Holmes, July 25, 1903, Bishop, *Roosevelt*, vol. i, p. 260; also Roosevelt to Root, Lodge, and Turner, Mar. 25, 1903, *Correspondence of Roosevelt and Lodge*, vol. ii, p. 5; and Roosevelt to Lodge, June 29, 1903, ibid., p. 37.

a neighbourly nor purely legal settlement was desired; power-politics in Anglo-American relations again subserved the aims of sectional politics in domestic affairs. Lodge, Root, and Turner were waiting to ascertain what they could 'afford' after Alverstone made his best offer; as politicians rather than as impartial jurists they only would concede a boundary line 'upon a *tenable* theory on which we can stand at home'. And expecting an early decision, Lodge invited Roosevelt's approval and further instructions about anything he and his associates 'ought to do or to know'.[1] The Senator was modest. An exponent of the most rigid nationalism, he needed no guidance from the White House.

For the Canadian commissioners there were in London few crumbs of comfort. While the various questions were still *sub judice*, Society in the capital and the press on both sides of the Atlantic echoed with the rumour that the Lord Chief Justice would vote for the American case.[2] This did not sweeten Canadian tempers and hampered Alverstone in his efforts to find a compromise and yet preserve the judicial demeanour of the tribunal. To Lodge the reasoning of counsel was frankly immaterial; the decision, he wrote to the President, rested with the commissioners and 'it does not depend on the arguments'.[3] Nor would the Foreign Office permit the negotiations to fail. Sir Michael Herbert having just died, his post at the Washington Embassy had to be filled. Lord Lansdowne 'several times' sent for Lodge to discuss with him a suitable appointment. 'We also', the Senator remembered, 'had naturally some talk about the tribunal.'[4] On this topic Canadian commissioners do not appear to have been similarly consulted.

As the crisis ripened the British Government became more intimately involved. It was on his own initiative that Alverstone, whose vote could effect either a victory for the United States or a fatal deadlock, had been endeavouring to arrange a compromise. But in winning him over to their side, Lodge and Root tried, at the beginning of October, to procure the help of a higher authority. Henry White was their intermediary and, visiting the Prime Minister at Wittingehame, he impressed upon his host the urgency of a settlement, the particular obstacle confronting the commissioners and the dire consequences of a disagreement. With the resignation in September of Joseph Chamberlain British politics had entered into a dramatic

---

[1] Lodge to Roosevelt, Sept. 24, 1903, ibid., p. 59.
[2] Skelton, *Laurier*, vol. ii, pp. 148–9; Dafoe, *Sifton*, pp. 227–8.
[3] Lodge to Roosevelt, Sept. 29, 1903, *Correspondence of Roosevelt and Lodge*, vol. ii, p. 61.
[4] *Proceedings LVIII Mass. Hist. Society*, p. 341, 'Memoir of H. C. Lodge'.

phase which the retirement from the Government of the Duke of Devonshire and others did not render any the less exciting. Yet White reported Balfour as having said on October 4 'that he attached far more importance to the agreement of the Tribunal than to any of the Cabinet questions and complications with which he was then bothered, and that he thought it would be little short of a disaster if the Tribunal broke up without a decision'. Alverstone, White had suggested, should be informed that the Government 'without in any way wishing to influence him' were very anxious not to have this happen. Of the steps taken, from the Prime Minister himself, his guest learned nothing further. Nevertheless, 'two days afterwards', wrote White to Hay, 'his confidential secretary, Saunders, who is a friend of mine, let me know very confidentially that he had had two interviews with Lord Alverstone'.[1] And thus were the engines of diplomacy again set in motion.

The Canadians now grew apprehensive. Henry White spoke to Arthur Balfour on October 4. Three days later Clifford Sifton, the agent in London for the Canadian side, sent a message in alarm to Sir Wilfrid Laurier. The arguments of counsel were not yet finished, but Sifton cabled to Ottawa that Alverstone had made up his mind to vote with the Americans and totally reject the Dominion's case. 'We all think that Chief Justice's intentions are unjustifiable, and due to predetermination to avoid trouble with the United States. Jetté and Aylesworth are much exasperated, and considering withdrawing from Commission.' To their withdrawal, however, Laurier would not consent. 'If they cannot get our full rights,' he flashed back, 'let them put up a bitter fight for our contention on Portland Canal, which is beyond doubt: that point must be decided in Canada's favour. Shame Chief Justice and carry that point. If we are thrown over by Chief Justice, he will give the last blow to British diplomacy in Canada. He should be plainly told this by our Commissioners.'[2] Alverstone remained the storm-centre. By his colleagues he was being pulled in opposite directions and the British Government did not leave him alone. But with the sober bent, if hardly the purpose, of a judge, he still struggled to reconcile conflicting views.

Before the tribunal counsel completed their arguments on October 8. As the Chief Justice and the American commissioners had not yet agreed upon the width of the Alaskan coastal fringe to which the United States was entitled, the dangers of Anglo-American estrangement were approaching a climax. On October 9 the Prime Minister

[1] White to Hay, Oct. 20, 1903, Nevins, *White*, p. 200.
[2] Dafoe, *Sifton*, pp. 228–9; Skelton, *Laurier*, vol. ii, p. 149.

and Senator Lodge met at the house of Henry White to review the
situation. Of Balfour's intense disquietude Lodge retained a vivid
recollection. 'All the world at the moment is talking about the Duke
of Devonshire's withdrawal from the Cabinet on account of Mr.
Chamberlain's protection policy; but I say to you frankly', the Prime
Minister declared, 'that that matter and all similar matters are as
nothing in my judgement, compared to the importance of this Alaskan
dispute. It is full of peril, and it must be settled.' By White, however, it was subsequently noted that, while appreciating Alverstone's
motives in attempting to do for Canada as much as possible, he himself had felt more cheerful about the outlook than those who did not
possess the professional skill to gauge accurately 'the undercurrent
of diplomacy'. For from its 'force and quiet working' he throughout
calmly expected the desired decision to emerge.[1]

The framing of the award occupied ten days. After the public
sessions, at the first meeting of the commissioners, the compromise
plan of the Chief Justice was to be again descried. Alverstone held
that Canada should be given the four islands at the mouth of the
Portland Channel; the boundary, in keeping with her contention, ran
to the north of them and not to the south. But the Chief Justice also
concluded and correctly, as Canadian writers now concede, that the
heads of the inlets belonged to the United States.[2] Alverstone's
scheme was that in return for her four islands Canada should recog-
nize American rights to a coastwise strip blocking the Yukon from
the sea. But, even if he thus accepted the main thesis of the United
States, the Chief Justice did not concur that her unbroken strip of
Alaskan territory must, in pursuing the sinuosities of the shore,
stretch everywhere 10 marine leagues in width; under the terms of
the Anglo-Russian Treaty of 1825 there were mountains, as the
Canadians asserted, along which the line should be drawn nearer the
sea. The American commissioners, however, strove for a fringe that,
by the mountains chosen to mark the boundary, would be almost as
wide as the one originally sought. On October 12 Alverstone read his
opinions to the other members of the tribunal. Reserving judgement,
the American commissioners raised no objection to the transference
of the four islands to the Dominion. But the width of the fringe per-
plexed them. They did not reach that question, Lodge wrote to
Roosevelt, and no actual vote had been taken on anything. He,
nevertheless, found the Chief Justice privately 'very set on having

---

[1] *Proceedings LVIII Mass. Hist. Society*, pp. 341–2, 'Memoir of H. C. Lodge';
White to Hay, Oct. 20, 1903, Nevins, *White*, pp. 200–1.
[2] James White, *Can. Hist. Rev.*, vol. vi, no. 4, Dec. 1925, p. 346; also Skelton,
Laurier, vol. ii, p. 150; Dafoe, *Sifton*, p. 232.

his selected summits and then creating a range which will narrow the strip'. This, Lodge observed, they could not admit. 'We may get our way but it will be either that or a disgreement.'[1] The final crisis was at hand. The invariable remedy had to be applied.

What happened at the end is not altogether obscure. When the decision was announced Joseph Choate, Ambassador of the United States at the Court of St. James's, dispatched a letter to John Hay substantiating the Canadian suspicion that the Big Stick of American diplomacy had once more been brought into play. 'On Wednesday last,' he reported to the Secretary of State, 'when there seemed to be a tendency to a deadlock between the Commissioners, I had an interview with Lord Lansdowne in which I pressed upon him very urgently the views of the President as expressed by him in our interview in June.'[2] What did Roosevelt tell Choate on that occasion? To the Ambassador he had said that the tribunal was the last chance of an agreement being reached by the free act of both parties; if it failed, not only would there be no arbitration but he would instead ask Congress for an appropriation to enable him to run the boundary 'on our own theory'.[3] And now in the middle of October failure appeared inescapable unless, on the width of the fringe, Alverstone should cease to differ from his American colleagues. To obtain their demands peaceably Choate therefore proceeded to reiterate harsh threats at the Foreign Office which previously had at least been conveyed to London in a more indirect and informal manner. How well such intervention served its purpose was speedily revealed. In his account to Hay the Ambassador continued:

'The upshot of our conversation was that the Commissioners, all four of them, must agree on the drawing of the line, and that if necessary we might ourselves agree on what would be a satisfactory line, and perhaps if necessary advise the Commissioners what we thought. But in view of the result so happily attained this part of the conversation is no longer important. I left satisfied that he and Mr. Balfour would, if they had not already done so, tell Lord Alverstone what they thought as to the necessity of agreeing upon that line, and that the present chance of settling the controversy ought not to be lost.'[4]

It may be noted as a matter of some piquancy that at that very time—on October 14, 1903—Great Britain and France had concluded a general treaty of arbitration. An harbinger of the Entente Cordiale,

---

[1] Lodge to Roosevelt, Oct. 12, 1903, *Correspondence of Roosevelt and Lodge*, vol. ii, p. 69.

[2] Choate to Hay, Oct. 20, 1903, Dennis, *Adventures*, p. 154.

[3] Roosevelt to Lodge, July 16, 1903, *Correspondence of Roosevelt and Lodge*, vol. ii, p. 39.

[4] Choate to Hay, Oct. 20, 1903, Dennis, *Adventures*, p. 154.

this instrument was a sign that by the British Government friends were being attracted and not repelled.

The impact of diplomacy on judicial interpretation soon made itself palpable. To the dismay of the Canadian commissioners, Alverstone, modifying his opinion of October 12 that the four islands at the mouth of the Portland Channel belonged to the Dominion, voted on October 17 to give two of them to the United States. When an Ambassador warns a Foreign Secretary—especially if the assistance of the Prime Minister has also been enlisted—it does not take many days for one feature of a treaty to assume an entirely fresh juristic meaning. Each party had contended for the four islands as a group; the boundary, it was stipulated by both sides, should be drawn either to the north of them or to the south. But the Chief Justice, a Solomon in judgement, now voted with his American colleagues that the line ran in the middle through the Tongas Passage; the group was thus divided in half, two of the islands being assigned to Canada and two to the United States. No argument, written or oral, which entailed that solution had been submitted to the tribunal. Alverstone, however, said afterwards that at the last moment an American member laid down the cession of the two islands as the condition upon which he and his compatriots would sign an award.[1] Theodore Roosevelt himself considered that on this question a certain leniency was permissible; as late as October 5 he had written to Senator Lodge that 'of course, we can yield on the Portland Canal Islands, if Alverstone goes with us on the main contention'.[2] The Chief Justice did what was required of him when he agreed that American territory followed the windings of the Alaskan coast round the heads of the inlets. But in London the representatives of the President were more Rooseveltian than Roosevelt and from them diplomatic pressure would not abate until the fulfilment of their further demands had been achieved.

The decision on the Portland Channel violated so cynically the judicial character of the tribunal that it discredited the whole award. Over the width of the coastal fringe the American commissioners wanted a 'tenable theory' on which they could stand at home. With advice from Downing Street ringing in his ears, Alverstone probably allowed them to take the two islands as a kind of compensation in that particular dispute. The United States, nevertheless, received a range of mountains which made the lisiére almost as wide as the one for which her spokesmen had contended; and when reproached by

[1] James White, *Can. Hist. Rev.*, vol. vi, no. 4, Dec. 1925, pp. 345–6; Dafoe, *Sifton*, pp. 231–2.
[2] Roosevelt to Lodge, Oct. 5, 1903, *Correspondence of Roosevelt and Lodge*, vol. ii, p. 66.

Sir Louis Jetté that, under the Anglo-Russian Treaty of 1825, coastal and not more inland mountains should have been selected, Alverstone retorted that he had to fight hard even to secure the boundary as settled.[1] Suited for the haggling and wrangling of the market-place, such methods ill befitted that cool, dispassionate weighing of evidence to which members of the tribunal were pledged. The United States won her 'main contention' that in southern Alaska the American fringe barred Canadian territory everywhere from access to the sea; she obtained a coastal strip the size almost of that for which her counsel had argued—and one somewhat wider than she might have procured from a purely judicial reading of the treaty or by friendly negotiation; and then her commissioners appropriated two of the four islands which Alverstone had assigned to the Dominion. With the exception of the last item there was in the American case strong support for the broad principles of the award. But with this Lodge, Turner, and Root were not satisfied. Through the British Government they cudgelled minor points out of Alverstone and by their conduct abundantly justified the Canadian objection to them as 'impartial jurists'. Neither as a judicial process nor as a diplomatic incident could the Dominion regard the delimitation of the Alaskan boundary with composure or restraint.

Canadian feeling was demonstrated by an exchange of messages between Clifford Sifton and Sir Wilfrid Laurier. When Alverstone switched his vote the former cabled from London that the two islands assigned to the United States commanded the entrance to the Portland Channel and destroyed the 'strategic value' of the other two. The course of the discussion, he added, had greatly exasperated the Canadian members of the tribunal who considered the settlement to have been prearranged. The two islands, Laurier replied, were transferred to the United States by no justifiable interpretation of the Anglo-Russian Treaty. 'It is one of those concessions which have made British diplomacy odious to Canadian people, and it will have most lamentable effect. Our Commissioners ought to protest in most vigorous terms.'[2] The award of the Alaskan boundary tribunal was signed on October 20, 1903. Lord Alverstone, Elihu Root, Senators Lodge and Turner affixed their signatures, but their Canadian colleagues abstained.[3] Sir Louis Jetté and Allen Aylesworth published instead an explanatory statement in which they announced that they had refrained from so doing because the findings of the commission

[1] Dafoe, *Sifton*, pp. 231–2; Skelton, *Laurier*, vol. ii, pp. 150–1.
[2] Sifton to Laurier, Oct. 17, 1903, Laurier to Sifton, Oct. 18, 1903, Dafoe, *Sifton*, p. 233.
[3] *U.S. Foreign Relations*, 1903, pp. 543–5.

were not judicial on the islands of the Portland Channel and the boundary marked by the coastal mountains. They had been powerless, they declared, to avert a sacrifice of the interests of their country, whose just rights were ignored.[1] By the assertion of American nationalism a counter-assertion of Canadian nationalism was thus evoked.

Against its southern neighbour whose will could be imposed so freely on the whole North American continent all the traditional prejudice of the Dominion sprang now to life. And as the medium of this latest injury, though he deserved sympathy rather than condemnation, Alverstone was not spared. At the Joint High Commission of 1898–9, the task of his predecessor, Lord Herschell, had been immeasurably more simple. The Spanish War having just finished, Anglo-American understanding had still to adapt itself to peace-time conditions. Would mutual barter furnish material, plastic in quality, out of which might lastingly be moulded its normal shape? Conscious of her new strength, the United States did not only prove intractable but upon her goodwill started to set a mounting price. If the adjustment of outstanding difficulties were to be accomplished, British policy would therefore have to be one of gratuitous concessions. Canada bore the brunt when Hay and Pauncefote signed their first isthmian agreement and she forfeited the opportunity, in return for the revision of the Clayton-Bulwer Treaty, of driving a bargain over the Alaskan boundary. The next blow fell when she was constrained to renounce all hope of neutral arbitration or adjudication; and then with the cards stacked against her even the American scheme was vitiated by the President's choice of 'impartial jurists'. During the summer and autumn of 1903 Theodore Roosevelt and his representatives in London issued to British Ministers categorical warnings which, had they emanated from European Chancelleries, might have jeopardized friendly relations. The fact that they had in the end the opposite result testifies eloquently to the attitude of conciliation adopted by Downing Street. Canadian resentment was intelligible. But the position of the Chief Justice must have been tormenting. American intimidation was to be resisted at the cost of English-speaking solidarity. Yet Alverstone did not yield at once. Although the judicial character of the tribunal was undermined from the outset, it took renewed pressure of every sort by Roosevelt, White, Lodge, and Choate through Chamberlain, Balfour, and Lansdowne before the Lord Chief Justice could finally be persuaded to join his American colleagues. For him further to have insisted upon the arid technicalities of the law would have been only to see them brushed impetuously

[1] Dafoe, *Sifton*, pp. 232–3.

aside by Rooseveltian action in Alaska. Canada was saved from the ensuing complications and Great Britain from a heavy loss in prestige and diplomatic friendship. Alverstone afterwards maintained that he differed from the Canadian commissioners 'purely in a judicial capacity'.[1] He had been judicious if not judicial. In a court which, through no fault of his, was no court, the interpreter of the law became the preserver of peace, the judge the arbitrator, the bench the custodian of policy.

The outcry in the Dominion was not that of a poor loser but the shrill anger of a litigant whose case, good or bad, had been accorded an unfair trial. Smarting under a certain lack of consideration from Great Britain, Canadian Ministers attributed such perfunctory treatment to their country's 'colonial' status and were resolved that henceforth, in the world-wide balancing of diplomatic accounts, the sensibilities of a young Dominion should never again be reckoned small coin. In October 1903, addressing the House of Commons at Ottawa, Sir Wilfrid Laurier therefore sounded the keynote for further constitutional advance. He regretted that, ás a self-governing Dominion, Canada did not possess the treaty-making power. 'It is important that we should ask the British parliament for more extensive powers, so that if we ever have to deal with matters of a similar nature again, we shall deal with them in our own way, in our own fashion, according to the best light that we have.'[2] What he would have done to cope with American military measures on the Alaskan frontier the Prime Minister of Canada did not say. But to that great Imperial development which is now expressed in the relationships of the British Commonwealth of Nations an immense and far-reaching stimulus had been given.

And so this boundary question would in its consequences exercise indirectly on world politics no negligible influence. Its settlement coincided, moreover, with the opening of Chamberlain's historic campaign for fiscal and administrative centralization between the various units of the British Empire. Yet he also was a leading advocate of Anglo-American understanding. In the Alaskan controversy these two ideals were at odds. Towards Chamberlain's doctrine the unresponsive attitude of the Canadian Liberal Government was for that reason based probably not only on economic grounds but on diplomatic and constitutional ones as well. In international affairs Canada then stood for a kind of Imperial disunification. But in the long run her views served to promote the unity of the British Empire. For it was weaker when the limitations on the Dominions were taut yet brittle, stronger

[1] Viscount Alverstone, *Recollections of Bar and Bench*, pp. 240–1.
[2] Skelton, *Laurier*, vol. ii, pp. 154–6.

when they were resilient, slackened, or dissevered. As Canada's autonomy evolved the danger dwindled of her regional quarrels entangling
the whole Empire. For in the latter, centripetal and centrifugal tendencies were, during 1903, arrested by each other but not rescinded.
Eventually, from them, in the external relations of Great Britain and
the Dominions, an essential elasticity emerged; a method was being
pragmatically attained to synthesize independence with common
responsibilities and a common allegiance. The unity of British nations
seemed feasible only with a democratic levelling-up in their status—
d'égal à égal. Contemporary practice and the Statute of Westminster
were products of a trend accelerated by the Alaskan dispute.

The animosities rekindled in 1903 against the United States contributed eight years later to the defeat by the electors of Canada of
a project for commercial reciprocity between those two countries. In
the Dominion the sense of injustice was, nevertheless, slowly but
definitely assuaged; and while the Alaskan decision caused, temporarily, much ill-feeling its permanent results were admirable. For
after 1903, with the major diplomatic barrier lifted and out of the
way, the pulsing continental intercourse of the two western nations—
economic, financial, social, and cultural—flowed more and more
through its natural channels. There were questions about which they
continued to differ—these affected matters such as boundary waters,
fisheries, and water-power; and over them Elihu Root as Secretary of
State and James Bryce as British Ambassador were to negotiate auspicious arrangements. Although, during the next quarter of a century,
she still provided the means of official communication, the need
steadily decreased for Great Britain to intervene between Ottawa and
Washington. Before 1903, in her attempt to improve relations with
the United States, the Dominion was an Achilles' heel; the claims of
a British State in North America might sometimes be asserted by
Downing Street to the detriment of its policy of English-speaking
friendship. But now a reverse and entirely beneficent process could
begin to operate. Friction with the United States to a considerable
extent provoked the demand from Ottawa for larger constitutional
powers; and yet as she acquired them, Canada gradually employed
her growing weight in the directing councils of the Empire to preserve
Anglo-American goodwill. So long, in fact, as that remained a living
force she would never be compelled to make a reluctant choice between
the exigencies of her continental situation and her wider loyalties to
the British Commonwealth. Canada's territorial position, the root of
past difficulties, could indeed be used henceforth to bind together and
not divide the English-speaking peoples.

During the next two decades the truth of that was shown on several important occasions. At the Imperial Conference of 1911 the practice of consultation in foreign affairs between Great Britain and the Dominions received a noteworthy fillip—and one, moreover, in which Anglo-American understanding was again concerned. The Asquith Ministry were proposing to revise the second Anglo-Japanese Alliance and to sign an arbitration treaty with President Taft's Administration in order to prevent the British Empire as the ally of Japan from being dragged involuntarily into conflict with the United States. Invited to attend a meeting of the secret Committee of Imperial Defence, the delegates to the Imperial Conference heard from Sir Edward Grey an outline of his policy. By thus enlightening the autonomous Dominions on the great diplomatic problems of the day the British Government tacitly recognized their lessening subordination. So, too, amends were offered to Canada for what she regarded as cavalier treatment meted out to her in the Alaskan dispute. But, above all, Asquith and Grey confided in Dominion representatives because they desired to reconcile British 'world policy' with Imperial interests and with Anglo-American friendship. From 1903 to 1911 the change was striking. Laurier's approval of what Grey sought to do at Washington and Tokio indicated that, to the future maintenance of Anglo-American solidarity, Canada would be no bar.[1]

But in upholding it she had an even more positive function to perform and of this, after the Great War of 1914–18, there was fuller evidence. At the Imperial Conference of 1921, Arthur Meighen, then Prime Minister of Canada, insisted that, for the sake of goodwill between the United States and the British Empire, the Anglo-Japanese Alliance should be allowed to lapse. The tables were turned. As the chief of the overseas Dominions and as a North American State, Canada had become the main champion of Anglo-American friendship. The attitude of her Government led up to the Washington Conference of that year, the peaceful adjustment for a decade of grave international rivalries on the Pacific and in the Far East, and the suspension of a building race in armaments between the greater naval Powers. Canada was carrying out the mediatorial role created for her by geographical proximity to the United States and equal partnership in the British Commonwealth of Nations: in the relations of the English-speaking peoples she now acted as a harmonizing factor.

Meanwhile in 1903 the Alaskan decision had been hailed by Americans with enthusiasm. It gave the United States much more than

[1] *Br. Docs.*, vol. vi, pp. 781–90; *Br. Docs.*, vol. viii, no. 427, p. 525; also ibid., pp. 503–605, and Trevelyan, *Grey of Fallodon*, pp. 203–4.

John Hay ever anticipated; the tribunal, in the words of the President, provided his country with 'the greatest diplomatic victory during the present generation'.[1] This may have been a frank admission of the award's non-judicial character; but it called attention to a welcome feat in foreign affairs which might strengthen the popular appeal of an Administration and party seeking in the next year to be returned to office. Under Theodore Roosevelt shirt-sleeve diplomacy had donned a coat of mail. Yet in December 1903, when he sent his annual message to Congress, the President declared that the Alaskan award furnished signal proof of the 'fairness and goodwill with which two friendly nations can approach and determine issues involving national sovereignty and by their nature incapable of submission to a third power for adjudication'.[2] It did, actually, nothing of the sort. Apart from the practical value of direct negotiation there was in principle, as distinguished from expediency, no valid reason for rejecting normal methods of arbitration or adjudication. As an example of how to deal with international disputes, the Alaskan settlement did not mark a constructive precedent. Along the rugged road of Anglo-Canadian concessions to the United States it was, in fact, merely another milestone.

For the course they had followed the British Government were, nevertheless, by the broad sequel to the Alaskan controversy, richly rewarded. If Canada failed to secure certain fragments of territory and a port to the Yukon, Great Britain preserved her friendship with the United States. In London, since the close of the nineteenth century, an underlying conviction had persisted that once their mutual disputes were liquidated—even if this were done at the expense of the Dominion—Anglo-American goodwill would be placed inexpugnably on firm ground. And so many things, not otherwise always endurable, were, in relations with the United States, yet endured. By his public virtues and shortcomings alike, Theodore Roosevelt well epitomized the American spirit of his day and age. During the Russo-Japanese War he laboured to restore peace and soon after this venture into world politics wrote to a British diplomatist that from his cordial attitude towards Great Britain he had never wavered. One of the best manifestations of it, he added, was his insistence 'upon having the Alaskan boundary settled right and taking sufficiently active steps to make the British Government understand the seriousness of the situation'.[3] In 1911, when no longer President but still a great tribune

---

[1] Hay to Mrs. Hay, Oct. 21, 1903, Dennett, *Hay*, p. 362; John W. Foster, *Diplomatic Memoirs*, vol. ii, p. 209.
[2] *U.S. Foreign Relations*, 1903, p. xviii.
[3] Roosevelt to Spring Rice, Nov. 1, 1905, Gwynn, *Spring Rice*, vol. ii, pp. 10–11.

of the American nation, Theodore Roosevelt observed that the Alaskan award composed 'the last serious trouble between the British Empire and ourselves as everything else could be arbitrated. I feel very differently towards England from the way I feel towards Germany'. For now, as he stated in his autobiography, the last obstacle to 'absolute agreement' between the English-speaking peoples had been removed.[1]

It was fortunate that the North American horizon grew brighter as the outlook darkened in Asia and Europe. Washington seemed content. From that quarter hostile distractions were inconceivable; as international conditions elsewhere deteriorated, no advantage of Great Britain would be taken by American Governments. Initiated under Lord Salisbury, the British policy of friendly informal reinsurance with the United States was in 1903 unassailably established. And indeed without the Alaskan award American association in 1917–18 with the Entente and Allied Powers might never have occurred. On the development of the *rapprochement* between Great Britain and the United States Senator Lodge left his stamp; his participation in events and lengthy subsequent experience as Chairman of the Senate Committee on Foreign Relations attached to his opinions a special authority. In Lodge's final view the solving of the Alaskan problem was more important than the Hay-Pauncefote Treaty for the construction of the isthmian canal; its importance, according to him, could not be over-estimated. 'If we had become involved in a war with England and Canada or in a serious clash on the boundary, not only would all the other questions have remained unsettled but the attitude of the United States towards England would have been of such a character as to have embarrassed us most seriously when the Great War of 1914 broke out.'[2] There was ultimately no better defence than this of the line adopted by Balfour and Lansdowne during the Alaskan controversy nor, in fact, of the general policy of amelioration pursued at Washington by the British Government since the turn of the century. Having willed the end—a good understanding with the United States—they had to will the means. And more than a decade later, when she fought against Germany with the rest of the British Empire, even Canada could deem herself wholly requited for the humiliation she once had suffered over some remote tracts of northern wilderness. The indispensable reinforcement brought by the United States to a common cause might never have been given if the Dominion fourteen years before had not paid the price for English-speaking solidarity.

[1] Roosevelt to Mahan, June 11, 1911, Taylor, *Mahan*, p. 203; Theodore Roosevelt, *An Autobiography*, p. 582.
[2] *Proceedings LVIII Mass. Hist. Society*, p. 342, 'Memoir of H. C. Lodge'

VIII

TOWARDS AN ANGLO-AMERICAN CONCERT

THE Russo-Japanese War of 1904–5 provided the first occasion for
the United States as a Great Power to take the initiative in a major
crisis of world politics. During that conflict Theodore Roosevelt
intervened in the diplomatic situation abroad to a degree exceeding
the efforts of any President before the advent of Woodrow Wilson.
Could Anglo-American co-operation be maintained even when exposed to the severest trial it had yet undergone in the wider sphere
of international affairs ? The mutual disputes of the English-speaking
Powers had in the main been adjusted and in China their interests
were similar. Great Britain, however, was the ally of Japan and
Germany the friend of Russia. Anglo-American relations were to be
complicated by those two facts. Prompted from Berlin and so that
he might succeed with his Far Eastern programme, Roosevelt took
a hand in the Moroccan controversy in which Great Britain and
France stood together. The peace of Europe and mediation in Eastern
Asia were thus interlaced. Moreover, throughout this time of crisis,
Germany tried desperately but, on the whole, unavailingly to detach
the United States from Great Britain. For although during the actual
Russo-Japanese peacemaking their policies diverged, the English-
speaking Governments were, at the final stage of the Far Eastern
settlement, to be in full accord.

After the Boxer Rebellion Russia did not abide by her promise to
withdraw from Manchuria. Tokio was afraid of Russian designs in
that province and in Corea; London and Washington objected to the
general Russian aggression in China. The Anglo-Japanese Alliance
ensued, and with it in April 1903 the British Foreign Secretary invited
the closest American collaboration. Lansdowne, indeed, went so far
as to assure Washington that Great Britain was 'prepared to follow
the United States step by step up to any point that may be necessary
for the protection of our common interests in China'.[1] And it was the
view of Senator Lodge that these were large enough to warrant action
by the American Government: 'To unite with England and Japan
in a protest is not an entangling alliance.'[2] Since 1898, however, the
Secretary of State had been learning his lesson in a hard school.

---

[1] Lansdowne to Herbert, Apr. 28, 1903, *Br. Docs.*, vol. ii, no. 227, p. 200; ibid.,
chap. xiii, pp. 197–252.
[2] Lodge to Roosevelt, May 21, 1903, *Correspondence of Roosevelt and Lodge*, vol. ii,
p. 15.

John Hay therefore preferred a course, politically much safer, of leaving to Anglo-Japanese diplomacy the defence of American Far Eastern policy. But at the end of 1903 relations between Japan and Russia were seriously aggravated. The partition of China seemed once more to be imminent; the Open Door, the prestige and commercial rights of the United States were again imperilled. And so the American asked the British Government to give them any information received from the Far East. With this request, Lansdowne, pleased that the United States evinced such concern, expressed his entire willingness to comply.[1] For by the Japanese the issue with Russia was about to be put to the arbitrament of the sword.

Meanwhile the European position was one of exceptional delicacy. Lord Lansdowne and Théophile Delcassé, the French Minister of Foreign Affairs, were in the midst of negotiations which soon culminated in the Entente Cordiale. France was the ally of Russia just as Great Britain was the ally of Japan. The Government in Paris were anxious therefore to avert a Far Eastern struggle so as to eliminate every possibility of a Franco-British collision. They did not suggest an ordinary mediation, but at London the French Ambassador thought that Great Britain, France, and the United States might tender Russia and Japan their 'good offices and sedative advice'.[2] To this move, however, the British Government were opposed. They wanted to secure the friendship of France, but they also had decided that in the Far East Japan must be allowed to scotch the Russian menace. If the Japanese were deprived of the opportunity then presented to them, Great Britain might incur their lasting resentment. As British Ambassador to the United States Sir Mortimer Durand had replaced Sir Michael Herbert. At the beginning of February 1904 he was instructed to ascertain—should the French proposal be broached at Washington—whether American ideas differed from those of his own Government.[3] With Great Britain the United States at that moment did not disagree. Yet a precedent had been established which in the summer of 1905 would cause Theodore Roosevelt considerable irritation. Nevertheless, by the Anglo-French Entente of April 8, 1904, the danger was dispelled that the Far Eastern conflict might embroil against each other the European allies of the two combatant Powers. To German rivalry on land and sea Great Britain countered by casting in her lot with France.

On February 10, 1904, two days after her gunboats had attacked

---

[1] Lansdowne to Durand, Dec. 31, 1903, *Br. Docs.*, vol. ii, no. 266, p. 228; also Dennis, *Adventures*, pp. 359–61; Dennett, *Hay*, pp. 403–6.

[2] Lansdowne to Monson, Jan. 27, 1904, *Br. Docs.*, vol. ii, no. 283, p. 240.

[3] Lansdowne to Durand, Feb. 5, 1904, ibid., no. 288, p. 243.

the Russian fleet near Port Arthur, Japan declared war. Before this happened the British Government had notified Tokio that they would fulfil their treaty obligation to prevent interference by a third Power or Powers.[1] They were, in brief, formally holding the ring for their ally as they had in 1898 informally warded off the enemies of the United States. For while Great Britain remained neutral—her neutrality being proclaimed on February 11—the service rendered by Japan to her western partner was of colossal value. In British policy honour and interest were thus intermingled.

Likewise neutral, Germany, on the other hand, was particularly well disposed towards Russia. A military and naval defeat for Japan would be a diplomatic defeat for Great Britain. Besides, German aspirations at Constantinople and in Asia Minor could not only have freer scope the more engrossed Russia became in the Far East, but pressure by her might further be relaxed on the German frontier and in the Balkans against the allied Empire of the Habsburgs. When war was declared Germany inspired the United States to suggest to the Powers that, for the duration of hostilities, China should be neutralized; from her plan, nevertheless, she omitted Manchuria and certain neighbouring regions. The American Government, adopting the proposal, stipulated, however, that the neutralized zone should include the whole 'administrative entity of China'.[2] And so at that juncture the Chinese Empire would not be dismembered. It was the aim of Count von Bülow, the Imperial Chancellor, to encourage Russia without damaging relations between Germany and other countries. For this reason he had to keep a check on the Kaiser who, obsessed with the idea of the monarchical mission of the Houses of Romanoff and Hohenzollern, could scarcely contain his horror at the lack of zeal being exhibited by the Tsar in the prosecution of the struggle. Preaching a crusade of Holy Russia against the Yellow Peril, William II railed at the barely tepid sympathy of Paris with St. Petersburg and the goodwill of the English-speaking world towards Japan. But Bülow wished to steer clear of a request from Russia to help repel the supposed danger to the white race, Christendom, and the civilization of Europe. German aid for the Russians meant war with Great Britain, the ally of Japan. For the Teutonic racial hysteria of his sovereign, the Chancellor substituted a saner programme of friendship with St. Petersburg while running no risks

[1] Lansdowne to Hayashi, Feb. 6, 1904, ibid., no. 291, p. 244; also Lansdowne to Edward VII, April 18, 1904, Newton, *Lansdowne*, pp. 308–9.

[2] *Br. Docs.*, vol. ii, no. 299, p. 252; Thayer, *Hay*, vol. ii, pp. 372–4; Roosevelt to Root, Feb. 16, 1904, Dennis, *Adventures*, p. 363; Bülow to the Kaiser, Feb. 18, 1904, Frederic Whyte (ed.), *Letters of Prince von Bülow*, pp. 38–9.

with Tokio or London.[1] Yet even these objects were in the end only partly attained. After 1905, in the wake of France, Russia turned to Great Britain, and at Washington also full success would elude the grasp of German diplomacy.

From the outset of the war British and American opinion had been at one with each other and to Downing Street that was a source of real satisfaction. 'Japan', the President observed, 'is playing our game.'[2] Nor was he unprepared to assist Tokio. From McKinley isolationism his experience of high office would appear to have carried Theodore Roosevelt no small distance. The step he took he described afterwards to the British diplomatist, Cecil Spring Rice.

'As soon as this war broke out,' the President narrated, 'I notified Germany and France in the most polite and discreet fashion that in the event of a combination against Japan to try to do what Russia, Germany and France did to her in 1894, I should promptly side with Japan and proceed to whatever length was necessary on her behalf. I, of course, knew that your Government would act in the same way, and thought it best that I should have no consultation with your people before announcing my own purpose.'[3]

If his memory served him aright this was a threat of direct intervention by the United States and one which revealed the depth of her agreement with Great Britain. For behind the scenes, in defence of their Far Eastern interests, the American Administration would have then been supplementing British localization of the conflict.

During 1904 it seemed, as a matter of fact, most improbable that the Germans and the newly Anglophile French would fly in the face of the passive protection accorded Japan by the Royal Navy. The policy he promulgated Roosevelt would therefore not be called upon to execute. Nor is it indeed inconceivable, no confirmatory proof having ever been adduced, that his account of this démarche, like that of what he did during the Anglo-German coercion of Venezuela, was much exaggerated or even wholly fanciful. Yet by his words at least he tacitly acknowledged the inefficacy in Eastern Asia of American non-interventionist principles. The President may not have deemed it wise to go as far as the British proposal of 1898 for closer association in China between Great Britain and the United States; he had, however, or said he had, at once discarded the feeble expedients to which at the turn of the century John Hay was confined. What Roosevelt believed it essential to do might have been obviated,

[1] Bülow's memorandum, Feb. 14, 1904, *Bülow's Letters*, pp. 36–8; Bülow, *Memoirs 1903–1909*, pp. 60–2.
[2] Nevins, *White*, pp. 183–5; Roosevelt to Theodore Roosevelt Jr., Feb. 10, 1904, Pringle, *Roosevelt*, p. 375.
[3] Roosevelt to Spring Rice, July 24, 1905, Gwynn, *Spring Rice*, vol. i, p. 478.

the entire drift of world politics deflected, by an acceptance of the earlier British invitation. And yet it is very doubtful whether, in belligerent measures abroad, Congress and the American public would have upheld him; even temporary support of the Anglo-Japanese Alliance he might, in any final test, have been compelled to abandon. But would not such a stand by the American Government have influenced the Chancelleries of Europe and left its mark before concrete sanctions were required? Of the President's action, granting that it actually took place, the British Foreign Office at the time had evidently no exact information; of the similarity of views prevailing between London and Washington it was nevertheless perfectly aware. And that, too, could be considered friendly reinsurance with the United States. American traditions did not permit her formally to enter into the ambit of the British diplomatic system. Yet from the beckoning enemy camp she had visibly moved away. Henceforth, by Rooseveltian participation in international affairs, it was rendered ever more important for Anglo-American solidarity that between the English-speaking Powers there should be a common outlook.

The sinews of war had to be procured in the western money-markets. Tokio turned to the City of London, where a provisional agreement was reached with a British financial group—the Hong Kong and Shanghai Banking Corporation, Parr's Bank and the Yokohama Specie Bank—for a loan of £10,000,000. Difficulties arose; Korekiyo Takahashi, the agent for Japan and later Prime Minister, explained subsequently how the full loan would not have been issued as soon as his Government desired were it not for the American banker and philanthropist, Jacob H. Schiff. Takahashi stated that the persecution of the oppressed Jews in Russia—of which the barbarous massacre at Kishineff had been a recent example—was a factor impelling Schiff to back Japan. For Schiff now arranged to float half of the Japanese loan through a New York group consisting of his own house, Kuhn, Loeb and Company, the National City Bank, and the National Bank of Commerce. According to Takahashi, Tokio regarded the transaction 'as a material manifestation of the moral support of our cause by the British and American nations'. Lord Lansdowne expressed his pleasure when the Japanese loan was taken up in the United States and to Schiff, about what he had done, King Edward VII spoke appreciatively. The first issue appeared in May 1904; in London and New York under the same auspices a second flotation for £12,000,000 followed in November.[1] There were four of these altogether and in 1905, during the Portsmouth Conference,

[1] Takahashi's memorandum, Cyrus Adler, *Jacob H. Schiff*, vol. i, pp. 213–30.

Schiff's salutary advice helped Tokio make its decision for peace. The State Department must have approved of the Anglo-American loans to Japan; the assistance was of a semi-diplomatic as well as financial nature; against the wishes of the Administration it would not have been proffered by the New York banking institutions. In 1904–5 Anglo-American *haute finance* as much as Anglo-American *haute politique* was thus co-operatively attached to the Japanese side. On the one the other could not have failed to interact.

As the arms of Japan went from triumph to triumph some of the European Governments diligently kept watch to ensure that from the settlement of the war their rivals gained no special advantage. Nor did Roosevelt witness with entire ease of mind the progress of events. Of the growing power of Japan he had quickly become apprehensive; and so, while admiring her military prowess, he did not favour the expulsion of the Russians from Eastern Asia but took the view that she should merely be entitled to the same paramountcy in the Yellow Sea as the United States enjoyed in the Caribbean. In June 1904 Takahira, the Japanese Minister at Washington, and Baron Kaneko, a prominent Japanese official, told him that Japan harboured no designs on the Philippines. The mastery of Corea rather than efforts to maintain the unity of China was the goal she set herself. Roosevelt gathered from the Japanese Minister that she hoped to drive Russia out of Manchuria and return it to the Chinese; Takahira felt, however, that they might not be capable of governing it themselves. From the President's account of his talk with the Japanese spokesmen it is apparent that at the time of the Far Eastern conflict an excellent opportunity was lost to establish on firmer foundations the territorial integrity of the Chinese Empire.

> 'I said that of course if we could get a Chinese Viceroy able to keep definite order under the guarantee of the Powers in Manchuria, that would be the best outcome; but that I did not know whether this was possible, or whether the Powers would even consider such an idea. The Minister was evidently very anxious that there should be a general international agreement to guarantee the autonomy of China in Manchuria.'[1]

Such notions were widely held by Japanese statesmen before Russia had met with overwhelming defeat. Twenty-eight years later under Lord Lytton the Commission of Enquiry of the League of Nations were to advocate analogous proposals as a way of restoring from Japan herself Chinese sovereignty in Manchuria.[2] Meanwhile,

[1] Roosevelt to Spring Rice, June 13, 1904, Gwynn, *Spring Rice*, vol. i, pp. 416–19.
[2] *Report of the Commission of Enquiry, League of Nations*, 1932, pp. 130–5; also MacDonald to Lansdowne, Nov. 22, 1904, *Br. Docs.*, vol. iv, no. 57 and enclosure, pp. 64–6.

throughout 1904, Roosevelt did not wish Japan to be so victorious that she could next menace the United States. He began therefore to hint that a peace treaty should be framed, the terms of which would leave the two belligerents counterbalancing each other in the Far East.[1] And in Anglo-American relations this policy was presently to be a matter of no slight importance.

In August President Roosevelt discussed his Far Eastern programme with the German Ambassador. As the friend of Russia, however, the Wilhelmstrasse walked warily.[2] The Germans, in short, wanted to co-operate with Washington without deserting St. Petersburg; what in fact they now desired was to entice the United States from her understanding with Great Britain and thereby impair the Anglo-Japanese front. By Roosevelt's typical exuberance in conversation the Kaiser had been perhaps misled.[3] For William II was in hot pursuit of the will-o'-the-wisp of a Russo-German alliance. He feared that after the war, with France as an intermediary, the British and the Russians would attempt to combine; and such an alignment he intended to forestall by himself uniting with the Tsar— from whom, in this instance, the suggestion had emanated.

'Of course', wrote Willy to Nicky, 'the alliance would be purely defensive, exclusively directed against the European aggressor or aggressors in the form of a mutual fire insurance company against incendiarism. It is very essential that Amerika should not feel threatened by our agreement. Roosevelt, as I know, owing to the innate American dislike to all coloured races, has no special partiality for Japan although England does her utmost to work upon American opinion in favour of the Japanese. Besides the Americans have a clear perception of the indisputable fact that a powerful Japanese Empire is a lasting danger to the American Philippines.'[4]

It appears to have been the object of the German Emperor by means of this vast and comprehensive aggregation to dissolve or weaken all those new friendships with which Great Britain was endeavouring everywhere to strengthen her diplomacy. And in it, through the medium of Russia, he would not only enrol France but also, by obtaining the goodwill of the United States, undermine Anglo-American solidarity.

[1] Roosevelt to Spring Rice, Mar. 19, 1904, Gwynn, *Spring Rice*, vol. i, p. 398; Roosevelt to Spring Rice, June 13, 1904, ibid., p. 419; Jusserand, *What Me Befell*, pp. 300–1.
[2] Bülow to the Kaiser, Aug. 31, 1904, *Bülow's Letters*, pp. 72–3; also Sternburg to the German Foreign Office, Aug. 12, 1904, *Grosse Politik*, xix. 534; Dugdale, *Germ. Dip. Docs.*, vol. iii, p. 199; Bülow to Sternburg, Sept. 5, 1904, *Grosse Politik*, xix. 541; Dugdale, *Germ. Dip. Docs.*, vol. iii, p. 200.
[3] Sternburg to the German Foreign Office, Sept. 27, 1904, *Grosse Politik*, xix. 541; Dugdale, *Germ. Dip. Docs.*, vol. iii, pp. 200–1.
[4] Willy to Nicky, Oct. 30, 1904, *The Kaiser's Letters to the Tsar*, p. 130. The two Emperors corresponded in English.

At one moment his dream seemed to be nearing realization. In October 1904 the Russian Baltic Fleet fired on some British trawling vessels off the Dogger Bank and for support, during the grave crisis that followed, the Tsar turned to Germany. By Bülow a suitable treaty was thereupon drafted, but Count Lamsdorff, the Russian Minister for Foreign Affairs, refused to sign it until Russia had consulted her French ally. With Paris, however, William II never could permit prior communication as the Entente Powers would thereby be enabled to nip in the bud his long-nurtured scheme for an anti-British continental league.[1] He was therefore compelled to defer the project—and one to which he reverted at Björko in July 1905—of using his fellow-monarch to detach the French from their British friends and so destroy the post-war prospect of a general accord between Great Britain and the Dual Alliance. Germany's chief interest, the Kaiser now argued, lay in cultivating Japan and the United States.[2] But at Washington, as at Tokio, the Germans were again handicapped by their benevolent attitude towards Russia. For Theodore Roosevelt sympathized with Japan even though he did not want her to become too powerful either in the Far East or on the Pacific. And it was thus the British rather than the German camp with which, to the chagrin of the Wilhelmstrasse, the American Government had most in common.

Could the Germans achieve a better understanding with the United States and yet retain the goodwill of Russia? To do that Bülow decided on a diplomatic campaign at Washington against both the Anglo-Japanese Alliance and the Franco-British Entente. By inculcating doubts in the President as to the character of the latter grouping the Chancellor tried to prove to him that Germany, encompassed by many pitfalls, could not safely afford to antagonize her Russian friend. With St. Petersburg Berlin still sought more intimate relations; but, pursuing a double course at Washington, Bülow attempted covertly to employ the existence of the Franco-Russian Alliance as a lever with which to separate the United States from Great Britain. Upon one thing the Wilhelmstrasse was obstinately resolved: that in the Russo-Japanese struggle neither London nor Paris should mediate and make peace. Whatever qualms Russia may have betrayed about her obligations to France, she had to be deterred from moving after the war closer to the Anglo-French Entente. For in the event of mediation by one of its members

---

[1] Brandenburg, *From Bismarck*, &c., pp. 211–17; Bülow, *Memoirs 1903–1909*, pp. 123–8; also *Bülow's Letters*, pp. 74–81.
[2] The Kaiser to Bülow, Dec. 28, 1904, *Grosse Politik*, xix. 346; Dugdale, *Germ. Dip. Docs.*, vol. iii, pp. 184–5; *Bülow's Letters*, p. 90.

Germany might find herself perilously isolated: France bringing Russia and Great Britain bringing Japan into a quadruple alliance— a *bloc*, moreover, which was to be cemented territorially by the partition of the Chinese Empire. To frustrate such machinations the Wilhelmstrasse determined to exploit the ceaseless interest which Theodore Roosevelt displayed in the settlement of the Far Eastern conflict. To incite the President against the dangers of a quadruple alliance—and his distrust of Russia was a convenient handle; to push the United States into the foreground as a mediator whom none of the Chancelleries would care to offend; to convert the American Government into an instrument of German world policy—this was the purpose of Bülow's far-reaching calculations.[1] By a well-conducted attack on the alleged motives of Anglo-French diplomacy in Eastern Asia, he might yet manage to split the ranks of the English-speaking Powers.

At Washington, in applying Bülow's stratagem, no time was lost. Port Arthur, the Russian fortress on the Pacific, had fallen on January 1, 1905, and Theodore Roosevelt now hoped that Japan would not get 'puffed up with pride . . . and turn against us'.[2] For the remainder of the war these misgivings perhaps rendered the President less sceptical than usual of German apprehensions. To the State Department on January 5 the Kaiser's opinion was conveyed that some of the Powers, headed by France, were forming a strong combination directed against the Open Door and the territorial integrity of China. 'The aim of this coalition is to convince the belligerents that peace without compensation to the neutral Powers is impossible.' The United States was asked by Germany to secure assurances that no such Machiavellian designs were entertained; American intervention would 'force the Powers to show their hands'. Baron Speck von Sternburg, the German Ambassador at Washington, explained afterwards that the Kaiser was afraid of a combination between Great Britain, France, and Russia to despoil China. Had William II been perfectly frank, and how close were his actual relations with the Tsar? John Hay was mystified, but he and the President acceded to the Kaiser's request—'1st, to nail the matter with him, and 2nd, to ascertain the views of the other Powers'. Inquiries were set on foot. Without an exception the reply of the neutral Governments was in favour of the Open Door and the territorial integrity of China.[3]

[1] Bülow to the Kaiser, Dec. 24 and 26, 1904, ibid., pp. 84–8.
[2] Roosevelt to Meyer, Feb. 6, 1905, Roosevelt to Trevelyan, Mar. 9, 1905, Pringle, *Roosevelt*, p. 380.
[3] Thayer, *Hay*, vol. ii, pp. 385–8; *U.S. Foreign Relations*, 1905, pp. 1–4.

Upon Far Eastern problems there had for a number of years been
an approximation in outlook between the English-speaking Powers.
But now the Germans were telling the American Administration that,
under French guidance, Great Britain was going to reverse her
traditional policy. Without the support of British diplomacy and the
Anglo-Japanese Alliance the United States in Chinese affairs stood
helpless; should the German charge be true, a situation of the utmost
gravity would therefore at once arise. Washington and Berlin disclaimed demands for concessions and special privileges in China
which might retard a settlement of the Russo-Japanese War; but
what if the British Foreign Office should not do likewise? Lansdowne's response, however, left nothing to be desired; by him Joseph
Choate was informed that the American Government could rely on
'the full concurrence' of Great Britain; 'our assent might indeed be
looked upon in the light of a foregone conclusion'.[1] In Downing
Street, then, no trace could be found of the supposed cabal of the
Powers to partition China. 'The answers from England and Italy',
John Hay noted, 'show clearly the extent of the Kaiser's illusion.'
French adherence soon followed. At what the whole performance
meant to the Emperor William the Secretary of State confessed himself puzzled. 'But there is no possible doubt that we have scored for
China.'[2] In Berlin Count von Bülow could sum up with an equal
satisfaction. According to him the American circular had disturbed
ideas cherished by France to unite with Great Britain and Russia
for the control of the Chinese Empire.[3] It was, in fine, his belief that
he had scored for Germany. Nor of such German allegations had the
last been heard.

During the Russo-Japanese War the new interests of the United
States on the Pacific and in the Far East would have themselves
sufficed to make the American Government cast aside self-restricting
theories of rigid aloofness. By the decision of the Wilhelmstrasse to
turn to account Washington's diplomatic independence this natural
tendency was, moreover, carried a stage further. But none of these
factors would have been quite so important were it not for the dynamic personality of Theodore Roosevelt. Restless, imaginative,
didactic, prone to wide-ranging speculation upon the whole domain
of world politics, he took a much less parochial view of the international responsibilities of the United States than any of his recent
predecessors. And in the winter of 1905, as John Hay, ill in health,

[1] Lansdowne to Durand, Jan. 14, 1905, *Br. Docs.*, vol. iv, no. 61, p. 69.
[2] Thayer, *Hay*, vol. ii, pp. 387–8.
[3] Bülow to the Kaiser, Jan. 15, 1905, *Bülow's Letters*, pp. 95–8.

sank into the background, the President assumed over American foreign affairs an almost continuous direction.

With Sir Mortimer Durand, the British Ambassador, Roosevelt had never been on confidential terms. At the time of his appointment influence was again exercised in London to arrange the transference as Secretary from the St. Petersburg to the Washington Embassy of the President's old friend, Cecil Spring Rice. But the attempt failed once more and the White House may have been exhibiting its annoyance when it neglected Durand on his arrival.[1] Nor can the diplomatic consequences of that be overlooked. Theodore Roosevelt had gathered around himself a private circle which included M. Jules Jusserand and Baron Speck von Sternburg, the French and German Ambassadors. To it Sir Michael Herbert had belonged, and Anglo-American relations were affected presently by the fact that Spring Rice could not fill his vacant place. For as the President became more and more absorbed in the Far Eastern situation he grew eager to exchange ideas with the British Foreign Office. But he said that his mind and Durand's did not meet and there was no one in the Washington Embassy with whom he felt he could talk freely. At the end of 1904, through Henry White, Roosevelt therefore asked the Foreign Office whether Spring Rice, then home from Russia on leave, might pay him a visit.[2]

Meanwhile to London the President had dispatched a preliminary statement of his position. Spring Rice, to whom it was addressed, handed it over to the Foreign Office—it being likewise brought to the attention of the Prime Minister, Arthur Balfour, and his brother Gerald Balfour, the President of the Board of Trade.[3] Roosevelt appeared to be proposing collaboration with Great Britain in the Far East within the limits permitted by the American Constitution, the diplomatic traditions of the United States, and pacifist sentiment in the English-speaking democracies. By Russia, he observed, these latter had been treated badly, while, on the other hand, in Eastern Asia the objects of Japan were those of all civilized Powers. Her numerous triumphs on the field of battle were, nevertheless, a source of anxiety; Europeans and Americans might be considered 'white devils' to be beaten in their turn; and it had been discovered that by the Japanese troops the United States was regarded as the damper of

[1] *Proceedings LVIII Mass. Hist. Society*, p. 341, 'Memoir of H. C. Lodge'; Gwynn, *Spring Rice*, vol. i, pp. 358–9, 368–75; Sir Percy Sykes, *The Right Honourable Sir Mortimer Durand*, p. 274.

[2] Roosevelt to White, Dec. 27, 1904, Nevins, *White*, p. 225; also Gwynn, *Spring Rice*, vol. i, pp. 432–5.

[3] Roosevelt to Spring Rice, Dec. 27, 1904, ibid., pp. 441–6; Gerald Balfour to Spring Rice, Jan. 17, 1905, ibid., p. 449.

their hopes in the Philippines and Hawaii. The President, however, did not think that there was much chance of a post-war agreement between Russia and Japan, in which France and Germany would participate. On the Asiatic mainland the ambitions of Tokio and St. Petersburg were too profoundly opposed; while if Japan forswore these and embarked on a career of oceanic expansion she would run up against western countries already entrenched in the Pacific area. To let Japan develop to a point consonant with the safety of American —and Dutch and British—possessions but not beyond that point; to leave her strong but not too strong as a counterpoise against Russia in Eastern Asia: such was the implication of the programme which Roosevelt outlined. 'So long as Japan takes an interest in Korea, in Manchuria, in China, it is Russia which is her natural enemy.'[1] And upon this policy, thus being roughly shaped, the President was to base his case for Anglo-American co-operation. Allied to Japan, the British Government could assist him to set up a balance of power in the Far East similar to that historically maintained by Great Britain on the European continent. Since the dawn of a new era in Anglo-American understanding six or seven years may have elapsed but, from the most effective use of it, John Hay had, outside the western hemisphere, always been debarred. And now during the Russo-Japanese War combined action in a great issue of world politics was for the first time sought not by London at Washington but by Washington at London.

In Roosevelt's analysis there was nothing suggestive of disloyalty by Great Britain towards her Oriental ally. As for the conception of a Far Eastern equipoise, it might be quite consistent with the terms Japan would herself demand at the end of the war. Later, and as the German Government predicted, though not by partitioning China, Russia composed her differences with the British and Japanese; and eventually, too, Great Britain had to acquiesce in the over-weighting of the Far Eastern equilibrium so that against Germany she might the more securely uphold the European balance of power. But at the close of 1904 Japan's probable conditions for peace, as reported to the British Foreign Office, were exceedingly modest. According to Marquis Ito, Elder Statesman and a former Prime Minister, Tokio would respect the Open Door and the territorial integrity of the Chinese Empire. Manchuria was to be restored to China and policed by Chinese, perhaps under Japanese officers. This force would be managed by 'the international committee of control' who were also to have charge in the north of the internationalized

---

[1] Roosevelt to Spring Rice, Dec. 27, 1904, Gwynn, *Spring Rice*, vol. i, p. 445.

Chinese Eastern Railway.[1] Japan, in brief, would submit conditions not unlike those favoured by Roosevelt in the summer of 1904. But with the progress of her victories her terms hardened and at the Portsmouth Conference she obtained for herself all Russian rights in Manchuria's southern railway. Plans to neutralize and internationalize Manchurian railways and government were to be revived at Washington by the Taft Administration and in 1932 by the Commission of Enquiry of the League of Nations. Nevertheless at the beginning of 1905, whatever the variations in motive, American, Japanese, and British policy were by no means incompatible.

As a matter of fact Arthur Balfour had drafted a long reply to the President's communication—addressed to Spring Rice it was perhaps intended ultimately for Roosevelt's perusal—which, though evidently never sent, yet discloses his deep sympathy with any proposal for co-operation between Great Britain and the United States. Sceptical of talk about the Yellow Peril, he agreed that they should consider together what peace terms would be in harmony with their interests and how they could prevent a post-war attempt by Russia to indemnify herself at the expense of China. The Prime Minister also wondered whether by some international scheme it would be possible to make China observe her pledges and thought, above all, that her territorial integrity might best be preserved by an Anglo-American treaty. No combination could be stronger than such a union between the English-speaking Powers; the obstacles to it would, he believed, be presented not by Great Britain but by the tradition and Constitution of the United States.[2]

For Downing Street the difficulty, then, was not one of Anglo-American collaboration. The British Government were merely embarrassed by Roosevelt's invitation to depute a diplomatist of junior rank to canvass high policy when an accredited Ambassador resided at Washington. But Lansdowne did not wish to refuse the President's request and Durand was willing that conventional etiquette should be disregarded. Spring Rice, being on leave, therefore found himself free to proceed on a private visit to the American capital. Before his departure, moreover, and despite the informal nature of the mission, he was acquainted at the Foreign Office with the views of the British Government.[3] Accompanied by Durand, Spring Rice first visited Roosevelt on February 5. The guest of Henry Adams, he stayed three days in Washington. And thus the

[1] MacDonald to Lansdowne, Nov. 22, 1904, *Br. Docs.*, vol. iv, no. 57, and enclosure, pp. 64–6.
[2] Blanche Dugdale, *Balfour*, vol. i, pp. 386–8.
[3] Gwynn, *Spring Rice*, vol. i, pp. 447–9.

President, through this semi-official envoy, was able more fully to expound to British statesmen the underlying purposes of his programme for the settlement of the Russo-Japanese War.

Early in 1905 Great Britain and the United States were forming what was, in effect, a Far Eastern concert. At the end of January the British and American Governments had agreed with each other to approve of terms which were stated to be among Japan's conditions for peace. She desired to retain Port Arthur and, above all, to establish a protectorate over Corea. The latter step would, however, require a partial revision of the Anglo-Japanese Alliance, and in February the President seems to have mentioned this to Spring Rice.[1] At any rate, on his return from Washington, when he reported to the Foreign Office, the British emissary discovered that Lord Lansdowne was—as he informed Roosevelt—'very much delighted at the messages which had reached him from the President. . . . In England, of course, as Chamberlain told me very earnestly, every thinking man is convinced of the absolute necessity for England of a good understanding with America—but they know, most of them—that they had better not say so. The King'—Edward VII had sent for Spring Rice—'as much as anyone.'[2]

Did Roosevelt in February refer to the possibility of the United States becoming the Far Eastern peacemaker and inquire whether she could count on British co-operation ? That he did so would appear to be indicated by a letter to John Hay in which Spring Rice described how his chief rejoiced at the news from Washington.

'Lord Lansdowne was nervous as to outward manifestations which he was anxious to avoid. But he had absolute confidence in you, as to the diplomatic side of the question. The King was (as you know) anxious and more than anxious to do everything in his power, and in fact his enthusiasm had to be damped by constitutional reminders. I should think you could be certain that we will follow your lead and that you will find us ready and anxious to take any action which you suggest beforehand.'[3]

Great Britain and the United States were neutral Powers. Publicly, during the Russo-Japanese War, they could utter no opinion about suitable terms or the making of peace. Nevertheless, on the eve of the battle of Mukden, they had attained a general understanding— and one which the German Government would try hard, but fail, to demolish. For, whatever now happened in the peace negotiations,

---

[1] See Chapter X below.
[2] Spring Rice to Mrs. Roosevelt, Mar. 13, 1905, Gwynn, *Spring Rice*, vol. i, p. 453. Spring Rice addressed his correspondence to Mrs. Roosevelt; the President always replied.
[3] Spring Rice to Hay, Mar. 15, 1905, ibid., pp. 462–3.

the fundamental unity of British and American policy was at the core of the Far Eastern settlement.

Theodore Roosevelt had perceived that for the success of his diplomatic programme Anglo-American collaboration would be essential. But this may not have been entirely feasible without a welcome change in the domestic politics of the United States. The English-speaking peoples had liquidated the most vexatious of their mutual disputes and in 1904, during the presidential election, the customary appeal to anti-British prejudice fell unprecedentedly flat. Remaining at the White House, Roosevelt was pleased that he had not procured his votes 'by any demagogic attack upon England'. But to a correspondent he also remarked that she had been well-disposed towards the United States since their country had grown so strong as to make amicable relations 'a matter of more moment to her than to us. If we quit building our fleet, England's friendship would immediately cool'.[1] These were half-truths with which a politician parried the thrusts of his critics. The facts upon which he framed his policy were much less narrowly conceived. For, no sooner did Roosevelt contemplate intervention in international affairs out-side the western hemisphere, than he came face to face with the cardinal importance to the United States of a closer understanding between the English-speaking Powers. The President in concert with the British Government was venturing into perilous realms of world politics. And in an emergency, if concrete backing were required, could he have relied on the support of the Senate? Justifiable un-certainty about that will help to elucidate some subsequent diffidence in Downing Street towards the practice rather than the principles of Rooseveltian diplomacy.

Apart from experience gained in dealing with the United States since 1898, there were fresh grounds for such dubiety. In December 1904 the British and American Governments had signed one of the arbitration treaties which John Hay was at that time nego-tiating with foreign Powers. They were based on the Anglo-French convention of 1903 and involved no consideration of the national honour or vital interests of the contracting parties. But the Senate amended them so that, before disputes could be submitted to arbitration, its consent as well as that of the Executive would be necessary. Senators representing States which had repudiated their bonds were afraid that foreign Powers might now be able to sue for payment and, as many of these were held by Englishmen, that Great Britain, above all, would be tempted to raise her claims. In February

[1] Bishop, *Roosevelt*, vol. i, pp. 346–8; Pringle, *Roosevelt*, p. 281.

1905 the Senate therefore amended the first treaty so that recourse to arbitration was on each occasion subject to its own assent even when the matters arbitrable had previously been defined. In this way, safeguarding itself against British or other demands to arbitrate, it reduced the general conventions to futility. Mortified at what had happened, the Administration thereupon decided to drop them altogether.[1] Nor was that the only difficulty which the Upper House then created. In the same month the Senate also had emasculated a fisheries treaty with Newfoundland, and it is significant that of this particular Anglo-American problem the President, throughout 1905, soft-pedalled controversial discussion.[2] For the statesman who intervened abroad in the paramount issues of the day could afford to tolerate no insular, pedantic treatment of comparatively minor questions. Over the Hay treaties and the Newfoundland fisheries, Roosevelt's policy of Far Eastern co-operation between the English-speaking Powers was, by the intransigence of Henry Cabot Lodge and his fellow-Senators, more likely to be hampered than facilitated.

Thus once again in foreign affairs the self-regarding attitude of the Senate offered a strange contrast to the collaborative programme of the White House and the State Department. In December 1904 when the arbitration treaty was signed with Great Britain, Joseph Choate, the American Ambassador at the Court of St. James's, deemed the moment opportune to retire. Submitting his resignation to Theodore Roosevelt, he wrote that the 'friendship and goodwill between the two countries which I was instructed by President McKinley to cultivate, as my chief duty, are now apparently perfect and are, I think, certain to remain so long after you are President'.[3] Yet, to the Hay agreements, as with the arbitration treaty of 1897, prejudice against Great Britain would shortly harden senatorial opposition. 'The anti-English hostility, which is always active in this country,' one observer reported from Washington, 'asserted itself affirmatively when the old arbitration treaty was before the Senate and carried the day to real glory. It is asserting itself now by indirection, using the southern bond argument as its chief vehicle.'[4] Other factors had no doubt also come into play. Among them were partisan politics; dislike of arbitration as a pacific method for settling international

[1] *U.S. Foreign Relations*, 1904, pp. 8–9; Willis Fletcher Johnson, *America's Foreign Relations*, vol. ii, p. 365; World Peace Foundation, *Arbitration and the United States*, pp. 513–21; Bishop, *Roosevelt*, vol. i, pp. 435–6.
[2] W. Stull Holt, *Treaties defeated by the Senate*, pp. 199–200; *Correspondence of Roosevelt and Lodge*, vol. ii, pp. 173–6.
[3] Choate to Roosevelt, Dec. 12, 1904, Edward Sandford Martin, *The Life of Joseph Hodges Choate*, vol. ii, p. 263.
[4] World Peace Foundation, *Arbitration and the United States*, p. 517.

disputes; and the desire of Senators to defend their treaty-making prerogatives against the usurpations of a President who had just constituted the Dominican Republic a fiscal protectorate of the United States. But a familiar hue and cry was not inaudible. 'The Clan-na-Gael', Hay noted, 'had worked more effectively than any one thought.'[1] After all the decisive British concessions to the United States, Senators could still be led astray by irascible Anglophobe minorities. At that stage, however, the damage they might do was small. For with years of tranquillity in Anglo-American relations the ancient myths perished. Yet in 1905 Great Britain could not fashion her policy so that, reckoning on positive assistance from the United States, she might prudently take diplomatic risks with other friendly and unfriendly Powers. Across her path lay the shadow of the Senate.

On the other hand, during the winter of 1905 the current understanding about the Far East continued to be the salient feature of Anglo-American relations. At signs of goodwill between Great Britain and the United States, German diplomatists habitually looked askance. From Washington Sternburg informed Bülow that the British were promoting the idea of a naval alliance between the English-speaking peoples; that Durand's first charge was to draw them together and isolate the Germans; and that by those who controlled *The Times* the attempt would be made to poison against Germany not only the British but also the American press and public opinion. According to the Ambassador, Spring Rice had turned his visit into a skilful manœuvre for the furtherance of British interests and for exercising an influence upon the President adverse to Germany and Russia. But in point of fact Roosevelt would also perhaps soon need German co-operation at St. Petersburg to carry out his Far Eastern programme. In February, therefore, he was very confidential with Sternburg and excessively critical of some tendencies in English social and political life. Nor is it indeed improbable that the President's amazing conversational indiscretions encouraged the German Government to imagine that they could subvert Anglo-American friendship.[2] They imagined in vain. On February 14 the Paris *Figaro* had published an article which, since it suggested that the Powers of Europe ally against Japan for the partition of China, fitted in well with the campaign at Washington already undertaken by the Imperial Chancellor. In this scheme the Germans at once detected the hand of Théophile Delcassé, the Foreign Minister of France,

[1] Thayer, *Hay*, vol. ii, p. 392.
[2] Sternburg to Bülow, Feb. 10, 1905, *Grosse Politik*, xix. 570; Dugdale, *Germ. Dip. Docs.*, vol. iii, pp. 215–18.

and hastened to bring it to Roosevelt's attention. But any thought of complicity on the part of the British Government the President instantly rejected; it was inconceivable in the light of their sympathies, their commitments to Tokio, and the recent Anglo-American understanding upon the prospective character of the Far Eastern settlement at the termination of the Russo-Japanese War. Yet the Wilhelmstrasse gradually would succeed in making him suspicious of France and with her Great Britain had become closely associated.[1] To German policy frequent imputations at Washington against Delcassé were, during 1905, again and again to render service.

The desire of the Emperor William to curry the President's favour had seldom been disguised. By it, moreover, and by the endeavours of his nephew to sow distrust of Great Britain in the United States, King Edward VII was especially angered.[2] Through Henry White, on the eve of his second term in the Presidency, the British monarch sent Roosevelt an oral message of congratulation reminding him that, despite efforts at persuasion by any other ruler or Government, Great Britain was the best friend of the United States; with the American nation, as in no other country, her Sovereign and people alike shared a community of interests and feelings.[3] The Inauguration took place on March 4, 1905, and for it Edward VII dispatched to Roosevelt a letter of the most cordial good wishes accompanied by a miniature of Walter Hampden out of the royal collection at Windsor.[4]

When the letter and gift were handed to the President by the British Ambassador they evoked from him a highly satisfactory statement upon Anglo-American relations. Roosevelt assured Durand 'of his firm resolve to stand in with us'. He said he would never take the Kaiser seriously and hinted at a view he then held that Englishmen exaggerated the significance of German naval expansion. Agreeing that the Anglo-American understanding about Japan's terms should be kept secret, the President asked in particular that nothing be allowed to reach the ear of the Wilhelmstrasse. 'He told me', the Ambassador reported to Lansdowne, 'the Emperor had been gravely alarmed at the idea of a Franco-Russo-Anglo-Japanese Alliance against him, also that the Emperor wished him to believe that the French and Russians had vainly tried to bring Germany into a

---

[1] Sternburg to the German Foreign Office, Feb. 17, 1905, *Grosse Politik*, xix. 575; Dugdale, *Germ. Dip. Docs.*, vol. iii, pp. 203–4; Roosevelt to Tower, Feb. 16, 1905, Tyler Dennett, *Roosevelt and the Russo-Japanese War*, pp. 82–3.

[2] Lascelles to Knollys, Mar. 24, 1905, Lee, *Edward VII*, vol. ii, p. 336.

[3] White to Roosevelt, Feb. 25, 1905, Nevins, *White*, p. 241.

[4] Edward VII to Roosevelt, Feb. 20, 1905, Lee, *Edward VII*, vol. ii, pp. 429–33; Bishop, *Roosevelt*, vol. ii, pp. 261–2; also Gwynn, *Spring Rice*, vol. i, pp. 452–3.

coalition against England.'[1] From Roosevelt's last remark may be deduced the extent to which William II, as coached by Bülow, was attempting to hoodwink the United States. Although the meeting at Björko of the two Emperors still lay ahead, the German Chancellor in the autumn of 1904 had himself drafted a treaty of alliance with the Tsar and the disappointment of his royal master had been intense when the Russian Government, mindful of their obligations to France, raised insuperable difficulties. Meanwhile the picture of his attitude towards Great Britain which the President painted to Durand appeared much less dismal than that being reproduced at Berlin by Baron von Sternburg.

The Ambassador's account was corroborated by Roosevelt's own letter of acknowledgement to Edward VII. To the King he in his turn sent a gift, a copy of some of his studies on the American West. 'I absolutely agree with you', the President observed, 'as to the importance, not only to ourselves but to all the free peoples of the civilized world, of a constantly growing friendship and understanding between the English-speaking peoples. One of the gratifying things in what has occurred during the last decade has been the growth in this feeling of good will.' Their larger interests and fundamental traits of character were the same; but, as he also added, of problems affecting the United States, the internal ones were gravest. 'In matters outside our borders, we are chiefly concerned, first with what goes on south of us, second with affairs in the Orient; and in both cases our interests are identical with yours.'[2] Of the progress that had been achieved in Anglo-American solidarity there could be no more authoritative recognition than this. To Roosevelt's mind the identity of interests between Great Britain and the United States, in the Far East as in the western hemisphere, seemed perfectly clear. Divergencies would, however, soon unfold themselves and in the summer of 1905 the attainment of common policies by the English-speaking Governments was to be an unexpected task of singular complexity.

[1] Durand to Lansdowne, Mar. 10, 1905, Sykes, *Durand*, pp. 280–1; Gwynn, *Spring Rice*, vol. i, pp. 453–5.
[2] Roosevelt to Edward VII, Mar. 9, 1905, Bishop, *Roosevelt*, vol. ii, pp. 262–3; Lee, *Edward VII*, vol. ii, p. 432.

IX

GREAT BRITAIN AND ROOSEVELTIAN DIPLOMACY

In the spring of 1905 the first Moroccan crisis was superimposed upon the diplomacy of the Russo-Japanese War, and as a result Anglo-American relations were swung into an ever-widening circuit of world politics. Since the close of the nineteenth century, in their alliance negotiations with Great Britain, the German Government had confidently reckoned that from her, Franco-British differences being eternally insoluble, they would in the long run be able to extract better terms. A minatory ruler, the incessant naval agitation combined with the vast land-power of Germany on the neighbouring continent, policies which again in 1905 and 1906 showed feeble insight into foreign psychology: all these factors, in the circumstances of British isolation in Europe, falsified the complacent German assumption. On April 8, 1904, the Entente Cordiale had been announced with a series of agreements composing Anglo-French disputes. Of them the principal one gave Great Britain a free hand in Egypt and France a free hand in Morocco—there also being secret articles to pave the way in the event of a future partition of the Shereefian Empire between Spain and France. With Italy, moreover, the latter had arranged matters beforehand and they were completed in October 1904 when Paris and Madrid signed a convention. Among historians the precise connotation of the Anglo-French secret articles, their ethical no less than their political import, is a theme of interminable debate.[1] At the time, however, their existence was probably unknown and in 1904 it looked as if the new friendship between Paris and London would be accepted by Germany with docility.

But no sooner had British objections been removed than France resolved to tighten her grip on Morocco. For an immediate pretext she could point to disorder in a land where her interests were not only large but which also was adjacent to her Algerian possession. In Berlin, however, the French plea rang hollow. For although he had obtained the special consent of other interested Powers, Delcassé had rashly omitted to do so with the one most capable of causing trouble. Germany now feared that in Morocco her commercial rights would be ignored and her claims as a signatory to the Madrid Convention of 1880 overridden. But at bottom her discomfiture sprang from the

---

[1] Anglo-French Agreement, *Br. Docs.*, vol. ii, pp. 385–95; also *Camb. Hist. of Br. Foreign Policy*, vol. iii, p. 340; Fay, *Origins of the War*, vol. i, pp. 162–5; Spender, *Fifty Years of Europe*, pp. 216–17.

unanticipated menace of an Anglo-French partnership. For the Entente shattered the foundation upon which the Wilhelmstrasse had framed its policy—that fundamentally Great Britain was more hostile to the Dual than to the Triple Alliance—and threatened to dislodge Germany from her continental pre-eminence. In 1904 Lansdowne and other Englishmen may have regarded friendship with France not as the forging of an immensely powerful diplomatic instrument but as a mere settlement of current differences. Yet British Ministers had themselves discussed with the German Government the project of an alliance and by them one with Japan had actually been concluded. From Downing Street the Chancelleries must therefore have received disavowals of positive political motives with an explicable incredulity. In appearance, if not in reality, Great Britain had chosen to terminate her European isolation by grouping herself with France rather than Germany. To sunder this alignment and safeguard their own prestige and diplomatic preponderance was the task to which henceforth the German Government dedicated themselves ;[1] and by contesting French conduct in Morocco they could undertake it the more readily because about that their protest did not lack justification. In March 1905 with the defeat at Mukden of France's ally, Russia, the opportunity for the first stroke had arrived; so far as European controversies were concerned she could for the moment carry little weight. By Germany in the battered crucible of Morocco the experiment of dissolving the Anglo-French Entente would now be essayed.

Doubting the wisdom of Bülow's calculations, the Emperor William was reluctant to follow his charted course. He nevertheless allowed himself to be overruled and on March 31, disembarking at Tangier, delivered a resounding speech in which he upheld the sovereignty of the Sultan of Morocco. Directed at France, this gesture was deliberately provocative. Would the Quai d'Orsay, as Berlin peremptorily demanded, consent to an international conference on Moroccan affairs ? Delcassé retorted in the negative. Would the British Government stand behind him in refusing such a conference ? For the execution of their Moroccan and Egyptian arrangements the two Powers were pledged to mutual 'diplomatic support', while, in any case, because of an agreement signed with her, Great Britain could not permit France to suffer. Lansdowne accordingly urged Delcassé to resist the German demand. And thus almost at once the Entente began to be something more than a simple adjustment of Franco-British difficulties. Without legal ties, as a consequence of the German challenge, it gradually assumed the outward character of a

[1] Bülow, *Memoirs 1903–1909*, p. 104.

defensive alliance. The spirit of war was spreading from the Orient, and Europe watched breathlessly.

At this juncture Germany addressed herself to the United States. She wanted Great Britain to influence France in favour of a Moroccan conference and fancied that Rooseveltian pressure at London would bring her success. To accomplish its object the Wilhelmstrasse fingered the chords of Anglo-American friendship. The method employed was to frighten the President about the poor prospects for a suitable settlement of the Russo-Japanese War if, as the result of a diplomatic reverse in Europe, the German Government were unable to help him in the Far East; and they underlined their thesis by warning him constantly against the danger of a coalition of Powers to appropriate and partition the Chinese Empire. For the Germans argued that in both China and Morocco the Open Door was confronted with the same enemies; the integrity of the Chinese Empire would first be preserved by preventing the subjugation of the North African territory. Roosevelt had his theory of a Far Eastern balance of power; Germany implied that the British and French by demolishing the balance in Europe were liable also to extinguish any hope of a collateral equilibrium in Eastern Asia. The scheme of the Wilhelmstrasse was to exploit the interest of the United States in the Far East and either to wean her away from Great Britain or, if that proved impossible, to use Anglo-American understanding for the advancement of German world policy.

More than three weeks before the Kaiser's speech at Tangier Bülow had ascertained that in Morocco Roosevelt would not oppose the legitimate aspirations of Germany.[1] Entirely misjudging the effect on the British Government of his master's challenge, he expected that their assent to a conference of the Powers would isolate France and compel her to yield. For with the President as a medium of persuasion the Chancellor sought to make them realize that in Morocco their trading interests, like those of Germany and the United States, were bound up with the Open Door and the maintenance of the *status quo*. At the proposed conference American sympathy with that policy would, he believed, bring Great Britain into line.[2] The road from the Wilhelmstrasse to Downing Street lay through Washington and in pursuing it the Germans spared no effort.

The Moroccan situation was, then, but one aspect of the larger problem to be solved by the suggested conference of the Powers.

---

[1] Dennis, *Adventures*, pp. 513–14; Roosevelt to Whitelaw Reid, April 28, 1906, Bishop, *Roosevelt*, vol. i, p. 468; also ibid., pp. 467–505.

[2] Bülow to the Kaiser, Apr. 4, 1905, *Bülow's Letters*, pp. 121–3; also ibid., pp. 114–15.

For through it Bülow sought also to crush everywhere the supposed designs of the Entente—designs which the United States would discover to be as iniquitous in China as they were for Germany nearer home. At the beginning of April Roosevelt was notified that William II had observed 'a close connection between France and England in the questions of the Far East and Morocco'; yet in the latter country British commercial and political interests were not those of a Franco-Spanish monopoly. The Emperor therefore thought that they had been renounced as the price of French assistance in China and more especially for the control of the Yangtse Valley. Nor was that the whole story. If Germany submitted meekly to the bullying of France over Morocco, Paris might next demand a revision of the Treaty of Frankfort. It was, however, still possible to protect the rights of others since the Kaiser understood that from Great Britain the Quai d'Orsay could rely only on 'diplomatic support'.[1]

About the President's response the Germans were over-sanguine. 'Through this attitude of America', Bülow recorded, 'England will be obliged to change her tone.' But, instead of acting at London as the Emperor requested, the Government of the United States assured France during the middle of the month that if she rejected the proposal for a Moroccan conference they would do the same.[2] Meanwhile from Berlin Roosevelt was being told that upon his views depended the decision of the British Cabinet.[3] No longer backed by Great Britain, France must relent. Would the President, as the Wilhelmstrasse so feverishly begged him to do, advise Downing Street to adopt the German plan? Could he, perhaps, be used as a wedge to split the Entente Cordiale?

The Germans did not only delude themselves about the extent to which Washington would swallow their anti-British allegations. They also over-estimated the possible influence of the United States on Lansdowne's policy. No one wished to minimize the value of Anglo-American friendship; the Moroccan crisis was, however, becoming as much a British as a French quarrel with Germany. Roosevelt would have to present a very strong case indeed before Great Britain could surrender to Berlin her support of France; and for such an undertaking he had neither desire nor inclination. By him British collaboration was required in the settlement he envisaged to terminate the Russo-Japanese War; obviously he could not afford to associate

---

[1] Sternburg to Roosevelt, Apr. 5, 1905, Dennis, *Adventures*, pp. 514–16; Bishop, *Roosevelt*, vol. i, pp. 468–9.
[2] Bülow to Kühlmann, Apr. 6, 1905, *Bülow's Letters*, p. 123; Jusserand, *What Me Befell*, pp. 313–15.
[3] Sternburg to Roosevelt, Apr. 13, 1905, Dennis, *Adventures*, p. 516.

himself with Germany against Great Britain and France—even if he were so disposed—on behalf of the Shereefian Empire; for its sake— and in it American interests were meagre—his Far Eastern programme might be shipwrecked irretrievably. On the other hand, the President also needed the goodwill of William II if only because of the service he could render in securing eventual Russian consent for the peace-making contemplated in Eastern Asia; to have turned down the Germans altogether would have thus been equally inexpedient. Towards the end of April Roosevelt consequently endeavoured to steer a middle course. For he now promised Germany to make inquiries of the British Government about their attitude towards the Moroccan situation;[1] and these, in the absence from Washington of Roosevelt and Hay, were left to Secretary Taft. The purpose of the United States was to obtain information but not to express an opinion; to play an impartial role and yet contribute to the slackening of Anglo-German tension. 'If we find that it will make the English suspicious,' the President warned Taft, '—that is, will make them think we are acting as decoy ducks for Germany—why, we shall have to drop the business.'[2] The procedure he intended to follow would be considerably more limited in scope than the American advocacy of a Moroccan conference for which the Wilhelmstrasse petitioned. The fact remained that in Downing Street any move of this sort was doomed inevitably to a frigid welcome.

For one thing, although anxious to uphold Anglo-American understanding, the British Foreign Secretary betrayed uneasiness as to Roosevelt's proficiency in the actual conduct of current diplomatic transactions. Early in April Lansdowne had been worried about the effect on St. Petersburg, and especially on Tokio, of the President's premature and imprudent efforts to start negotiations for peace;[3] and such a preliminary appraisal of his skill in mediating between Russia and Japan could not but permeate the almost simultaneous treatment of Moroccan affairs. American intervention in the broader issues of world politics was a novelty of exceptional significance; in the eyes of a cautious Foreign Office it had, nevertheless, still to prove its full capacity. For Great Britain, moreover, the guiding principle at that time was a tenacious fidelity to those of her friends who were under fire. Anything which touched French and Japanese policies— particularly if it emanated from Berlin—affected British interests as well. Nor did Lansdowne believe that the United States and Japan

---

[1] Roosevelt to Sternburg, Apr. 20, 1905, Bishop, *Roosevelt*, vol. i, pp. 473–4.
[2] Roosevelt to Taft, Apr. 20, 1905, ibid., pp. 471–3.
[3] Lansdowne to Hardinge, Apr. 3, 1905, Newton, *Lansdowne*, p. 322.

were likely to be misled by the endeavour of the Germans to ingratiate themselves with these two countries.[1] The truth would seem to be that, by the formation of the Anglo-French Entente and the victories of her Japanese ally, the diplomatic self-confidence of Great Britain, so badly shaken during the South African War, was steadily being restored. If the British Government were alienated elsewhere, Roosevelt could not succeed with his programme in the Far East. At any rate Downing Street now felt itself in a position to rebuff the President's awkward inquiry. By London he certainly would not be encouraged to assist the Germans in a contest throughout which Lansdowne counselled Delcassé to maintain a bold front.

This was evident at the end of April immediately after the visit of Roosevelt's representative to the British Ambassador. Taft spoke of the German fear that 'England is going to support France in some important declaration of policy with regard to Morocco'. As for the President, he sought only to improve relations between Germany and Great Britain and to dissipate the idea that the one meant to attack the other. Durand, however, denied British apprehensions on that score; even had they wished to do so the Germans were much too weak at sea to make the attempt. The United States, Taft explained, 'does not care a cent about Morocco'; between Germany and France she did not have the slightest desire to take sides. 'My impression is', the Ambassador cabled to Lansdowne, 'that President wants to know your views about the situation in Morocco, probably for communication to German Emperor.'[2]

To Durand's message the British Foreign Secretary replied with vigour. 'So far as we are concerned,' the Ambassador was informed, 'you may safely reassure President, we have not and never have had any idea of attacking Germany, nor do we anticipate that she will be so foolish as to attack us. There is at this moment so far as I am aware no subject of dispute between the two Powers, or any reason why their relations should not be of a friendly description.' Roosevelt, in brief, would be asked courteously not to interfere; whatever Anglo-American goodwill signified it scarcely could become a roundabout agency for the exercise, through Washington, of German pressure upon the Entente. One further remark of Lansdowne's dealt with the Moroccan question in a manner which critics of the secret articles may consider somewhat disingenuous; for he asserted that the Anglo-French agreement 'contained nothing detrimental' to the interests of other countries. According to him the attitude of France, as contrasted

[1] Lansdowne to Lascelles, Apr. 9, 1905, ibid., p. 334.
[2] Durand to Lansdowne, Apr. 26, 1905, *Br. Docs.*, vol. iii, no. 82, pp. 67–8.

with that of Germany, was very forbearing and conciliatory. Nor could the Foreign Secretary understand why any international complication should be created unless the German Government were 'determined to take advantage of what was at most a diplomatic oversight in order to make mischief or to disturb the *status quo*, e.g., by demanding cession of a Moorish port'. Thus British countered German accusations at Washington and Lansdowne dismissed Delcassé's previous neglect of Germany as a paltry excuse for the dangerous unrest into which Europe had so abruptly been plunged. By him Durand was admonished finally 'to say nothing which could be interpreted as an invitation to the President to act as mediator between us and Germany'.[1] Instigated by Berlin, the offer of good offices from the United States met with a firm refusal.

Roosevelt had been politely snubbed. For the British Ambassador made it clear to Taft—and the fruitless outcome of the American effort was communicated to Baron Speck von Sternburg—that against Germany his Government were giving France whole-hearted support. The elaborate calculations of the Wilhelmstrasse that the President would urge Lansdowne, who in turn could induce Delcassé, to consent to a Moroccan conference were patently fallacious. Durand chided Roosevelt for paying heed to Potsdam. 'He said', Taft wrote to the President at the beginning of May, 'that they in England were quite familiar with the vagaries of the German Emperor and understood how your anxiety might be aroused by his extraordinary suspicions and unfounded imaginings.'[2] The gibe penetrated. As a result of what had happened Roosevelt now did his best to emphasize to Spring Rice, to the French Ambassador, and to Senator Lodge— soon to be in England—that he could not be deceived by the Kaiser.[3] In so doing he was, even on general grounds, unfeignedly sincere. But in the spring of 1905, with the approach of the long-awaited negotiations to settle Far Eastern affairs, he found it all the more necessary to combat the belief, prevalent in the highest British quarters, that he had fallen victim to the wiles of William II. When later, and again prompted by Germany, the President undertook further steps during the Moroccan crisis they were, it may be noted, in the direction of Paris and away from London.

Throughout May there was still no conference in sight. After the

---

[1] Lansdowne to Durand, Apr. 27, 1905, *Br. Docs.*, vol. iii, no. 83, p. 68.

[2] Taft to Roosevelt, May 2, 1905, Dennett, *Roosevelt and the Russo-Japanese War*, pp. 184–5.

[3] Roosevelt to Spring Rice, May 13, 1905, Gwynn, *Spring Rice*, vol. i, pp. 469–71; Jusserand, *What Me Befell*, p. 267; Roosevelt to Lodge, May 15, 1905, *Correspondence of Roosevelt and Lodge*, vol. ii, p. 123. 'Undoubtedly', he observed, 'with Russia weakened Germany feels it can be fairly insolent within the borders of Europe,' ibid.

Kaiser's speech at Tangier an agreement to convene one would have signalized the triumph of German diplomacy over the Entente and to that Great Britain could not tamely submit. None the less, unabashed by the failure of the recent American inquiry, Germany persisted on the course she had chosen. The dismemberment of China, Anglo-French policy in Morocco, the dangers to Washington and Berlin alike of a new grouping of the Powers: such were the topics of the impassioned messages with which the Emperor untiringly bombarded the White House. Time and again Roosevelt was assured that, since in accepting a conference the British would indubitably follow his example, the solution for all these problems lay in his hands.[1] Meanwhile, under the guidance of the Wilhelmstrasse, the Sultan of Morocco himself put forward the German suggestion. Upon how they should treat it a definite decision by France, Great Britain, and the United States could no longer be shelved.

At the beginning of June Whitelaw Reid, newly appointed as American Ambassador to the Court of St. James's, presented his letters of credence. With him the President sent word of his pleasure that on the major diplomatic questions the English-speaking Powers were so much in accord, and he expected that this satisfactory state of affairs would continue.[2] Anglo-American understanding was instantly reflected in the way the two Governments handled the Sultan's proposal. Lansdowne had resolved to discourage it and he had heard indirectly that the United States did not favour it either.[3] Having told the French Ambassador that he would try to persuade her to reject the proposal, Lansdowne at once discussed it with Whitelaw Reid. Since she was represented at Tangier the United States would be concerned in the matter. To the British Foreign Secretary the proposal seemed ill-advised; he could in fact conceive of no procedure less likely to bring about the reforms needed by Morocco than a conference of ten or a dozen Powers, some of whom were without any real interest in the country. 'We should', he said, 'certainly oppose it.' How was it regarded by the United States? With the views that had been conveyed to him the American Ambassador expressed 'general concurrence' and cabled to Washington Lansdowne's opinion of the Moroccan proposal 'as unfortunate, and as possibly planned to embarrass France'.[4] For their dissident

---

[1] Bishop, *Roosevelt*, vol. i, pp. 469–71; German memorandum, May 31, 1905, Dennis, *Adventures*, p. 517.
[2] Lansdowne to Durand, June 5, 1905, *Br. Docs.*, vol. iv, no. 75, p. 82.
[3] Lansdowne to Bertie, June 5, 1905, ibid., vol. iii, no. 109, p. 89.
[4] Lansdowne to Durand, June 5, 1905, ibid., no. 110, p. 90; Bishop, *Roosevelt*, vol. i, p. 475.

policies Great Britain and Germany were each seeking Roosevelt's approval. What was the American attitude?

At Washington the German Government enlisted no support. To their Ambassador the President had observed that so long as France objected the United States could not adhere to the proposal for a conference of the Powers. This news was wired by Durand to Lansdowne on June 5;[1] and then for the next few days Europe reverberated with the fall of Delcassé. For French antagonism to the suggested conference he had been primarily responsible and, as the peril of war intensified, its Foreign Minister was overthrown by a panic-stricken nation. On June 7 Whitelaw Reid confirmed the stand adopted by his Government. To Lansdowne the American Ambassador was authorized to repeat what Roosevelt had said in Washington to Sternburg and Jusserand—'that he did not see how the United States could take part in any Conference as to Morocco unless France acquiesced'. And at that stage the common Anglo-American outlook manifested itself by further talk between Whitelaw Reid and the Foreign Secretary about the Moroccan situation and the effect upon it of Delcassé's resignation. 'We agreed', Lansdowne recorded, 'that in the circumstances it would be better to "mark time" so far as the proposed Conference was concerned.'[2] Against Great Britain and France, German diatribes in Washington were for the moment of no avail. The United States was waiting to take her cue from Paris.[3]

But now French and American policy underwent a decisive change. In Paris Delcassé's portfolio had been assumed by Maurice Rouvier, the Prime Minister of the Republic; Cabinet and people alike recoiled from the prospect of a rupture with Germany; to the Sultan's proposal, given certain conditions, Rouvier and his colleagues might be not unwilling to accede. They claimed German recognition of the special rights of France in Morocco, acknowledgement by the Wilhelmstrasse that her existing arrangements with other Powers were valid; but, provided Berlin and Paris could agree in advance upon a programme for the conference, Rouvier would yield to the German demand. From London the French retreat was witnessed with feelings of surprise and regret not untinged with scorn.[4] Before this occurred, by Rooseveltian mediation between the disputants, Anglo-American friendship might have been acutely strained. But now

---

[1] Lansdowne to Cambon, June 6, 1905, *Br. Docs.*, vol. iii, no. 112, p. 91.

[2] Lansdowne to Durand, June 7, 1905, ibid., no. 113, p. 91.

[3] Jusserand to the French Foreign Office, June 6, 1905, Jusserand, *What Me Befell*, pp. 316–17; Sternburg to the German Foreign Office, June 8, 1905, *Grosse Politik*, xx. 421; Dugdale, *Germ. Dip. Docs.*, vol. iii, pp. 230–1.

[4] Lee, *Edward VII*, vol. ii, p. 344; Newton, *Lansdowne*, p. 341; also *Br. Docs.*, vol. iii, no. 152, pp. 118–19.

at Paris, Entente solidarity having suddenly been relaxed, it had become possible for the President to work towards European assuagement behind Lansdowne's back. For in no other fashion could Anglo-American understanding have escaped altogether unscathed. The French might surrender of their own volition; American pressure to make them do so would have been deemed in London an unwarranted interference with the Franco-British partnership. And thus, too, for the first time in a major diplomatic crisis, Great Britain might have found herself on one side, the United States and Germany on the other. Privately disappointed at the fate of Delcassé, the British Government still openly opposed the coveted concession. That his activities should not come to their notice Roosevelt in the succeeding weeks doubtless took precautions. As soon as Delcassé resigned Germany accepted the Sultan's invitation.[1] The initiative being left thenceforth by Great Britain to France, the Quai d'Orsay and the Wilhelmstrasse proceeded with their negotiations, the President of the United States threw his weight into the scales, and in the end all the interested Powers consented to participate in a Moroccan conference.

On June 7 Whitelaw Reid had shared Lansdowne's view that upon the Sultan's proposal it would be well to 'mark time'. But instead of doing this or continuing to follow in the footsteps of France, the head of his Government shortly attempted to take the lead and sway her in the framing of policy. What altered the American attitude? The President was spurred into action by a sensational message from Germany that the Entente might begin a general war—one in which the partition of China would be involved—just when he sought to make peace between Russia and Japan and with British help establish in the Far East a self-protective balance of power. The Germans charged, as they had been doing for six months, that Great Britain had become implicated in a plot which, if carried out, must have undermined the bases of Anglo-American co-operation and ruined his own programme for settling East Asiatic affairs. That Roosevelt hearkened at last to their asseverations may in some degree have been due to the fact that they synchronized with British hesitancy to urge his ideas upon Japan in the negotiations now pending with Russia.[2] For without assistance from Downing Street the President's Far Eastern endeavours would be rendered less certain of fulfilment—with the contentions of the German Government being

[1] Bunsen to Lansdowne, June 8, 1905, ibid., no. 115, p. 91.
[2] State Department to Whitelaw Reid, June 15, 1905, Dennett, *Roosevelt and the Russo-Japanese War*, p. 211.

correspondingly endorsed. They had, moreover, been awakening his distrust of Delcassé, whose intrigues were supposedly intended to bring about the failure of American intervention so that Great Britain and France, promoting their own selfish interests, might become the Russo-Japanese peacemakers.[1] On his course Roosevelt was, then, to a considerable extent impelled by anxiety to repress the outbreak of a European war which, if the Germans were correct, would have stultified his diplomacy in the Orient. For although he still needed her support, his faith in Great Britain had sensibly been impaired. After the fall of Delcassé, when he advised France to adopt the proposal for a Moroccan conference, the President intervened in the rivalries of Europe that he might the more securely achieve the peace settlement for which he was striving in the Far East.

The memorandum of June 11, submitted to Roosevelt by the German Ambassador, fully exemplified the tactics at Washington to which his Government had resorted. In theme, assailing the world-wide designs of Great Britain and France, it encircled the globe. The logical inference to be drawn from it was that, with Germany repulsed by the British and French over the Moroccan question, the United States would single-handed be unable to defend against the Entente the threatened integrity of the Chinese Empire.

> 'Mr. Rouvier (who has shown himself distinctly friendly to Germany and has been opposing Mr. Delcassé) has indirectly informed the German Chargé d'Affaires in Paris that England has made a formal offer to France to enter into an offensive and defensive alliance with England which would be directed against Germany.'

This, however, French Ministers had not as yet accepted; they preferred rather to tempt Germany into an agreement by intimating that she might be granted a slice of Moroccan territory. But if the Germans did not assent, and being pledged to the Sultan they were honour-bound to reject a French bribe, the Entente would become a military alliance.

> 'My people', the Kaiser declared, 'are sure that England would now back France by force of arms in a war against Germany, not on account of Morocco, but on account of Germany's policy in the Far East. The combined naval forces of England and France would undoubtedly smash the German navy and give England, France, Japan and Russia a more free hand in the Far East, and Russia might try to cede a portion of China to Japan as a war indemnity, instead of parting with the island of Saghalien. The previous destruction of the German navy undoubtedly would be welcomed by these powers.'

[1] Howe, *J. F. Rhodes*, pp. 122–3; Gwynn, *Spring Rice*, vol. ii, p. 10.

It was, none the less, also stated that the French were then displaying a more conciliatory spirit and the British Government had asked for time to consider the Sultan's proposal. William II therefore again implored the President to serve the cause of peace by hinting in London and Paris that he thought a conference would furnish the best means of solving the problem. 'In case you should not feel inclined to take this step the Emperor believes that your influence could prevent England from joining a Franco-German war, started by the aggressive policy of France in Morocco.'[1] The Wilhelmstrasse aimed with care and deliberation. For, from their European target, these shots ricochetted on to the whole fabric of American Far Eastern diplomacy.

Untrue as the German tale may have been about the attitude of Great Britain in Eastern Asia, it was not entirely groundless with regard to European affairs. Fantastically distorted, it sprang from the desire of the British Government to have a general discussion with the French 'in anticipation of any complications to be apprehended' at that critical juncture. Delcassé favoured such consultation, but Rouvier's Cabinet, terrified of Germany, shrank back and the Foreign Minister, as the Kaiser insisted, had to relinquish his post.[2] What the French Government then declined so hastily they were urgently to request seven months later. It was, furthermore, a curious sense of loyalty to the Entente which allowed a report of Lansdowne's exceedingly confidential overtures to reach the receptive ear of the Wilhelmstrasse. In Berlin, to Bülow and Holstein, the British Ambassador at once denied that an offensive-defensive alliance could have been tendered; King Edward VII pronounced the story 'nearly as absurd as it is false'; and on June 16 the British Foreign Secretary assured the German Ambassador that Great Britain and France had not been conspiring against Germany. The official contradiction of the rumour Count Metternich accepted 'unreservedly'.[3] But at Washington the Germans were not likely to retract their allegations since, by switching these sinister currents on to the White House, they had managed finally to move the Rooseveltian machinery.

The President was now convinced that a European war might be imminent. This calamity, as he afterwards recollected, he tried to

[1] Sternburg to Roosevelt, June 11, 1905, Bishop, *Roosevelt*, vol. i, pp. 476–7.

[2] *Br. Docs.*, vol. iii, nos. 94 and 95, pp. 76–8; also André Maurois, *King Edward and His Times*, pp. 172–7; Maurice Paléologue, *The Turning Point*, pp. 246, 248–50, 258, 261–6; G. P. Gooch, *Before the War*, vol. i, pp. 56–61, 175–81.

[3] Lascelles to Lansdowne, June 12, 1905, *Br. Docs.*, vol. iii, nos. 97 and 98, pp. 79–82; Lansdowne to Lascelles, June 16, 1905, ibid., no. 99, pp. 82–3; also chap. xviii, ibid., pp. 72–87.

stave off not only for the sake of France and civilization but also because of his own Far Eastern peacemaking. Besides, he was at that moment seized with a sudden fit of indignation against the British Government for pushing the Quai d'Orsay to an extreme; France, he argued, would bear the brunt of the struggle on land while the Royal Navy swept the seas.[1] Roosevelt spoke therefore to the French Ambassador about the German message and said he was not going to approach Great Britain. He thus would show his esteem for France and indicate how little he wanted to diminish her role or to separate the Entente partners. Although indisposed to take the Kaiser seriously, he advised Rouvier to be prudent. The President wondered whether to agree to a conference which must have negligible results would not be a lesser evil than the offer—repudiated by the French—of a German zone of influence in Morocco.[2]

Since the Moroccan crisis arose in the first instance from a Franco-German question it was quite proper that Roosevelt should turn to Paris rather than London. But the campaign at Washington conducted by the Wilhelmstrasse had been concentrated no less on the nefarious character of British ambitions. In all likelihood the President preferred to deal with Paris instead of with London because of Lansdowne's refusal in April to countenance his intervention between Germany and Great Britain; by another similar rebuff the Anglo-American concert, on which he was relying for the consummation of his Far Eastern policy, would have been damaged irrecoverably. And so to preserve amicable relations with Downing Street and yet thwart possible British designs in Europe and Eastern Asia, Roosevelt probably resolved to exercise his persuasive powers upon the French alone. He did this, moreover, just when it appeared that, if Berlin acquiesced substantially beforehand in the maintenance by France of her Moroccan interests, the Quai d'Orsay might consent to a conference and soothe Germany's ruffled susceptibilities. Galvanized into action by an Anglophobe canard from William II, the President was labouring for a proposal the acceptance of which would present German diplomacy with a spectacular victory.

Towards the end of June the negotiations were making slow progress and agreement between Berlin and Paris seemed still distant. Lansdowne continued to disapprove of the Sultan's proposal, but the Germans believed that Roosevelt was now supporting them.[3] In any

---

[1] Bishop, *Roosevelt*, vol. i, pp. 475–7.
[2] Jusserand to the French Foreign Office, June 14, 1905, Jusserand, *What Me Befell*, pp. 317–18; Bishop, *Roosevelt*, vol. i, pp. 477–8; also Paléologue, *The Turning Point*, pp. 275–6, 278.
[3] *Br. Docs.*, vol. iii, pp. 96–100; Sternburg to Roosevelt, June 18, 1905, Bishop,

event it is hardly credible that the British Government were aware of what the Emperor had alleged at the White House; apprised of such insidious calumnies they could never have remained silent. Nor did the Quai d'Orsay venture to acquaint its partner with the news that the President was advocating a Moroccan conference. At London the French Ambassador told Lansdowne on June 21 that William II had been in communication with Roosevelt. The latter, however, was quoted as merely stating that he would be guided by the decision of those Powers who possessed special interests in Morocco, and notably by that of France.[1] So far as Downing Street knew, the attitude of the United States—aloof and passive, if sympathetic towards the French—had undergone no change. More than a week had elapsed since the President was incited by the Germans to recommend at Paris a course which Great Britain condemned. Of his conversion the British Government were evidently uninformed and likewise ignorant of the fact that their supposed policy in Europe and Eastern Asia had in the most recent exchanges become a vital element.

From the fall of Delcassé the expected relief of Franco-German tension was not forthcoming. The Quai d'Orsay appeared ready to accept the 'idea of a conference', but the Wilhelmstrasse, inscrutable and bellicose, could not be satisfied. To avert the danger of war the French Government appealed hurriedly to Washington. It was now Germany's turn to be checked and Roosevelt endeavoured to flatter the Kaiser into acquiescence.[2] But the Wilhelmstrasse, discontented with Rouvier's deft ambiguities, wished France also to take a straight line; on June 24 it accordingly again asked for a Moroccan conference, even though a preliminary programme had not yet been adopted.[3] Next day at the White House the French Government redoubled their efforts. Suggesting to the President what could be done 'in order to avoid the break with which Germany would seem to desire to menace us', Jusserand elicited from him a promise to remonstrate with William II in terms severely appropriate to the gravity of the position.[4]

Roosevelt did this at once when he told the German Ambassador

---

Roosevelt, vol. i, p. 481. There is nothing in the relevant British and American sources to confirm Sternburg's report—*Grosse Politik*, xx. 442; Dugdale, *Germ. Dip. Docs.*, vol. iii, pp. 231–2—that some intimation of the President's views had been given to Durand.

[1] Lansdowne to Bertie, June 21, 1905, *Br. Docs.*, vol. iii, no. 126, p. 97.

[2] French Minister of Foreign Affairs to Jusserand, June 23, 1905, Bishop, *Roosevelt*, vol. i, pp. 478–80; Roosevelt to Sternburg, June 23, 1905, ibid., p. 482.

[3] *Br. Docs.*, vol. iii, no. 132 (*b*), pp. 103–5; Bülow to William II, June 25, 1905, *Bülow's Letters*, pp. 137–9.

[4] Jusserand to the French Minister of Foreign Affairs, June 25, 1905, Bishop, *Roosevelt*, vol. i, pp. 480–1.

that since in principle a conference was on the point of being granted the favourable opportunity should not be spoiled by needless trifling. 'As you know, I made up my mind to speak to France rather than to England, because it seemed to me that it would be useless to speak to England; for I felt that if a war were to break out, whatever might happen to France, England would profit immensely, while Germany would lose her colonies and perhaps her fleet.' Assisted by the President, the Emperor had obtained an unanticipated triumph; should war, in spite of that, still occur, the 'high and honorable fame' of William II might be clouded; he could, in brief, act either with magnanimity or, as it was hinted, run the risk of estranging the United States.[1] At the beginning, in response to German accusations against British and Entente policy, Roosevelt, with the object of preserving peace and his Far Eastern plans, had intervened at Paris; yet in the end, and for the same reasons, it was French anxiety which inspired the pacific counsel proffered by him to Potsdam and the Wilhelmstrasse. For the goodwill of the United States Germany had vied with Great Britain since 1898; and just then, when confronted by a new European combination, she could not have chosen a more unpropitious time to jettison American friendship. For to have spurned the President's advice would have been irrevocably to range the sympathies of the White House with the Entente Powers and to have banished the last chance of a better understanding between Washington and Berlin. On the German Government Rooseveltian candour must have had a most salutary effect.

The situation now rapidly improved. Germany and France paused at the brink of war; by June 28 it could be seen from London that all signs pointed to an agreement. Rouvier said to a British diplomatist that his parting from Delcassé was no cause for throwing himself 'dans les bras de l'Empereur et sur son cou'; Roosevelt had helped to render such Gallic embraces superfluous; within the next ten days France secured recognition by Germany of her special privileges in Morocco and in return accepted the Sultan's proposal. A detailed agenda for the conference had yet to be negotiated; but on July 8 communications were exchanged and a declaration signed which safeguarded the fundamental interests of France in the Shereefian Empire.[2] The extrinsic diplomatic success rested with Berlin; a sop to their pride was one of the things the Germans wanted. Intrinsically the French had achieved a further political advance for the subjugation of Morocco.

---

[1] Roosevelt to Sternburg, June 25, 1905, Bishop, *Roosevelt*, vol. i, pp. 483–5; also Paléologue, *The Turning Point*, p. 283. [2] *Br. Docs.*, vol. iii, pp. 103–18.

Before this, Roosevelt had suggested a formula to Paris and Berlin which was important chiefly because it evoked an outburst of gratitude from Sternburg, whose impulsive language obligated the German Government at the future conference to adopt the decision of the White House upon disputed points;[1] and in the winter of 1906, during the deadlock at Algeciras, they were to be reminded by the President of that inconvenient pledge. Negotiations for the defined programme of the Moroccan conference lasted until September 28, when the draft was signed; in the course of the summer of 1905 both parties turned frequently to their American mediator; but, as the peril of war receded in Europe, the Far Eastern peacemaking attracted most attention.[2] Meanwhile, early in July, Lansdowne had discussed with the French Ambassador the manner in which the conference ought to be organized. He desired the inclusion of those Powers who were likely to take the view of the Entente and did not dissent from Cambon's opinion that the United States should participate.[3] Downing Street may have been unaware of the fact that Roosevelt, deviating from the British attitude, had pursued at Paris an active policy of his own; by Lansdowne he was nevertheless still correctly regarded as a friend of the Anglo-French grouping. For getting them out of an impasse the President received thanks from the Quai d'Orsay and the Wilhelmstrasse; and then in the same month Great Britain and the United States expressed their willingness to join in the conference.[4] At London and Washington as well as at Paris the Germans had thus attained their immediate goal, and that being so the first stage of the Moroccan crisis now drew to its close.

But the danger it revealed in Anglo-American relations had not entirely been obliterated. Roosevelt's initial effort after the German message of June 11 might have brought him into a serious misunderstanding with Great Britain. Fortunately, as he started to advocate a Moroccan conference when France herself was veering towards one, he could work for the acceptance of the proposal within the limits of his antecedent agreement with the Entente Powers. By the President it had, nevertheless, been shown that for Anglo-American friendship there might, under prevailing diplomatic conditions, be new hazards in store. Prior to 1914 the central characteristic of the international order was tense competition on a large scale between sovereign States, singly or in groups, for European and indeed universal preponderance.

[1] Jusserand, *What Me Befell*, pp. 319–21; Bishop, *Roosevelt*, vol. i, pp. 486–7.
[2] *Br. Docs.*, vol. iii, pp. 117–47; Bishop, *Roosevelt*, vol. i, p. 488.
[3] Lansdowne to Lister, July 6, 1905, *Br. Docs.*, vol. iii, no. 143, p. 114.
[4] *Correspondence of Roosevelt and Lodge*, vol. ii, pp. 164, 166; *Br. Docs.*, vol. iii, no. 151, p. 118; ibid., no. 160, p. 122.

Seeking friends and allies they endeavoured perpetually in strength of arms and policy to surpass their opponents. Germany could not divorce the United States from Great Britain; that result Roosevelt wisely eschewed. Yet he palpably was influenced to an extent which, in the short run, served German purposes. By mediating at Paris the President inadvertently assisted the assault of Germany on the Franco-British Entente. Similarly, in essaying to restrain the Kaiser he was still trying on both sides to stifle a European conflict. For if one began, and the alleged designs of the Entente were imposed upon the Far East, he would be unable to complete the Russo-Japanese peacemaking to which he had set his hand. American interest in Eastern Asia had been utilized by the Wilhelmstrasse with an eye to its own aims in Morocco and Europe. In quite that precise form the same situation could never perhaps recur—although on each other, since the end of the nineteenth century, European and Far Eastern affairs have unceasingly interacted. But it did demonstrate that to the contagious alarms of its enemies Anglo-American solidarity, as it existed in the peculiarly competitive circumstances of world politics before 1914, was not immune. A more collective and less anarchic system of international relations would tend to restrict their scope. At any rate, one in which Anglo-German rivalry for American good-will was a typical feature always presented a potential threat of bedevilment to English-speaking amity.

From the outset, however, Roosevelt had frankly sympathized with France—even though the Germans imbued him with the belief that by Delcassé and Lansdowne the French were being driven along the road to war. Striving over Morocco to dissever the Entente, Germany then made her most strenuous attempt before 1914 to separate London and Washington. The vicissitudes of that undertaking exhibited the degree of its failure. The United States stood four-square behind France: in other words, indirectly and finally, with Great Britain. For the latter Power a fresh problem in Anglo-American relations was, nevertheless, rearing its head. Since 1898 she had in the western hemisphere assiduously been adapting her policies to those of the United States. But now in 1905 Roosevelt assumed a lead in general world affairs, and in that larger theatre Anglo-American harmonization might again be essential. Bound to Japan and France, Great Britain had, however, become internationally less of a free agent. Yet, while the web of British commitments had been stretched, so also did the ramifications of Anglo-American friendship seem to be extending. By the Moroccan question only one phase of this development was illuminated. In the Far East it rose to its full height. With the maintenance of Anglo-Japanese unity would the British-American concert, at the very hour for which Roosevelt had been waiting and preparing, prove itself incompatible ? Or could they, as had been expected early in 1905, easily be reconciled ?

To these queries, when Theodore Roosevelt first shouldered the burden of peacemaking in the Far East, no definite answer could be afforded. His heated insistence during the summer of 1905 upon a speedy termination of the war may partly have been due to the seeds of suspicion planted in Washington by the German Government. For when he found Lansdowne to be withholding from Japan counsels of moderation, he perhaps wondered whether this did not give some colour to William II's distrust of the Entente. Yet, if the President feared that by such diffidence his scheme of Far Eastern settlement would be imperilled, an air of vacillation in British policy was at the time unavoidable. With Russia abased and Japan victorious, the prospect of an agreement between London and St. Petersburg began to reappear. And for Great Britain that had been rendered all the more desirable not only by her association with Russia's ally, France, but also by the continental military predominance of Germany which the Russian defeat accentuated. Nor were the Germans slow to point out this tendency to Roosevelt—the charge about a quadruple alliance to partition China being ceaselessly ingeminated—in the hope of exacerbating his doubts of British good faith.[1] The fact of the matter was that from the peace negotiations Lansdowne sought wholly to keep clear. For if Japan were urged by him to submit modest demands he would provoke her resentment, while to suggest rigorous ones would needlessly prolong Anglo-Russian hostility and Great Britain now wished the trend to be the other way.

The climax of the Moroccan crisis overlapped the opening stage of the Far Eastern pacification and at the beginning of June world politics as surveyed from London were in a precarious state. Between Russia and Japan Theodore Roosevelt might have then become the intermediary on whom all eyes were fixed; his programme for a balance of power in Eastern Asia he may even have fashioned in accordance with the previous Anglo-American understanding. Nevertheless, thanks to the fulsome care so notoriously lavished on him by the Kaiser, the British Foreign Office probably regarded his proposals as often Germanic in origin. Apprehensive of inexpert diplomacy and with the outlook obscure, Lansdowne on every ground

---

[1] Sternburg to the German Foreign Office, May 17, 1905, *Grosse Politik*, xix. 602; Dugdale, *Germ. Dip. Docs.*, vol. iii, p. 205. For Anglo-Russian relations *Br. Docs.*, vol. iv, pp. 183–218.

preferred to temporize while the President arranged the peace. But the more circumspect the British attitude the less patience Roosevelt had with it. Thus there again emerged what may be considered a permanent difficulty for Anglo-American collaboration in international affairs. The United States was a Power remote from Europe and Asia, formally isolationist despite her labours in 1905, without wide political affiliations abroad. Great Britain, in contrast, stood necessarily at the centre of an intricate network of sensitive ties, Imperial and foreign. It would have been reckless of her to adopt tactics which might win a march and lose the battle. She had entered into special relations with Japan and France. To safeguard these connexions and yet keep secure American friendship was the task she set herself and successfully accomplished. For the moment the Germans might fancy they were making headway at the White House. Actually the community of interest in the Far East between Great Britain and the United States, which the two Governments had foreseen and discussed, was in the end the foundation of Roosevelt's policy.

In Tsushima Straits during the last week of May the Japanese sank the Russian Navy and from Tokio the President received an invitation to bring the adversaries together to treat for peace. So discreet was Great Britain in her relations with Japan, and so little collusion had there been between the latter Power and the Entente, that the Japanese were now constrained to ascertain British views through the medium of the White House. Lansdowne, however, informed Roosevelt that he could have no opinion about the terms Japan might demand from Russia until he perceived the impression produced by Tsushima on the 'temper and expectations of both belligerents'.[1] Meanwhile to St. Petersburg the American Government were planning to tender pacific advice.

In that capital there reigned a stubborn refusal to acknowledge the Russian débâcle. For the sake of her general policy, so as to save Russia from a total collapse, Germany, however, wanted the war brought to a quick finish. And besides, the mediation of the United States rather than that of the Entente Powers had long been one of her objectives; William II was eager therefore and, by means of his personal friendship with the Tsar, in an excellent position to cooperate. Nevertheless, much as Roosevelt required German help,

---

[1] Durand to Lansdowne, June 2, 1905, *Br. Docs.*, vol. iv, no. 71, and message of June 3, pp. 78–9; Dennett, *Roosevelt and the Russo-Japanese War*, pp. 210–11; also Durand to Lansdowne, June 5, 1905, *Br. Docs.*, vol. iv, no. 73, pp. 79–80. For Roosevelt's peacemaking Bishop, *Roosevelt*, vol. i, pp. 374–424; Dennis, *Adventures*, pp. 389–420; Dennett, *Roosevelt and the Russo-Japanese War*, pp. 189–235.

he declined energetically to become the cat's-paw of Potsdam's Russophile aspirations. In Washington evidence of this was supplied on June 5, when the British Embassy learned from the President that the Kaiser had not only urged the Tsar to parley with Japan but had also described Roosevelt as the 'person best suited to make an appeal to the Japanese to grant reasonable terms'; and, furthermore, that William II had requested his fellow-monarch either to communicate with the President through the ordinary channels or to authorize him to work on behalf of Russia at the White House. Roosevelt, whose sympathies were with Japan, was not caught unawares. Later on he himself might have sought reasonable terms; but, while desirous of an early peace, he unhesitatingly rejected the role of broker for any settlement which commended itself particularly to Russo-German diplomacy. 'The President said', it was reported to the British Foreign Office, 'he thought it time to act at once as he did not wish to be asked by Russia to approach Japan in the sense suggested and least of all through the instrumentality of the German Emperor.' And so at St. Petersburg Roosevelt began to exercise direct pressure, proposing simultaneously to the Quai d'Orsay that the French should do likewise. By the method of combined representations from the United States, Germany, and France—of whom the second was Russia's friend and the third her ally—he hoped the Tsar's obstinacy towards ending the war would be overcome.[1] The Kaiser, however, had shown his hand. After that the British Government, loyal to their Japanese ally, discounted with an intelligible scepticism all subsequent talk of 'reasonable terms'.

It was at this juncture that Whitelaw Reid, the successor to Joseph Choate, had arrived in London to occupy the post of American Ambassador. Towards his country the British Government and Royal Family appeared very warmly disposed but, owing to the critical situation in Europe, they were, as he wrote to the President, exceedingly careful about every step.[2] With Lansdowne, Reid had his first interview during the week in which the United States made it plain that she would join in a Moroccan conference only if France consented to participate. To the Foreign Secretary the new Ambassador conveyed an extremely cordial message from Theodore Roosevelt

'who had instructed him to express the satisfaction with which he had observed the close correspondence which existed between the policy of

[1] Durand to Lansdowne, June 5, 1905, *Br. Docs.*, vol. iv, no. 74, pp. 80–1; also *The Kaiser's Letters to the Tsar*, pp. 183–90; Bishop, *Roosevelt*, vol. i, pp. 384–5; Dennett, *Roosevelt and the Russo-Japanese War*, pp. 221–2; Jusserand, *What Me Befell*, p. 301. For German policy Brandenburg, *From Bismarck*, &c., pp. 231–3.
[2] Cortissoz, *Whitelaw Reid*, vol. ii, p. 305.

His Majesty's Government and that of the United States on the most important international questions. The President had no reason to doubt that the diplomacy of the United States and that of Great Britain would be found moving upon parallel lines in the future.'

Lansdowne reiterated his view that it was impossible to form an opinion as to the attitude of Russia and Japan until the effect on them of the Russian naval catastrophe could be estimated. Before concluding this auspicious conversation, Reid spoke with unqualified approval of Sir Mortimer Durand, the British Ambassador at Washington.[1] But Durand had never really enjoyed the confidence of the White House, and the President was even then directing Senator Lodge to intimate in London, should the opportunity occur, that Spring Rice might well replace him. Afterwards, as the Far Eastern peacemaking got under way, the absence from Washington of the British Ambassador aroused a feeling that it had been deliberately contrived so that his Government should have as little as possible to do with the negotiations.[2] The goodwill he lost, which was already small, he could not regain. In the Far East Anglo-American collaboration had still to be put to the test.

At St. Petersburg Roosevelt's mediation bore fruit within several days. The Tsardom itself was seething with revolutionary disaffection; Delcassé, moreover, had just fallen on the Moroccan issue; and the Russians, immobilized in the Far East, were confronted with the added humiliation, if Germany invaded France, of being unable to fulfil their obligations and assist their western ally. Defeat in war, the imminence of a social upheaval at home, the Kaiser's assurance that the United States would shield him from a Carthaginian peace— all these induced Nicholas II to acquiesce.[3] To American diplomacy high credit was ascribed for a brilliant performance. By June 12 both Russia and Japan had formally accepted the President's offer of good offices and agreed to appoint plenipotentiaries.[4] Whether or not the peace conference should meet in the United States had yet to be decided. Before this and other matters were arranged there was no armistice.

To the victor, Tokio now held, belonged the spoils. So as to conceal their own internal difficulties the Japanese even professed to the British Minister that it was the Russians, and not they, who were seek-

---

[1] Lansdowne to Durand, June 5, 1905, *Br. Docs.*, vol. iv, no. 75, p. 82.

[2] Roosevelt to Lodge, May 24, 1905, *Correspondence of Roosevelt and Lodge*, vol. ii, p. 125; Roosevelt to Lodge, June 5, 1905, ibid., p. 133; Dennett, *Roosevelt and the Russo-Japanese War*, p. 211.

[3] For American activities Bishop, *Roosevelt*, vol. i, p. 386; *U.S. Foreign Relations*, 1905, pp. 807–24; also *Br. Docs.*, vol. iv, nos. 77 and 78, p. 85; no. 86, ibid., pp. 89–90.

[4] Bishop, *Roosevelt*, vol. i, pp. 388–9; *Br. Docs.*, vol. iv, no. 83, pp. 86–8.

ing peace.[1] For their conditions stiffened as their triumphs mounted. At Washington the Japanese Minister told Durand that if Russia entered into negotiations she had better be prepared 'to make large sacrifices in money and possibly in territory'.[2] This was a strong hint, the force of which Lansdowne must fully have appreciated, that Japan would not be baulked of her prey; and to it, with every reason to be thankful for what her ally had done, Great Britain could scarcely object. Her trade had been freed of Russian competition in the Yangtse Valley while throughout China that of France, French funds being frozen up in Russia, would henceforth decrease. Furthermore, to the British Empire Russia had become less of a military and diplomatic menace; curbed at last she might cease presently even to be antagonistic. But prior to that change it was necessary to hem her round by augmenting Japanese power; and indeed to impair the growth of Japan—a growth which at that time could only take place at the expense of Russia—would be to expedite the Kaiser's scheme of luring the Tsar into an alliance. On Great Britain the lesson had been impressed by the Moroccan crisis that it was no moment for friendships to languish or lapse. The revision of the first Anglo-Japanese Alliance, then being secretly and concurrently discussed, betokened, as will be seen, how little she intended that this should happen. By a Government which encouraged France to resist the German challenge it did not seem likely that from the vanquished Russians Japan would be advised to forgo her hard-won rights.

It was here that in British and American policy a significant disparity of emphasis began to exhibit itself. Information from the German Emperor kindled Roosevelt's fears that unless Japanese terms were modest Russia might prolong the conflict and there would be no peace.[3] He was, moreover, also perturbed by an intemperate campaign in Japanese newspapers for immense territorial acquisitions on the Asiatic mainland. A protectorate over Corea would not suffice: a loud clamour had developed for the wresting from China of Manchuria and Mongolia and for the seizure by Japanese troops of all Siberia east of Lake Baikal. To Arthur Balfour the President's view was voiced by Whitelaw Reid, who remarked that while Japan might appropriate the island of Sakhalin, the Russians should retain eastern Siberia and merely be driven out of Corea and Manchuria · for Roosevelt argued that Japan could ill afford to pay the huge cost of further conquest in the north. The American Ambassador

[1] Compare ibid., no. 83, pp. 86–8 with Bishop, *Roosevelt*, vol. i, pp. 382–4.
[2] Durand to Lansdowne, June 8, 1905, *Br. Docs.*, vol. iv, no. 79, p. 85.
[3] Sternburg to Roosevelt, June 11, 1905, Bishop, *Roosevelt*, vol. i, pp. 386–7.

said to the Prime Minister that Great Britain ought to persuade Tokio to lower its demand for an indemnity to a point which St. Petersburg could not reject. 'Yes,' Balfour responded, 'but still one would like to have that "point" translated into pounds, shillings and pence.'[1] Senator Lodge was on the eve of a visit to England and the opinions of the President were disclosed to him for communication to the British Government. At the agitation against Japan among his own compatriots Roosevelt evinced considerable anxiety. Troubled by the phenomenal rise of that Oriental nation he was concerned about the strengthening of the American Navy to frustrate possible dangers from her on the Pacific as from Germany on the Atlantic. With British support he therefore sought to arrange that Russia be 'left face to face with Japan so that each may have a moderating action on the other'.[2] Ostensibly mediating in a purely disinterested spirit the President was in fact also pursuing his special aim of a Far Eastern balance of power. His sympathies remained with Japan rather than with Russia; he wanted to see her aggrandized and hoped to possess her friendship. But an early termination of the war and a lack of severity in her terms was imperative lest with additional victories or rich gains she should next be able to threaten American interests. Allied to Japan, the British Government were then haunted by few of these premonitions. And so to Washington in the summer of 1905 the pace of the peacemaking was a matter of more importance than to London.

In the negotiations would Great Britain assist the United States? On June 13 an exchange of cables between Durand and Lansdowne indicated her position. The British Ambassador thought Roosevelt would have liked him to urge upon Takahira the desirability of moderation in the Japanese peace terms. In Washington, he reported, there seemed to be a feeling that at Tokio the British Government might properly exercise their influence towards that object. To his Japanese colleague Durand so far had avoided making any such suggestion. It was not his business to do that and he supposed Great Britain 'would probably be reluctant to take any step which could embarrass Japanese'. His surmise proved accurate. Replying to him, the Foreign Secretary described the attitude of the Ambassador as being in accordance with that of his Government and, failing contrary instructions, was to be maintained.[3] Despite the general

---

[1] Cortissoz, *Whitelaw Reid*, vol. ii, pp. 306–7.
[2] Roosevelt to Lodge, June 16, 1905, *Correspondence of Roosevelt and Lodge*, vol. ii, p. 153; also ibid., pp. 130–5, 138–56.
[3] Durand to Lansdowne, June 13, 1905, *Br. Docs.*, vol. iv, no. 81, p. 86; Lansdowne to Durand, June 13, 1905, ibid., no. 82, p. 86.

Anglo-American understanding Lansdowne had now adopted a policy of strict aloofness. William II alone was at the President's disposal.

At British disinclination to follow his lead Roosevelt, during the middle of the month, began to show alarm. It was an arduous task to settle with the Japanese and Russians the preliminaries of their peace conference; a message to Whitelaw Reid revealed his irritation that, as between Germany and Great Britain, the latter appeared the more averse from helping him. 'The President desires you to find out', the State Department directed, 'whether the English Government really does wish for peace or not.'[1] Yet at that time in conversation with Durand he displayed none of this acerbity. 'President says', the British Ambassador cabled to Lansdowne, 'that our attitude of reserve seems to him wise and proper, and that any advice given by us hereafter will come with double force.'[2] In point of fact Roosevelt had evidently decided that with Durand not much could be done and instead tried at London to advance his contentions through other channels.

By the Foreign Secretary and the American Ambassador these questions were discussed on June 16. King Edward VII had told Reid previously that he considered it best for the Russians and Japanese to be left to conduct their negotiations alone. With this view, said the Ambassador, the President agreed; but he also believed that Tokio could later usefully be advised not to submit extreme demands. Reid next referred to the American impression that Great Britain 'might be likely to create difficulties in the way of peace by encouraging Japan to insist upon excessive terms'. That idea Lansdowne stoutly denied. But the British Government could scarcely advise Japan about her terms when they did not know what she proposed to ask.[3] In the report of the American Ambassador the Foreign Secretary was quoted as stating that he 'had heard unofficial rumours and persons were hinting that England might not so much want peace at the moment as other things'. Nothing could be more abhorrent, Lansdowne had observed, than the thought that any action of the British Government might tend to prolong bloodshed. But upon Japan it was, in the circumstances, quite another matter for them to bring any pressure to bear.[4] Great Britain's standpoint had been defined and to alter it Roosevelt could do little.

[1] State Department to Whitelaw Reid, June 15, 1905, Dennett, *Roosevelt and the Russo-Japanese War*, p. 211.
[2] Durand to Lansdowne, June 16, 1905, *Br. Docs.*, vol. iv, no. 84, p. 88.
[3] Lansdowne to Durand, June 16, 1905, ibid., no. 85, p. 89.
[4] Reid to the State Department, June 17, 1905, Dennett, *Roosevelt and the Russo-Japanese War*, p. 211; also Bishop, *Roosevelt*, vol. i, p. 396.

In 1905 Cecil Spring Rice was a bridge-builder between Downing Street and the White House. Because of his peculiar faculty in that respect—the President's mediation being anticipated—he had been recalled from his post at the St. Petersburg Embassy for consultation by the Foreign Office; and to him on June 16 Theodore Roosevelt turned again. As he intended it to be, the President's letter of that date was handed to Lord Lansdowne—Spring Rice having been selected by Roosevelt as a medium for communication with the British Government in a manner less formal and more comprehensive than he deemed feasible through the existing diplomatic agencies. The President did not disguise the effect on his mind of Japan's formidable victories, of her capacity soon to put her expansionist ideals into practice. The attitude of his Administration, as portrayed by him, was one of friendship with Tokio while maintaining an efficient navy prepared for every eventuality. In the negotiations he had furthermore obtained help from the Emperor William, and he mentioned his wish that at the proper time the British should likewise assist him. These were shrewd remarks, for they implied that, among the foreign Powers represented at Washington, Germany, as a result of her sole co-operation, might take first place. Roosevelt thereupon stressed the wisdom of an early peace. The possession of East Asia would not compensate Japan for the losses incurred by an extra year of fighting; what he wanted was a settlement in which each belligerent 'will be in a sense the guarantor of the other's good conduct'. His theory of a Far Eastern balance he thus restated, and although to secure it he sought British collaboration he still opposed—apart from his efforts in the world crisis of 1904–5—the abandonment of isolation as a general policy. For the President asserted that if Japan were ever to become a menace the American people would be saved by their own exertions 'and not by an alliance with anyone else'. By events before and after 1905 the defect of such reasoning was laid bare; if, outside the western hemisphere, the United States shunned proportionate obligations she hardly could expect the sort of international system that might serve her needs or claim her sympathy to be established. But upon a fundamental departure from the traditions of his country even Theodore Roosevelt did not have the temerity to venture; between complete detachment and full participation his activities were, on the whole, the best conceivable compromise. And so he requested Great Britain to support a mediation in which a laudable altruism was leavened with a potent admixture of national self-interest. To Spring Rice he expressed his hope that the British Government 'will not permit any feeling that they would like to see both combatants exhausted to prevent them doing all they can to bring about peace. Germany and France should make their influence felt by making Russia willing to yield what she ought to yield; and England should make her influence felt in making the Japanese terms not so severe that Russia, instead of granting them, would prefer to continue the war.'[1]

The United States thus summoned Great Britain to uphold their common front upon Far Eastern affairs.

In the Foreign Office when the President's letter was received on July 9 it created an immediate stir. Spring Rice saw Lansdowne at once and they arranged that the Foreign Secretary should speak to Whitelaw Reid three days later. Meanwhile, summarizing Lansdowne's views in a memorandum for dispatch to the American Government, Spring Rice framed a document which may be considered an authoritative exposition of British foreign policy during the critical summer of 1905. To him Lansdowne had emphasized that in the Far East British interests required a stable peace; with the President, the King and Balfour's Cabinet were here in entire agreement. But Great Britain in letter and spirit was bound to Japan. She could not, as other Governments wished her to do, urge Tokio to waive certain conditions. There was a difference between an impartial friend and a sworn ally. France might attempt to influence Russia since the Dual Alliance did not apply to the Far East while Germany and the United States were free to advise both sides. For Spring Rice contended that 'honour commands us to abstain from putting any pressure whatever on Japan to abstain even from actions which may eventually entail very severe sacrifices from us under the Treaty'. The Foreign Secretary, moreover, had no information which pointed to extreme terms beings demanded by Japan. He nevertheless invited Roosevelt to communicate with him should that occur. Outlining his policy to Spring Rice for transmission to the President, Lansdowne did not dilate upon the advantages from the Russo-Japanese War which had accrued to the safety of the British Empire but on the risks endured. There were dangers in Asia such as the possibility of a clash with Russia when Great Britain was recuperating from the South African conflict and the Anglo-French Entente itself might have been imperilled. Nor did the British Government want Russia—whose downfall had made the Turks more refractory—excluded from the Pacific, if only because she would then seek an outlet for her energies in the Near and Middle East. And indeed on any broad judgement her ruin—perhaps the Foreign Secretary thus

[1] Roosevelt to Spring Rice, June 16, 1905, Gwynn, *Spring Rice*, vol. i, pp. 472–4.

hinted at a post-war Anglo-Russian *rapprochement*—was undesirable. 'But the most serious aspect of the question'—and at this stage the British apologia became a neat attack on Roosevelt's friendship with the Kaiser—'is the general balance of power in Europe.' The Moroccan crisis—the Germans seizing the opportunity with Russia prostrate ınd Austria confused—was the price paid for Japan's success. The British fleet could not prevent an invasion of France, and Great Britain might have to organize a land army to protect that country from annihilation or from being 'turned into a province of Germany, to be directed as a subservient ally against herself'. At the forthcoming Moroccan conference the political independence of France would have to be preserved. Nor could the inferiority of the British and French democracies in military striking-power be overlooked.[1] On her European and Asiatic commitments Great Britain, faced with so grave an international situation, proposed to keep an exceedingly firm grasp.

The Foreign Secretary's explanatory survey, of which Spring Rice sent an account to Washington, was followed on July 12 by an official statement to the American Ambassador:

> 'I mentioned to Mr. Whitelaw Reid to-day', Lansdowne wrote to Durand, 'that it had come to my knowledge that we were supposed by the Government of the United States to be lukewarm in our desire for peace between Japan and Russia, if indeed we did not regard with a certain amount of satisfaction the continuation of a struggle out of which both parties would emerge greatly weakened for some time to come. It was, I said, unnecessary for me to assure His Excellency that no Power was more desirous of seeing peace restored than this country.'

And as an earnest of that the Foreign Secretary cited a recent speech of the Prime Minister's delivered at a banquet given to the American Ambassador on his arrival in England. 'Mr. Whitelaw Reid said that he did not believe that the President entertained this view, although it was one which might possibly have been suggested to him by interested parties.'[2]

There were from St. Petersburg and Berlin unremitting endeavours to destroy Roosevelt's confidence in Great Britain. But that the enfeeblement of Japan was not one of her motives the revision of the Anglo-Japanese Alliance soon illustrated since, as a matter of ordinary common sense, for her to seek the exhaustion of a partner to whom heavier treaty responsibilities were then being assigned would be for her to work to her own detriment. John Hay had lately been in

---

[1] Spring Rice to the Secretary of State, July 10, 1905, Gwynn, *Spring Rice*, vol. i, pp. 474–8.
[2] Lansdowne to Durand, July 12, 1905, *Br. Docs.*, vol. iv, no. 87, p. 91.

London, where he discussed the international outlook with British statesmen; and to his absence from Washington Baron Speck von Sternburg attributed an American attitude in Far Eastern and Moroccan affairs less Anglophile than usual and more consonant with the principles of German diplomacy.[1] Mourned by all friends of English-speaking solidarity, John Hay died on July 1. As Secretary of State he was replaced by Elihu Root, with the President, however, remaining in direct charge of the Administration's foreign policy. Meanwhile, despite the fact that they had agreed to negotiate, the Russians and Japanese were still fighting, and in London the prospects for the success of the American mediation did not rate high.[2] Angered by this, Roosevelt complained to Sternburg that he was hampered by the refusal of Great Britain to exercise a moderating influence upon Japan. 'Aha!' William II noted triumphantly, 'Now America sees for the first time where the real disturber of the world's peace lies!'[3] For, to the American Ambassador, the German Emperor and Prince von Bülow were busily traducing perfidious Albion. If Roosevelt's intervention failed, Germany expected that 'Delcassé's plan of indemnifying Belligerent and Mediator at the expense of China' would be tried anew—those favouring it naturally doing their best to prolong the war. The alleged scheme was the familiar one in which the Quai d'Orsay and Downing Street were to become the Far Eastern peacemakers: Russia and Japan would each annex portions of Chinese territory and for their services the British and French were to be similarly rewarded. Great Britain, the Germans argued, preferred the war to terminate in this way 'by advancing her own interests at the same time'.[4] In June these grotesque accusations had excited the President to persuade France to adopt the proposal for a Moroccan conference. But they had at last outlived their usefulness; for them, in the news from London and in the progress of the preliminary Far Eastern negotiations, there was no corroborative evidence. So Roosevelt merely replied to Berlin that he would not submit 'to such action by any of the Powers'. To the Kaiser, for co-operating with him at St. Petersburg, he was, nevertheless, very grateful.[5]

At that juncture, and for a delusive interval, the Russophile

[1] Sternburg to the German Foreign Office, June 17, 1905, *Grosse Politik*, xx. 442; Dugdale, *Germ. Dip. Docs.*, vol. iii, pp. 231–2.

[2] Reid to Roosevelt, June 23, 1905, Bishop, *Roosevelt*, vol. i, p. 396.

[3] Sternburg to the German Foreign Office, July 5, 1905, *Grosse Politik*, xix. 613; Dugdale, *Germ. Dip. Docs.*, vol. iii, pp. 205–6.

[4] Tower to Roosevelt, July 13, 1905, Dennett, *Roosevelt and the Russo-Japanese War*, pp. 233–5.

[5] Roosevelt to Tower, July 27, 1905, Bishop, *Roosevelt*, vol. i, pp. 401–2.

proclivities of Potsdam came finally within an ace of fulfilment. On July 24, although Russia had been included in the German indictment of Franco-British intrigues, William II did not scruple to sign with the Tsar a secret treaty of alliance. About what had happened when the two Emperors met at Björko there was in the Chancelleries of Europe much nervous speculation. From St. Petersburg the British Ambassador reported that between the Russian and German monarchs a greater degree of intimacy had ensued; nor did it seem likely that the Tsar would accept the President's mediation; rather than concede to Japan the terms she desired Nicholas II really wanted to continue the war.[1] In the eyes of Downing Street these circumstances were bound to throw grave doubt on the sincerity of the Kaiser's support at St. Petersburg of the Rooseveltian peace efforts. And so to the British Government the American contention that Germany but not Great Britain was acting for the general good must, therefore, have appeared as a patent sign of the President's naïveté. At any rate, to William II the Tsar had made it plain that, as a consequence of German advice, the Russians were relying on Roosevelt to reduce Japanese demands to what they considered reasonable limits.[2] Regarded in Berlin and St. Petersburg as their mainstay, the President would have been even more astonished had he also then known of the role cast for the United States alongside the Kaiser's anti-British continental league. But on that subject London and Washington were not to be enlightened until the autumn.

By Björko international uncertainties were deepened. Yet, oddly enough, Theodore Roosevelt chose that very time to dispatch a tart rejoinder to the Lansdowne-Spring Rice defence of British policy. Pitched in a key of rebuke, his comment on a ministerial explanation was obviously again destined for perusal by the Foreign Secretary. 'Don't you think you go a little needlessly into heroics,' the President inquired of Spring Rice, 'when you say . . . "that honour commands England to abstain from putting any pressure whatever upon Japan to abstain from action which may eventually entail severe sacrifices on England's part"?' At Tokio he merely asked her to do what William II and the French Government were doing at St. Petersburg; but for all his reproachful impatience the President here revealed the extent of the misapprehension under which he laboured. The aims of Germany were not above suspicion while, after the Moroccan crisis, it was pure self-interest for France to advocate

---

[1] Hardinge to Lansdowne, Aug. 1, 1905, *Br. Docs.*, vol. iv, no. 91, pp. 95–6.
[2] The Kaiser to Bülow, July 25, 1905, Spectator, *Prince Bülow and the Kaiser*, p. 177.

measures which would curtail the further weakening of her Russian ally. To Spring Rice the President expressed approval of the British attitude of preventing a hostile coalition against Japan—one which at the outset of the war he also had adopted. During the summer of 1905 he nevertheless was baffled by the reluctance of the British to give their ally, for her own sake, the same sort of beneficial advice that the French were urging on Russia.[1] Of assistance from London Roosevelt accordingly now had no great expectations.

It was with keen distress that Spring Rice witnessed even the slightest rift develop within the Anglo-American lute. On August 10 before the tribunal of the White House he therefore attempted once more to arraign Germany as the chief menace not only to Great Britain but to the peace and liberties of Europe as well. Bent on dispelling the effect of William II's co-operation with Roosevelt and using the information which had arrived at the Foreign Office from St. Petersburg, the British diplomatist wrote questioningly of the Kaiser's activities at Björko and of his honesty of purpose in the Russo-Japanese negotiations.[2] Prior to that and with considerable exactitude, Spring Rice had warned Gerald Balfour, now President of the Local Government Board, of what the German Emperor was saying at Washington about the Anglo-Japanese group. Meanwhile in London the King and leading statesmen spoke to Senator Lodge and Francis B. Loomis, the First Assistant Secretary of State.[3] In British policy there was, however, no change.

Downing Street did not share Roosevelt's anxieties. By it Tokio instead of Washington or Berlin—and still less St. Petersburg—was, quite simply, regarded as the best judge of the interests of Japan. Besides, nothing indicated officially that her terms would be exorbitant, while the British Foreign Office did not seem to be aware of the fact that even for the victor, so depleted were her resources, an early peace had become essential.[4] Seeking to lower Japanese demands, Russia and Germany might try hard to secure American help; that Great Britain would lend herself to such transparent manoeuvres was, however, highly improbable. In order to counteract the Kaiser's success at the White House, Spring Rice suggested that the British Government should again put on record their desire for peace. But, although he watched the President's mediation with the utmost

[1] Roosevelt to Spring Rice, July 24, 1905, Gwynn, *Spring Rice*, vol. i, pp. 478–9.
[2] Spring Rice to Mrs. Roosevelt, Aug. 10, 1905, ibid., pp. 483–5; also Hardinge to Lansdowne, Aug. 1, 1905, *Br. Docs.*, vol. iv, no. 91, pp. 95–6.
[3] Spring Rice to Gerald Balfour, July 29, 1905, Gwynn, *Spring Rice*, vol. i, pp. 481–3; Spring Rice to Mrs. Roosevelt, Aug. 10, 1905, ibid., p. 483.
[4] Dennett, *Roosevelt and the Russo-Japanese War*, p. 214.

benevolence, Lansdowne made no move.[1] Silently and vigilantly, London was waiting for the results of the Portsmouth Conference.

When, therefore, in August 1905 the peacemaking formally began, the Far Eastern concert of Great Britain and the United States did not appear to be in a very robust condition. Theodore Roosevelt was piqued by British passivity—even though he received the good wishes of Edward VII for the happy conclusion of his endeavours with grace and warmth.[2] Had Anglo-American friendship suffered? Continued disagreement would have wrought irreparable harm. But more unifying forces had quietly been at work. The negotiations for the renewal of the Anglo-Japanese Alliance were at an end and in the framing of the revised treaty the interest shown by the United States was of capital importance. From the fall of Delcassé until the Portsmouth Conference British and American policies diverged. As shaped in the western hemisphere, an understanding between the English-speaking Powers, when applied to European and Asiatic problems, might not always hold fast. If the Germans rejoiced their jubilation was premature. On the basis of the Far Eastern settlement and on the broad principles of world affairs, Great Britain and the United States were, during the latter months of 1905, to be in complete harmony.

[1] Spring Rice to Lansdowne, Aug. 6, 1905, Gwynn, *Spring Rice*, vol. i, pp. 480–1; Lansdowne to Spring Rice, Aug. 7, 1905, ibid., p. 486.
[2] Wallace to Knollys, Aug. 9, 1905, Lee, *Edward VII*, vol. ii, pp. 433–4.

X

THE FAR EASTERN UNDERSTANDING

WHEN the Anglo-Japanese Alliance was revised in 1905 the English-speaking Powers attained the peak of a common Far Eastern policy. By the new treaty Roosevelt's scheme for a Far Eastern equipoise seemed to have been substantially underwritten; at the end, despite differences which had arisen, he himself testified that to the success of his peacemaking its signature was a decisive contribution. During the negotiations between the two allies the British Government refused, moreover, to agree to anything that might injure or leave Anglo-American friendship out of account. And of their results the President did not only take a favourable view but, soon after, by explicitly confirming the approval he had given, administered to the Kaiser's fond dream of a vast combine against the Anglo-Japanese group a further sharp check. Yet within a few years of the Peace of Portsmouth the chief weakness of American endeavours was again manifest. Once more had the United States as a Great Power fallen between two stools; for if she assisted in refashioning a major instrument of international relations she also had maintained her orthodox isolationist position. By his cordial attitude in 1905 towards the Anglo-Japanese Alliance Theodore Roosevelt brought his country nearer to diplomatic commitments abroad than any modern President before Woodrow Wilson. But, outside the western hemisphere, there was for American interests, short of full participation in world politics, no direct safeguard.

For what reason, more than a year and a half before it expired, did the Anglo-Japanese Alliance undergo revision? To that the answer must first be sought in the widespread repercussions on two continents of the defeat of Russia. In Asia, as they recoiled from the Pacific, the Russians, it was believed, might now expand on the northern frontiers of India, while in Europe the comparative military power of Germany had by their collapse been correspondingly enhanced. For Great Britain, therefore, the German menace on land—of which the Moroccan crisis was an omen—marched abreast with that on sea. To some extent, however, these dangers could be met by strengthening her connexion with Japan. That nation had just displayed its indomitable fighting qualities and to it the British Government might not only assign the protection of their Far Eastern interests but also engage its support for the defence of India. The

Japanese would, on the whole, look after Asia; Great Britain, in turn, could concentrate on European affairs. On the other hand, to Japan, exhausted by her own remarkable exploits, the renewal of the Alliance would imply a British guarantee of whatever she might manage to acquire in the peace settlement. For Russia may have met with temporary reverses; she was nevertheless still capable, with all her wealth and huge untapped resources, of attempting at no distant date to avenge herself on her diminutive adversary. And such being the general considerations, when the two allies negotiated the required changes, their relations with the United States were not lost from sight.

But more particularly the Anglo-Japanese Alliance had to be revised so that Japan could assume control over Corea. The preamble and Article I obligated the two contracting parties to maintain the independence and territorial integrity of the Corean as well as the Chinese Empire.[1] The encroachments of Russia on that hapless realm were among the main causes of the Far Eastern conflict. At the beginning of 1905 by the British and American Governments it had therefore been held that after the war Japan should establish her supremacy at Seoul. On January 23 Sir Mortimer Durand cabled Roosevelt's opinion that if the Japanese continued to withstand Russia they ought to retain Port Arthur, the Russian ice-free fortress on the Pacific, and 'paramount influence in Corea'. To this, in their reply two days later, the British Government fully assented. The Foreign Minister of Japan had informed Great Britain that one of the indispensable conditions of peace would be for Corea to come into the 'exclusive sphere of Japanese influence' within which no special Russian interests were to be allowed. It was felt in London that the demands of Japan were not excessive and Durand received instructions to communicate them to Roosevelt verbally and in the strictest confidence. On January 30 the Ambassador responded that the President entirely agreed with the views expressed in the British message of January 25. Roosevelt did not think that Russia would consent to the Japanese terms, but to them prima facie he saw no objection.[2]

In this matter he argued first of all that the helplessness of the Coreans, their inability to strike a blow in their own defence, would alone justify a Japanese protectorate.[3] But, secondly, by another idea revolving in his mind, Roosevelt was no doubt also actuated. For the disposition of Corea appears to have been a basic element in his

[1] Text, Br. Docs., vol. iv, no. 118, pp. 128–31.
[2] Note on 'Position of Japan in Corea', ibid., p. 156.
[3] Dennett, Roosevelt and the Russo-Japanese War, pp. 110, 161; Bishop, Roosevelt, vol. i, pp. 380–1.

scheme of augmenting Japanese power within well defined limits—
and at no cost to the United States—so as to counterbalance Russia
in Eastern Asia.

Perceiving that the desired alterations could not be accomplished
without a revision of the Anglo-Japanese Alliance, the President most
probably recommended this course to Downing Street. In February
when Cecil Spring Rice visited him it would seem to have been mentioned. On his return from Washington the British diplomatist
reported to the Foreign Office and then in a letter to Roosevelt described Lansdowne's attitude. 'He for his part', Spring Rice wrote to
the President, 'is quite determined to play up. The difficulty lies
with the Liberal Party; but Lord Rosebery, Grey and Haldane were
all ready to continue the alliance with Japan, and, as you see, they
have all made speeches to that effect.'[1] During the summer of 1905
the President's approval of the Anglo-Japanese Alliance would be
carried a stage further. Meanwhile, in March the British Ambassador
told him that King Edward VII was much pleased with his language
when the Japanese terms had been discussed. The Foreign Secretary
had requested that their views be kept secret. 'Ah, that's right—
that's right,' Roosevelt observed. 'As long as they stick to that I
shall feel quite comfortable. Whatever you do, don't let anything
get round to Germany.'[2] It was thus a spirit of genuine amity in
which at the outset Great Britain and the United States had
arrived at their understanding about the prospective Far Eastern
settlement.

In London this naturally produced considerable gratification. With
the question of modifying and renewing the agreement the two allies
began to deal towards the end of March. At their first conversation
on the subject Viscount Hayashi, the Japanese Minister, inquired of
Lord Lansdowne whether there was any chance of their being joined
by the United States. In Japan, he remarked, no combination could
be more important or more popular. But his experience of American
isolationism impelled the British Foreign Secretary to dash Japanese
hopes in that direction.

'I said', Lansdowne noted, 'that I had had frequent discussions with
the United States Government with regard to affairs in the Far East,
and that I had good reasons for knowing that their policy was eminently
friendly to Japan, and I thought I might say identical with ours. There
was therefore every reason for anticipating that American influence
would be exerted upon the same lines as ours. The United States
Government were however notoriously opposed to the idea of entangling

[1] Spring Rice to Mrs. Roosevelt, Mar. 13, 1905, Gwynn, *Spring Rice*, vol. i, p. 453.
[2] Durand to Lansdowne, Mar. 10, 1905, ibid., p. 455.

themselves in foreign alliances, and although I should expect to find them moving upon parallel lines with us, I doubted whether they were likely to do more.'[1]

Nor did Lansdowne overlook the potential value of American friendship to British strategy in the Pacific. In May the negotiations were complicated by the attempt to formulate a text suited to the new naval and military circumstances consequent on the defeat of Russia. The original treaty did not become operative until a third party interfered. The Foreign Secretary now offered to amplify it and, in the event of an attack even by one hostile country, put at Japan's disposal the whole of British sea-power. Russia, he contended, must seek eventually to crush her and would desist only when confronted with the united fleets of the two allies. But if Russia were precluded from reprisals in the Far East she might threaten British interests more seriously upon the Indian frontier and in other parts of Asia. As compensation for Great Britain's proposed naval liability he therefore asked Japan to give military assistance for the defence of India.[2] Tokio, however, had also been approaching the same problem, but from a different angle; for it was more concerned about the amount of immediate help that would be at hand and less with the ultimate measure of support which might elsewhere be forthcoming. Since 1902, in consonance with notes exchanged supplementing their agreement, each signatory had, so far as possible, maintained available for concentration in the waters of the Extreme East a naval force superior to that of any third Power; and in 1905 Japan did not want these efforts to be relaxed. By a secret and separate article attached to her draft treaty of May 26, she accordingly stipulated that the two contracting parties should each endeavour 'to maintain at all times in the Far East a naval force superior in strength to that of any third Power having the largest naval force in the Far East'.[3] But here Great Britain objected. For by this proviso the special function of Anglo-American understanding in the system of British security had been ignored.

It will be recollected that during 1904 Sir John Fisher undertook to reorganize the Royal Navy as a spear-head against Germany in the North Sea. And then at Tsushima in May 1905 the Russian fleet under Rojdestvensky was routed by Togo and the Japanese. At sea

---

[1] Lansdowne to MacDonald, Mar. 24, 1905, *Br. Docs.*, vol. iv, no. 111, p. 121. For the negotiations ibid., pp. 120–82.

[2] Lansdowne to MacDonald, May 17, 1905, ibid., no. 115, pp. 124–5; MacDonald to Lansdowne, May 25, 1905, ibid., no. 117, pp. 126–8; also Balfour to Edward VII, June 9, 1905, Blanche Dugdale, *Balfour*, vol. i, pp. 389–90.

[3] Note of January 30, 1902, *Br. Docs.*, vol. iv, p. 131; Japanese Draft Heads of Agreement, May 26, 1905, ibid., footnote, no. 118, pp. 128–9.

the Russian danger had for the moment ceased to exist; of most British war vessels the Admiralty could now safely proceed to denude the Far East. But from Tokio the British Minister informed the Foreign Office that the Japanese Government would probably dissent; with the secret article submitted by Hayashi on May 26 the suggested withdrawal was not altogether compatible. Holding his ground, none the less, Lansdowne endorsed the opinion of the Assistant Under-Secretary of State for Foreign Affairs that by the agreement of 1902, reproduced in the separate article of the new draft, Great Britain was only bound 'to keep a stronger naval force in Far Eastern Waters than any third Power. With 7 armoured cruisers we should be far stronger than any third Power except possibly the U(nited) S(tates) who have three Battleships, but nothing worth mentioning in the cruiser class'.[1] Against the American Navy, to the mind of the British Foreign Office, the stipulations of the revised treaty would not apply. But at the beginning of June the Japanese reiterated their claim and Lansdowne deemed it of sufficient gravity to place before the Cabinet.[2]

What troubled the British Government was plainly exhibited in their counter-draft of June 10. The disputed Japanese article had been altered. It now provided that the two signatories should each endeavour 'to maintain at all times available for concentration in the waters of the Far East a naval force superior in strength to that of any European Power in those seas'.[3] To the Japanese Minister Lansdowne explained the full meaning of the change. The British Government would, he said, keep the required naval force available for concentration, but would not necessarily maintain it within the actual waters of the Far East.

'We had also stipulated that each party should maintain a force superior in strength not to that of any other Power, but to that of any European Power in those seas. This was done in order that we might not be compelled to level our fleets up to the strength of the naval force maintained by the U(nited) S(tates) in or near the Far East. We did not consider it at all likely that we should be at war with the United States and unless this exception were made Great Britain and Japan would each be obliged to maintain a superfluous number of ships.'[4]

Such a declaration by the Foreign Secretary, reflecting in the midst of a major diplomatic transaction Great Britain's policy of informal

[1] MacDonald to Lansdowne, June 1, 1905, and Minute, ibid., no. 122, p. 133.
[2] MacDonald to Lansdowne, June 2, 1905, ibid., no. 123, p. 133; Lansdowne to MacDonald, June 3, 1905, ibid., no. 124, pp. 133–4.
[3] Ibid., no. 155, p. 169.
[4] Lansdowne to MacDonald, June 10, 1905, ibid., no. 126, p. 137.

reinsurance with the United States, outweighed entirely the purely technical aspect of the economies contemplated. Under the sheltering arms of the Anglo-Japanese Alliance and English-speaking friendship the British Admiralty, shifting its sleepless vigil from the Pacific and other outlying regions to the North Sea, could to its European problem henceforth devote its undistracted attention. And indeed, without either or both of these two political attachments, Fisher's strategic reorientation of the Royal Navy would have been much less far-reaching if not wholly impracticable.

Could the advantages of Anglo-American friendship be reconciled with the terms of the new treaty? The Japanese Government were not unamenable, and on June 23 by their second draft accepted the British contention that the allied naval forces in Far Eastern waters should each have a strength superior only to that 'of any European Power'. A proposal from Great Britain for a large specified amount of Japanese military support in the war-time defence of India they nevertheless rejected. Japan throughout preferred instead that the nature of the assistance to be given for the maintenance by the allies of their respective interests in Eastern Asia and India should be arranged and periodically revised by the naval and military authorities of the two countries.[1] In the light of Anglo-American goodwill the British Government were reducing their Far Eastern naval preparations. It is not inconceivable that the refusal of Japan to adopt definite Indian commitments was an immediate result.

With her view, however, the British General Staff expressed agreement. For strategic reasons they regarded consultation as more advisable than a rigid definition in advance of the character of the assistance to be given.[2] But with his second draft Lansdowne on July 1 insisted that the Japanese should be ready to send an expeditionary force for service in India. Japan had consented to the exclusion of the United States from the allied naval calculations in the Far East. If she did this, expecting in return that her military obligations could remain unspecified, she was disappointed. She therefore suggested the deletion from the treaty of all exact naval and military stipulations and to her proposal Great Britain ultimately

---

[1] For various drafts Br. Docs., vol. iv, pp. 165–9; also Lansdowne to MacDonald, June 23, 1905, ibid., no. 128, p. 141.

[2] Grierson to Sanderson, June 16, 1905, ibid., no. 127, and Enclosure, pp. 137–40. The General Staff managed to pack into one extraordinary comment evidence that they were blind to strategic realities over the greater part of the Pacific area and oblivious of the true sentiments of British peoples everywhere. It ran: 'In the military contingency of the United States being hostile, Japanese troops could advantageously be employed against the Philippines, and also against the States themselves, thus indirectly assisting in the defence of Canada,' ibid., p. 140.

acceded. About the conditions under which in defence of their respective interests in the regions of Eastern Asia and India armed assistance should be given, the armies and navies of the two Powers were, by Article VII of the final text, pledged only to periodical consultation.[1] If the British Government had been willing to offer her a larger degree of naval support in the Far East, would Japan have accepted specified measures of military aid for the protection of their Indian Empire? By Great Britain, because of the friendly attitude of the United States and the American Navy, the former step was considered a wasteful one—and no increase in Japanese reluctance to undertake precise Indian commitments could induce her to abandon so rational a stand.

Nevertheless, the omission of the secret articles left Great Britain with more latitude to determine and vary the amount of her naval strength in the Far East. Not only was Japan her ally and the United States her friend but in devising and implementing the British fleet reorganization the Admiralty had been burdened with no inflexible strategic engagements. On the other hand, the general treaty obligation turned out less satisfactory in the end than it had at first appeared. To the Japanese Minister Lansdowne had said that he did not want Great Britain to assume 'a new and formidable *military* liability'; yet she did, in fact, seem afterwards to have assumed on land and sea one liability as onerous as it was undesired. Article II of the final text stipulated that:

> 'If by reason of unprovoked attack or aggressive action, wherever arising, on the part of any other Power or Powers either Contracting Party should be involved in war in defence of its territorial rights or special interests mentioned in the preamble of this Agreement, the other Contracting Party will at once come to the assistance of its ally, and will conduct the war in common, and make peace in mutual agreement with it.'[2]

To the aspirations of Downing Street nothing could have been more totally alien or repugnant than the idea of the Anglo-Japanese Alliance, as now framed, ever being theoretically capable of placing the English-speaking peoples on opposing sides. In the summer of 1905 even Theodore Roosevelt, despite his anxiety about the growth of Japanese ambitions, did not foresee how speedily his apprehensions of antagonism between the United States and Japan would be fulfilled. And so the one grave danger which ensued, leading in 1911 to the revision of the second Anglo-Japanese Alliance, was the one least

[1] For course of discussion, ibid., no. 130, p. 144; no. 134, p. 147; no. 136, p. 150; no. 141, p. 153; no. 142, p. 154; no. 148, p. 160; no. 150, p. 161. For draft variations and final text, ibid., no. 155, pp. 165-9.
[2] Ibid., no. 155, p. 166.

envisaged. For indeed from the start to the requirements of Anglo-American understanding Lansdowne had at every stage been endeavouring scrupulously to conform.

Of that the negotiations about the future status of Corea afforded further proof. To Japanese ascendancy over that country the British and American Governments had agreed at the beginning of the year. The question to be decided was the terms upon which it should be sanctioned by the modified alliance. On June 23 Tokio indicated its aims in Article III of its revised draft:

> 'Japan possessing special paramount political, military and economic interests in Corea Great Britain recognizes the right of Japan to take such measures of guidance, control and protection in Corea as she may deem proper and necessary to safeguard and advance those interests, provided always that such measures do not infringe the principle of equal opportunities for the commerce and industry of all nations.'[1]

Having consented to help defend India against Russian aggression, the Japanese were counting upon their Corean reward. But in Corea Great Britain did not wish to impair the legitimate position of third parties. In the second British draft the Corean article therefore terminated with the words significantly altered: 'provided always that such measures do not infringe the Treaty rights of other nations or the principle of equal opportunities for their commerce and industry.'[2] But at Tokio this attempt to preserve the Open Door encountered the most obstinate resistance. The British reservation, it was argued, would accord other Powers equality with Japan in her special region and might even guarantee Russia's existing privileges.[3] In reply Lansdowne frankly confessed the source of his misgivings. While setting up her paramountcy in Corea Japan might encroach on the rights of a third Power and become engulfed in war with it. Would she, the Foreign Secretary inquired, then expect British assistance? He proposed a double solution: firstly, to substitute the words 'are not contrary to established treaty rights' for the words 'do not infringe the treaty rights of other nations'; and secondly, that between London and Tokio there should be an exchange of notes which would make it clear that Japan had no intention of summoning Great Britain to her aid in such a dispute.[4]

---

[1] *Br. Docs.*, vol. iv, no. 155, p. 166; also MacDonald to Lansdowne, June 29, 1905, ibid., no. 129, pp. 142–3.

[2] Ibid., no. 155, footnote 3, p. 166; Lansdowne to MacDonald, July 1, 1905, ibid., no. 130, p. 143.

[3] MacDonald to Lansdowne, July 8, 1905, ibid., nos. 131 and 132, pp. 144–5; Lansdowne to MacDonald, July 14, 1905, ibid., no. 134, p. 146; Lansdowne to MacDonald, July 18, 1905, ibid., no. 136, p. 149.

[4] Lansdowne to MacDonald, July 18, 1905, ibid., no. 136, p. 150; also Lansdowne

Believing with the Japanese Minister that his Government would approve of the note, the Foreign Office in the revised British draft of July 19 eliminated all reference to established treaty rights. But Hayashi and Lansdowne were too optimistic. On July 25 Sir Claude MacDonald, the British Minister at Tokio, spoke to Viscount Katsura, the Prime Minister of Japan. Katsura was perfectly candid. He said that the omission rendered Article III acceptable to Japan, but its good effects were nullified by the note to be exchanged after the signature of the treaty.[1] A situation of inordinate perplexity had thus arisen. Because of Japanese policy in Corea Great Britain did not propose to fight the United States nor indeed any other Power. But, for such potential British support, Tokio, under cover of the new Alliance, was at that juncture presumably striving. Screened by the treaty, Japan might perhaps exploit Corea with less fear of challenge from a third party.

In an endeavour to wear down Tokio's obduracy, the British Foreign Secretary now resorted to direct mention of the United States. His sympathies Theodore Roosevelt had, during the Far Eastern struggle, scarcely bothered to conceal; upon Katsura, by pointing to the amicable relations subsisting between Japan, Great Britain, and the United States, it might therefore still be possible to exercise an emollient influence. To Sir Claude MacDonald Lansdowne cabled on July 26 that the suggested note could be amended; 'all we desire is that we should not be compelled to go to war say with the U(nited) S(tates) in the event of a violation of established Treaty rights by Japan'. Nor did Hayashi in London think that the latter would invoke British assistance in such a case—one which was anyway unlikely to occur.[2] But MacDonald's response from Tokio did not sound very reassuring. To Katsura the British Minister had already remarked that the Japanese could hardly expect Great Britain to go to war with a Power or Powers whose established treaty rights they had infringed—'and I instanced the United States as being a Power with whom Japan was at present on exceedingly friendly terms'. On July 25, however, Katsura did not acknowledge the persuasive force of this contention; within the ambit of Tokio's calculations the American Government came perhaps as much as any other. 'Though I pressed him,' MacDonald added, 'Prime Minister avoided giving me a definite answer.'[3]

to MacDonald, July 19, 1905, ibid., no. 137 and Enclosure 2, pp. 150–1; Balfour to Lansdowne, July 19, 1905, ibid., no. 138, p. 151.

[1] Lansdowne to MacDonald, July 21, 1905, ibid., no. 141, p. 153; MacDonald to Lansdowne, July 25, 1905, ibid., no. 142, pp. 153–4.

[2] Lansdowne to MacDonald, July 26, 1905, ibid., no. 143, p. 154.

[3] MacDonald to Lansdowne, July 28, 1905, ibid., no. 144, p. 155.

But during the next week Katsura's attitude was to undergo a most auspicious change, and for it the United States would herself be principally responsible.

Into the maelstrom of world politics, while Great Britain and Japan were thus negotiating with each other, Theodore Roosevelt had been planning to take another deep plunge. By the traditionalist Senate he might be prevented from joining the Anglo-Japanese Alliance;[1] with Japan, in the last week of July, he reached, nevertheless, an explicit understanding which in effect served at both Tokio and Washington as an important reinforcement for British policy. This understanding he achieved through W. H. Taft, the American Secretary of War, who, being on a mission to the Philippines, had arranged to visit the Japanese capital. With Viscount Katsura Taft first exchanged ideas on July 27 and four days later Roosevelt—to whom a report had been sent—cabled him that his discussion with the Prime Minister of Japan was 'absolutely correct in every respect'. The President instructed the Secretary of War to tell Katsura that 'I confirm every word you have said'.[2] The two statesmen agreed that a memorandum bearing the date of July 29 represented their views. From it further evidence may be gleaned of the close relations prevailing in the summer of 1905 between the United States and the Anglo-Japanese Alliance.[3]

At the outset Katsura denied to his American visitor that Japan wished to wrest the Philippines from the United States. Rather than allow them to fall to one or several of her colonial rivals, Great Britain in 1898 had urged President McKinley to annex them. And now, seven years later, it was to her a matter of some considerable moment that between friend and ally they should furnish no grounds for Far Eastern dissension. Taft mentioned the rumour, circulated by American Russophiles, that Japan's victory would be 'a certain prelude' to her aggression on the Philippines. He thought, however, that in the archipelago neither native misrule nor the control of a hostile European Power could be to her interest, but orderly government by a strong and friendly nation such as the United States. 'Count Katsura confirmed in the strongest terms the correctness of his views on the point and positively stated that Japan does not harbor any aggressive designs whatever on the

[1] Dennett, *Roosevelt and the Russo-Japanese War*, p. 20; Roosevelt to Kennan, May 6, 1905, ibid., pp. 115–16.

[2] Pringle, *Roosevelt*, pp. 383–4; Roosevelt to Taft, July 31, 1905, ibid., p. 384.

[3] For memorandum of July 29, 1905, Dennett, *Roosevelt and the Russo-Japanese War*, pp. 112–14. It was written in English and the awkwardness of its language is therefore ascribed to Japanese draftsmanship, probably that of Viscount Katsura himself. Ibid., p. 112.

Philippines.'[1] With this unequivocal disclaimer of alleged threats to the American dependency in the Pacific, the Prime Minister paved the way for a favourable pronouncement by the President's emissary on the wider aims of Japan. And thus reassured Taft in turn could afford to reveal the attitude of the United States towards the Anglo-Japanese Alliance and the disposition of Corea.

Dealing with the general diplomatic question, Katsura proposed a tripartite agreement. The maintenance of peace in the Far East was, he declared, Japan's fundamental policy. 'In his own opinion the best, in fact the only, means for accomplishing the above object would be to form good understanding between the three governments of Japan, the United States, and Great Britain which have common interests in upholding the principle of eminence.' The Prime Minister realized that American isolationism was an obstacle and he perceived how impossible it would be for the United States to adhere to a formal alliance with foreign countries. But he could see no reason why 'some good understanding or an alliance in practice if not in name, should not be made between these three nations, in so far as respects the affairs in the Far East'. In those regions, and for the benefit of all Powers concerned, peace might thereby easily be safeguarded. Taft, in reply, had of necessity to refer to the restrictions under which Rooseveltian diplomacy laboured; none the less, by the tone and substance of his observations its broad range and character were abundantly indicated. It was, he said,

'difficult, indeed impossible, for the President of the United States of America to enter even to any understanding amounting in effect to a confidential informal agreement, without the consent of the Senate, but that he felt sure that without any agreement at all the people of the United States was so fully in accord with the people of Japan and Great Britain in the maintenance of peace in the Far East that whatever occasion arose appropriate action of the Government of the United States, in conjunction with Japan and Great Britain, for such a purpose could be counted on by them quite as confidently as if the United States were under treaty obligations to take (it).'[2]

Cordial and sympathetic, an utterance of this kind obviously denoted no mere expression of ordinary goodwill, even though it scarcely meant that the United States would, as Katsura desired—'in practice if not in name'—become an unofficial member of the Anglo-Japanese Alliance. Yet between Tokio and Washington it did bring a *rapproche-*

---

[1] Katsura also voiced indignation at anti-Japanese propaganda of the Yellow Peril variety. Memorandum of July 29, 1905, ibid., pp. 112–13.
[2] Memorandum of July 29, 1905, ibid., pp. 113–14.

ment into being which was at that time to be of the greatest value. For therewith the American Government accorded Japan an added sense of security against Russia and Germany, hoping perhaps that at the Portsmouth Conference her demands would be less stringent than they anticipated. And thus, too, of the Rooseveltian peace-making in the Far East, the Taft-Katsura understanding may be reckoned as a notable feature.

On the negative expedients to which John Hay had been confined it also no doubt registered a certain advance. Yet, however marked the tendency towards co-operation with Great Britain and Japan, the United States was still loath to adopt an effective programme for continuous participation in the politics of Eastern Asia. On the other hand, within the constricting limits of traditional isolationism, an American Administration had voiced unmitigated approval of the Anglo-Japanese Alliance—an approval from Washington excelling any that it had ever before received and than after 1905 it was ever to receive again. Taft's remarks constituted, moreover, the third suggestion during the international crisis of those years that in particular circumstances the United States might collaborate abroad with some, and against other, Powers. At the beginning of the Russo-Japanese War Roosevelt had notified Berlin and Paris, or claimed to have done so, that, should Japan be molested by a hostile European coalition, he would go to her support; then in June 1905 he had promised France, if she accepted the proposal for a Moroccan conference, to take 'very strong grounds' against any German unfairness; and now in July came the assurance of 'appropriate action' when called for along with Great Britain and Japan. Mainly temporary in intent, these intimations may have bound him to no fixed commitments. They were, all the same, highly illuminating as tacit admissions of the fact that only by abjuring her self-imposed continentalism could the United States, even for brief periods, play adequately the role of a Great Power. That whenever she intervened in world affairs she should do so on the British side or in consonance with British interests was one aspect of the friendly reinsurance with her which Downing Street had pursued since 1898. Copious German messages about the evil machinations in China of Great Britain and Japan may have flooded the White House; the Taft-Katsura understanding conduced finally to demonstrate that by the President they had been given short shrift. He may have remained perturbed at Lansdowne's hesitancy about advising Tokio to frame moderate conditions for peace; this was a problem not of principle but of method. Fundamentally in the conduct of their Far Eastern policies the English-speaking Governments had seldom been less at variance.

It was fortunate that the exchange of views between Taft and Katsura coincided with British insistence that her recognition of Japanese paramountcy in Corea must not embroil Great Britain in a conflict with the United States or any other Power. For in July Taft also disclosed to Katsura the favourable attitude of President Roosevelt— an attitude of which the British Government had been apprised for the past six months—towards Japan's Corean move. To the American statesman the Japanese Prime Minister had explained the importance of solving a question which was the direct cause of the Far Eastern struggle. If Corea were left to herself she would relapse into her old habit of signing treaties with foreign Governments. To avoid a recurrence of the previous confusion and to preclude another war, Japan felt constrained to take some definite step. The justness of these arguments Taft did not refute. He expressed it as his personal opinion that 'the establishment by Japanese troops of a suzerainty over Korea to the extent of requiring that Korea enter into no foreign treaties without the consent of Japan was the logical result of the present war and would directly contribute to permanent peace in the East'. Although he thought the President would concur, he was, he stated, speaking of this and other matters without special authority.[1] But everything he had said Roosevelt promptly endorsed and instructed him to inform Katsura accordingly. About the Philippines, the Anglo-Japanese Alliance, and Corea, so far as an informal understanding would permit, the United States and Japan were in full agreement.

Upon the current negotiations between London and Tokio, the influence of that fact was almost at once discernible. Taft and Katsura did not examine the precise point which made the British Government apprehensive. In Tokio, however, the position had been transformed. On July 25 Katsura was evasive when Sir Claude MacDonald instanced the United States as a friendly Power with whom the Japanese could hardly expect Great Britain to fight because they had violated established treaty rights in Corea. Cabling the next day in the same sense to the British Minister, Lansdowne offered to amend the draft of the proposed note. By its recipient a paraphrase of this message was sent to the Japanese Prime Minister and MacDonald interviewed him on July 30. But in the meantime the Taft-Katsura understanding had supervened. There was now no hedging as there had been five days before and no effort to burke the question. Fresh

[1] Memorandum of July 29, 1905, Dennett, *Roosevelt and the Russo-Japanese War*, p. 114.

from his discussion with the American representative, Katsura told the British Minister that Lansdowne's message of July 26 had 'very considerably cleared up the situation'. Japan, he observed, did not contemplate the infringement of existing treaty rights—whereupon MacDonald suggested that if such a confidential assurance were cabled by the Japanese to the British Government the draft note might either be modified or rendered unnecessary. Since Katsura had appeared willing to consider how he could meet Lansdowne's wishes, the latter regarded the outlook as much more hopeful.[1] On the Corean reef the Alliance was, it seemed, no longer in danger of foundering.

During the negotiations with Japan Lansdowne had been keeping Anglo-American relations under constant scrutiny. And so, when the Corean difficulty was most acute, he decided to ascertain the exact attitude of President Roosevelt towards the terms of the new treaty —the Government of the United States, it is noteworthy, being the only non-signatory of whom such inquiries were undertaken. Several purposes were thus accomplished. Firstly, by consulting the President, Lansdowne might make a gesture of friendship and attempt to show that the proposed changes consorted with the ideas previously exchanged between the English-speaking Powers on Far Eastern affairs. Secondly, if Roosevelt found no fault with the articles submitted, if he detected in them nothing inimical to his own country, there was probably little need to fear that the Alliance could ever provoke an Anglo-American conflict; a consideration, moreover, which applied as much to the *casus foederis* as to Corea. To Lansdowne as to every one else the future lay hidden. But it was true none the less that in any subsequent crisis, should Japan align Great Britain against the United States, it might fairly be asserted that Theodore Roosevelt had known the conditions beforehand; whatever the consequences, although every precaution had been taken, the motive was incontrovertibly pacific. The revision in 1911 of the second Anglo-Japanese Alliance thus heralded no novel departure but merely the adaptation to altered circumstances of a guiding principle. The President was not informed that in the Far East the British Government had insisted upon omitting the American Navy from their strategic calculations. But to him all the crucial treaty engagements then being drafted were frankly communicated.

Lansdowne cabled to Durand on July 29. To a paragraph in the preamble dealing with the preservation of the independence and integrity of the Chinese Empire and with the maintenance of equal

---

[1] MacDonald to Lansdowne, July 30, 1905, *Br. Docs.*, vol. iv, no. 146, pp. 156–7; MacDonald to Lansdowne, July 31, 1905, ibid., no. 147, pp. 157–9.

opportunities for foreign commerce and industry, the Ambassador was instructed to draw the special attention of the President as being one 'which is in close accordance with his policy'. Article II defined the *casus foederis*. The Foreign Secretary stated that the new treaty differed from its predecessor 'mainly in that contracting parties will come to one another's assistance if either of them is involved in war owing to unprovoked attack even of a single Power'. This clause, directed to the defence of British and Japanese interests in the regions of Eastern Asia and India, was the one which afterwards would create a serious problem for Anglo-American friendship. At the time, however, Roosevelt did not subject it to critical analysis, doubtless because of the very cordial relations still existing between Japan and the United States. But the framing of the Corean article was what really worried the British Government. Lansdowne transmitted it to Durand in a form palatable to Tokio and as included in the final text; he did not mention his proposal to exchange a note with Japan exempting Great Britain from participation in a war resulting from a Japanese violation of established treaty rights in Corea. For the contested formula Lansdowne was anxious to elicit Roosevelt's approval. 'This Article', he cabled, 'to which Japan attaches the utmost importance seems to us in accordance with President's views'; and he referred the Ambassador to the discussion with Roosevelt in January of that year about Japanese paramountcy in Corea. Francis B. Loomis, the First Assistant Secretary of State, had been visiting England and from him Lansdowne gathered that to the Corean article the United States in all likelihood would not object.[1]

Durand interviewed Roosevelt on August 3, three days after the latter had confirmed the understanding reached at Tokio between Katsura and Taft. Designed to strengthen Japan's position and enable her to pursue her aims in Corea unobstructed by further Russian encroachments, the Anglo-Japanese draft stipulations tallied with what the President through official and semi-official channels had been advocating to Downing Street for many months. Towards the fulfilment of Roosevelt's plan of a Far Eastern balance, the goal of his current endeavours, they would indeed provide the political groundwork. When, therefore, the British Ambassador went to see the President at Oyster Bay so as to acquaint him with the principal terms of the new treaty an adverse judgement was most improbable. 'He accepted it', Durand recorded, 'at once without demur.' Although Roosevelt did not believe that Great Britain required Japanese help for the defence of India he thought the Russians must now realize the

---

[1] Lansdowne to Durand, July 29, 1905, ibid., no. 145, pp. 155–6.

hopelessness of an attack.[1] His views, it was evident, had suffered no change; at its inception in fact the second Anglo-Japanese Alliance gave promise of being an element not of discord between the English-speaking Powers but of harmony. During the negotiations two of the major difficulties encountered—the naval and the Corean—sprang chiefly from Lansdowne's attitude towards the United States. In British policy the conservation of Anglo-American solidarity had again been revealed as a vital factor.

In London, at the beginning of August, good news, then, arrived from both Washington and Tokio. Katsura was prepared to compromise. Having on the highest authority just learned that the United States would not hinder Japan's penetration of Corea, he safely could satisfy Great Britain about a very remote contingency. But for domestic and international reasons no one was to know that he had done so; if nothing were announced on that score Russia and other Powers would steer clear of Corea lest the allies join forces against them. Nor were notes to be exchanged between Tokio and London. By Katsura, however, the British Government were assured that in the imaginary circumstances of a violation of established treaty rights in Corea they would not be obliged to support Japan.[2] The last serious hitch had been overcome. Another matter, less strenuously debated, was also adjusted about explanations to be offered of the article concerning the defence of India. Lansdowne and Hayashi signed the agreement on August 12, 1905. But it was decided to refrain from publication as yet. The Portsmouth Conference would be dealing with some of the same questions and the signatories did not wish to present it with a *fait accompli* nor to assume responsibility for its possible break-down because of prior arrangements into which they had entered.[3]

On the other hand, the British Government wondered whether one exception should not be made from this general rule and their American friend alone informed that the task of revising the Alliance had formally been concluded. The President, moreover, was still displeased that they boggled at urging moderation in the Japanese peace terms.[4] If, then, they now divulged to him the actual signature of

---

[1] Durand's memorandum, Sykes, *Durand*, pp. 285–6. The date of this conversation may have been Aug. 2, and not Aug. 3. Roosevelt to Reid, Aug. 3, 1905, Bishop, *Roosevelt*, vol. i, p. 403.

[2] MacDonald to Lansdowne, Aug. 3, 1905, *Br. Docs.*, vol. iv, no. 148, pp. 159–60; Lansdowne to MacDonald, Aug. 8, 1905, ibid., no. 151 and Enclosure, pp. 161–3; MacDonald to Lansdowne, Aug. 11, 1905, ibid., no. 153, p. 164.

[3] Lansdowne to MacDonald, Aug. 3, 1905, ibid., no. 150, pp. 160–1; Lansdowne to MacDonald, Aug. 8, 1905, ibid., no. 151, pp. 161–2. For text, ibid., no. 155, pp. 165–9.

[4] Durand's memorandum, Sykes, *Durand*, pp. 285–6.

the new treaty he might altogether cease to suspect that they were standing wilfully aloof from positive co-operation. On August 12 Durand asked for instructions and King Edward VII presumed that it would soon be desirable to tell him. 'I am most anxious to show the President that we trust him completely,' Lansdowne cabled back on August 16, 'but can we be quite sure that the secret would be kept.' The matter was left to the discretion of the Ambassador[1]—the upshot being that Durand withheld the information until after the Treaty of Portsmouth had been signed. He apparently felt that the secret would not be kept. In Theodore Roosevelt the British Ambassador had perhaps as little confidence as the former had in him.

Meanwhile on August 10, 1905, the Russo-Japanese Peace Conference, meeting under American auspices at Portsmouth, New Hampshire, had begun its labours. Japan was represented by Baron Komura, her Minister for Foreign Affairs, and by M. K. Takahira, her Minister at Washington; Russia by Count Witte, an ex-Finance Minister and future Prime Minister, and by Count Rosen, her newly appointed Ambassador to the United States. Quick to capture the goodwill of the American press, the Russians were skilfully displacing the Japanese as popular favourites. Eight points of the proposed treaty were settled with celerity; the plenipotentiaries were at loggerheads over two questions: the restoration to Russia of the island of Sakhalin and whether she should pay Japan a war indemnity. This stage they reached on August 16, and Roosevelt thereupon undertook to break the dead-lock so as to ensure the consummation of his peacemaking.

At St. Petersburg he was seconded by the Emperor William from whom flowed in an endless stream perfervid denunciations of Franco-British chicanery. Working also through his own Ambassador, the President dispatched three personal messages to the Tsar. As a result of these efforts Nicholas II was persuaded to cede the southern half of Sakhalin, but he would not yield even the modest indemnity to which Roosevelt deemed the victorious Japanese entitled. Japan, in the meantime, had been striving for the whole island of Sakhalin and a large indemnity to replenish her empty coffers. Would such demands bar the way to peace ? Genuinely afraid that this might happen, the President now addressed to the Japanese Government two powerful letters—cabled home by his friend Baron Kaneko—arguing the advantages to Japan herself of an early termination of the war.[2] The

---

[1] Durand to Lansdowne, Aug. 12, 1905, *Br. Docs.*, vol. iv, no. 157, p. 170; Lansdowne to Durand, Aug. 16, 1905, ibid., no. 158, p. 170.

[2] For the negotiations Bishop, *Roosevelt*, vol. i, pp. 404–12; Dennett, *Roosevelt and the Russo-Japanese War*, pp. 236–77; Dennis, *Adventures*, pp. 410–12; *Br. Docs.*, vol. iv, pp. 96–106; Gwynn, *Spring Rice*, vol. i, pp. 486–9.

auguries were, however, none too bright. Roosevelt blamed the Russians most for not admitting themselves vanquished, while the Japanese were wrong to risk a prolongation of the struggle in order to obtain a monetary recompense. He was, moreover, still vexed with Great Britain because she gave him no diplomatic assistance at Tokio corresponding to that which France and Germany were supposed to be proffering at St. Petersburg. About advising Japan to be reasonable the British Government had, he said, been 'foolishly reluctant'.[1]

Nevertheless at Downing Street the President on August 23 again tried to exercise pressure. In a letter to the British Ambassador he reiterated his contention that Japan should withdraw demands which would bring not peace but a renewal of the conflict and to Lansdowne the next day Durand sent a summary of Roosevelt's statement.

> 'He has told Japanese that the opinion of the civilized world will not support them in continuing the war merely for the purpose of extorting money from Russia. He thinks that they would be right in continuing the war if Russia refused to cede Sakhalin but in as much as they wish to hold all they have taken it is difficult to see what possible claim they have for a heavy indemnity. President points out that if Japanese continue the war all they can possibly get is Eastern Siberia which they do not want, and this after great expenditure and loss of life with the feeling of the civilized world turning against them and a possibility of reverses. It seems to him the greatest act of friendship to urge Japan in her own interest not to follow a course which may do her great damage and can do her no real benefit.'

To Durand's message the British Foreign Secretary appended a minute which was wholly of a piece with the policy he had pursued from the start:

> 'This is a suggestion that we should press the Japanese to make further concessions.
> 'Were we to do so our advice would not be taken and would be resented.
> 'I am in commun(icatio)n with Mr. Balfour as to the course to be taken.'[2]

The British Government were in an extraordinarily awkward predicament. Since June their case for abstention had been explained to the President frequently and at length. Besides, so far as they knew, the fault was not that of Tokio but of St. Petersburg. Nor could her ally be expected willingly to dissuade Japan from a natural desire

---

[1] Roosevelt to White, Aug. 23, 1905, Nevins, *White*, p. 267; Bishop, *Roosevelt*, vol. i, p. 408; Dennett, *Roosevelt and the Russo-Japanese War*, pp. 257–8, refers to an appeal on Aug. 18 from Roosevelt to Durand.

[2] Durand to Lansdowne, Aug. 24, 1905, *Br. Docs.*, vol. iv, no. 97, and footnote, pp. 104–5.

for a settlement on her own terms—more especially as the latter now appeared ready to modify her conditions and compromise on the indemnity, although definitely insisting on some such payment.[1] None the less, should the dispute about it cause a resumption of the war, Great Britain, having remained inactive, could not easily be absolved from a certain responsibility. A situation of this kind had furthermore been forecast by the Kaiser as one of his fancied Anglo-French intrigues, and on her at Washington he was always waiting to steal a march. Indeed, on many grounds, the effect would be deplorable if Roosevelt were subsequently to attribute the failure of his peacemaking to British apathy or indifference. And thus at a critical juncture Great Britain found herself again torn by the necessity of riding with the American hounds while hunting with the Japanese hares—a ticklish problem with the graver recrudescence of which she was afterwards to become more and more uncomfortably familiar.

The British Government, attempting to reconcile their two affinities, managed, however, to unite deference towards the sensitive pride of their ally with the maintenance of Anglo-American friendship. Without comment Lansdowne transmitted to Tokio a copy of Durand's cablegram. In this fashion, although Great Britain did not commit herself to any particular opinion, the character of Roosevelt's efforts at London was brought to the notice of the Japanese Government. At the final Council held in Tokio, so Durand informed the President, his message had been taken into consideration.[2] And with Roosevelt the British Foreign Office may have co-operated in yet another manner. On August 25 unofficial news of the conclusion of the second Anglo-Japanese Alliance seems to have been disclosed to the press.[3] While the stipulations of the revised treaty did not affect the precise details under dispute at Portsmouth, the circulation of the rumour conveyed the impression at home and abroad that to Russian browbeating the Japanese Government would henceforth be relatively insusceptible. Fortifying their hands, it thereby enabled them to surrender their claim for an indemnity and the whole island of Sakhalin without tacitly confessing that, impotent even in victory, they must still cling to the Russian chariot-wheels. Nor was the President disposed to ignore the useful function which Great Britain had discharged. 'I did not get much direct assistance from the English Government,'

[1] MacDonald to Lansdowne, Aug. 20, 1905, ibid., no. 95, pp. 102–3; MacDonald to Lansdowne, Aug. 24, 1905, ibid., no. 96, pp. 103–4.
[2] Durand to Roosevelt, Aug. 31, 1905, *Correspondence of Roosevelt and Lodge*, vol. ii, p. 188; also ibid., pp. 177–90.
[3] Dennett, *Roosevelt and the Russo-Japanese War*, p. 257. But was the source Japanese rather than British? Lansdowne to Barrington, Sept. 2, 1905, *Br. Docs.*, vol. iv, no. 160, p. 171.

he wrote to the American Ambassador at London, 'but I did get in-direct assistance, for I learned that they forwarded to Japan my note to Durand, and I think that the signing of the Anglo-Japanese treaty made Japan feel comparatively safe as to the future.'[1] To the Presi-dent's last appeal, as he himself acknowledged, Great Britain had responded in no unhelpful spirit.

At this point Rooseveltian adjurations in London were supplemented by singularly opportune financial advice. Jacob H. Schiff had not only sponsored the flotation of Japanese bonds in the United States; through his German connexions he also had arranged for the third and fourth loans to be taken up in Germany. Nevertheless, at the Portsmouth Conference, further assurance of a fresh supply of funds was needed by Japanese representatives so as to show themselves capable, should their demands be rejected, of prolonging the conflict.[2] But the war expenditures of Japan had rocketed steeply upward—her national indebtedness having soared from 600,000,000 to 2,400,000,000 yen, the annual interest being estimated at 110,000,000 yen.[3] While to her American bankers these exact figures were in all probability unknown, they swiftly perceived that for Japan to be saved from financial ruin an early peace had become essential. Of the vast diminution in Japanese pecuniary and material resources the British Foreign Office may not have been conscious.[4] But the emphasis with which Roosevelt dwelt on that primary fact might indicate that he was in consultation, among others, with Jacob Schiff. Such an assump-tion is supported by the timeliness—and it may have been but a coin-cidence—of an extremely important letter which Schiff dispatched to the Japanese spokesmen at Portsmouth just when the moderating activities of the President were at their height. If the war continued, Schiff wrote on August 25 to tell Takahira and Komura, Russia could employ her huge gold reserves, or even temporarily abandon the gold standard. To Japan, on the other hand, those expedients were not available; her position threatened therefore to be more difficult. By Schiff's own firm, Kuhn, Loeb and Company, she would not be left in the lurch. 'What I do apprehend, however, is that the money markets of the United States, England, and Germany will, with the belief of a war à outrance, no longer be prepared to finance Japan's requirements to any great extent.'[5] This communication, ostensibly volunteered by a foreign friend to whom the Japanese Government had every

[1] Roosevelt to Reid, Sept. 11, 1905, Bishop, *Roosevelt*, vol. i, p. 415.
[2] Takahashi's memorandum, Adler, *Schiff*, vol. i, pp. 224–6.
[3] Gotaro Ogawa, *The Expenditures of the Russo-Japanese War*, p. 252.
[4] Dennett, *Roosevelt and the Russo-Japanese War*, p. 214.
[5] Schiff to Takahira, Aug. 25, 1905, Adler, *Schiff*, vol. i, pp. 231–2.

reason for gratitude, betokened the one sort of pressure they obviously could not resist. In view of that, because of what now happened, should Jacob Schiff be numbered among the chief peacemakers of 1905 ? Was Theodore Roosevelt endeavouring to influence Tokio not only from the White House, not only and with less hope of success through the British Government, but also with that peculiarly compulsive dialectic which Wall Street alone could marshal ?

On August 29, to every one's surprise, the Japanese plenipotentiaries backed down. The Russians had rejected their claim for a large indemnity and only were willing to cede to Japan the southern half of the island of Sakhalin. Forced either to accept peace on these terms or renew the struggle, the Japanese decided on the former course. Under the Treaty of Portsmouth, which was signed on September 5, 1905, Russia agreed that Japan should possess paramount rights in Corea. As for Manchuria, it would be evacuated by the troops of both Powers and restored to the sovereignty of China. Yet in that province Japanese predominance was inaugurated by the transference to Japan of the southern section of the Manchurian railway—and she also inherited Russian interests in the Liaotung Peninsula which included Port Arthur and its environs.[1] On the Asiatic mainland the foundations for her future expansion were thus firmly established.

The President was duly elated at the turn events had taken. To the success of his mediation the Treaty of Portsmouth bore striking testimony, and in its provisions the Rooseveltian theory of a Far Eastern balance of power appeared, for a delusive spell, to be embodied. Yet one constructive idea, to which in 1904 he and the Japanese had subscribed, seems to have vanished: that, namely, of guaranteeing the autonomy of China in Manchuria—the management of her police and railways—by means of an international committee of control. Nevertheless, since his main objects had been accomplished, the President could feel the utmost satisfaction. Around him during a major diplomatic crisis world politics had rotated and in attempting to safeguard American security he had at the same time served humanity and won universal renown.

As soon as the Treaty of Portsmouth had been signed it was feasible officially to announce to the interested Powers the conclusion of the second Anglo-Japanese Alliance. Durand acted at once. Communicating with Roosevelt on September 5, he implied that the British Government deserved credit, for by the prompt conclusion of the

---

[1] For Treaty *Br. Docs.*, vol. iv, no. 101, pp. 107–11; *U.S. Foreign Relations*, 1905, pp. 824–8.

agreement they enabled Japan the more easily to moderate her demands.[1] Five days later Lansdowne cabled to the Ambassador that, if desirable, it should be explained to the President why the actual signature of the revised Alliance had not been divulged to him previously. Durand, however, perceived nothing indicative of Roosevelt having taken offence. 'President writes to me', he replied, 'that he has no doubt that the signing of the Treaty was a powerful factor in inducing Japan to be wise and reasonable as to terms. His letter is quite pleasant in tone.'[2] Meanwhile the contents of the Alliance were imparted to the French and Russian Governments on September 8— the covering dispatch which Lansdowne submitted to them carrying, significantly enough, a plain intimation of American approval of Corea's altered status; and then in the middle of the month Germany was informed, publication following on September 27.[3] The second Anglo-Japanese Alliance and the Treaty of Portsmouth were the twin pillars on which rested the Far Eastern settlement. That they would be interdependent Theodore Roosevelt had long foreseen; the conclusion of the one, as he freely admitted, helped in the end to attain the completion of the other. Between the English-speaking Powers the common policy sought by the President since 1904 was, despite the cleavages which had occurred, finally achieved.

At the time Roosevelt himself bore witness to this fact, but in later years he reverted to his old complaint. In his autobiography the ex-President remarked that during the negotiations, although he tried to enlist the aid of other Governments, he obtained assistance only from the German Emperor.[4] Published, however, in 1913, that volume had been written after the evident break-down of his scheme for protecting American interests through a Far Eastern equilibrium and subsequent to the onset of a potentially serious complication in English-speaking friendship bred by ill will between Japan and the United States. The truth was that in September 1905 Roosevelt fully acknowledged the effective role which Great Britain had performed.[5] And of what he had done the President sent a review to Spring Rice who in turn forwarded it to Balfour and Lansdowne. The Japanese, he fancied, might have procured the northern half of Sakhalin. 'But

[1] Durand to Roosevelt, Sept. 5, 1905, Dennett, *Roosevelt and the Russo-Japanese War*, p. 258.

[2] Lansdowne to Durand, Sept. 10, 1905, *Br. Docs.*, vol. iv, no. 173, pp. 179–80; Durand to Lansdowne, Sept. 11, 1905, ibid., no. 176, p. 181. The full text was conveyed to the American Government on Sept. 28, *U.S. Foreign Relations*, 1905, p. 487.

[3] *Br. Docs.*, vol. iv, no. 166, pp. 174–5; no. 172, pp. 177–9; no. 177, p. 181; no. 180, p. 182.

[4] Roosevelt, *Autobiography*, p. 586.

[5] Roosevelt to Reid, Sept. 11, 1905, Bishop, *Roosevelt*, vol. i, p. 415; Durand to Lansdowne, Sept. 11, 1905, *Br. Docs.*, vol. iv, no. 176, p. 181.

on the whole it is all right, and I think the peace is just to Russia and Japan, and also good for England and the United States.'[1] On the British side praise of Roosevelt's efforts, and the success with which they had been crowned, was warm and unstinted. Anglo-American relations were, at the close of the Russo-Japanese War, in a state of unalloyed cordiality.[2]

Yet so also were those between Potsdam and the White House. Prior to the Portsmouth Conference and with the Moroccan crisis in mind, Roosevelt had not only pronounced Germany a European danger but even had envisaged the possibility of a naval attack by her on the United States. To Durand he said that if the Germans seized Holland he would take over Dutch possessions in the West and he presumed that in Java and elsewhere Great Britain would do likewise.[3] By September, however, the President's attitude was much less censorious. William II had co-operated with him at St. Petersburg and upon this he commented to Spring Rice appreciatively.[4] But such a metamorphosis was hardly to the taste of a British diplomatist who always endeavoured to indoctrinate Roosevelt with his own profound conviction of the native German aptitude for international mischief. From his post at the St. Petersburg Embassy, to which he had now returned, Spring Rice accordingly attempted to pick up the threads once more. At the end of September and the beginning of October, in three letters to the President, he again portrayed Germany as the supreme menace to the peace of Europe and ascribed to American mediation alone the fact that against their own wishes Russia and Japan had agreed to the terms of the Portsmouth Treaty. By its recipient Roosevelt's account of his activities had been submitted to Lord Lansdowne. Answering the President, Spring Rice quoted the Foreign Secretary as having observed that Roosevelt had 'done a big thing, and I for one take off my hat to him'.[5] Through his analyses of the European situation there ran a single, dominant theme: the threat of Russia becoming subservient and France being subordinated to a German policy the ultimate aim of which was the overthrow of British world-power. They prefaced a more important correspondence dealing with an alleged attachment—to which Spring

[1] Roosevelt to Spring Rice, Sept. 1, 1905, Gwynn, *Spring Rice*, vol. i, p. 489.

[2] Durand to Roosevelt, Aug. 31, 1905, *Correspondence of Roosevelt and Lodge*, vol. ii, p. 188; Lodge to Roosevelt, Sept. 7, 1905, ibid., p. 191; Reid to Roosevelt, Sept. 11, 1905, Bishop, *Roosevelt*, vol. i, p. 413; Sykes, *Durand*, p. 287.

[3] Ibid., pp. 287–8.

[4] Roosevelt to Spring Rice, Sept. 1, 1905, Gwynn, *Spring Rice*, vol. i, p. 489; also Roosevelt to Lodge, Sept. 2, 1905, *Correspondence of Roosevelt and Lodge*, vol. ii, p. 188.

[5] Spring Rice to Mrs. Roosevelt, Sept. 26, 1905, Gwynn, *Spring Rice*, vol. i, pp. 490–4; Spring Rice to Mrs. Roosevelt, Oct. 5, 1905, ibid., pp. 495–8; Spring Rice to Mrs. Roosevelt, Oct. 10, 1905, ibid., pp. 498–501.

Rice already had referred—between the United States and the vast project then under discussion for a continental combine.

In July 1905 from the Tsar's yacht on the Baltic the Kaiser had thrown a large pebble into the troubled waters of world politics and there was scarcely a Great Power that did not feel affected by the mysterious Russo-German collaboration which seemed as a result to portend. After some delay, moreover, a few of the ripples spread even to Washington. For at Björko the two Emperors had signed a secret treaty of alliance—one to which France, supposedly chastened by the Moroccan crisis, would be compelled to adhere and whose example many of the smaller nations were expected to emulate. Conflicting with the Dual Alliance, the arrangement was finally turned down by Count Lamsdorff, the Russian Minister for Foreign Affairs; St. Petersburg had been left without the least glimmer of hope that the French could be lured supinely from their Entente with Great Britain in order to enter the German fold. At Berlin the regal handiwork enjoyed no happier fate. The first article stipulated that if one of the two signatories were attacked by a European Power the other would aid it in Europe with all its forces on land and sea; but against the Kaiser's insertion of the words 'in Europe' Prince von Bülow protested energetically. William II may have restricted the treaty to Europe so as to avoid any obligation to go to the assistance of Russia in an Asiatic quarrel between her and Great Britain; this, however, meant also that Russian help would not be forthcoming where the Chancellor considered it could best be used—in operations on the frontiers of India. Bülow's resignation his Sovereign refused to accept. 'According to English ideas,' the Chancellor had written to the Emperor, 'India and Canada are the only two vulnerable points of the British Empire.'[1] Nor did the signature of the Björko Treaty prove to be a matter remote from the most recent phase of Anglo-American relations, inasmuch as it clearly vindicated the Fabian policy adopted by Great Britain during the Rooseveltian peacemaking. Seeking to arrest the further decline of Russian strength, the Kaiser's was no disinterested purpose but one directly inimical to her. That in his co-operation at St. Petersburg there had been sound reason to suspect ulterior motives events presently would demonstrate.

In Count Witte the Emperor William found a zealous coadjutor. Journeying home in September from the Portsmouth Conference, the Russian plenipotentiary visited him at Rominten. Witte shared his

---

[1] Bülow to the Kaiser, Aug. 3, 1905, Bülow, *Memoirs 1903–1909*, p. 134; also ibid., pp. 130–44; *Bülow's Letters*, pp. 143–89; Fay, *Origins of the World War*, vol. i, pp. 171–7. For text of treaty *Br. Docs.*, vol. iv, p. 95.

host's ambition to subvert in the Occident the new structure of British diplomacy—the Entente Cordiale and friendship with the United States; as a means of driving apart the English-speaking Powers they both took for granted and relied upon American hostility towards the Anglo-Japanese Alliance. A letter from the Kaiser to the Tsar delineated in a quaint yet graphic English style his discussion with Count Witte.

> 'He is a firm advocate of a Russo-German-France Alliance which as he tells me will be gladly "Cotaoygé" by America—for the maintenance of the Peace & *statu quo* in the world, the balance of which has been disturbed by the Anglo-Japanese Treaty. He was consequently very agreeably surprized when I told him of our work at Bjorkoe. It is the grouping of Powers which is the most natural—they being the representants of the "Continent"—& will have the consequence of drawing all the other lesser Powers in Europe into the orbit of this great block. Amerika will stand on the side of this "Combination". Firstly from the "Racial" point of view, they are decidedly "White" anti "Yellow". Secondly politically, from fear of Japan on account of the Philippines upon which the Japanese have cast longing eyes, their loss would impair the American position in the Pacific. Thirdly from the dangerous competition of the Japanese trade sustained by very cheap labour & without the cost of long transport with its tariffs for freight & for the passage of the Suez Canal. The sums to be paid for its passage being a heavy tax on the whole *European* commerce. The same thing will be the "Panama Canal".'

And thus anticipating for their scheme the support of the United States, the Kaiser proceeded to expound to Nicholas II its central object:

> 'The "Continental Combine" flanked by America is the sole & only manner to effectively block the way to the whole world becoming John Bull's private property, which he exploits at his heart's content after having, by lies & intrigues without end, set the rest of the civilized nations by each others ears for his own personal benefit.'

This pernicious tendency had, moreover, been active in the Moroccan question—the French being hypnotized by Great Britain to oppose Germany. But the future interests of France lay with the Russo-German coalition, and of that William II wanted Russia to remind her, to advise the Quai d'Orsay that such 'Anglomania' must now be stopped.[1]

Early in October 1905, after Witte's return to St. Petersburg, the French Government were much disquieted at the strength of Germanophile propensities in the Russian capital. What they desired was no close union with Germany but on the contrary one with

[1] Willy to Nicky, Sept. 26, 1905, *The Kaiser's Letters to the Tsar*, pp. 210–12; also Bülow, *Memoirs 1903–1909*, pp. 163–6; Brandenburg, *From Bismarck*, &c., pp. 233–43.

themselves between their ally and Great Britain. Discomfited by the project for a continental coalition and by the virulence of Witte's tirades against the Anglo-Japanese Alliance, M. Bompard, the French Ambassador, confided on October 4 in Sir Charles Hardinge, his British colleague. Between Russia, Germany, and the United States was a combination possible ? Hardinge did not think so; as far as the United States was concerned, the relations of the President with Great Britain and Japan, and his attitude towards the Open Door, which both Powers were pledged to maintain, rendered the idea 'in the highest degree improbable'. And then on the same day, to the British Ambassador himself, Count Lamsdorff, the Russian Minister for Foreign Affairs, echoed his Government's fury at the fact that the revised Anglo-Japanese Alliance contemplated assistance from Japan against Russia for the defence of India. Any comprehensive adjustment of differences between London and St. Petersburg, such as had been mooted before the Far Eastern struggle, would, he said, have as a result to be again postponed.[1] But what seemed particularly disconcerting were the views attributed to the United States. Writing from St. Petersburg on October 5, Spring Rice hastened therefore to bring them to Roosevelt's immediate attention. France, he pointed out, was being placed in a painful dilemma. If her ally insisted upon her joining the anti-British compact it would be hard for her to refuse; and yet by participating she must inevitably weaken the Entente Cordiale on which depended the European equilibrium. 'The French are also very nervous as to the attitude of the United States. It is being said here that the U.S. are inclined to enter into a combination or an understanding hostile to England and Japan, which would make it even more difficult for the French to stand out.' On the other hand, if Germany attacked Great Britain or France successfully, the country not attacked would be put in an untenable position; and that, he averred, was why as a matter of self-preservation they were obliged to back each other up.[2] By October 10, however, Spring Rice deemed a Russo-German declaration conceivable but unlikely. To the President he nevertheless recounted how Witte was still raging against Great Britain for having signed the second Anglo-Japanese Alliance.[3] One further letter completed a series which elicited from the White House a prompt and noteworthy response.

This was caused by a conversation on October 14 between Lamsdorff and Bompard. Obtaining a full account from the latter,

[1] Hardinge to Lansdowne, Oct. 4, 1905, *Br. Docs.*, vol. iv, no. 195, pp. 205–7.
[2] Spring Rice to Mrs. Roosevelt, Oct. 5, 1905, Gwynn, *Spring Rice*, vol. i, pp. 496–7.
[3] Spring Rice to Mrs. Roosevelt, Oct. 10, 1905, ibid., p. 500.

Hardinge reported it at length to the British Foreign Office. His French colleague had contended that, as the ally of Russia, France was entitled to hear Lamsdorff's opinion of the revised Anglo-Japanese Alliance; and having thus been urged the reluctant Minister unburdened himself with the utmost vehemence. Upon the other Powers in Asia, and despite the pre-war Anglo-Russian negotiations, Great Britain and Japan were attempting to impose their will; a proceeding the upshot of which was, he asserted, 'deep dissatisfaction not merely in Russia but also in Germany and the United States'—something challenged in turn in a marginal comment of Lansdowne's as being quite unsupported by evidence. What she had done in Africa, Lamsdorff told Bompard, Great Britain was now doing in Asia. It had to be stopped, as indeed it would be, by a quadruple coalition—a counterpoise in the Far East to the Anglo-Japanese Alliance maintaining there an equilibrium similar to that which the Dual and Triple Alliances maintained in Europe; 'a combination of Russia, France, Germany, and the United States would serve that purpose.' By the French Ambassador the Russian Minister was, however, at once informed that, after her experience during the Moroccan crisis, his country could join no Russo-German group; as an alternative he suggested that the action of the other Powers be assimilated to that of Great Britain and Japan. To Hardinge Bompard conveyed his impression that the admitted German endeavours at St. Petersburg were regarded by Lamsdorff without enthusiasm if not with disrelish. But he emphasized the remarks of the Russian Foreign Minister, made for the second time, about American discontent with the Anglo-Japanese Alliance. 'The danger of such an attitude on the part of the United States Government', it had seemed to the French Ambassador, 'would consist in the fact that Russia might be disposed to enter into a coalition with Germany and the United States while she would be unwilling to enter into an agreement with Germany alone.' To this Hardinge had replied that the Anglo-Japanese Alliance, upholding equal opportunities for foreign trade and the integrity and independence of China, was in tune with American policy; in the United States no signs of opposition were evident. At the British Foreign Office the importance of what Lamsdorff had said was directly perceived. Lansdowne and the Assistant Under-Secretary of State noted that the Anglo-Russian negotiations could not, for the moment, be resumed and that the Russians were being strongly pressed by the German Emperor. They also noted that they had had no indication of American views since the Government of the United States had received the text of the second Anglo-Japanese Alliance, 'but when the substance was communicated to the President, he appeared quite satisfied'.[1]

Yet in the interval a change might have occurred. For one thing the British Government realized that at Washington, thanks to his co-operation with the Rooseveltian peacemaking, the German Emperor had gained considerable ground; to them, they had learned, comparisons drawn by the President were distinctly unflattering. In the circumstances a fresh and authoritative elucidation of American policy was essential and towards securing it Spring Rice set himself unhesitatingly to work—the step he `took being approved by Gerald Balfour, the President of the Local Government Board, through whom he kept in touch with the Prime Minister. Bompard spoke to Lamsdorff on October 14. A day later, from the British Embassy at St. Petersburg, Spring Rice again wrote to the President. He depicted the sharp annoyance of the Russians at the revision of the Anglo-Japanese Alliance and the disappointment of the Entente that as a consequence Anglo-Russian differences were less likely than ever to be composed. Furthermore, upon France the disagreeable choice was being forced of either joining Russia in the anti-British continental league or of staying out, isolated in Europe, while Germany supplanted her with her ally—a matter which brought him to the heart of his exposition. Japan, Spring Rice observed, needed peace and wished for greater stability in central Asiatic affairs.

'But yesterday the French Ambassador had an interview with Lamsdorff in which L. used very violent language against England and said that a continental coalition was the right and proper answer to the Anglo-Japanese alliance. England, he said, had insulted civilization in her South African War and now again in her East Asiatic alliance. "Il faut mettre fin à tout ça." He added that if France refused to join she would be left alone. The United States were in favour of this course, as the American Government was hostile to the Anglo-Japanese arrangement as they thought it a menace to their own interests.'

Witte, moreover, talked in an even stronger vein than the Foreign Minister and their language indubitably mirrored that of the Russian Court. Bompard was perturbed. 'He is very anxious', Spring Rice stated, 'to know whether it is true that America is favourable to the proposed combination and, if so, in what manner the American Government has made it known here.'[2]

In the meantime Théophile Delcassé had recently disclosed what he regarded as a promise from Great Britain during the Moroccan

---

[1] Hardinge to Lansdowne, Oct. 14, 1905, *Br. Docs.*, vol. iv, no. 198, pp. 211–12.
[2] Spring Rice to Mrs. Roosevelt, Oct. 15, 1905, Gwynn, *Spring Rice*, vol. i, pp. 501–2; also Gerald Balfour to Spring Rice, Oct. 25, 1905, ibid., pp. 503–4.

crisis to afford France naval and military assistance against Germany. This revelation by the former Foreign Minister—speedily disavowed in both London and Paris—tended perhaps to show that in world politics the Entente was a somewhat provocative factor. Any such idea Spring Rice earnestly denied, but to Roosevelt he pointed out, chiefly by historical analogy, that Great Britain could not remain indifferent while German aggression upon France dislocated still further the European balance of power. Since a continuance of the existing irritation would be intolerable, he pleaded in conclusion for 'a quieting word' from the United States.[1]

On the President the effect of Spring Rice's communications was instantaneous, and his reply attested once more to the diplomatic importance of their private correspondence. For it did not only confirm the understanding in the Far East between Great Britain and the United States; it also was a long and thorough résumé of Anglo-American relations as a whole. The letters he received from Spring Rice, Roosevelt wrote on November 1, often gave him 'the chance to set things right'. This was so with respect to Witte's assertion that the United States shared Russian hostility towards the second Anglo-Japanese Alliance. The President had been quick to explain his attitude to the French and Japanese representatives.

> 'In accordance with your request I saw Jusserand at once and told him what Witte had said, and asked him immediately to cable to his Government that so far from this being true, I had seen the treaty in question before it was ratified, both the English and the Japanese giving me the substance thereof; and that I had told both nations in answer to their requests that I entirely approved of the treaty, was glad that it had been negotiated, and believed that it was advantageous to the peace of Asia, and therefore, to the peace of the world. By my direction, Taft reiterated this in a talk with the Japanese Prime Minister, Katsura; saying specifically, that we entirely approved of the Japanese position about Korea as set forth in the Anglo-Japanese Treaty, and as acknowledged in the Treaty of Portsmouth. Jusserand told me that he entirely understood my position, and that he believed the French Government did, but that in any event he would cable just what I had said. Root also, of course, understands my position and cordially sympathises with me. I informed Takahira to-day of what I had told Jusserand and shall ask Root to let Durand know also.'[2]

It was impossible for Roosevelt to be more precise. The notion entertained in Potsdam and St. Petersburg that the United States might attach herself to the European combine had swiftly and incontestably been blotted out.

---

[1] Spring Rice to Mrs. Roosevelt, Oct. 15, 1905, ibid., pp. 502–3.
[2] Roosevelt to Spring Rice, Nov. 1, 1905, ibid., vol. ii, p. 8.

The remainder of the President's letter was devoted to a candid and more general survey of international affairs. For the Russian autocracy he professed no admiration, but he liked the Japanese, who were becoming less resentful of a peace settlement from which all they desired had not been obtained. About Anglo-German antagonism Roosevelt considered Spring Rice's pessimism to be well founded, and there was in the way of a remedy nothing for him to suggest. When he first succeeded to the Presidency, suspecting Germany of serious designs upon South America, he had himself ventured unofficially to impress on the Kaiser that the violation of the Monroe Doctrine by territorial aggrandizement in the Caribbean area meant immediate war with the United States. Since then, although liable to be upset by tariff disputes, relations with Germany had been on the mend. Nor did Roosevelt approve of the attitude adopted by William II during the Moroccan crisis. But Delcassé's subsequent conduct '—together with the fact that, as I am now pretty sure, Delcassé really wished to prevent peace between Russia and Japan, or at least its coming through American efforts—has made me very uncertain whether the Kaiser did not have just cause for apprehension from Delcassé's policy'. Spring Rice had wound up with an appeal to the President for help to keep Europe tranquil. To this, however, he retorted that, while circumstances might again warrant mediation abroad, his main duty was at home and he did 'not intend to go into peace-making as a regular business'. On Anglo-American solidarity Roosevelt laid special stress. 'As to your own country, I have never wavered. I feel that England and the United States, beyond any other two powers, should be friendly with one another, and what I can legitimately do to increase the friendliness will be done.'[1]

These were words of honest conviction and at the White House during the same month the President repeated the views thus expressed in the presence of Elihu Root and W. H. Taft, the Secretaries of State and War. While he did not esteem highly the governing capacities of Arthur Balfour's Cabinet, he 'thought more of England than of any other foreign country'; she was more sincerely the friend of the United States.[2] The significance of such sentiments, doubly important at the close rather than the beginning of his unprecedented diplomatic labours, cannot be gainsaid. In their mutual contacts, in their outlook on world politics, the English-speaking Powers had elevated their relations to a new plane of concord and goodwill.

[1] Roosevelt to Spring Rice, Nov. 1, 1905, Gwynn, *Spring Rice*, vol. ii, pp. 8–11.
[2] Howe, *J. F. Rhodes*, pp. 120–3.

William II now encountered a final rebuff. Stubborn resistance in St. Petersburg from the French Ambassador wrecked the scheme for a counter-combination to the Anglo-Japanese Alliance; by the fourth week of October the prospects were already less faint for an amelioration of Anglo-Russian animosities.[1] In Europe, therefore, the President's contribution served to accelerate the new trend. But it did more. For Roosevelt had dispelled any misgivings that, as a result of the peace negotiations, Anglo-American friendship may have met with a set-back; instead, the Far Eastern understanding between Great Britain and the United States was unimpeachably reaffirmed. Spring Rice exulted and informed Roosevelt of the immense relief experienced by Entente diplomatists at the assurances which arrived from Washington.[2] Afterwards, enumerating in a report to the British Foreign Office the principal reasons for the failure of the Kaiser's project, he included among them 'the repudiation by the President of the United States of the intentions attributed to him'.[3] And Spring Rice himself, as the one to whose initiative this repudiation was due, had demonstrated once more the value of the confidence he enjoyed at the White House to his country's diplomacy. For through him, and at a decisive turning-point in international affairs, it had again been shown that the American Government were prepared informally to range themselves on the British side.

That Lansdowne had abstained from direct participation in the Rooseveltian peacemaking there was later small cause to regret. With the terms of settlement the people of Japan, having been denied an indemnity and the cession of the northern half of Sakhalin, were exceedingly disgruntled; only from the signature of the strengthened Anglo-Japanese Alliance could some measure of consolation be derived. For what had happened at Portsmouth they blamed the President, and he became the object of a bitter anti-American outburst. On the Pacific coast of the United States a corresponding impulse against Japan and Japanese immigration was, furthermore, shortly to gather and swell, while everywhere in that country men now looked askance at her rapid political and commercial expansion. If then at Tokio, as Roosevelt wished him to do, Lansdowne had tendered counsels of moderation, Great Britain might also have incurred Japanese wrath —with the revised Alliance, so far as it reposed on a moral basis of

---

[1] *Br. Docs.*, vol. iv, nos. 201–3, pp. 214–18; Gwynn, *Spring Rice*, vol. i, p. 503; ibid., vol. ii, p. 7.

[2] Spring Rice to Mrs. Roosevelt, Nov. 27, 1905, ibid., vol. ii, p. 11.

[3] The others were the French refusal and Lamsdorff's objection to an agreement with Germany alone. Spring Rice to Grey, Feb. 12, 1906, *Br. Docs.*, vol. iv, no. 209, pp. 224–5.

popular assent, being thus sabotaged from the outset. The storm he
had aroused did not, however, disturb the President's equanimity.
With their territorial, diplomatic, and economic gains and their new
status as a sea-power the Japanese had, he thought, little ground for
complaint and by November were, he believed, taking more rational
views.[1]

Such, too, was his frame of mind when he approved of Japan's
arrangements in Corea, begotten by the defeat of Russia, the second
Anglo-Japanese Alliance, and the Treaty of Portsmouth. There,
during the war, the Japanese Government had established a virtual
suzerainty and in November 1905 they induced the Emperor at Seoul
to yield to Tokio the supervision of his foreign relations—a long step
towards the eventual annexation of 1910. By the end of December
China, the nominal sovereign of Manchuria, had consented, moreover,
to the transference to Japan of Russian rights in that province; under
the Treaty of Peking she accordingly accepted the Portsmouth settlement.[2] In Japan's Corean move the American Government promptly
acquiesced. As soon as they were notified that she had become the
legal medium for the conduct of Corean foreign policy they recalled
their diplomatic mission from Seoul and Elihu Root gave instructions
that business with Corea should be transacted through Tokio.[3] With
the latest developments on the mainland of Eastern Asia, the United
States, in consonance with the Anglo-American understanding and
the Taft-Katsura discussion of July, had, by so doing, thus publicly
signalized her agreement.

From the turn of the century to the settlement of 1905, events in the
Far East, the varying shifts in the distribution of power, cast on the
subsequent course of international affairs an ever-deepening shadow.
If Russia had won the war with Japan, Clemenceau told Grey in 1908,
her future being confined entirely to Asia, European politics would
have seen the last of her.[4] The full and tragic import of this remark
the next decade inexorably revealed. Blocked in the Far East, Russia
and Pan-Slavism, their outward pressure sleeplessly renewed, would
beat against the Austro-German fabric in eastern Europe, in the
Balkans, and at the Straits, until suddenly in 1914 the whole continent
was set aflame. To Downing Street the final rift between the Russian
and German Governments may at first have been no unwelcome

---

[1] Roosevelt to Harvey, Sept. 6, 1905, Dennett, *Roosevelt and the Russo-Japanese War*, pp. 263–4; Roosevelt to Spring Rice, Nov. 1, 1905, Gwynn, *Spring Rice*, vol. ii, pp. 9–10.

[2] Chang, *The Anglo-Japanese Alliance*, pp. 105, 108, 110.

[3] Root to the Japanese Minister, Nov. 24, 1905, *U.S. Foreign Relations*, 1905, pp. 613–14; also Sykes, *Durand*, p. 299.

[4] Grey of Fallodon, *Twenty-Five Years*, vol. ii, p. 291.

spectacle. Nevertheless, in the Orient the British policy of support for Japan, with which the United States had so notably if informally associated herself, was destined ultimately to sap the primacy of Great Britain. As the chief Asiatic Power none suffered more if the prestige of the West were lowered in the East. Yet she had aided the Orient as championed by Japan to overcome one of the mightiest Empires of the Occident. Inescapably, on the awakening multitudes of Asia who dwelt under the British Crown, the success of her ally would act as a nationalist stimulus. And besides, among the Japanese themselves, far-reaching political and economic ambitions now struck root. To a growing extent on their attitude would henceforth depend not only the question of equal opportunities for foreign trade and the independence and territorial integrity of China but also the security and peace of much of the Pacific area. More and more over a vast stretch of the earth's surface vital British interests are still being affected by the results of an alliance with which Japan lifted herself to world power.

And yet what other policy was there for Great Britain to pursue ? In the Far East, because first of the Russian and then of the German menace, she needed above all an efficient ally. Relying therefore increasingly on Japan, she had been left by American isolationism with no sure alternative. Of this, indeed, Theodore Roosevelt seemed aware and to bestow his blessing on the Anglo-Japanese Alliance went as far as his national traditions and constitutional prerogatives permitted. None the less, within a few years, by those in charge of American finance in China and American strategy on the Pacific, that instrument was regarded as detrimental to their interests. And so to Great Britain the delicate task again presented itself of harmonizing the friendship of the United States with the intricate responsibilities of a widely dispersed Empire. For in 1905 a major difficulty had been perpetuated. Seeking to profit by the establishment of a favourable Far Eastern régime, the American Government were consistently unable to commit themselves to its maintenance. The purpose of Roosevelt's mediation was to obtain at no real cost to his own country a balance of forces between Russia and Japan which would reduce commercial monopoly in Eastern Asia, preclude political domination by a single Power, and safeguard the American position throughout the whole Pacific region. But Great Britain, beset with thickening preoccupations in Europe, now evinced herself not indisposed to modify her customary Chinese policy if she could unite the two former belligerents in a common front with the Entente against the Austro-German system. Such an attempt, moreover, the settlement of 1905

—the victory of Japan, the second Anglo-Japanese Alliance, and the Treaty of Portsmouth—had at last rendered practicable. During the autumn when the Germans reiterated their warning about the danger in the Far East of a quadruple grouping it was the President's opinion that continued Russo-Japanese differences would conserve the objects of his programme.[1] But once those differences were adjusted a partnership for exploitation replaced the East Asiatic equipoise and the sanguine diplomatic theory of the White House ceased, quite simply, to apply.

The fundamental fact was that Washington could not, and London would not, control the further shaping of events, the redistribution of power in the Far East. Towards co-operation with Great Britain the American Government may have displayed a pronounced inclination. They could, however, offer no formal guarantees of tangible assistance —the naval and military sanctions which in the last resort might underlie combined diplomatic action—such as would allow that encumbered Power to curtail, attenuate, or totally refashion other essential engagements. In Eastern Asia the Rooseveltian balance was shortlived. Like John Hay before him, the President, toying with heresy, found himself embarrassed by the isolationist faith, the dogma of American non-participation. To the consequences of that all experience from the days of McKinley and Salisbury pointed infallibly. The potential strength of collaboration between the English-speaking peoples, to the immeasurable loss of mankind, was in practice seldom adequately exercised. The problem remains. But among the currents and cross-currents of the period one in particular can be distinguished. The United States as never before had assumed a role of world leadership and the complex diplomacy of 1905 concluded as it began, whatever the intermediate divagations, with Anglo-American understanding fully unimpaired.

[1] Bülow to Sternburg, Oct. 29, 1905, and note, *Grosse Politik*, xix. 641; Dugdale, *Germ. Dip. Docs.*, vol. iii, pp. 206–7.

XI

THE UNITED STATES AND THE EUROPEAN POWERS

THE Far East had been pacified, but appeasement in Europe had yet to come. By the conference at which the Powers agreed to assemble the Moroccan problem still awaited settlement. Since Theodore Roosevelt had been drawn into the dispute at the outset it was improbable that he could disregard the attempt now made to reach a lasting solution. For the main object of his intervention in international affairs may have already been achieved; until the Algeciras Conference in the winter of 1906 would restore to Europe a fuller measure of calm it was, nevertheless, not really complete. Several questions, therefore, are pertinent. When the President again acted, where was his influence exerted the more weightily—at London, Paris, or Berlin? And, further, were his efforts such as would commend themselves to the British Government? At Algeciras Anglo-American friendship did not, as a matter of fact, undergo any serious reverses, yet in the current struggle of world politics the Conference was to mark a decisive stage.

Before it met, however, English-speaking amity had been evidenced in a number of ways. Thus, during the autumn of 1905 when a British cruiser division paid a courtesy visit to the United States it was accorded an extremely hospitable reception. In London, moreover, Edward VII had become intimate with Whitelaw Reid, the new American Ambassador, while with the President himself the King remained on the most cordial terms.[1] And to envenomed Anglo-German relations all this provided a heartening contrast—at a time especially when Germany's rejoinder to the laying down of the British *Dreadnought*, that gigantic symbol of their competition on the seas, was a German Big Navy campaign. Nor did the Emperor William help to ease matters. Opening the Reichstag in November, he singled out Japan, Russia, and the United States as the Powers with whom the relations of his Government were good and friendly— the inference being that with Great Britain and France they were merely correct.[2] And such European tension would, in the nature of things, react upon English-speaking friendship. The more acute

---

[1] Sykes, *Durand*, p. 288; Cortissoz, *Whitelaw Reid*, vol. ii, pp. 347–8; Lee, *Edward VII*, vol. ii, pp. 434–7.
[2] *Camb. Hist. of Br. Foreign Policy*, vol. iii, pp. 304–5; Spender, *Campbell-Bannerman*, vol. ii, p. 246.

their rivalry, the more the British and Germans strove for American goodwill.

Meanwhile, in Great Britain the Unionist star was waning rapidly and that of the Liberals rising fast. On October 21, 1905, Sir Edward Grey, generally regarded as the likeliest successor to Lord Lansdowne, denied in a celebrated speech that when they attained office the Opposition would revise British foreign policy. For them as for the Conservatives it consisted of three cardinal and immutable features. 'The first is the growing friendship and good feeling between ourselves and the United States, a matter of common ground and common congratulation to all parties in this country.' And the others, as Grey enumerated them, were the Anglo-Japanese Alliance and the Franco-British Entente.[1] To the German Ambassador the Liberal statesman, R. B. Haldane, soon to be Secretary for War, talked privately in the same sense. He told Count Metternich, who reported their discussion to the Imperial Chancellor, that Grey and the entire party wished to assuage Anglo-German antagonism. 'But England's good relationship with America,' said Haldane to the Ambassador, 'the Entente Cordiale and the Japanese Alliance are the foundations of a foreign policy to which the whole of England subscribes.'[2] And principles thus enunciated, hard in any case to overrate, were all the more significant when uttered by spokesmen for a Government destined to be at the helm throughout the next decade and under whom the British Empire would accept and withstand the supreme challenge of 1914.

The Prime Minister, Arthur Balfour, resigned on December 4, 1905. Led by Sir Henry Campbell-Bannerman the Liberals assumed the reins a week later, Sir Edward Grey, as expected, going to the Foreign Office. The first member of the Diplomatic Corps to call upon him was the American Ambassador—a gratifying circumstance which did not pass unnoticed. One outstanding question, the old dispute over Newfoundland fisheries, still bothered the two Governments, but they at once agreed that it could be settled amicably. That, in fact, did actually happen, and the arbitration to which it was afterwards submitted, as compared with the earlier treatment of the Alaskan boundary, well exemplified the progress of Anglo-American understanding. To Whitelaw Reid—who described the conversation to the President—the Foreign Secretary spoke in warm tones of his earnest desire for permanent good relations with the United States. Before that, in his speech of October 21, he had to their constant cultivation

---

[1] Trevelyan, *Grey of Fallodon*, pp. 90–2.
[2] Bülow, *Memoirs 1903–1909*, p. 196.

given first place; and he was glad to hear that his remarks on this subject had been communicated by the Ambassador to Washington. Grey also mentioned his esteem for the President and voiced the hope of visiting the United States and making Roosevelt's acquaintance.[1] By the Prime Minister himself the foreign policy of the new Government was outlined during December in an address at the Albert Hall. Referring to Anglo-American friendship, Campbell-Bannerman felicitously declared that 'with the United States we are bound by the closest ties of race, tradition and fellowship'.[2] In this, as in other directions, the continuity of British policy would be maintained.

From Washington the outlook for Anglo-American friendship was at the end of 1905 no less favourable. About Newfoundland Elihu Root, the Secretary of State, seemed to be content and, as Durand put it, Senator Lodge had for the moment ceased to trouble. With needless gloom, however, the British Ambassador foresaw a possible danger to Great Britain if Roosevelt, whom he did not consider Anglophile in tendency, were to obtain mastery over the Senate. Perhaps Durand here confused the President's unamiable attitude towards himself with official policy, while his relations with Root were scarcely more satisfactory.[3] For this unfortunate state of affairs the Ambassador may not have been altogether blameless; certainly in the diplomatic circles of his own country there also were murmurings against him. His personal foibles, the President's preference for Spring Rice, the probable suspicion of the White House that in his interpretation to Downing Street of the Rooseveltian peacemaking Durand had been none too sympathetic—all these factors, it may be presumed, had much to do with what eventually occurred. On both sides, prior to Root's final 'cleaning the slate' between Great Britain and the United States, it was deemed best that the Ambassador should relinquish his post.[4] Durand may or may not have been justly handled. But if London and Washington were to preserve a congenial atmosphere for the business yet to be done, his removal in October 1906 was unavoidable.

At the beginning of the year, however, Durand had been instructed to assure the President that towards the United States Grey's policy would be the same as Lansdowne's. To this message Roosevelt replied that his views likewise had not altered. While he desired the United States to be on good terms with all nations, he regarded Great Britain 'as the one country with which America ought to be on terms of close

[1] Reid to Mrs. Roosevelt, Dec. 12, 1905, Cortissoz, *Whitelaw Reid*, vol. ii, pp. 319–23.

[2] Spender, *Campbell-Bannerman*, vol. ii, p. 208.

[3] Sykes, *Durand*, p. 289.   [4] Ibid., pp. 296–310.

and confidential friendship'; and as long as he was President that would be the chief principle of his foreign policy. Wishing to give an example of co-operation by the United States, he cited the prompt recall from Seoul of the American Legation when Japan in November 1905 took over the conduct of Corean foreign relations. This, Roosevelt told the British Ambassador, was meant to show the world 'his unreserved acceptance of the Anglo-Japanese Treaty, and his intention to act loyally in support of it'. The Russian, German, and even the French Governments were dubious as to the wisdom of the step and had, he said, been watching him with anxiety. 'He spoke with some indignation about the report that he had disapproved of the Anglo-Japanese Treaty and was ready to join with others in thwarting it.' Roosevelt urged Durand to explain his attitude to Jules Jusserand, the French Ambassador. In response the British representative was able to observe that of the President's position he had had no doubts since his visit to Oyster Bay in August 1905, when his host 'unreservedly approved the treaty'. Roosevelt himself suggested as the only conceivable foundation for the rumour the gratitude he had expressed to the Kaiser for assistance received during the Russo-Japanese peacemaking.[1]

Such, then, was the state of English-speaking friendship on the eve of the Algeciras Conference. Of the goodwill of the United States the British Government were now so sure that in Anglo-American relations Lord Grey of Fallodon remembered nothing from 1905 to 1912 of sufficient interest to be included in his memoirs; during the Conference whatever had been done from Washington was, he averred, unknown in London at the time, and he became cognizant of it only after Roosevelt had retired.[2] The British Government, it is true, were not entirely aware of the kind of influence exercised at Berlin by the President. Yet the Foreign Office, as the records indicate, had, when he again intervened, been apprised from the start; and, besides, the whole episode would appear to have been discussed a number of months later in a most cordial private correspondence that had sprung up between Grey himself and Theodore Roosevelt.[3] Grey may have forgotten, but by the outcome of pressure from the White House he was, before the Conference terminated, to be exceedingly perturbed.

Nevertheless, the spirit in which the American Government decided to participate is beyond cavil. Henry White, recently appointed Ambassador at Rome, was selected as First Delegate from the United

---

[1] Sykes, *Durand*, p. 299.
[2] Grey of Fallodon, *Twenty-Five Years*, vol. ii, p. 85.
[3] Grey to Roosevelt, December 2, 1906, Trevelyan, *Grey of Fallodon*, pp. 114–16, 142–3.

States—a fact signifying in itself that her representation had largely been entrusted to one who, while attached to the London Embassy, did much to foster Anglo-American understanding. But the sympathies of the Second Delegate, Samuel Gummeré, her Minister at Tangier, were reputed to be pro-German. Referring to this towards the end of 1905 in a communication to White, Root remarked that the United States was not to be thrown 'into even apparent antagonism to the Anglo-French *entente*' or manœuvred into breaking it up. 'It is useful to us,' he wrote, 'as well as agreeable.'[1] And that point of view was reflected in a message sent by Durand to Grey on January 11, 1906. The Secretary of State had informed the British Ambassador that at Algeciras his Government considered few of their national interests to be involved. 'The American Delegates have been instructed to stand for the open door, to interfere as little as possible in other matters, to use their influence for peace, and to avoid any action which could tend to weaken Anglo-French *entente*.'[2]

For English-speaking friendship this policy was of high importance. Downing Street may have suspected the Germans of seeking a naval station on the Atlantic coast of Morocco.[3] The real issue lay deeper. Since the days of Elizabeth, and as during those of Louis XIV and Bonaparte, England's safety and independence had demanded not only that she protect the territorial integrity of the Low Countries but also resist the claim to preponderance of the strongest European Power or combination of Powers. Should Germany, by extorting a diplomatic victory at Algeciras, manage to dissolve the Entente partnership, the French might be constrained to join their Russian ally in that anti-British continental *bloc* to which the Emperor William unceasingly aspired. And so by helping France to secure German assent to her special position in Morocco, Grey demonstrated that, in accordance with time-honoured maxims of self-preservation, Great Britain would again lean towards the weaker side and contest the domination of Europe from Potsdam. And in such circumstances the attitude of the United States might be no negligible factor.

Steps now taken in the Entente capitals revealed the alarm that prevailed at Europe's uneasy truce. For Grey had not been many weeks in office when the Quai d'Orsay pressed him to endorse Lansdowne's Moroccan policy—something in fact which he did at Berlin as well as Paris. British and French experts envisaging hypo-

---

[1] Root to White, Nov. 28, 1905, Nevins, *White*, pp. 267–8; also Roosevelt to White, Aug. 23, 1905, ibid., p. 267.
[2] Durand to Grey, Jan. 11, 1906, *Br. Docs.*, vol. iii, no. 236, p. 217; also Jusserand to the French Government, Jan. 11, 1906, Jusserand, *What Me Befell*, p. 322.
[3] *Br. Docs.*, vol. iii, no. 200, p. 162; ibid., no. 227, pp. 208–9.

thetically the contingency of a war with Germany had, moreover, already initiated their discussion about naval and military assistance to France from Great Britain; and in January 1906 these historic conversations received Grey's approval—a move in which Campbell-Bannerman, the Prime Minister, Lord Ripon, the Lord Privy Seal, and Haldane, the Secretary for War, but not the full Cabinet, had been consulted.[1] To German truculence the main answer was thus the strategic alignment, then secretly begun, which the Entente Powers in 1914 would at once bring into operation.

The Moroccan Conference itself opened at Algeciras, Spain, on January 16, 1906. Wedded to the restriction of French ascendancy in the Shereefian Empire, Germany strove to defend the sovereignty of the Sultan, to safeguard in his domains equality of opportunity for foreign trade, and to institute reforms of an international character. For her this seemed an unwonted role, and British opinion remained convinced that her object was the more far-reaching one of discomfiting and demolishing the Entente so as to become the undisputed arbiter of Europe. At Algeciras the organization of the State Bank and the supervision of the police in the Moroccan ports—the principal instruments for establishing administrative supremacy by a foreign Power—were the chief subjects of controversy. The supervision of the police would, in particular, give control over Morocco's outlets; if the French, in conjunction with the Spaniards, could procure the management of the police, the economic and political future of the country would rest in their hands. Towards a solution of this problem, as the one most hotly debated, Theodore Roosevelt was therefore to bend his energies—at first to the annoyance of Berlin and then to that of London, Paris, and Madrid, but with the constant aim in mind of preventing a German triumph over France and the Entente.

To Algeciras Sir Arthur Nicolson had been sent as the British delegate and M. Paul Révoil as the French, while the German spokesmen were Herr Joseph von Radowitz and Count Tattenbach. Between the two camps headed by these representatives, Henry White and the Italian Marquis Visconti Venosta quickly found themselves called upon to mediate. Early in the Conference the American Government were inclined to entertain a plan which would have diminished both German and French interference in Morocco; advocated also by de Lanessan, a French journalist, it was one that Germany started to back.[2] But France demanded for herself and Spain, as the Powers

[1] Br. Docs., vol. iii, pp. 169–203; Grey of Fallodon, Twenty-Five Years, vol. i, pp. 69–112; Trevelyan, Grey of Fallodon, pp. 126–40; Paléologue, The Turning Point, pp. 313–14, 317.
[2] Br. Docs., vol. iii, nos. 250 and 251, pp. 231–3; ibid., no. 256, p. 235.

possessing the greater proportion of foreign interests, the supervision of the Moorish police; and subscribing to her contention, Henry White persuaded his Government to reject the German scheme.[1] The Conference was at an impasse. So White advised the American Government to transmit the French terms to the Kaiser himself. These were that France and Spain should furnish the Sultan with instructors, commissioned and non-commissioned officers, to organize the police in the coast towns of Morocco and supervise their payment.[2] Along such lines intervention by Roosevelt would range the United States behind the Entente.

At Washington the Germans blundered in their tactics. It was useless for William II to attempt again to manipulate European diplomacy by playing upon the susceptibilities of the President. The Far Eastern conflict had been settled and Anglo-American friendship confirmed; Roosevelt was less likely than before to credit German allegations—indeed, if anything, he tended henceforth to over-emphasize the merits of the French case. The proposals submitted to him by the Wilhelmstrasse included one that several of the Great Powers, each with a port on the Atlantic, should direct the police in separate districts. As an alternative it was also intimated that a minor Power might be charged with their organization—no pro-French countries being stipulated.[3] But in the American capital these schemes merely kindled distrust. Recognizing the preponderant interests of France and Spain, the President, who was in close touch with Jules Jusserand, the French Ambassador, now suspected the Germans of endeavouring to partition Morocco. 'Germany', he subsequently recounted, 'sought to impress us with the fact that all the other Powers but England were in her favor.' Yet it had been discovered that Russia and Italy were also opposed to the acquisition in Morocco of a German sphere of influence. Roosevelt, moreover, was afraid that if the Conference failed trouble between France and Germany would ensue.[4] Meanwhile in the isolationist Senate objection had been raised to the presence at Algeciras of an American plenipotentiary; in London the French Ambassador, Paul Cambon, pointing this out to the Foreign Secretary, therefore expected no action from the United States. But Roosevelt ignored domestic criticism and at Algeciras Henry White, showing considerable im-

[1] Ibid., nos. 262 and 263, pp. 239–40; ibid., no. 269, p. 244; ibid., no. 275, pp. 246–7. Also Dennis, *Adventures*, pp. 501–2; Harold Nicolson, *Lord Carnock*, pp. 183–6.
[2] Nicolson to Grey, Feb. 11, 1906, *Br. Docs.*, vol. iii, no. 275, pp. 246–7; Nicolson to Grey, Feb. 12, 1906, ibid., no. 276, pp. 247–8.
[3] Nicolson to Grey, Jan. 25, 1906, ibid., no. 256, p. 235.
[4] Roosevelt to Reid, Apr. 28, 1906, Bishop, *Roosevelt*, vol. i, p. 489.

patience with the Germans, told Nicolson and Révoil that further postponement of the police question—the most important item on the agenda—would cause him to apply for permission to leave the Conference.[1] It was at this juncture that the American views were put forward.

As a result of inquiries from Washington Henry White suggested the solution which the President proposed to William II. About the forthcoming intervention by the United States, Nicolson had kept the British Foreign Office fully informed. The American project incorporated substantially the basic French demands.[2] Communicated by Root to the German Ambassador on February 19, it stipulated that the Moroccan police should be Moorish in personnel and owe allegiance to the Sultan. For their upkeep funds were to be supplied by the State Bank in the stock of which, except for a small French preference, all the Powers concerned would share equally. As for their management, they were to be instructed and supervised by French and Spanish officers, commissioned and non-commissioned, nominated for appointment to the Sultan by their respective legations. The annual report of the senior officers was, however, to be presented not only to the Moroccan Government but also to that of Italy— a concession urged on the French by Henry White—who in turn would pass it on to the other Powers; international rights in Morocco being by implication thus acknowledged. And, finally, the Open Door for foreign trade and enterprise was to be maintained.[3] By recommending his plan to the Kaiser, Roosevelt, to keep the peace of Europe, again made inroads on American tradition.

At the Conference Germany refused point-blank to accept the French demands and Grey regarded the outlook as one of the utmost gravity. Pondering cheerlessly the chances for peace or war, he felt that if British honour and prestige were to be upheld at home and abroad, and an understanding reached with Russia, French anticipations of armed support from Great Britain must not be disappointed. At the Foreign Office it was, however, the opinion of the Under-Secretary of State that, in the Moroccan dispute, by strong indications of British solidarity with France, Germany would almost certainly be deterred; but if, on the other hand, Great Britain were now to forsake them the French must indubitably unite with their Russian ally in the Kaiser's long-cherished design of an anti-British

[1] Grey to Bertie, Feb. 15, 1906, Br. Docs., vol. iii, no. 286, pp. 255–6; Nicolson to Grey, Feb. 16, 1906, ibid., no. 289, p. 259.
[2] Compare Br. Docs., vol. iii, no. 286, pp. 255–6 with Nevins, White, pp. 272–4; also Br. Docs., vol. iii, nos. 275 and 276, pp. 246–8; minutes, ibid., no. 308, p. 272.
[3] Root to Sternburg, Feb. 19, 1906, Bishop, Roosevelt, vol. i, pp. 489–91.

continental league.[1] Should there be a rupture at Algeciras, war would, sooner or later, nearly be inevitable. Yet, whatever happened, the British Government were compelled to follow France lest for European purposes they leave themselves isolated and friendless. As critical for Great Britain in that respect as it was for her partner, such was the situation in which Roosevelt bestirred himself to achieve a settlement.

Would the Conference fail? It was hoped by Nicolson in that event to saddle Germany with the apparent blame for the break-down. Since the French had been gaining ground on the police question the Germans wanted to defer it until the problem of the State Bank had been completely thrashed out. Nicolson waited therefore for an opportunity to secure an open vote on the subject of the police. Nor did he count on Henry White. 'The United States Representative is, I know,' Nicolson wrote to Grey, 'personally in favour of the French view; but considerations of home politics, such as the relations between the President and the Senate, and the desire of the American public not to take a decided line in differences between two European Powers, may force him to maintain silence.'[2] The moment arrived on March 3. At the plenary session, thanks to a manœuvre by Nicolson, the Conference registered the opinion that it should proceed at once with the question of the police. With him there voted the representatives of France, Spain, Italy, Portugal, Russia, and Holland. Henry White, on behalf of the United States, did the next best thing. Together with the Belgian and Swedish delegates he expressed his willingness to adopt the views of the majority—as if there were any doubt of what they would be. In wishing to give further precedence to the question of the bank only Austria-Hungary and Morocco stood with Germany.[3] By a vote of ten to three the Germans were rebuffed and the United States had gone as far as she could outwardly to associate herself with the Entente. The lesson hastened an agreement.

Meanwhile Roosevelt's scheme had also been rejected. Three of his four suggestions were acceptable but, fearing an exclusive monopoly, the German Government declined the key proposal that French and Spanish officers should instruct and superintend the Moorish police. By them the President was, nevertheless, invited to mediate

---

[1] Grey's memorandum of Feb. 20 and Hardinge's notes of Feb. 23, 1906, *Br. Docs.*, vol. iii, no. 299, pp. 266–8.

[2] Nicolson to Grey, Feb. 25, 1906, ibid., no. 312, pp. 274–5; also ibid., no. 294, p. 262; ibid., no. 300, p. 268.

[3] Nicolson to Grey, Mar. 3, 1906, ibid., no. 323, p. 282; ibid., no. 326, pp. 283–4; also Nicolson, *Carnock*, pp. 187–90.

ın some other manner.[1] Apprehensive of a deadlock at the Conference, Roosevelt did not consider this reply at all propitious. From a private source he had learned that in the estimation of the Emperor William, Prince von Bülow, and Admiral Tirpitz their forces were ready and sufficiently powerful to overwhelm the British and French on land and sea alike.

> 'The trouble is,' wrote the President to Whitelaw Reid, 'that with Russia out of the way as she now is, Germany firmly believes that she can whip both France and England. I have excellent reason for believing that the German Naval authorities are as confident as the German military authorities, and believe that England is relying still upon the memory of the Nelsonic triumphs and that they would have a first-class chance of temporarily crippling or driving off her fleet; while the military men firmly believe that an army of fifty thousand Germans landed in England would with but little difficulty take possession of the entire island.'[2]

Such a disaster, Germany thus becoming mistress of the seas and suzerain of a vast colonial empire, no American statesman could ever afford to witness unmoved. At one bound, in a world order repellent to her national genius, the United States would be herself confronted with a fundamental challenge to corporate self-respect and material well-being. For if in the western hemisphere the British Empire was reinsured by Anglo-American friendship, the downfall of Great Britain must conversely have meant a German threat everywhere to the dependencies, sea-routes and international trade, to the whole position indeed of the United States as a major Power. Roosevelt would have been less prone perhaps than Hay or Mahan to couch the argument in broad terms of safeguarding not only American security but also the common democratic interests of the English-speaking peoples; and since he was still inclined to scout Germany's vaunted superiority in arms over Great Britain he must have felt the danger to his own country—one which a decade later would actually arise—to be as yet pretty remote.[3] All the same, as a matter of elementary prudence, the President may have been animated in part at least by some rough, half-instinctive calculation of this sort—a surmise which from start to finish American policy did nothing to belie. At any rate having once toiled for an equilibrium in Eastern Asia, Roosevelt now seemed to be intervening for the sake of the Entente to preserve the European balance.

In the Wilhelmstrasse there could be no shadow of doubt as to

---

[1] Sternburg to Roosevelt, Feb. 22, 1906, Bishop, *Roosevelt*, vol. i, pp. 491–3.

[2] Roosevelt to Reid, Mar. 1, 1906, Cortissoz, *Reid*, vol. ii, pp. 329–30; also Jusserand's message, Mar. 2, 1906, Jusserand, *What Me Befell*, pp. 323–4.

[3] Jusserand's message, Mar. 2, 1906, ibid., pp. 323–4.

his attitude. For to it on March 7 and with characteristic trenchancy Roosevelt had again propounded his own plan while refusing to ask France for further concessions. By him the Kaiser was reminded of how at Germany's bidding he had urged the French Government, with strong assurances of a fair solution, to consent to the Conference; of how, too, at Washington Baron Speck von Sternburg had promised German support for a decision by the President should disagreement occur. Calling upon the Emperor William to adopt his proposals, Roosevelt described them in terms strangely prophetic of the contemporary principle underlying the system of territorial Mandates associated with the League of Nations. According to him they implied the abandonment by the French of their claim in Morocco to exclusive control; instead France and Spain would have accepted a joint mandate from all the Powers to whom they would be answerable for the maintenance of equal rights and opportunities— and with Germany's declared object in Morocco being thus accomplished, she would, he added, have thereby won a notable diplomatic triumph as well. But the President warned the Kaiser not to press the French farther than the measure of concession embodied in his scheme. For then, if the Conference failed, 'the general opinion of Europe and America would be unfavorable, and Germany would lose that increase of credit and moral power that the making of this arrangement would secure to her, and might be held responsible, probably far beyond the limits of reason, for all the evils that may come in the train of a disturbed condition of affairs in Europe'.[1] On Berlin the force of these remarks was not likely to be lost.

Roosevelt's message exhibited the absolute futility of trying to detach the American Government from their friends. Nor was it only at Washington that the efforts of Berlin were having an effect the opposite of that intended: the Russians also were becoming restive; while, as the French had opportunely allowed the rumour of the Franco-British military conversations to filter out, it appeared that instead of being shattered by the hammer-strokes of German diplomacy the Entente had been welded into closer unity. Coupled at Algeciras with the vote of March 3, which Nicolson had so adroitly turned to good account, these facts induced in the Wilhelmstrasse a pronounced change of heart—the conduct of its Moroccan policy having already been removed from the hands of Holstein who resigned in the following month.[2] To a compromise plan sponsored by

[1] Root to Sternburg, Mar. 7, 1906, Bishop, *Roosevelt*, vol. i, pp. 493–5.

[2] *Br. Docs.*, vol. iii, no. 398, pp. 332–4; *Grosse Politik*, xxi. 567; Dugdale, *Germ. Dip. Docs.*, vol. iii, p. 249.

Austria-Hungary Germany now pinned her faith. In the second week of March, when this project was submitted, the Conference heaved visibly a great sigh of relief. As its main feature it contemplated that the police at seven Moroccan ports should be under the supervision of French and Spanish instructors; at the eighth, however—the port of Casablanca—German interests were largest and it therefore was to be entrusted to a Swiss or Dutch officer, presumably sympathetic to Germany, who also would be the Inspector-General of the entire police organization. A settlement seemed feasible at last.[1] But at Algeciras, as new difficulties were encountered, optimism ebbed.

While Great Britain approved of the Austro-German scheme, France was stubbornly opposed. Since the Germans were in retreat the Quai d'Orsay wanted a full surrender—a desire which the news from Washington of the very frank language employed at Berlin by Theodore Roosevelt did nothing to abate.[2] Paris insisted that, although the Inspector-General might be the subject of a minor third Power, all eight ports must be placed under Franco-Spanish tutelage; in Morocco German influence was to be reduced to a minimum. And at that stage, when Great Britain favoured the Austro-German proposal, a brief internal crisis flared up within the Entente itself. Detecting disloyalty, the French affirmed that their partner was deserting them—an allegation which Grey and Nicolson treated with the contempt it deserved. Public opinion, remarked the Foreign Secretary, would realize that Casablanca was not a point about which French obduracy could be justified; the British Government were resolved none the less, if the Conference broke down, to persist in their support of France.[3] Nor did the pertinacity of the Quai d'Orsay go unrewarded. In the middle of March everything indicated, as indeed for some time it had tended to do, a further withdrawal by the German Government; they would compromise if compensated in the question of the State Bank.[4] And then to their deep chagrin the Chancelleries perceived that they had omitted to reckon with Theodore Roosevelt.

From the outset the American proposals had scarcely been to the liking of the Wilhelmstrasse, and now that Germany was adhering to her ally's solution it felt even less enamoured of them. Responding

[1] *Br. Docs.*, vol. iii, nos. 331 and 332, pp. 288–9; ibid., no. 334, pp. 289–91; ibid., no. 338, pp. 294–5; Nicolson, *Carnock*, pp. 190–1.

[2] Grey to Bertie, Mar. 9, 1906, *Br. Docs.*, vol. iii, no. 333, p. 289; Nevins, *White*, p. 276.

[3] *Br. Docs.*, vol. iii, nos. 335–61, pp. 292–310; Grey of Fallodon, *Twenty-Five Years*, vol. i, pp. 104–12.

[4] *Br. Docs.*, vol. iii, nos. 358 and 359, pp. 307–8; ibid., no. 362, pp. 310–11; ibid., no. 364, pp. 311–12.

on March 13 to Roosevelt's communication of March 7, William II attempted therefore to dispose of them by extolling the Austrian scheme. The latter, he asserted, did not only cover the President's idea of international control but also was acceptable to most of the other Powers; while, on the other hand, to submit fresh suggestions would be merely to cause added delay—this reply of the Kaiser's being followed by a German appeal to the traditional interest of the United States in the doctrine of the Open Door against the dangers in Morocco of Franco-Spanish monopoly.[1] But Roosevelt's partiality for France and his distrust of Germany were in full swing; on his previous activities as peacemaker there would it seemed still have to be put a brisk finishing touch. To Berlin during the next week he delivered a blunt retort.

The most important expression of his views was contained in a note of March 17 from Elihu Root to the German Ambassador. The American Government deemed the Austrian plan, but not the French demands, an assault on the principle of the Open Door. For they contended that it presaged the partition of Morocco into three separate spheres of interest—four ports to be organized by the French, three by the Spanish, and one by the Swiss or Dutch; and this, too, just when France had yielded to the idea of internationalization by offering to become jointly with Spain a mandatory in Morocco for all the Powers. From the President himself, moreover, Sternburg also had heard that he did not intend to counter the Austrian project with another American proposal; if adopted at Algeciras it would be accepted by him. But, in order to show where the United States had stood, Roosevelt threatened, should the Conference break down, to publish his correspondence with certain Powers. To the Wilhelmstrasse its Ambassador likewise reported how Root had stigmatized the German attitude as pettifogging and unworthy of a great nation; Germany had lost her strong position at the Conference and would soon forfeit the confidence of the world.[2] Was Washington, within the bounds of American isolationism and without infringing diplomatic correctitude, beginning to fidget for its Big Stick?

In no direction could the Germans make headway. That Franco-Spanish ascendency over Morocco was not to be arrested and the Anglo-French Entente dissevered by invoking the Open Door policy

[1] Sternburg to Roosevelt, Mar. 13, 1906, Bishop, *Roosevelt*, vol. i, pp. 495–7; message of Mar. 14, ibid., p. 497.

[2] Root to Sternburg, Mar. 17, 1906, ibid., pp. 497–9; ibid., p. 500; Sternburg to the German Foreign Office, Mar. 18, 1906, *Grosse Politik*, xxi. 302; Dugdale, *Germ. Dip. Docs.*, vol. iii, pp. 246–7.

of the United States had been clear for some time; what none could foresee was the downright fashion in which Roosevelt would discountenance the one project that might still redeem their diplomacy from the painful ignominy of total failure. Such, nevertheless, had been the irony of events that the attack on the Austrian plan came not so much from the more intimate partisans of France as from that very quarter to which the Germans had looked for aid and understanding. Isolated at Algeciras, Germany's purely European problem was, in all conscience, awkward enough. But now, as if this did not suffice, she appeared to be also imperilling that trans-Atlantic friendship for the promotion of which, at the expense of Anglo-American solidarity, she had striven so diligently. The Wilhelmstrasse was swift to relent. On March 19 the Chancellor cabled to Washington a denial of German bellicosity and renounced any desire to quibble over details. During the Russo-Japanese War Germany and the United States had worked well together; their good relations, which mattered more to him than the whole Moroccan dispute, Bülow wished to maintain.[1] Conveying the gist of this message to the President, Sternburg laid stress on one particular feature of the American proposal: the 'cooperation of French and Spanish officers to be about equally divided in each of the ports'; for to such a 'mixed system', along with an Inspector-General to whom France had in principle already agreed, his Sovereign was at length willing to assent.[2] And as to the further consideration that, thus interpreted, the American scheme would fall on the other camp like a bomb-shell, Berlin may have been silent but not insensible.

Towards an Entente victory at Algeciras, the President had, nevertheless, now made an extremely valuable contribution. For through Rooseveltian suasions Germany abandoned her claim to an inspector at Casablanca who would be the subject of a minor pro-German Power—a pivotal concession, the chief idea of the Austrian plan being thus discarded, on which, whatever else might yet happen at the Conference, she could not jib or go back. The most notable phase of the American intervention, it was subsequently recognized as such by Roosevelt and Henry White themselves. Of the President's activities during the Algeciras Conference, Grey of Fallodon in his reminiscences seemed to have no recollection. But he did recall a conversation with Theodore Roosevelt in 1910 when the ex-President, visiting England, spoke to him of what had been done from Washing-

---

[1] Bülow to Sternburg, Mar. 19, 1906, *Grosse Politik*, xxi. 309; Dugdale, *Germ. Dip. Docs.*, vol. iii, pp. 247–8.

[2] Sternburg to Roosevelt, Mar. 19, 1906, Bishop, *Roosevelt*, vol. i, pp. 499–500.

ton to make the Kaiser yield over Casablanca. And with their talk in mind Grey wrote afterwards of how 'Roosevelt believed, and from what he told me had reason to believe, that the part he took influenced a peaceful solution'.[1]

Meanwhile at Paris and Algeciras Austro-German diplomacy had been smoothing the path for a final compromise. By the Quai d'Orsay the conciliatory temper of Germany was attributed to a statement of continued support for France communicated to Berlin from St. Petersburg.[2] But to what degree had it been evoked by Roosevelt's firm stand? Did the Germans go on retreating because they anticipated a counter-offensive on the rival group from the White House? Their surrender at any rate would be diminished materially by an American arrangement impairing the efficacy of French and Spanish control over the Moorish ports and to that extent mitigating the prospective success of the Entente. In agreeing with the President, by putting her Moroccan policy in line with that of the United States, did Germany at the eleventh hour still hope to snatch the semblance of a qualified victory from the jaws of an otherwise almost inescapable defeat?

At the Conference Nicolson had heard from Henry White that the American Government objected to the Austrian plan because it implied the partition of Morocco into three exclusive spheres of influence. But as soon as he learned the exact terms of their latest message to Berlin he realized that for the Entente the United States had inadvertently produced an unexpected set-back. The purpose of the American note, he hastened to inform the Foreign Secretary, was 'to place French and Spanish instructors at each port conjointly with a strict surveillance over them'—a scheme which France would oppose and Germany accept and which he himself regarded as impracticable and likely to breed incessant friction.[3] To London news such as this was most unwelcome. The Entente had just been on the verge of extracting German consent to separate control by the French or Spanish, according to their preponderant interests, at each Moroccan port. And now with Germany's approval—information on that point being presently conveyed to Nicolson by Henry White—the United States was advocating a 'mixed system' of superintendence rather than the distribution, as they saw fit, of the eight Moroccan ports between France and Spain. Berlin, moreover—so Nicolson gathered

[1] Grey of Fallodon, *Twenty-Five Years*, vol. i, pp. 121–2; also White to Root, Apr. 14, 1906, Nevins, *White*, pp. 279–80.
[2] *Br. Docs.*, vol. iii, nos. 358–64, pp. 307–12; ibid., no. 375, p. 317.
[3] Nicolson to Grey, Mar. 17, 1906, ibid., no. 359, p. 308; Nicolson to Grey, Mar. 19, 1906, ibid., nos. 365–7, pp. 312–14.

—had advised the Austrians, who were preparing a new project, to frame any further proposals on the American model.[1]

Grey's irritation was undisguised. Nor did the fact that this stumbling-block had been interposed by a Power so friendly to the Entente render the matter any the less deplorable. To Nicolson the Foreign Secretary expressed his regret that a fresh plan should be brought forward when the Austrians were about to modify theirs satisfactorily, and with unaccustomed asperity told the Austrian Ambassador that he 'was afraid there were too many peacemakers at work'. By the United States 'an unworkable proposal' had, he said, been suggested, 'which introduced an unfortunate complication'.[2] Speaking in a similar vein to the Spanish Chargé d'Affaires, whose Government objected to it on the ground that it would lead to the establishment of French police at Tetuan, Grey observed that Great Britain, France, and Spain 'must all three continue to act together as we had been doing'. Paris and Madrid should, he felt, allocate the Moroccan ports to each other—it being assumed by him that such was their view as well.[3] By a curious turn of events, on the eve of a favourable adjustment, the Entente Powers found themselves obstructed not from Berlin but from Washington.

Delicate in any case, Grey's position became even more so when the American Government, informing him on March 22 of Germany's acquiescent attitude, solicited for their project British support. This, of course, the Foreign Secretary could not give unless he was disposed to undertake a complete reversal of the whole Entente policy pursued by Lansdowne and himself, with all those hazardous consequences it had been designed purposely to circumvent. Yet, on the other hand, an outright refusal might have done harm to Anglo-American friendship and resulted in a closer understanding between Potsdam and the White House; William II for one would assuredly have accounted the Moroccan battle well lost which, after many years of sedulous endeavour, left him at Washington in serene possession of the field. It was, then, essential to proceed with care in disabusing the President of his oddly ingenuous notions about the high internationalist aims of the Entente. Replying to Washington's request, Grey therefore stressed an interpretation of the American scheme unintended by its sponsor, yet which did not only concede the French demands but which the Powers were eventually to adopt. 'If this means', he cabled to Durand, 'that France and Spain, who are to do the work, are to

---

[1] Nicolson to Grey, Mar. 21, 1906, *Br. Docs.*, vol. iii, nos. 368 and 370, pp. 314–15.
[2] Grey to Nicolson, Mar. 20, 1906, ibid., footnote, no. 366, p. 313; Grey to Goschen, Mar. 21, 1906, ibid., no. 371, pp. 315–16.
[3] Grey to de Bunsen, Mar. 21, 1906, ibid., no. 372, p. 316.

arrange with each other how the police are to be distributed I think it would provide basis for a settlement. But if on the contrary it is to be insisted that French and Spanish police are to be mixed in dual organization at each port I fear this would not be accepted and would be quite unworkable.' To the Secretary of State the British Ambassador was to make that clear and keep in touch with Jules Jusserand, his French colleague. 'We in common with United States are most anxious to see the Conference end in agreement but everything depends upon the point I have explained and I trust influence of the President, which has been so beneficially exercised, will be able to arrange it satisfactorily.'[1]

The British assumption was not erroneous that in Paris the American proposals were likely to arouse small enthusiasm. Roosevelt would have been incensed had he known that the French ascribed German paternity to the plan which he had so sternly imposed upon a reluctant Wilhelmstrasse—the President, in the version of the Quai d'Orsay, having been prompted to father it by the Kaiser, who was supposed to have approached him independently of Bülow. Anyway, Léon Bourgeois, the French Foreign Minister, now asked that Durand be directed to co-operate with Jules Jusserand either in urging Roosevelt to withdraw his project entirely or, if it were too late for that, in persuading him to wait at least until a compromise scheme could be devised. Responding on March 23 as Bourgeois desired, Grey charged Durand to back Jusserand in whatever action he might wish to take.[2] From Algeciras and the European capitals the diplomatic front had for the moment shifted to the United States.

At Washington, however, there was no need for combined representations by the Entente Ambassadors. In the first place the Moroccan interests of the United States, as compared with those in Far Eastern affairs, were meagre; in the second, for the President to show himself determined to have his own way in the solution of a transatlantic dispute would have been for him, should the rumour leak out, to court an isolationist onslaught at home. Nor did he seek in the slightest to collaborate with Germany against France and Great Britain. Jusserand, moreover, had evidently been acquainting Roosevelt with the views of the Entente and when Durand's instructions arrived his colleague had decided that concerted pressure should not then be applied. In point of fact, for what had occurred, the French Ambassador, who was on very friendly terms with the President,

---

[1] Grey to Durand, Mar. 22, 1906, ibid., no. 374, p. 317.
[2] Bertie to Grey, Mar. 22, 1906, ibid., no. 375, pp. 317–18; Grey to Durand, Mar. 23, 1906, ibid., no. 377, p. 318.

levelled part of the blame at the Quai d'Orsay; on the subject of the Moroccan police his own Government should, he believed, have been less tardy to inform Roosevelt of their contentions.[1] At the Conference the damage was soon repaired. The United States without delay altered her course.

News of the decisive change in the attitude of his Government was dispatched to Henry White at Algeciras on the evening of March 23, and communicated in Washington to the British Ambassador the day after. Reaffirming the broad principle of internationalization, they now modified their proposal for officers of mixed nationalities. The Inspector-General would be impartial in supervising on behalf of all the Powers the execution of the mandate. But so long as France and Spain accepted 'a joint responsibility for every port' the United States did not mind whether at some ports their instructors were employed together or at others separately. 'All this distribution of officers can and should be settled as a matter of detail between the two mandatory Powers which undertake the preservation of order, and provided that it is understood that mandate is joint and not several and the responsibility is universal and not local or distributive.'[2] Theoretically Roosevelt thus still upheld his own conception of the system to be established. But in effect, for practical purposes, he supported France. At Washington, by the Anglo-French Entente, the Germans had again been repulsed.

Yet Roosevelt did not relinquish his own solution ungrudgingly. Although from his criticism none of the principal antagonists were to be spared, it was with the conduct of British policy that he seemed at this juncture particularly to find fault. 'My impression after seeing French Ambassador and Secretary of State', Durand cabled to Grey, 'is that U(nited) S(tates') Gov(ernmen)t consider us as opposed to Germany and possibly inclined to push France too far. Neither President nor Secretary of State have discussed Morocco Conference with me,' he added, reflecting thereby the lack of confidential relations between the Administration and himself, 'and I have asked no questions till yesterday: but I know that President used to think us unduly suspicious of Germany if not unduly hostile.'[3] Upon some of each other's activities the English-speaking Governments looked, towards the end of the Conference, with an appreciable measure of disapprobation. This being, however, but a transient mood it was quick to fade and pass away.

[1] *Br. Docs.*, vol. iii, footnote, no. 381, p. 321; Jusserand, *What Me Befell*, p. 323; also Roosevelt to White, Apr. 30, 1906, Nevins, *White*, p. 280.

[2] Durand to Grey, Mar. 24, 1906, *Br. Docs.*, vol. iii, no. 380, pp. 320–1.

[3] Durand to Grey, Mar. 24, 1906, ibid., no. 381, p. 321; also Nicolson, *Carnock*, p. 195.

In the meantime the Austrians had also rejected the American scheme and dropped their suggestion about Casablanca. The negotiations could therefore be resumed.[1] Unable to rely on help from the United States and virtually isolated in Europe, the Germans now yielded on the subject of French and Spanish instructors in the eight Moorish ports. The Conference was nevertheless endangered by a Franco-German controversy over the ultimate control of the police. But with Henry White as intermediary Germany accepted an Entente formula that the reports of the Inspector-General, whom the Powers later agreed should be a Swiss, were to go to the Diplomatic Corps at Tangier as well as to the Sultan of Morocco.[2] Over the problem of the State Bank she also came to terms with France. It was decided that the shares should be divided between the Powers signatory to the new treaty, the French being allowed to take a larger portion of the capital than the others. The last difficult hurdle had been cleared. Minor problems were similarly adjusted. The Moroccan Jews suffered grievous disabilities, and in expressing hope for their better treatment by the Sultan the British delegate supported his American colleague.[3] Signing the treaty on April 7, the representatives at Algeciras had concluded their labours. Germany may temporarily have won her point that in Morocco rather than an overt French protectorate there should be a simulacrum of international authority. The actual victory, as events would indicate, rested with France.

For his most recent excursion into international peacemaking Roosevelt was thanked both by Berlin and Paris. But while their Washington Ambassadors were exempt from his censure, he did not think the French or German Governments had been wholly 'straightforward'.[4] When the Senate ratified the Algeciras Treaty it stipulated that participation in the Conference by the United States signified no change from her traditional attitude of abstaining from the settlement of European questions. The fact was none the less that the Administration had repeatedly contravened the strict letter of American isolationism. And, apart from assistance given the Entente through Washington by Roosevelt and Root, Henry White's Anglophile sympathies had often been employed to advantage in Algeciras itself. At its termination he described to the President how he had persuaded the German representatives that Great Britain did not want

[1] *Br. Docs.*, vol. iii, nos. 378 and 379, pp. 318–20.
[2] Ibid., nos. 382–4, pp. 321–5; ibid., no. 386, pp. 326–7.
[3] Dennis, *Adventures*, pp. 500–1; *Br. Docs.*, vol. iii, no. 388, p. 328; ibid., no. 392, pp. 329–30; also Moon, *Imperialism and World Politics*, pp. 206–7.
[4] Roosevelt to Reid, Apr. 28, 1906, Bishop, *Roosevelt*, vol. i, pp. 489 and 500–3; Roosevelt to White, Apr. 30, 1906, Nevins, *White*, p. 280.

to break up the Conference so as to drive France into war and enable the Royal Navy to destroy their fleet. This idea White combated stoutly 'every time the German delegates mentioned it to me, which was quite frequently for a time, and I am glad to say that before the Conference ended they were convinced that I was right and that the rôle played by England was a useful one'.[1] The special position of the United States, midway between the two groups, had been utilized by Henry White in a manner conducive to the maintenance of Anglo-American friendship. 'It was felt all through the Algeciras Conference', Grey himself wrote to Roosevelt in December 1906, 'that American influence was not being used against France and us.'[2]

Meanwhile, misgivings were entertained by Englishmen and Americans alike at the unwearying attempts of William II to insinuate himself into Roosevelt's good graces. King Edward VII shared these apprehensions and so did the Ambassador of the United States to the Court of St. James's. 'The truth is', Whitelaw Reid reported in June to the President, 'that the Emperor's assiduous efforts to cultivate the most intimate relations with you have attracted the attention of all the Chancelleries in Europe, and a common comment upon it is that the Emperor overdoes his love-making as he does his diplomacy, with a certain German confidence in the value of brute vigor in either pursuit!' At this stage, moreover, the Secretary of State wished to renew the process begun at the close of the nineteenth century and complete the settlement of such Anglo-American differences, affecting Canada and Newfoundland, as were still unresolved. In London, after the Algeciras Conference, what Whitelaw Reid strove therefore to dispel was any feeling—the suspicion of a growing friendship between Germany and the United States—that might jeopardize Root's programme in advance.[3]

The President in reply was at once reassuring and wholly typical. Of his activities during the Moroccan crisis he had already sent Whitelaw Reid an exhaustive account.

'In this Algeciras matter', Roosevelt observed to the worried Ambassador, 'you will notice that while I was most suave and pleasant with the Emperor, yet when it became necessary at the end I stood with him on his head with great decision. . . . As for the Germans, I really treat them much more cavalierly than I do the English, and I am immensely amused at the European theory (which cannot, however, be the theory of the French Government) that I am taken in by the Kaiser. I am very polite to him, but I am ready at an instant's notice to hold my own. In

[1] White to Roosevelt, Apr. 8, 1906, Nevins, *White*, p. 281; also Dennis, *Adventures*, pp. 508–9.
[2] Grey to Roosevelt, Dec. 2, 1906, Trevelyan, *Grey of Fallodon*, p. 142.
[3] Reid to Roosevelt, June 19, 1906, Cortissoz, *Whitelaw Reid*, vol. ii, pp. 330–1.

the same way my policy with Japan is to be scrupulously polite, to show a genuine good will toward her, but to keep our navy in such shape that the risk will be great for Japan if it undertakes any aggression upon us.'[1]

Events themselves would supply a fuller answer. With Canada and Newfoundland the outstanding questions were soon adjusted and, as the former assumed increasing control over her own external relations, trouble of that sort afflicted Anglo-American friendship less and less. But even in 1906 it did not seem as if on the mutual affairs of Great Britain and the United States Rooseveltian intervention in world politics had impinged adversely.

Nor was the President insincere in his remarks about the Kaiser. Towards Germany the Moroccan crisis imbued Roosevelt with an ineradicable sense of mistrust. During the summer of 1906 the British Government, desirous of promoting a limitation or reduction of armaments, had sought his co-operation—he being invited by Grey to take the initiative on this topic at the second Hague Conference and asked by Grey's colleague, R. B. Haldane, the Secretary for War, to exercise his influence on William II in favour of such a course. But although the general object was one of which he approved, he pointed out in response how vast a misfortune it would be for the free peoples to disarm while 'military despotisms and military barbarism' did not; and recalling from the Anglo-German coercion of Venezuela to the Algeciras Conference his experiences with the Kaiser, the President was frankly sceptical of what he could accomplish at Berlin. 'That I can work with France and England', he explained to Henry White, 'I have no doubt'; of Germany and William II he could not speak with equal assurance.[2]

Such sentiments Grey at any rate was unlikely to discourage. In the English-speaking world he may have held religion and a common language, if not Anglo-Saxon race feeling—a subject on which he displayed sounder judgement than Joseph Chamberlain—to be strong bonds. 'But, more than all this,' he wrote to Roosevelt at the end of 1906 in a fine confidential survey of British policy, 'I should say that some generations of freedom on both sides have evolved a type of man and mind that looks at things from a kindred point of view, and a majority that has a hatred for what is not just or free.'[3] In friendship with the United States, as in other aspects of his statecraft, Grey could carry on where his predecessor had left off; carry on, now that an era

---

[1] Ibid., pp. 332–3; also Roosevelt to Reid, Apr. 28, 1906, Bishop, *Roosevelt*, vol. i, pp. 467–503.

[2] Nevins, *White*, pp. 249–51; Roosevelt to White, Aug. 14, 1906, ibid., pp. 498–500; also Trevelyan, *Grey of Fallodon*, p. 206.

[3] Grey to Roosevelt, Dec. 2, 1906, ibid., pp. 114–16, 142–3.

of goodwill had replaced the simmering hostility of the past century, amplify and enrich by cordial private relations with leading Americans no less than by prudent regard in the conduct of public business for the great and abiding principles of English-speaking amity.[1] For what had been planted under Salisbury and Lansdowne it was Grey's lot to bring nearer to fruition.

To the American Government their exertions during the Algeciras Conference were long a source of pride. They only remembered that, by compelling Germany to consent to the Rooseveltian proposal for French and Spanish instructors at each of the eight Moroccan ports, the United States had done much to force her to abandon her demand —and one to which she could not revert—for Casablanca. The commotion provoked in London, Paris, and Madrid by the President's scheme for officers of mixed nationalities was forgotten; and in the account which Roosevelt himself wrote of his Moroccan diplomacy its hurried withdrawal is not mentioned. To the American contribution at Algeciras the Secretary of State referred during the spring of 1906 in conversation with the British Ambassador. He told Durand that the ambition of the Kaiser had been to procure a port opposite Gibraltar. Great Britain, said Root, did not seem to mind and it really was saved by the United States.[2] In 1905, at the close of the Far Eastern conflict, the President had continued to sympathize with the Anglo-Japanese Alliance. And as then, so now, at the termination in 1906 of the Moroccan Conference, by standing with the Entente against Germany, the United States was, at bottom, in full accord with British interests.

Wherever they turned the febrile endeavour of the Germans to insert a wedge in the Anglo-French grouping had thus miscarried. Between the Entente partners there was developing instead a livelier consciousness of a common obligation to stem the surging Teutonic flood. 'The Germans', Grey noted ominously a few months after the adjournment of the Conference, 'do not realize that England has always drifted or deliberately gone into opposition to any Power which establishes a hegemony in Europe.'[3] And, in its current phase, as another outcome of this tendency, signs of the Anglo-Russian *rapprochement* were multiplying with a further aftermath in Germany's growing dread of 'encirclement'. It besides speedily became evident that over Morocco the sway of France and Spain would proceed unchecked. But in 1905–6 the Chancelleries, magnifying portentously

---

[1] Trevelyan, *Grey of Fallodon*, pp. 159–62, 197–209, 303–22.
[2] Sykes, *Durand*, p. 501.
[3] *Br. Docs.*, vol. iii, no. 418, p. 359; also ibid., no. 391, p. 329; no. 396, p. 331; Grey of Fallodon, *Twenty-Five Years*, vol. i, p. 112.

the picayune details of finance and police supervision, did not rock Europe for the benefit of that country. Nothing less had been at stake than the prestige of those massive combinations, now deploying against each other in the most formidable array, with whose fortunes the independence of Great Powers would henceforth be indissolubly bound up.

Such being the state of affairs, and since the British as well as the French were concerned in the quarrel with Germany, every step taken by Washington was, for good or ill, liable to involve Anglo-American relations. From the start, however, Roosevelt had favoured the cause of the Entente Powers: whatever he did, and he desisted as soon as their disapproval was manifest, he fancied to be in their interest. Even if the President considered that the British were urging the French beyond reasonable limits it had not been rendered impossible for Great Britain to reconcile her European connexion with her American friendship. And yet on a very much smaller scale there was a strange resemblance between what had happened in March 1906 and the Russo-Japanese peace negotiations of the previous summer. On each occasion Roosevelt believed that from an associated Power the British Government were withholding counsels of moderation; on each occasion, anxious to sever the tie between London and Washington, Germany co-operated with the United States. But at neither time did Great Britain swerve from her commitments and at the White House in the long run the Germans could reap no profit. On both sides of the Atlantic the designs of Potsdam had been utterly confounded. From the Far Eastern and Moroccan crises until 1914 the German campaign at Washington would never be revived with equal intensity. Concomitant with the rise of Anglo-American friendship, William II's jealous attempt to disunite the English-speaking peoples had, like his grandiose vision of an anti-British continental league, gone abjectly amiss.

But one special factor affecting them had for the second time within two years emerged with fresh significance. Governed principally hitherto by restricted questions of mutual interest, relations between Great Britain and the United States might, it appeared, now be influenced to an extent almost as important by their more indirect contacts in the general sphere of world politics. That they should try to work hand in hand and bring to bear upon international affairs their concerted weight and matchless power was the dream of Hay and Chamberlain at the close of the nineteenth century. But the story may have been less happy once the United States, comparatively untrammelled by external engagements, essayed to pursue an active

T

course of her own. For then she might swiftly have found herself at variance with an Imperial Government on whom devolved multifarious responsibilities stretching to every corner of the earth. But, despite his propensity to figure in the international limelight, even Theodore Roosevelt could not break the fetters of his country's isolationist tradition. The fact was that by them every movement abroad towards positive and sustained Anglo-American co-operation had invariably been impeded; and yet they none the less may also have debarred any consequent dissension of a grave nature over differences of opinion and policy. Nor if she had ventured continuously to assume the initiative in world politics would the United States have lacked enmity and opposition; acting alone, she could not do much. And who in those circumstances her partner would have been is, in view of the new attitude towards each other of the English-speaking peoples, hardly to be doubted. On the whole, however, from the Far Eastern and Moroccan crises until the Wilsonian interlude, the United States maintained her customary aloofness; between 1906 and the Great War of 1914–18 she did not again intervene decisively in the chief European controversies. But with the other and more formal ramifications of the British diplomatic system it was no less necessary for Great Britain always to harmonize Anglo-American understanding.

Since the days of McKinley and Salisbury the friendship between the English-speaking peoples had undergone stringent tests—bilateral and multilateral—only to survive puissant and flourishing. In their mutual disputes they had surmounted the main obstacles, and those that remained would be settled by methods consonant with this achievement; on the wider stage of world politics Great Britain was free to protect herself against the German menace, knowing that her major interests were securely reinsured in the western hemisphere and most probably wherever the diplomacy of the United States would be exercised. Before 1914 additional questions were to arise—the second Hague Conference, the financing of Chinese railways, Japanese immigration and the revision of the second Anglo-Japanese Alliance, Panama tolls, and Mexican revolution; yet, however intractable the subject, there had now been created in Anglo-American relations a saving and indestructible spirit of fundamental solidarity. The proof of this, if proof were needed, came with the participation of the United States in the Great War of 1914–18. At first during that conflict it looked as though the earlier labours of Anglo-American conciliation were in dire peril of being swept irretrievably away. They could in the end attain no more splendid vindication than the final effort made by the United States, her entry turning the scales at the last, in victorious defence with others of the liberties of mankind.

It was, then, in the closing years of the nineteenth century and the opening years of the twentieth that a legacy of ill will began to be converted into the existing friendship of the English-speaking peoples. Nothing but evil would have ensued—for them and for the distribution of power all the world over—had the chance not been seized at that critical time. And yet in the era of amelioration their relations were scarcely tranquil; before so protracted, so exasperating a task, Governments less resolute might easily have lost heart. For, as if in a microcosm, the formative period had shown many of those complex elements perpetually at work in the shaping of British and American policies which still unite, divide, and unite again the English-speaking peoples. To analyse them is therefore not only to reveal past difficulties. Properly gauged they may afford a standard by which to assess practically the permanent grounds of agreement and fellowship, a touchstone in the present, a guide for the future.

What was true in a preceding age is equally true to-day. Associated together and taking the lead with other nations of goodwill, the British Commonwealth and the United States might yet collaborate for their own welfare and for that more universal welfare from which it is inseparable. The problems they faced in a former generation are not entirely dissimilar from those confronting them now; in world politics the collective preponderance of the law-abiding is inexpugnably the one sure foundation for the rule of law. Between them they command unsurpassable resources of wealth and power; between them may be decided not only their own fate but that of humanity everywhere. In the contemporary ordeal of civilization they are permitted neither by the duty owed to the principles they have inherited nor by the invincible amplitude of their joint strength to evade their high burden or cast it off; if their common ideals based not on a single racial origin but on freedom, social justice, and enlightened progress are to prevail the plain compulsion is upon them to act in unison with foresight, with wisdom, with courage. They may succeed; they dare not fail. But, whatever the result, however they play their part, in the annals of the twentieth century the theme of Anglo-American friendship will, it is certain, find a central place.

WORKS CITED

ADAMS, HENRY. *The Education of Henry Adams*, Boston, 1918.

ADLER, CYRUS. *Jacob H. Schiff*, vol. i, London, 1929.

ALVAREZ, ALEJANDRO. *The Monroe Doctrine*, New York, 1924.

ALVERSTONE, THE RT. HON. VISCOUNT. *Recollections of Bar and Bench*, London, 1914.

ASPINALL, ALGERNON E. *The British West Indies*, London, 1912.

ASQUITH, THE RT. HON. H. H. *The Genesis of the War*, London, 1923.

BACON, ADMIRAL SIR R. H. *The Life of Lord Fisher of Kilverstone*, two volumes, London, 1929.

BEARD, CHARLES A. *The Idea of National Interest*, New York, 1934.

BEMIS, SAMUEL FLAGG (ed.). *American Secretaries of State and Their Diplomacy*, vol. ix, New York, 1929.

BERNSTORFF, COUNT. *My Three Years in America*, London, 1920.

BISHOP, JOSEPH BUCKLIN. *Theodore Roosevelt and His Time*, vol. i, New York, 1920.

BRANDENBURG, ERICH. *From Bismarck to the World War*, London, 1927.

British and Foreign State Papers, 1901–1902, vol. xcv, London, 1905.

BUCHAN, JOHN. *Lord Minto*, London, 1924.

BUCKLE, GEORGE EARLE (ed.). *The Letters of Queen Victoria*, Third Series, vol. iii, London, 1932.

BÜLOW, PRINCE VON. *Memoirs 1897–1903*, London, 1931.

—— *Memoirs 1903–1909*, London, 1931.

BYWATER, HECTOR C. *Sea-Power in the Pacific*, London, 1921.

—— *Navies and Nations*, London, 1927.

CHANG, CHUNG-FU. *The Anglo-Japanese Alliance*, Baltimore, 1931.

CLARK, J. REUBEN. *Memorandum on the Monroe Doctrine*, Washington, 1930.

CLARK, STEVENS, ALDEN, and KRAFFT. *A Short History of the United States Navy*, Philadelphia, 1927.

CORTISSOZ, ROYAL. *The Life of Whitelaw Reid*, vol. ii, London, 1921.

COWLES, ANNA ROOSEVELT. *Letters from Theodore Roosevelt to Anna Roosevelt Cowles, 1870–1918*, London, 1924.

DAFOE, JOHN W. *Clifford Sifton*, Toronto, 1931.

DENNETT, TYLER. *Americans in Eastern Asia*, New York, 1922.

—— *Roosevelt and the Russo-Japanese War*, New York, 1925.

—— *John Hay*, New York, 1933.

DENNIS, ALFRED L. P. *Adventures in American Diplomacy, 1896–1906*, New York, 1928.

DUGDALE, BLANCHE E. C. *Arthur James Balfour*, vol. i, London, 1936.

DUGDALE, E. T. S. (ed.). *German Diplomatic Documents, 1871–1914*, vol. iii, London, 1930.

ECKARDSTEIN, BARON VON. *Ten Years at the Court of St. James', 1895–1905*, London, 1921.

EWART, JOHN S. *The Kingdom of Canada and Other Essays*, Toronto, 1908.

FAY, SIDNEY BRADSHAW. *The Origins of the World War*, vol. i, New York, 1928.

FEIS, HERBERT. *Europe the World's Banker, 1870–1914*, New Haven, 1930.
FISH, CARL RUSSELL. *The Rise to World Power*, New Haven, 1919.
FISHER, LORD. *Memories*, London, 1919.
—— *Records*, London, 1919.
FITZROY, SIR ALMERIC. *Memoirs*, vol. i, New York, 1926.
FOSTER, JOHN W. *Diplomatic Memoirs*, vol. ii, Boston, 1909.
GARVIN, J. L. *The Life of Joseph Chamberlain*, vol. iii, London, 1934.
GOOCH, G. P. *History of Modern Europe, 1878–1919*, New York, 1923.
—— *Before the War*, vol. i, 'The Grouping of the Powers', London, 1936.
GOOCH, G. P., and TEMPERLEY, HAROLD (eds.). *British Documents on the Origins of the War, 1898–1914*, various volumes, London.
GRANT, N. F. (ed.). *The Kaiser's Letters to the Tsar*, London, 1920.
GREY OF FALLODON, VISCOUNT. *Twenty-Five Years, 1892–1916*, two volumes, London, 1925.
Grosse Politik (Die Grosse Politik der Europäischen Kabinette, &c.). Citations are from Dugdale's *German Diplomatic Documents*, vol. iii.
GWYNN, STEPHEN. *The Letters and Friendships of Sir Cecil Spring Rice*, two volumes, London, 1929.
HEADLAM-MORLEY, SIR JAMES. *Studies in Diplomatic History*, London, 1930.
HENDRICK, BURTON J. *The Life of Andrew Carnegie*, vol. ii, Garden City, N.Y., 1932.
HILL, HOWARD C. *Roosevelt and the Caribbean*, Chicago, 1927.
HOLT, W. STULL. *Treaties defeated by the Senate*, Baltimore, 1933.
HOWE, M. A. DE WOLFE. *James Ford Rhodes*, New York, 1929.
JOHNSON, WILLIS FLETCHER. *America's Foreign Relations*, vol. ii, New York, 1921.
JUSSERAND, J. J. *What Me Befell*, London, 1933.
KENWORTHY, J. M., and YOUNG, GEORGE. *Freedom of the Seas*, London, 1928.
KNAPLUND, PAUL (ed.). *Speeches on Foreign Affairs, 1904–1914, Sir Edward Grey*, London, 1931.
LATANÉ, JOHN HOLLADAY. *A History of American Foreign Policy*, Garden City, N.Y., 1927.
LEAGUE OF NATIONS. *Appeal by the Chinese Government, Report of the Commission of Enquiry*, Geneva, 1932.
LEE, SIR SIDNEY. *King Edward VII*, vol. ii, London, 1927.
LODGE, HENRY CABOT (ed.). *Addresses and Presidential Messages of Theodore Roosevelt, 1902–1904*, New York, 1904.
—— *Selections from the Correspondence of Theodore Roosevelt and Henry Cabot Lodge, 1884–1918*, two volumes, New York, 1925.
LONG, JOHN D. *The New American Navy*, vol. ii, London, 1904.
MACKINTOSH, ALEXANDER. *Joseph Chamberlain*, London, 1914.
MARTIN, EDWARD SANDFORD. *The Life of Joseph Hodges Choate*, vol. ii, London, 1920.
Massachusetts Historical Society, Proceedings LVIII, 'Memoir of Henry Cabot Lodge', April 1925.
MAUROIS, ANDRÉ. *King Edward and His Times*, London, 1933.
MOON, PARKER THOMAS. *Imperialism and World Politics*, New York, 1928.
MORSE, H. B., and MACNAIR, H. F. *Far Eastern International Relations*, Shanghai, 1928.

Mowat, R. B. *The Life of Lord Pauncefote*, London, 1929.
Nevins, Allan. *Henry White*, New York, 1930.
Newton, Lord. *Lord Lansdowne*, London, 1929.
Nicolson, Harold. *Lord Carnock*, London, 1930.
Ogawa, Gotaro. *The Expenditures of the Russo-Japanese War*, New York, 1923.
Olcott, Charles S. *William McKinley*, vol. ii, Boston, 1916.
Paléologue, Maurice. *The Turning Point, Three Critical Years, 1904–6*, London, 1935.
Papers relating to the Foreign Relations of the United States, various volumes, Washington.
Pringle, Henry F. *Theodore Roosevelt*, London, 1931.
Rippy, J. Fred. *Latin America in World Politics*, New York, 1928.
Ronaldshay, The Rt.' Hon. The Earl of. *The Life of Lord Curzon*, vol. i, London, 1928.
Roosevelt, Theodore. *An Autobiography*, London, 1913.
Rose, J. H., and Others. *The Cambridge History of the British Empire*, vol. vi, Cambridge, 1930.
Skelton, Oscar Douglas. *Life and Letters of Sir Wilfrid Laurier*, vol. ii, London, 1922.
—— Article in *Queen's Quarterly*, Kingston, February 1932.
Smalley, George W. *Anglo-American Memories*, Second Series, London, 1912.
Spectator. *Prince Bülow and the Kaiser*, London, 1931.
Spender, J. A. *The Life of the Right Hon. Sir Henry Campbell-Bannerman*, two volumes, London, 1923.
—— *Fifty Years of Europe*, London, 1933.
Steed, Henry Wickham. *Through Thirty Years, 1892–1922*, vol. i, London, 1924.
Straus, Oscar S. *Under Four Administrations*, Boston, 1922.
Sykes, Brigadier-General Sir Percy. *The Right Honourable Sir Mortimer Durand*, London, 1926.
Tansill, Charles Callan. *The Purchase of the Danish West Indies*, Baltimore, 1932.
Taylor, Charles Carlisle. *The Life of Admiral Mahan*, London, 1920.
Thayer, William Roscoe. *John Hay*, vol. ii, Boston, 1916.
Townsend, Mary Evelyn. *The Rise and Fall of Germany's Colonial Empire, 1884–1918*, New York, 1930.
Trevelyan, George Macaulay. *Grey of Fallodon*, London, 1937.
Ward, Sir A. W., and Gooch, G. P. (eds.). *The Cambridge History of British Foreign Policy*, vol. iii, Cambridge, 1923.
White, Andrew Dickson. *Autobiography*, vol. ii, New York, 1905.
White, James. Article in *The Canadian Historical Review*, vol. vi, No. 4, Toronto, December 1925.
Whyte, Frederic (ed.). *Letters of Prince von Bülow*, London, 1930.
William II, ex-Kaiser. *My Memoirs 1878–1918*, London, 1922.
Williams, Mary Wilhelmine. *Anglo-American Isthmian Diplomacy*, Washington, 1916.
Woodward, E. L. *Great Britain and the German Navy*, Oxford, 1935.
World Peace Foundation. *Arbitration and the United States*, Boston, 1926.

INDEX

Adams, Henry, and Anglo-American understanding, 35; on the Hay-Pauncefote Treaty, 102; Spring Rice his guest, 179.
— John Quincy, 130.
Aguinaldo, 31, 71.
Alabama claims, 143.
Alaska, purchased from Russia by U.S., 38, 140, 143; Roosevelt sends troops to, 137–8, 149.
Alaskan boundary dispute, 38–40, 42–7, 99, 129, 136, 252; postponement of permanent settlement, 121; Roosevelt demands settlement, 126; Hague Court suggested for, 140–1; Treaty, 142–3, 147–8, 152; composition of tribunal, 143–9; treaty ratified, 147–8; meetings of the tribunal, 153–62; award signed, 160; Canadian delegates did not sign, 160–1.
Algeciras, Spain erects and abandons batteries for heavy guns in, 29.
— Conference, deadlock at, 201, 257–60; and Anglo-American understanding, 251, 254; and the organization of State Bank, 256, 259, 269; and the direction of the police, 256–9, 262–8; Austrian plan at, 262–9; Treaty signed, 269, 272; U.S.A. proud of part in, 272.
Alsace-Lorraine, annexation of, 5; France would not renounce, 72.
Alverstone, Lord, member of Alaskan tribunal, 148, 152–62.
Anglo-American Arbitration Treaties, 3–4, 181–3.
— — understanding, up to 1898, 1–16; Joseph Chamberlain's efforts for, 3, 21–6, 29–31, 33, 35, 69, 162, 180, 271, 273; John Hay's efforts for, 21–5, 28, 33, 49, 75, 178, 180, 212–13, 260, 273; the Spanish War's part in, 17–36, 41, 59; suspense and delay, 37–58; lull in 1899 and 1900, 59; German jealousy a factor in, 60, 87, 104–6, 200; a cardinal point of Anglo-German negotiations, 92–3; part of special emissaries in, 98; second Hay-Pauncefote Treaty indicates growth of, 103–4; Cecil Rhodes's work for, 108; Venezuelan enterprise harmful to, 114–19, 121–2; effect of Anglo-Japanese alliance on, 95–6, 130, 217, 219–33, 245, 249, 254, 272; naval importance of, 133–5; strategic advantages reciprocal, 134; eventually improved by Alaskan settlement, 163–4; during the Russo-Japanese War, 170,

173, 179–81, 183–5, 203–4; initiative from Washington in Russo-Japanese War, 178; foundation of Roosevelt's Far Eastern policy, 181, 190–1, 198, 204; Roosevelt's Moroccan action shows new hazards, 201–2; not in robust condition at opening of Portsmouth Conference, 216; revision of Anglo-Japanese Alliance and, 220–4, 245, 249, 254, 272; cordial at close of Russo-Japanese War, 239, 253; Roosevelt on his unwavering belief in, 246; the Algeciras Conference and, 251; future of, 275.
— French Convention of 1903, 181.
— — Entente; see Entente.
— German Alliance suggested, 15, 22, 25, 86, 89–90, 187.
— Japanese Alliance (1902), first consideration of, 14, 84; Lansdowne and, 56, 94; effected, 86–7, 94, 167, 187; raises Japan to world power, 93–4; neutralizes Kaiser's support of Russia, 129–30; makes anti-Japan pact rumour unlikely, 184; effect on British policy, 190, 202–3; prevents Britain from counselling moderation to Japan, 210–12, 214, 228, 247–8.
(1905) First Revision, 216–35, 238–9, 247, 250; approved by Roosevelt, 94, 217, 219–33, 245, 249, 254, 272; and British sea-power, 220–3; and the defence of India, 220, 222–4, 231–2, 242; unforeseen danger of Article II, 223–4, 231; and Corea, 224–5, 229–32, 249; attacked by Witte, 242, 244–5.
(1911) Second Revision, 15, 90–1, 164, 223, 274.
— Russian Treaty (1825), 140, 143, 144, 145, 153–4, 157, 160.
Apia, 63.
Armaments, limitation of, 59, 62, 271.
Armour, Mr. Justice, member of Alaskan tribunal, 148.
Asquith, H. H., criticizes Joseph Chamberlain, 24–5; his government and the Two Power Standard, 133; his government and the Anglo-Japanese alliance, 164.
Australia, opposed to German colonial expansion, 66–7; her views and alliance negotiations with Germany, 91; arrangement with, for squadrons in adjacent waters, 130.
Austria-Hungary, and the Triple Alliance, 5; ambassador accuses Britain of criminal short-sightedness, 20; con-